Perilous Options

Perilous Options

SPECIAL OPERATIONS
AS AN INSTRUMENT OF
U.S. FOREIGN POLICY

Lucien S. Vandenbroucke

New York   Oxford
OXFORD UNIVERSITY PRESS
1993

Oxford University Press

Oxford New York Toronto
Delhi Bombay Calcutta Madras Karachi
Kuala Lumpur Singapore Hong Kong Tokyo
Nairobi Dar es Salaam Cape Town
Melbourne Auckland Madrid

and associated companies in
Berlin Ibadan

Library of Congress Cataloging-in-Publication Data
Vandenbroucke, Lucien S.
Perilous options : special operations as an instrument
of U.S. foreign policy / Lucien S. Vandenbroucke.
p. cm. Includes bibliographical references and index.
ISBN 0-19-504591-2
1. United States—History, Military—20th century.
2. United States—Foreign relations—1945–1989. 3. Special
operations (Military science)—United States—History—20th century.
4. Special forces (Military science)—History—20th century.
I. Title.
E840.4.V36 1993
973.92—dc20 93-11332

1 3 5 7 9 8 6 4 2

Printed in the United States of America
on acid-free paper

To Donna

Preface

The idea of this study originated in early 1980, when, as a graduate student in political science, I was writing a seminar paper on the U.S.-sponsored landing in 1961 by anti-Castrist exiles at Cuba's Bay of Pigs. Significant new material had recently become available on this disastrous bid to overthrow Cuban Premier Fidel Castro. In the late 1970s, the U.S. government had declassified parts of the report produced shortly after the debacle by a White House appointed board of inquiry. Author Peter Wyden had also shed new light on the affair with his just-published *Bay of Pigs*. As I was reviewing this material for my paper, in April 1980 the United States staged the ill-fated Iran rescue mission, an equally disastrous attempt to rescue fifty Americans held hostage at the U.S. embassy in Tehran.

A few months later, while reading the unclassified version of the Pentagon's postmortem on the Iran mission, I was struck by the fact that some of the same problems that had plagued the Bay of Pigs venture had surfaced again in the Iran raid. Even the language of the two reports was at times eerily similar. Testifying to the board of inquiry on the Bay of Pigs, Special Assistant for National Security Affairs McGeorge Bundy spoke ruefully of the lack of objective review that had characterized the Cuban plan. "In the future the President... should hear something from other than advocates," he observed. Almost 20 years later, the Special Operations Review Group that prepared the Pentagon's report on the failed Iran raid wrote: "The hostage rescue plan was never subjected to rigorous testing and evaluation by qualified, independent observers and monitors short of the Joint Chiefs of Staff themselves."[1]

I began to wonder whether the failure of these two operations, as well as of similar ones conducted between the Cuban and Iranian fiascoes, was not due at least in part to recurrent, systemic problems in the way the United States plans and executes such operations. Such was the genesis of the present study of U.S. strategic special operations since World War II. These are, as explained in more detail in the first chapter, commando-type strikes, conducted after detailed review at the highest levels of the U.S. government, staged in an attempt to solve major problems of U.S. foreign policy. The study is anchored on in-depth cases studies of the 1970 U.S. raid to Sontay in North Vietnam and the 1975 *Mayaguez* operation, in addition to studies of the Bay of Pigs and the Iran hostage rescue mission.

The reader may ask why the study does not also examine several other apparently related operations the United States has conducted since World War II: the 1954 overthrow of the leftist regime of President Jacobo Arbenz in Guatemala, the 1964 "Dragon Rouge" operation to rescue Westerners held by insurgents in the Congo, and the 1991 rescue of Americans and citizens from more than a dozen other countries threatened by civil war in Somalia. The reason is that although these three undertakings bear some resemblance to the operations described in the case studies, they are not truly U.S. strategic special operations.

Despite similarities between the Guatemala venture and the Bay of Pigs, the former was not a true strike operation. Arbenz's overthrow, covertly engineered by the CIA, was primarily a psychological, not a military, operation. Although the CIA assembled a small force of Guatemalan exiles, they did next to no fighting. After advancing a few miles from Honduras into Guatemala and engaging Arbenz's forces in desultory skirmishing, the exiles stayed put and let CIA psychological warfare bring Arbenz down. Broadcasts by a CIA clandestine radio and a few bombing raids in Guatemala by CIA contract pilots, flying World War II–era fighters, convinced the Guatemalan population and the military that an invasion by a much larger force was under way. Abandoned by his demoralized armed forces, Arbenz resigned. Psychological warfare was also part of the CIA's Cuban plan. But, unlike Guatemala, the Bay of Pigs called for a major military strike. Success in Cuba was predicated upon the ability of twelve hundred well-armed invaders to defeat roundly the much larger forces they would encounter upon landing, triggering a wave of popular revolt in Cuba.

In "Dragon Rouge," the United States lent logistical support to a Belgian operation. U.S. transport planes flew Belgian paracommandos from Belgium to Stanleyville (now Kisangi), in what was then known as the Congo and is today Zaire. The paratroopers assaulted the city, rescuing several hundred Westerners, including a number of Americans, from Congolese insurgents who were holding them hostage. Because the operation was planned and executed primarily by Belgium, it falls outside of the purview of this study, which focuses on U.S. operations.

The 1991 "Eastern Exit" operation occurred as the Somali capital of Mogadishu was engulfed in civil war and armed looters rampaged through the city. In a long-distance helicopter raid, U.S. Marines and Navy special operations forces evacuated almost three hundred U.S. and other citizens holed up in the U.S. embassy. The rescuers arrived after looters, who had already had traded gunfire with the embassy's security guards, threatened to overwhelm them. Dramatic as the plight of the embassy occupants was, however, it fell short of being a major U.S. foreign policy crisis. The assailants had no particular desire to challenge U.S. interests; they were simply looking for another target to loot. Neither the White House nor the U.S. public perceived the situation as a major foreign policy problem. Thus there was not the same extended White House consideration and debate of the plan and monitoring of its execution that characterizes strategic special operations, setting them apart from ordinary special operations, and contributing to their special dynamics.[2]

One of my reasons for writing this study was the conviction that the United States has suffered too many setbacks in strategic special operations, and too many lives have been lost in these undertakings, because the same mistakes have been repeated time and again. Hence, this work is meant for a broader audience than just students of political science, in the hope, in particular, that it might also be read by decision makers and military officials who may one day have to plan, evaluate, and perhaps execute yet another U.S. strategic special operation. The book therefore eschews extensive political science theorizing, which would interest but a specialized audience. At the same time, in an effort to ensure that the book's generalizations are as factually accurate as possible, the case studies draw extensively from primary material, including a large volume of material declassified for this study under the Freedom of Information Act (FOIA).

In the course of this project, I have incurred a debt of gratitude to a number of institutions and individuals. The University of Connecticut at Storrs gave me intellectual guidance and financial support, without which I could not have completed this endeavor. I wish to extend special thanks to professors Larry W. Bowman, Elizabeth C. Hanson, and Harold Seidman of the Department of Political Science, and to Professor Thomas G. Paterson of the Department of History, for their invaluable suggestions and constant support. I am also grateful to professors Mark A. Boyer and John Rourke, also of the University of Connecticut, and to Dr. Thomas Ofcansky and James E. Baker for their careful reading of earlier versions of the manuscript and many good suggestions. Dr. Uri Bar-Joseph, a fellow student of the Bay of Pigs, generously shared with me the fruit of his own archival research and his trenchant insights, for which I am most grateful. I further thank Captain Lionel

Krisel for sharing with me findings from his own exhaustive investigation of the Bay of Pigs. I also wish to express my appreciation to Ambassador Thomas C. Mann and Vice Admiral George P. Steele for their helpful comments on earlier drafts of chapters of this manuscript.

I am also grateful to the Brookings Institution, which offered me both financial support and an opportunity to broaden my understanding of national security affairs during the 1983–1984 academic year I spent there as a research fellow. At Brookings, I benefited particularly from the insights and advice of Dr. Richard K. Betts, Dr. Thomas L. McNaugher, Michael K. MccGwire, and Dr. John D. Steinbruner, to whom I extend my deep appreciation. I was also fortunate to receive a research grant from the National Science Foundation, which enabled me to conduct interviews and pursue research at manuscript and document collections throughout the country. I am grateful for this support.

A significant number of persons involved in the events chronicled in the following pages took the time to share with me, in often lengthy interviews, their recollections of these episodes of our history. A number of informed observers also were willing to give me the benefit of their insights. The names of most of those interviewed appear in the bibliography, although a few, due to special sensitivities, will stay unnamed. To all I extend my thanks. The staffs at the many university and presidential libraries where I did research were invariably professional and helpful. Historians with the U.S. armed forces, particularly those with the Pacific Air Forces in Hawaii, did a remarkable job tracking down and declassifying hundreds of documents in response to my many Freedom of Information requests. To Shirley Sontag, Freedom of Information Manager at Headquarters, Pacific Air Forces, Hickam Air Force Base, and Sergeant Roger Gernigan, previously of the Office of Air Force History at Bolling Air Force Base, I am especially grateful for their unfailing professionalism and helpfulness.

To two people I owe special thanks. Professor J. Garry Clifford has been both a mentor and a friend. He patiently guided this work as it progressed from seminar paper to Ph.D. dissertation and finally to its present shape, offering throughout penetrating criticism and sound advice. My wife Donna provided keen advice and support at every step of the way. Without them, this work would not be; to both I am deeply grateful.

Part of this study was written as I was working for the U.S. Department of State. This work, however, is based entirely on material obtained from the public record and in unclassified interviews. Moreover, the views herein are entirely my own. They do not reflect the opinion of the U.S. government or any of its branches, of the Brookings Institution, or of any individual who helped with this project. Any mistakes are my responsibility alone.

McLean, Virginia
December 1992   L. S. V.

Contents

Perilous Options

ONE

Patterns of Failure

One of the oldest forms of war is the *coup de main*. Throughout the history of warfare, small parties of warriors, operating with limited resources and without hope of reinforcement, have repeatedly conducted sudden strikes—frequently deep within enemy lines—relying on shock, surprise, speed, and maneuver to defeat an often numerically superior enemy. In the past 40 years, such strikes have occurred in almost every conflict arena, from the swamps of Cuba to the desert of Iraq.

Most such undertakings are daring yet minor operations meant to achieve limited military objectives. Occasionally, however, a country will mount such a strike to achieve major foreign policy goals. This was the case when in 1943 German paratroopers freed Italian dictator Benito Mussolini from a remote locale in Italy's Gran Sasso mountains, where he was being held after his overthrow by antifascist forces. A more recent example is the 1976 Entebbe raid. Demonstrating Israel's commitment to the security of Jews worldwide and its implacable hostility to terrorism, Israeli commandos rescued the passengers of an Israeli airliner whom Palestinian terrorists were holding at Uganda's Entebbe airport.

The United States is no stranger to high-stakes *coups de main* of this sort. Since World War II, U.S. forces or their surrogates have launched several such strikes aimed at achieving major U.S. foreign policy objectives. In early 1961, the U.S. government feared that the leftist regime of Cuban leader Fidel Castro, which was drifting increasingly close to the Soviet bloc, threatened the stability of the entire Western Hemisphere. In the spring of that year, a force of Cuban exiles, trained and

organized by the U.S. Central Intelligence Agency (CIA), struck at the
Bay of Pigs in an ill-fated bid to topple the Cuban leader.[1]

Almost a decade later, one of the key foreign policy concerns of the
United States had become the release of the American prisoners of war
(POWs) held in North Vietnam. In November of 1970, U.S. commandos raided the Sontay prison camp outside Hanoi in a bold but unsuccessful bid to release over sixty POWs the Pentagon thought might be
there. Five years later, the Ford administration faced a sudden crisis
when, only few days after the collapse of the U.S.-backed regimes in
Cambodia and South Vietnam, forces of Cambodia's new Communist
government seized the U.S. freighter *Mayaguez* with forty crewmen
aboard. The administration feared that unless the United States reacted
vigorously, its allies and foes alike would conclude that it had become a
"helpless giant" unable to defend its interests. Less than three days after
the ship was seized, the White House dispatched Marines to the tiny island of Koh Tang in the Gulf of Thailand, where the crew was thought
to be held. In early 1980, the entire nation was gripped with concern
over the fate of the fifty Americans held hostage at the U.S. embassy in
the Iranian capital of Tehran. In April of that year, U.S. forces launched
a daring but abortive raid to free the hostages.[2]

These strikes, which sought to achieve major foreign policy aims
rather than just tactical objectives, represent a special form of U.S. *coup
de main*. Given the importance of their objectives, such strikes can be
called strategic special operations. These are secret military or paramilitary strikes, approved at the highest level of the U.S. government after
detailed review. Executed in limited time and with limited resources,
they seek to resolve through the sudden, swift, and unconventional application of force major problems of U.S. foreign policy.[3]

Strategic special operations present specific characteristics. The highest civilian and military authorities in the White House and the Pentagon closely monitor the preparation and execution of such raids. During
the Bay of Pigs, President Kennedy personally directed the movements
of individual Navy ships supporting the operation. Strategic special operations, moreover, are usually joint endeavors involving several U.S.
military services and civilian government agencies. For example, each of
the four military services as well as the CIA took part in the Iran
mission.

Strategic special operations are also high-risk ventures for they seek
to achieve difficult objectives in a single bid, with deliberately limited
means. Because failure in such operations is typically both highly visible
and dramatic, the ensuing damage to U.S. prestige tends to be great, as
evidenced by the Bay of Pigs and Iran fiascos.

The U.S. strategic special operations listed above displayed an additional characteristic as well: they were all seriously flawed. The Bay of
Pigs invaders were routed almost upon landing. The Sontay commandos
raided an empty camp. U.S. troops in the *Mayaguez* operation landed at

the wrong island, to rescue a crew that, as it turned out, already was being freed. The Iran rescue force aborted its mission before even reaching Tehran.

This lackluster record raises a central question. Did U.S. performance in these episodes merely reflect poor luck and the unique circumstances of each operation? Or are there recurrent problems in the preparation and execution of U.S. strategic special operations that help explain their disappointing outcomes? Drawing upon the available historical evidence, this study examines in depth, in search of an answer, four U.S. strategic special operations conducted since World War II: the Bay of Pigs invasion, the Sontay raid, the *Mayaguez* operation, and the Iran rescue mission.

Admittedly, this selection may not represent all the strategic special operations undertaken by the United States since World War II. During the 1991 Persian Gulf war, U.S. and allied forces apparently conducted at least one operation that may qualify as a strategic special operation. In the closing days of the war, in an ultimate effort to drag Israel into the conflict, Iraq moved twenty-nine Scud missiles to its western border for a barrage attack against Israel. If conducted, this attack probably would have triggered large-scale Israeli retaliation against Iraq. This, in turn, would have gravely strained the coalition against Iraq, which included a significant number of Arab states. U.S. intelligence detected the deployment of Scuds and small teams of U.S. and British commandos slipped into western Iraq, helped locate the command and control centers for the missiles, and called in air strikes that destroyed several of them. So far, however, information on this mission is limited chiefly to a few sketchy press articles, precluding serious study. The following work thus focuses on the four postwar strategic special operations for which significant information is available.[4]

Comments by key players in these operations and well-informed observers suggest that similar difficulties indeed have regularly plagued U.S. strategic special operations. These remarks highlight several recurrent problems. The first is faulty intelligence. In the Bay of Pigs, the planners told the White House that Castro's troops were largely demoralized and unlikely to resist effectively an invasion by CIA-backed exiles. In reality, Castro's forces proved motivated and well-organized; they held their ground and relentlessly drove the invaders back into the sea. As Richard M. Bissell, the CIA mastermind of the invasion, later conceded, a chief cause of failure was that Castro's forces "moved more decisively, faster and in greater force than anyone had anticipated."[5]

Poor intelligence characterized the Sontay operation as well. U.S. forces successfully raided a POW camp on the outskirts of Hanoi only to discover that the North Vietnamese had moved the prisoners months earlier. Nor had U.S. intelligence identified a military installation bristling with enemy troops only minutes from the POW camp. U.S. forces stumbled across this enemy installation when part of the raiders, confusing it for the POW camp, landed there by mistake, triggering a fierce firefight in which the installation's occupants were neutralized. Without this fortuitous mix-up, the raiders would have run a serious risk of ambush by the hostile force as they withdrew from the camp. Intelligence shortcomings also marred the *Mayaguez* operation. The Marines assaulted Koh Tang Island expecting to face a handful of Cambodian Communist (Khmer Rouge) irregulars. They encountered a well-entrenched force of two hundred or more seasoned regular Khmer Rouge troops.

A second recurring problem in strategic special operations appears to be insufficient coordination and cooperation between the services and agencies involved. A major criticism of the Iran rescue mission is that it was entrusted to an ad hoc force of disparate units from the four services that failed to perform as a cohesive team. As Colonel Charles A. Beckwith, commander of the Army's Delta Force team that was supposed to free the American hostages at the U.S. embassy in Tehran, later commented: "In Iran we had an ad hoc affair. We went out, found bits and pieces, people and equipment, brought them together occasionally and then asked them to perform a highly complex mission. The parts all performed, but they didn't necessarily perform as a team. Nor did they have the same motivation."[6]

Beckwith's comments echoed the complaints of participants in earlier strategic special operations. After the Bay of Pigs, military commanders who had supported the operation spoke bitterly of the difficulty of working with their CIA counterparts. The Marines who landed at Koh Tang complained vehemently about the close air support they received from the Air Force. Such complaints are hardly surprising. Interservice coordination has been a recurrent problem of U.S. military operations for much of the past few decades, from the Vietnam war to the Grenada invasion.[7]

The comments of key participants in these events suggest that there is an additional recurrent problem in strategic special operations: the senior decision makers who evaluate and approve these operations often receive poor information and advice. After the Bay of Pigs, President Kennedy was furious about the advice he had received from the Joint Chiefs of Staff (JCS). His brother Attorney General Robert F. Kennedy, a member of the secret White House board that conducted the postmortem of the fiasco, termed the JCS's study of the invasion plan "disgraceful.... They really didn't give it the attention that was necessary and study that was essential and didn't analyze the facts."[8] In the wake of the Sontay raid, White House Special Assistant for National Security Affairs Henry A. Kissinger criticized the military's briefing of the White House. Although the military had intelligence suggesting that the prisoners might have been moved, Kissinger asserted, "none of the briefings that led to the decision to proceed had ever mentioned the possibility that the camp might be empty."[9]

In some instances strategic special operations may seem like the only solution to otherwise intractable major foreign policy problems. Moreover, they promise, if successful, to settle these problems at a single stroke with limited means. This gives rise to another recurrent problem. Decision makers can become insidiously attracted to strategic operations, to the point of engaging in wishful thinking, in which hopes distort perception and wishes are mistaken for reality.

There is evidence of wishful thinking in several of these operations. Reflecting on Kennedy's decision to authorize the Cuban invasion, former presidential adviser Arthur S. Schlesinger, Jr., wrote:

> One further factor no doubt influenced him: the enormous confidence in his own luck. Everything had broken right for him since 1956. He had won the nomination and the election against all the odds in the book. Everyone around him thought he had the Midas touch and could not lose. Despite himself, even this dispassionate and skeptical man may have been affected by the soaring euphoria of the new day.[10]

Looking back, Richard M. Bissell, the chief CIA architect of the operation, conceded that the planners had engaged in wishful thinking about the scheme.[11]

Moreover, it appears almost 20 years later that wishful thinking played a part in the ill-fated Iran rescue mission. In his book on the operation, former Delta Force commander Beckwith recalls that before the raid he had misgivings about the helicopter crews. Despite their key role in the operation, he apparently wished the problem away. As he wrote: "On the other hand, everyone wanted to have confidence in these leathernecks. If not them, who? If not now, when? The Marines got the benefit of the doubt."[12]

Another common complaint by participants in strategic special operations is that senior military or civilian officials far from the theater of operations often exercise excessive control over mission execution. Navy commanders were shocked during the Bay of Pigs when President Kennedy told them where to station individual ships off Cuba. Military and CIA officials involved in the invasion further complained that the White House had made key tactical decisions without seeking the military's advice. Following the debacle, the JCS privately complained bitterly that the president had canceled without consulting them a key D-Day air strike, gravely weakening the invasion plan. During the *Mayaguez* operation, on-scene commanders were dismayed when the Commander in Chief of U.S. forces in the Pacific (CinCPac), located thousands of miles away in Hawaii, tried to direct the movements of individual units and planes on or above Koh Tang. Key on-scene commanders spoke acidly after the operation about the intrusive and excessive guidance they received from CinCPac and senior military commanders in Washington.

The various comments by key participants in a variety of strategic special operations suggest that similar problems indeed did plague several of these operations, contributing to their unsuccessful outcomes. The next seven chapters examine in depth the four case studies, probing for detailed evidence of seemingly recurrent problems: faulty intelligence, poor interagency and interservice cooperation and coordination, inadequate information and advice provided to decision makers, wishful thinking, and overcontrol of mission execution from afar. The concluding chapter evaluates the evidence, identifying which of these problems do recur in strategic special operations. It also suggests steps that can help avoid these problems and ensure that future strategic special operations are conducted more wisely and with a greater chance of success.

TWO

Plotting against Castro

In November 1959, Castro's revolution was barely eleven months old. In the opinion of Washington policymakers, however, it had lasted long enough. Following Castro's takeover of Cuba, relations between the United States and its small island neighbor had rapidly deteriorated. Convinced that the United States was hostile to his revolution, Castro quickly began confiscating American property on the island. In the summer and fall of 1959, he accused the United States of encouraging the counterrevolutionary activities of anti-Castrist exiles and charged that the United States threatened Cuba with "economic strangulation."[1] U.S. political leaders, in return, increasingly were alarmed by Cuba's anti-American rhetoric and the active participation of Communists in Cuba's new regime.

In a November 5, 1959, memorandum to President Dwight D. Eisenhower, Secretary of State Christian A. Herter noted with concern that Castro "has tolerated and encouraged the infiltration of Communists and their sympathizers into important positions in key governmental institutions, the armed forces, and organized labor. . . . The international Communist apparatus has made it clear that it sees in the advance of Castroism the best chance of achieving its immediate objectives." Herter's conclusion was blunt: "The prolonged continuation of the Castro regime in Cuba in its present form would have serious adverse effects on the United States position in Latin America and corresponding advantages for international Communism."[2]

Eisenhower was not one to dismiss this threat lightly. Early in his

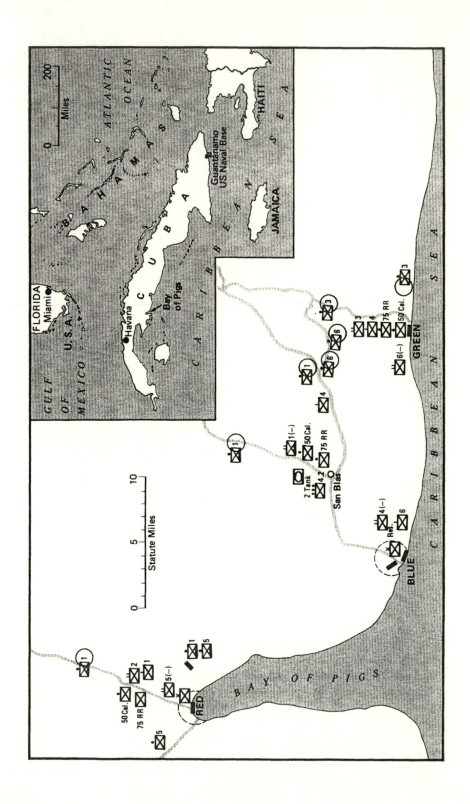

administration, he had displayed strong opposition to leftist regimes in the hemisphere. In the spring of 1954, he had authorized a major covert CIA operation that toppled the leftist government of Jacobo Arbenz in Guatemala.[3] As Eisenhower approached his last year in office, he was no more tolerant of Latin America's radical Left. By the fall of 1959, his administration had already decided on a clear agenda and timetable on Cuba: it had to be brought back into the Western fold within a year. As expressed in a State Department document of November 1959:

> The immediate objective of the United States with respect to Cuba is the development of a situation in which, by not later than the end of 1960, the Government then in control of Cuba should, in its domestic and foreign policies, meet at least minimally the objectives and standards indicated in the OCB Regional Operations Plan for Latin America which sets forth the basic United States policy objectives for Latin America countries.

To achieve this objective, the document continued, the United States gave priority to encouraging "opposition by suitable elements presently outside of the Castro regime with a view towards a step-by-step development of coherent opposition."[4]

Within the U.S. government, the CIA was particularly eager to check Cuba's leftward drift. In mid-December 1959, Colonel J. C. King, head of the agency's Western Hemisphere Division, sent a memorandum to CIA Director Allen W. Dulles stating that Cuba was in the grip of a "far left" dictatorship that threatened U.S. interests throughout Latin America. King suggested that "thorough consideration be given to the elimination of Fidel Castro." Barely a month later, Dulles raised the issue with the Special Group, the secretive interagency committee that oversaw CIA covert operations during the Eisenhower administration. According to the minutes of the Special Group meeting of January 13, 1960, Dulles "noted the possibility that over the long run the U.S. will not be able to tolerate the Castro regime in Cuba, and suggested that covert contingency planning to accomplish the fall of the Castro government might be in order."[5] As the new year wore on, Dulles found an increasingly receptive audience for his suggestions to remove Castro. On January 23, 1960, Eisenhower commented to Secretary of State Herter that Castro was "a man who is going wild and harming the whole American structure." In March, Herter wrote to a close friend that "the breach between ourselves and Castro is almost unhealable."[6]

It is within this heated atmosphere that the CIA first proposed concrete steps to weaken Castro. In early 1960, Allen Dulles asked to meet with the president to discuss a program of harassment of Castro. Dulles proposed a plan to sabotage Cuban sugar refineries. As Special Assistant to the President for National Security Affairs Gordon Gray later recalled, Eisenhower's reply was: "Allen, this is fine, but if you're going to make any move against Castro, don't just fool around with sugar refineries. Let's get a program which will really do something about Castro."[7] The agency had received the nod to begin plotting Castro's downfall.

Within weeks, the CIA drafted its policy paper "Program of Covert Action against the Castro Regime," calling for the creation of a unified Cuban opposition outside Cuba, a powerful anti-Castrist propaganda campaign, the development of a "covert intelligence and action organization within Cuba," and the formation of a "paramilitary force outside of Cuba for future guerrilla action." The president approved the policy paper on March 17, and the agency began implementing its proposals without delay. Underlying the agency's scheme was the belief that it could turn Castro's own techniques against him. The plan's basic concept was for a small guerrilla group to infiltrate Cuba, as Castro and his companions had done in 1956, and develop a strong underground opposition. The CIA hoped that eventually this would lead to a general popular revolt.[8]

At this point, however, covert action was just an option the White House was exploring. Throughout the spring and summer of 1960, the administration mounted a diplomatic offensive against Castro. It hoped that the Organization of American States (OAS) would agree to strong collective action, including economic sanctions and a break in diplomatic relations with Cuba.[9]

There was nothing unusual, however, about the U.S. willingness to consider covert action against Cuba. Since World War II, U.S. policymakers had come to view covert operations as merely another instrument of foreign policy. The Truman administration successfully used covert operations in the Italian elections of 1948 and against the Huk insurgency in the Philippines in 1952–1953. The Eisenhower administration held covert action and its practitioners in high esteem. In 1953, a CIA coup toppled leftist Prime Minister Mohammad Mossadegh in Iran, restoring the power of the shah. The next year, the agency engineered the overthrow of the leftist Arbenz regime in Guatemala. For administration officials in early 1960, contingency planning for covert action against Castro was a quasi-automatic response.[10]

CIA confidence in covert action ran especially high. Buoyed by its successes in Iran and Guatemala, the agency was, in the words of former CIA general counsel Lawrence R. Houston, "riding an optimistic wave."[11] CIA operatives referred to the Guatemala precedent repeatedly as they plotted against Castro. The agency assigned many of the same people who had engineered Arbenz's downfall to the new project. In 1954, Richard M. Bissell, then in charge of CIA "Special Projects," had been heavily involved in the Guatemala operation. Now, as the CIA's deputy director for plans (covert action), Bissell was the driving force behind the Cuban scheme. Bissell's deputy, Tracy Barnes, had also been part of the agency's Guatemala team. So had E. Howard Hunt, the Cuban project's political action chief, and David A. Phillips, one of chief propaganda specialists working on the project.[12]

Inside the agency, Bissell was known as a brilliant achiever who did the impossible—although many in the CIA also thought him reckless and mistrusted his administrative skills. He had developed the U-2 spy plane program in less than twelve months, when the Air Force had estimated it would take up to six years. Bissell believed in exerting tight personal control. In his own words, he had run the U-2 operation as a "private duchy." He brought the same operating style to the Cuban project. Instead of being run out of the agency's Western Hemisphere Division, the venture fell to an *ad hoc* task force, JMF/ATE, headed by Bissell. With an independent task force, he could control the planning personally.[13]

Within weeks of Eisenhower's initial approval, the CIA recruited a first cadre of Cuban exile fighters, who covertly began guerrilla training at a U.S. Army installation in the Panama Canal Zone. Meanwhile, CIA operatives undertook to bring together the scores of fractious Cuban exile groups in Miami. By late May, the CIA had cajoled the major exile organizations into forming the Democratic Revolutionary Front (Frente Revolucionario Democrático). The loosely united front included groups from a broad political spectrum. The CIA carefully excluded organizations linked to the discredited Batista dictatorship that Castro had overthrown.[14]

By May, a powerful radio transmitter went on the air at Swan Island, off the Honduran coast. "Black" radio operations had been key to success against Arbenz. Weeks before the Guatemalan coup, the CIA had set up a clandestine radio station in Honduras. By declaring to originate from a rebel base inside Guatemala, its broadcasts suggested that a strong anti-Arbenz movement operated in that country. They galvanized the regime's opponents and helped demoralize its supporters. Later, when 150 anti-Arbenz exiles—supported by a few antiquated fighters flown by CIA pilots who dropped bombs on Guatemala's cities— crossed from Honduras into Guatemala, the clandestine radio greatly inflated the invaders' strength. It broadcast orders to imaginary rebel groups throughout the country, instructing them to move hundreds of nonexistent troops. The broadcasts confused Arbenz loyalists and convinced them they faced an overwhelming foe. Even though the invaders engaged in only a few desultory skirmishes with Arbenz's forces, the latter panicked, and Arbenz fled into exile. With a like strategy in mind, the CIA operated "Radio Swan" in the guise of a Cuban exile radio, beaming its broadcasts to Cuba, hoping to stir unrest.[15]

When Eisenhower approved the CIA planning document, he was merely exploring one possible option against Castro. But as 1960 wore on and U.S.-Cuban relations kept deteriorating, the covert scheme gained momentum. In the spring of 1960, Cuba established diplomatic relations with the Soviet Union and received its first shipment of Soviet oil. By then Eisenhower was confiding to close advisers his wish to see Castro "sawed off." That summer, Castro nationalized U.S. oil refineries in Cuba. The administration slashed Cuba's quota for sugar sales to the United States. In Herter's words, the situation was "critically bad."[16]

The administration was increasingly frustrated with diplomacy. The president had become cynical about the prospects of multilateral action against Cuba. In February 1960, Eisenhower deplored the OAS's unwillingness to condemn Castro. Speaking to Senator George Smathers of Florida, he observed that although everybody in Latin America "says something should be done, they seem to want it done clandestinely—a policy . . . approximating gangsterism." Two months later, Eisenhower noted with dismay that U.S. efforts to convince the OAS of the Communist threat in Cuba had resulted in "almost a zero." An August 1960 meeting of the OAS ministers of foreign affairs brought more disappointment. Despite heavy U.S. lobbying, the ministers' public statement merely condemned Sino-Soviet interference in the hemisphere without mentioning Cuba by name.[17]

The administration realized, however, that overt unilateral U.S. action held little promise. The president was gravely concerned about the negative reaction it could trigger throughout the hemisphere. Meeting with congressional leaders in mid-1960, Eisenhower stressed that "our neighbors . . . resist the unilateral nature of the Monroe Doctrine. . . . If we were to try to accomplish our aims by force, we would see all of these countries [of Latin America] tending to fall away and some would be communist within two years."[18]

U.S. decision makers thus found the idea of secretly overthrowing Castro increasingly appealing. The president, who in the past had made his peace with "gangsterlike" covert action when it advanced U.S. interests, soon paid more attention to the CIA's plan. Normally, he kept his distance from the agency's covert dealings, delegating supervision to the Special Group. As Gordon Gray later recalled, this case was different.

> I'm not sure that Cuba was held strictly in accordance with Forty Committee [Special Group] procedures. I'm inclined to think . . . that this was between the President and the CIA and then others who were brought in from time to time who normally would have been members of the Forty Committee. . . . All these meetings [on Cuba] took place in the President's office. The Forty Committee, as such, never met in the President's office.[19]

Yet despite Eisenhower's personal attention to the project, overall supervision of the planning was loose. The agency's covert branch enjoyed considerable autonomy during the Eisenhower years. In the words of General Andrew J. Goodpaster, then a key member of the White House staff, the CIA was, at the time, a "weakly controlled business." It enjoyed broad discretion in planning the Cuban venture. Beyond the meetings in the president's office, there was limited outside review of CIA preparations. CIA headquarters, in turn, exercised uneven control over its people in the field.[20]

By late summer 1960, the agency had assembled a force of several hundred Cuban exile volunteers. Guatemala's right-wing President Miguel Ydigoras provided the CIA secret bases in his country, where the exiles began to train. But as fall approached, the agency grew skeptical about organizing an effective guerrilla movement within Cuba. As Bissell later recalled:

> Efforts during the late summer and autumn to build an underground... specifically to establish contact with guerrilla groups, to send in a radio operator and technician to each so that they'd communicate to the outside, to identify and recruit agents in fishing villages who were reliable people with whom communications would be possible, for infiltration by small boats, all of these efforts failed abysmally.[21]

CIA thinking gradually changed. Instead of relying on guerrilla action alone to overthrow Castro, the agency—expanding on the Guatemalan precedent, where a ragtag handful of exiles had "invaded" Guatemala—now contemplated landing a well-armed and organized strike force several hundred men strong on the Cuban coast. According to this scenario, the shock of the invasion, coupled with the CIA's propaganda and strategic bombing by exile planes, would incite Cubans to revolt and throw Castro loyalists into disarray. The agency hoped that in the ensuing chaos, Castro's regime would disintegrate. As Bissell described it, the revised concept contemplated "some sort of landing, of a significant force to act as a catalyst in inducing, ultimately, a revolutionary situation in Cuba."[22]

The decision to modify the plan was, as Bissell later recalled, essentially an "internal" shift. Apparently, the agency decided on, and began to implement, the new concept without fully informing the president or the Special Group. On November 4, the CIA ordered its operatives in Guatemala to limit guerrilla training to no more than sixty men. The remainder of the Cuban volunteers, now known as the Brigade, was to receive "conventional military training" for a combined amphibious and airborne assault. The president first learned of the changes on November 29. In early December the agency briefed the Special Group on its new concept. On neither occasion was there any objection to the revised plan.[23]

Most of the U.S. government, however, knew next to nothing about the Cuban venture. In Washington, the CIA shrouded the project in secrecy, keeping only a handful of presidential advisers and key bureaucrats informed. Even the Department of Defense knew little. Under Secretary of Defense James H. Douglas, a member of the Special Group, accompanied sometimes by Secretary of Defense Thomas S. Gates and JCS Chairman General Lyman L. Lemnitzer, attended the CIA briefings on the project. Few other Pentagon officials had any inkling of the plan. In Guatemala, however, knowledge of the mysterious training bases soon was widespread. It could have hardly been otherwise. The population of Retalhuleu, site of the Brigade's air wing, was over several thousand. More than a hundred townspeople, including the mayor, belonged to the local Communist party. Nor was the CIA's presence discreet. Albert C. Persons, one of the CIA air instructors, later described the "secret" air base: "The railroad from Tapachula to Guatemala City and San Jose [ran] along the edge of the field just outside the fence. . . . We often stood on the roof outside the penthouse to wave to the people on the trains. They always waved back."[24]

By October, reports about the exile force in Guatemala had surfaced in the Guatemalan press. They caught the attention of Latin American watchers in the United States. The information made its way to a prominent American with a special interest in the administration's Cuban policy: Democratic presidential candidate John F. Kennedy. By then the senator from Massachusetts had already received two CIA briefings covering, among other topics, Cuba. Although the exact content of these briefings remains unknown, it appears that in a meeting on July 23, 1960, with Kennedy, CIA Director Dulles had told Kennedy that the United States was "training Cuban exiles as guerrilla leaders and recruiting from refugees for more such training."[25]

As the 1960 presidential campaign entered its last weeks, Kennedy castigated the outgoing administration's inaction against Castro. In October, Kennedy proclaimed: "We must attempt to strengthen the non-Batista democratic anti-Castro forces in exile, and in Cuba itself, who offer eventual hope of overthrowing Castro. Thus far these fighters for freedom have had virtually no support from our government."[26]

Following Kennedy's election in November 1960, tensions with Cuba continued to grow. In December, a worldwide conference of Communist parties, meeting in Moscow, exhorted Cuba "to follow the Soviet example of peaceful development." Cuban National Bank President Ernesto "Che" Guevara publicly endorsed the message. On January 2, 1961, capping two years of steadily deteriorating relations, Castro gave the United States forty-eight hours to reduce its diplomatic staff in Havana. The United States broke diplomatic relations the next day.[27]

In his last three months in office, Eisenhower showed mounting interest in the CIA plot, reviewing the covert planning no fewer than six times. He encouraged the planners to step up their efforts. In a meeting of November 29, 1960, he wondered: "Are we being sufficiently imaginative and bold, subject to not letting our hand appear; and (2) are we doing the things we are doing, effectively." The United States, he said, should be "prepared to take more chances and being more aggressive." On January 3, 1961, he urged the planners to see how the "splendidly trained" exiles in Guatemala "can do anything useful," and spoke of "helping to mobilize a stronger invasion force so that a failure in the first effort would not wipe out the whole project." The month before, he had appointed Ambassador Whiting Willauer coordinator of the administration's Cuban policy, including the CIA plan. In 1954, Willauer, as U.S. ambassador to Honduras, had been closely involved in Arbenz's overthrow.[28]

The CIA needed few exhortations to be imaginative and bold. CIA officials seem to have had few qualms about unilaterally changing the plan from a guerrilla infiltration to a large-scale amphibious landing, and informing the president after the fact. Nor was this the only time when the agency "took chances," even without orders. In mid-1960, part of Guatemala's military revolted against President Miguel Ydigoras. The beleaguered strongman asked for the help of the exiles training in Guatemala as he moved to quash the revolt. The CIA chief in Guatemala flashed the request to Washington, where it reached Bissell in the middle of the night. Bissell promptly contacted Department of State's assistant secretary for inter-American affairs, Thomas C. Mann, who explained that he could not authorize U.S. intervention. The matter, Mann concluded, would have to wait until morning. Convinced that the local CIA chief's position was untenable, Bissell approved on his own the use of the Brigade. As it turned out, the CIA commander had already thrown the trainees into the battle. Agency planes flown by CIA pilots attacked a rebel-held airstrip, where a planeload of exiles tried to land. When the administration learned the next morning what was under way, it ordered that the trainees stay at their bases. Ydigoras crushed the rebellion with loyalist troops.[29]

While the agency pressed ahead with its project and Eisenhower became more and more involved, the president-elect kept his distance from the scheme. The CIA briefed Kennedy a few weeks after the election. During the campaign, the agency had mentioned to him in passing some of its anti-Castrist activities. Now Dulles and Bissell described the Cuban project in detail. As Bissell later recalled, Kennedy was "astonished at the scope of what was going on." But he did not object. Kennedy did not, however, pay close attention to it until after the inauguration. The outgoing administration was determined to stay in charge until it left the White House. Kennedy was happy to respect this desire and did not seek to involve himself in policy decisions before he took office.[30]

In the early days of 1961, the agency found it increasingly difficult to keep its plans secret. The *New York Times* of January 10, 1961, carried a front-page story on the exile force in Guatemala. Meanwhile, Castro predicted publicly that the United States would invade Cuba before the end of the month. As the size and visibility of the operation grew, so did doubts inside the agency. Several CIA officials began to question the wisdom of a project that had become the CIA's largest covert operation ever. Their doubts surfaced in various ways. In January, Pat M. Holt, a staffer on the Senate Foreign Relations Committee, received hints from CIA contacts that he should look into the agency's Cuban activities. Other CIA officers voiced concern at agency headquarters. As the Eisenhower administration drew to a close, Richard Drain, chief of operations for the Cuban project, protested to Bissell that the venture had become too large. The original scheme, Drain pointed out, was to send in people "in Castro fashion" and see what happened. Now the CIA was mounting "something that if we had not done World War II and Korea would have been seen as a big military operation." Bissell cited Guatemala as evidence the operation would succeed. Drain loyally swallowed his doubts.[31]

By inauguration day, the agency had invested considerable human, material, and emotional resources into the project. Scores of CIA personnel were involved, training hundreds of exiles and assembling an exile navy and air force to support the Brigade. Although the CIA had not yet drawn up a formal "plan" detailing when, where, and how the exiles might be used, among the CIA planners the idea of landing a strike force as a catalyst for revolutionary turmoil had firmly taken hold. For the executive branch, the ever-deteriorating relationship with Cuba, the existence of a now-powerful exile force, and the CIA's eagerness to strike at Castro were strong incentives to move against the Cuban regime. The project's momentum continued to grow.

But although Eisenhower had become increasingly receptive to the scheme, he never gave the final go-ahead to execute the plan. Nor did the outgoing administration decide how far the United States should support the Brigade if it did go into action. In the last days of the administration, CIA, State Department, and Department of Defense officials met to review the plan. They "assumed" that final operations "would not be triggered unless the U.S. Government were prepared to do everything else needed overtly or covertly . . . to guarantee success."[32] Ultimately, however, the questions of whether to use the Brigade and, if so, of the degree of support the United States should give it were left for the new administration to decide.

At the same time, Eisenhower clearly indicated his favored outcome. At a late November 1960 meeting on the plan, the president observed that he would soon meet the president-elect. Eisenhower said that he planned to raise the covert scheme and hoped that Kennedy's "response would be that he would follow the general line." Meeting again with Kennedy on January 19, 1961, Eisenhower was more forceful yet. Speaking of the guerrilla forces opposing Castro, the outgoing president stated that "it was the policy of this government to help such forces to the utmost. At the present time, we are helping train anti-Castro forces in Guatemala. It was his recommendation that this effort be continued and accelerated."[33] One of Eisenhower's last acts in office was to pass the Cuban project on to his successor with a ringing endorsement.

THREE

Debacle at the Beachhead

On January 20, 1961, John F. Kennedy took the oath as the thirty-fifth president of the United States. Eight days later, the CIA briefed the new administration in depth on the Cuban project. Attending were the president, Vice President Lyndon B. Johnson, Secretary of State Dean Rusk, Secretary of Defense Robert S. McNamara, Attorney General Robert F. Kennedy, JCS Chairman General Lyman L. Lemnitzer, Assistant Secretary of Defense for International Security Affairs Paul H. Nitze, and Special Assistant for National Security Affairs McGeorge Bundy. CIA Director Dulles and Bissell's deputy Tracy Barnes outlined a detailed operational plan, which called for the Brigade, now over eight hundred men strong, to stage a daylight amphibious and airborne assault on the Cuban coastal city of Trinidad. While the Brigade landed, its air wing would destroy Castro's air force and other strategic targets throughout the island. As soon as the exiles secured a beachhead, they would proclaim a Cuban provisional government, which the United States could then recognize.

The CIA planners anticipated that much of the population of Trinidad, where anti-Castrist sentiment was strong, would actively support the Brigade, as would hundreds of guerrillas operating in the nearby Escambray Mountains. The planners hoped that consolidation of a beachhead and proclamation of a provisional government would trigger a revolutionary situation that would sweep Castro away. As they saw it, "The scale of the operation, a display of professional competence and determination on the part of the assault force would ... demoralize the

Castro militia, cause defections therefrom, impair the morale of the Castro regime and induce widespread rebellion."[1]

An internal planning document of the CIA task force dated January 4, 1961, anticipated that Castro could be brought down within weeks:

> The initial mission of the invasion force will be to seize and defend a small area. . . . There will be no early attempt to break out of the lodgement for further offensive operations unless and until there is a general uprising against the Castro regime or overt military intervention by United States forces has taken place.
>
> It is expected that these operations will precipitate a general uprising throughout Cuba and cause the revolt of large segments of the Cuban Army and Militia. The lodgement, it is hoped, will serve as a rallying point for the thousands who are ready for overt resistance to Castro but who hesitate to act until they can feel some assurance of success. A general revolt in Cuba, if one is successfully triggered by our operations, may serve to topple the Castro regime within a period of weeks.[2]

If the Brigade ran into problems, the invaders could retreat into the rugged Escambrays and keep fighting as guerrillas.[3]

The new administration paid close attention to what became known as the Trinidad plan. In early 1961 the agency's prestige was high. As Kennedy observed: "I don't care what it is, but if I need some material fast or an idea fast, CIA is the place to go. The State Department is four or five days to answer a simple yes or no." Moreover, both Dulles and Bissell had close ties to the Kennedy White House. Dulles, who had been on friendly terms with Kennedy for years, was the first person Kennedy appointed to the administration. As Rusk later recalled, this gave him "a special aura, [suggesting] that somehow, the CIA had a special relationship to the President." Dulles was also friendly with presidential advisers McGeorge Bundy and Arthur M. Schlesinger, Jr.[4]

Richard Bissell's connections to the new administration were also close. As former CIA Deputy Director for Intelligence Robert Amory, Jr., later observed: "I think [Kennedy] regarded Dick as probably one of the four or five brightest guys in the whole Administration." Soon after the 1960 election, Walt W. Rostow, McGeorge Bundy's future deputy on the National Security Council (NSC), suggested to Kennedy that he seek a detailed briefing on the intelligence community. As Rostow later recalled, "I said to him once there must be someone you really trust inside the intelligence community. . . . You tell me who that is and let me talk to him. . . . His answer was Dick Bissell." Bissell's ties to McGeorge Bundy and Walt Rostow dated back to their student days at Yale. Another of Bissell's Yale friends was Bundy's brother William P. Bundy, the new deputy assistant secretary of defense for international security affairs. Bissell and Schlesinger were also friends.[5]

The agency's standing and the personal prestige of its directors lent authority to the Trinidad plan. The Kennedy administration had additional reasons to consider it carefully. Kennedy and his advisers came into office convinced that the cold war was a mortal struggle that the United States was in danger of losing. As he warned in his State of the Union address on January 30, 1961, "Each day the crises multiply. Each day their solution grows more difficult. Each day we draw nearer the hour of maximum danger.... the tide of events has been running out and time has not been our friend."[6]

The president and his advisers viewed Cuba as a worrisome threat. Testifying to the Senate Foreign Relations Committee in the wake of the Bay of Pigs, Rusk noted that when the new administration came into office, Cuba "seemed to be moving very fast under totalitarian regime under Communist control.... It had become a center of subversion against other American states.... There was also the prospect which had to be taken into account that Cuba might become a Sino-Soviet bloc missile base in this hemisphere right close to our own coastline." Years later, former secretary of defense McNamara recalled that there was then a mood of "hysteria" about Cuba.[7] For Kennedy and his advisers, the CIA project thus had undeniable appeal. Its success would remove at one stroke a major threat to U.S. interests and provide an important victory in the cold war.

The president and his advisers were also impressed by the argument that any decision to commit the Brigade had to be made quickly. As the new administration reviewed the Trinidad plan in late January and early February 1961, the CIA stressed that if the invasion was put off much longer, Castro's security apparatus would grow so strong that the landing would fail to trigger a popular revolt. Summarizing the CIA argument in a memo to Rusk, State Department Assistant Secretary Mann noted that the intelligence community was "unanimously of the opinion that time is running against us in Cuba in the sense that a declining curve of Castro popularity is offset by a rising curve of Castro control." The agency also emphasized that Cuba would soon receive Soviet-made jet fighters, which could crush any invasion unless the United States provided air support.[8]

The CIA had other powerful arguments in favor of acting quickly. Guatemalan President Ydigoras, faced with rising domestic criticism for harboring the Cuban exiles, had asked the United States to remove the trainees by March 1961. Moreover, Guatemala's rainy season would begin soon, bringing training to a halt. The CIA added that the exile force was at peak readiness; its effectiveness would erode if it waited much longer. As Schlesinger noted in a February 11 memo to the president, this created "great pressure within the government in favor of a drastic decision with regard to Cuba." Speaking after the invasion, Bissell conceded that this pressure "was very strong."[9]

Nor could the administration ignore domestic politics. Kennedy had won the election by a slim margin of 118,000 votes and was worried about his Republican opposition, which he considered "belligerent."[10] Canceling the operation would leave him open to attack. During the campaign Kennedy had advocated strong U.S. support for Cuba's "fighters for freedom." Eisenhower had strongly endorsed the CIA project during the transition. If Kennedy disbanded the Brigade, he would face what Dulles termed the "disposal problem." The disgruntled trainees would accuse the president of selling them out. Kennedy's right-wing critics would denounce his campaign rhetoric as a sham and accuse him of making his peace with Castro when Eisenhower would have swept him away. Dulles later confided to *New York Times* journalist Tom Wicker that he had suggested to Kennedy "repeatedly, without ever saying so explicitly," that if he "canceled the project, he would appear less zealous than Eisenhower against communism in the hemisphere."[11]

The incoming administration thus had strong incentives to authorize a prompt landing by the Brigade. Kennedy nonetheless had misgivings about the scheme. At the January 28 meeting on Cuba, the president authorized "a continuation and accentuation of current activities of the CIA." He simultaneously asked the JCS to review the invasion plan. In a February 8 meeting on Cuba, Kennedy worried about the scale and visibility of the landing. According to the minutes, "The President pressed for alternatives to a full-fledged 'invasion'.... Could not such a force be landed gradually and quietly and make its first major military efforts from the mountains—then taking shape as a Cuban force within Cuba, not as an invasion force sent by the Yankees?"[12]

Kennedy made clear to the JCS that he would not send U.S. personnel into combat to support the Brigade. He made the same point to Admiral Robert L. Dennison, Commander in Chief Atlantic, when the latter called on the White House on February 9. Dennison had learned about the invasion plan when the CIA requisitioned a landing ship dock (LSD) from his command. He asked whether he might have to "bail out" the CIA force if it ran into trouble. Kennedy's reply was a flat no; U.S. forces would not be "overtly involved."[13]

The president had questions of his own for the military but did not receive as candid a reply. Told to review the Trinidad plan, the Joint Chiefs instructed a small team from the Joint Staff to study the project. Major General David W. Gray, who headed the team, was "shocked" by the briefing the CIA gave. The planners provided no written document; the Joint Staff officers "had to pull it out of them."[14] Eventually, they learned enough to write a detailed evaluation. What they discovered was sobering. Although the Brigade was well equipped, the invasion was a potential logistical nightmare.

The plan called for more than eight hundred heavily armed exiles to seize a beachhead around Trinidad on Cuba's west coast and, aided by volunteers from the city, to hold their ground against counterattacks until defections and uprisings swept the island. The Joint Staff team discovered, however, that the Brigade had neither received nor was scheduled to receive amphibious training.[15] The team also identified critical flaws in the logistics of the plan.

The Brigade's limited shipping allowed "no margin for miscalculation or unforeseen contingencies." Moreover, no one in the Brigade was familiar with the loading of the ships. They would learn how the matériel was distributed aboard "immediately prior to D-Day while at sea." There were no constituted ship platoons for unloading; the CIA expected that the boats would somehow "be off-loaded by contract labor." The Joint Staff team found the shore party personnel and equipment "inadequate" to handle the heavy loads on the beach. The team's conclusion was grim: "The personnel and plans for logistic support are marginal at best. This operation may be supported logistically on an austere basis during an unopposed landing.... Against moderate, determined resistance, this plan will fail to provide adequate logistic support."[16]

Yet the JCS's criticism was cautious. They were keenly aware that this was a CIA, not a military, plan. As Chief of Naval Operations Admiral Arleigh A. Burke later recalled: "Over and over again we asked: 'Can we not put our logistic people on this?' The [president's] answer was: 'No. This is a CIA operation. It is not a military operation. You will not become involved in this. I do not want the United States to appear to be an aggressor.'" Lemnitzer likewise "was told a number of times by the CIA representatives that this was not our operation." Moreover, as Lieutenant General Earle G. Wheeler, director of the JCS Staff, later noted, the JCS had "tremendous difficulty in getting information out of the agency." This reinforced their perception that they were not responsible for the project. In the words of Deputy Secretary of Defense Roswell L. Gilpatric, the military came to view the project "more from the standpoint of an interested bystander than a principal."[17]

The JCS thus concluded that it was not their role to be overly critical. According to Burke, "Saying it is not a military operation did have a very strong effect on the whole damn thing. We did keep our hands off more. You can't be told every time you come into the room, 'All we want is what we are going to ask you. It is not your operation. You are not responsible for it.'... pretty soon you commence to believe it." He conceded the JCS "didn't speak up loudly enough."[18] Lemnitzer also was reluctant to dwell on the shortcomings of the plan. As he subsequently explained: "You couldn't expect us, any one of the Chiefs' level, to say this plan is no damn good, you ought to call it off; that's not the way you do things in government. You had a directive to put a force ashore; [the CIA] were doing their best in the planning, and we were accepting it. The responsibility was not ours." Wheeler explained in like terms why the military "didn't step forward and say, 'This ain't going to go.'" "This was not per se a military operation," he observed.[19]

The JCS had additional reasons to mute their criticism. It made little sense to antagonize an agency as powerful as the CIA over a project peripheral to the military's vital interests. Moreover, the JCS wanted Castro removed. In a January 1961 memorandum to McNamara, they warned of "a great and present danger that Cuba will become permanently established as a part of the Communist Bloc, with disastrous consequences." The primary U.S. goal in Cuba, they urged, "should be the speedy overthrow of the Castro government."[20]

The JCS evaluation thus was guarded. In the opinion of JCS Staff Director Wheeler, the Trinidad plan was "a shoestring that couldn't have possibly succeeded against any sort of organized resistance at all." Discussing the plan with the other chiefs, Marine Corps Commandant General David M. Shoup mused: "If this kind of an operation can be done with this kind of a force with this much training and knowledge about it, then we are wasting our time in our divisions, we ought to go on leave for three months out of four." But the JCS report on "Trinidad" was mild and hedged. In it the chiefs explained that the "evaluation of the current plan results in a favorable assessment...of the likelihood of achieving initial military success." "Timely execution of this plan," they added, "has a fair chance of ultimate success."[21]

The Joint Chiefs qualified the statement by cautioning that "ultimate success will depend upon political factors, i.e., a sizeable popular uprising or substantial follow-on forces." They also noted that the "assessment of the combat worth of assault forces is based upon second and third hand reports." They urged that an independent military team evaluate the Brigade and review the logistics plan, noting that "personnel and plans for logistic support are marginal at best. Against moderate, determined resistance logistic support as presently planned will be inadequate." The chiefs confined the more specific criticisms of the Joint Staff team to the annexes of the JCS report.[22]

The chiefs themselves did not present their views to the president. Instead, Bissell summarized their conclusions at a February 8 White House meeting, attended by the president and his chief national security advisers, including Rusk, McNamara, Lemnitzer, Dulles, McGeorge Bundy, Special Assistant to the Secretary of State Adolf A. Berle, and assistant secretaries Nitze, Mann, and Bundy. Bissell reported that "the JCS, after careful study, believed that this plan had a fair chance of success—'success' meaning ability to survive, hold ground, and attract growing support from Cubans. At the worst, the invaders should be able to fight their way to the Escambray and go into guerrilla action." Bissell apparently said nothing about the specific weaknesses the JCS had identified. Neither did Lemnitzer. As a result, the JCS's reservations were lost upon the White House. In a memorandum for Kennedy prepared a few hours before the meeting, McGeorge Bundy wrote: "Defense and CIA now feel quite enthusiastic about the invasion."[23]

Agreeing that the military should evaluate the Brigade firsthand, Dulles asked the JCS to send a team to Guatemala. In late February, three officers from the Joint Staff spent forty-eight hours with the Brigade. The Army expert found the infantry personnel "amazing" and their morale "high." But the officers also had serious concerns. The air expert stressed that although surprise was key to success, the invasion was an open secret. He noted that "with a communist infiltrated town approximately one mile from the airfield, and a railroad on one side of the base and a highway on the other . . . the Castro-Communists will know when the main invasion force is airlifted from Retalhuleu to Puerto Cabezas." Finding security at the staging base at Puerto Cabezas in Nicaragua just as poor, he concluded that Castro likely would know when the Brigade embarked for Cuba.[24]

The air expert's conclusion was equally bleak: "The odds are about 85 to 15 against surprise being achieved in the attack against Castro's Cuba. If surprise is not achieved, it is most likely that the air mission will fail. As a consequence, one or more of Castro's combat aircraft will likely be available for use against the invasion force, and an aircraft armed with 50 caliber machine guns could sink all or most of the invasion force." The logistics expert believed that "logistically the operation would likely fall apart." He warned that the Brigade would be unable "to sustain itself logistically for an extended operation," and estimated that the force had a "marginal capability of operating for a period of thirty days."[25]

The JCS endorsed the team's findings and passed on its report to the secretary of defense. But in their cover memo, the chiefs again proved circumspect. They suggested that the CIA seek to improve the security of the Brigade's activities, adding vaguely that if security could not be enhanced, "the chances of success of the CIA Para-Military Plan should be reevaluated." Alluding to logistical weaknesses, they recommended that a military logistics expert train the Brigade. But despite the glaring weaknesses uncovered by the evaluation team, the chiefs avoided strong criticism, concluding guardedly that "from a military standpoint, since the small invasion force will retain the initiative until the location of the landing is determined, the plan could be expected to achieve initial success. Ultimate success will depend on the extent to which the initial assault serves as a catalyst for further action on the part of anti-Castro elements throughout Cuba."[26]

Having put their reservations on paper, the JCS did not raise them again. There is no evidence the JCS mentioned to the president the findings of the evaluation team. Indeed, the military rarely spoke up about the project. As a result, the civilian decision makers were left with the impression that the Joint Chiefs approved the scheme. The Taylor Board, which conducted the White House investigation into the Cuban debacle, concluded that the JCS "took active part in considering changes to the plan as it developed into final form, did not oppose the plan and by their acquiescing in it gave others the impression of approval."[27]

The chiefs did speak up once, when the plan threatened major military interests. At one meeting, Rusk suggested that the exiles land in eastern Cuba, where they could retreat, if pressed, to Guantánamo Bay, a U.S. enclave on the island and the site of a major U.S. base. As Rusk later recalled: "The JCS did not want Guantánamo involved in this. They expressed themselves very forcefully." As Schlesinger wrote a few days after the invasion, "Rusk at one point proposed the use of Guantánamo for certain operational purposes; Lemnitzer and Burke expressed horror at the idea. Rusk later said to me that they were perfectly ready to put the President's reputation on the block but wouldn't let anyone touch their precious Guantánamo."[28]

Thus in early 1961 the White House had misgivings about the project. The JCS had reservations of their own but declined to press them, and the White House never realized the extent of their doubts. The CIA, in contrast, relentlessly pushed for the invasion. While Dulles and Bissell were the chief advocates, CIA Deputy Director Major General Charles P. Cabell, Tracy Barnes, and Jack Hawkins, a Marine Corps colonel on loan to the agency who was military commander of the invasion task force, often joined them at White House briefings. In part, their enthusiasm reflected the conviction that Castro was a threat who had to be removed. As Bissell later explained: "We saw him as a very major threat to the stability of the Caribbean and Latin America." Moreover, after months spent on the plan, many in the CIA had become, in Bissell's words, "deeply committed to it emotionally."[29]

The CIA had additional reasons to push for the invasion. Created in 1947, it quickly had become a major player in foreign affairs, waging in the process fierce turf battles with bureaucratic rivals. In the mid-1950s, for example, the agency had engaged in protracted struggle with the Air Force for the control of U-2 reconnaissance flights. A spectacular victory in Cuba was certain to consolidate its leadership role. Bissell also had personal stakes involved. Kennedy was thinking of him to replace Dulles when the elderly director retired.[30] A brilliant coup would enhance his chances of getting the job.

The agency representatives became strong advocates. As one White House adviser put it, "Allen and Dick didn't just brief us on the Cuban operation, they sold us on it." Testifying before the Taylor Board, McGeorge Bundy likewise observed that the planners "became advocates, rather than impartial evaluators of the problem." Bissell later conceded that "the pressure of circumstances, but also a pressure applied through people, including myself—was very strong."[31]

In their enthusiasm, the CIA advocates overlooked negative information. Nowhere was this more evident than in the assessment of the potential for uprisings and defections, which were crucial for success. Unless the landing prompted widespread rebellions and defections, Castro's 250,000-strong armed forces and militia would quickly overrun the Brigade.

The reports of the CIA's Directorate for Intelligence—the agency's analytical branch—gave little reason to assume that Castro's control would disintegrate once the exiles landed. In a January 27, 1961, study, the CIA's Board of National Estimates reported "that while Castro will probably continue to lose popular support, this loss is likely to be more than counterbalanced by the regime's increasingly effective controls over daily life in Cuba and by the increasing effectiveness of its security forces." In a follow-up study of March 10, the board concluded that Castro was "firmly in control" and "likely to grow stronger rather than weaker as time goes on." Noting that popular support for the regime was fading, the board nonetheless found "no signs that such developments portend any serious threat to a regime which by now has established a formidable structure of control."[32]

Such downbeat information had little influence on the planners' assessment of the situation within Cuba. The reports of the Directorate for Intelligence might have received more attention had the directorate been involved officially in the Cuban venture. In early 1961, however, it was the CIA's practice not to inform its analytical branch of the operations of the Directorate for Plans. The Directorate for Intelligence provided no formal input into the plan. The planners focused instead on fragmentary reports of opposition from CIA agents on the island, which reported that "more and more men are taking to the hills to fight Castro," and "large numbers of militiamen have refused to fight."[33]

The CIA planners did not just overlook negative information. They also tried to suppress views that could harm the project. In the closing days of the Eisenhower administration, Brigadier General Edward G. Lansdale, then special assistant for special operations to the secretary of defense, became alarmed when he learned that the CIA was preparing an "over the beach landing . . . the most difficult military operation of all." Lansdale spoke up at a December 1960 meeting of the Special Group. Dulles angrily interrupted him, snapping, "You're not a principal in this!" After Under Secretary of Defense James H. Douglas insisted that Lansdale be allowed to speak, Lansdale outlined why he thought the plan would fail. After the meeting, Dulles came up to Lansdale, whose association with the CIA had been long and close, urging him to refrain, "for old times' sake," from further criticism.[34]

In the following months CIA Inspector General Lyman B. Kirkpatrick, Jr., grew disturbed by internal CIA "gossip" about the operation. Although not officially informed of the project, he was approached by several midlevel members of the CIA task force who, "terribly upset about the haphazard organization of the plan," feared it "would blow up." Kirkpatrick asked Dulles for permission to investigate the project, but "Dulles didn't want to hear about it."[35]

The agency also failed to mention some negative facts about the plan. It stressed the Brigade's superb training, morale, and fighting ability but kept silent, however, when the Brigade mutinied in early 1961 against the leader the CIA put in charge of the force. As Schlesinger later wrote, the White House was left with the impression "that life in the Brigade could not be happier." Nor did the advocates mention that the Brigade would include, alongside a core of well-trained troops, scores of eleventh-hour recruits with little or no training at all.[36]

The White House faced forceful advocates of the project, disposed to overlook and sometimes withhold unfavorable information about the scheme. The other decision makers were at a disadvantage in evaluating the proposal. Stressing the need for security, the CIA disclosed the plan to only a handful of people outside the agency—chiefly the president and a few of his advisers. The latter included Secretary and Assistant Secretary of State Rusk and Mann, Secretary and Assistant Secretary of Defense McNamara and Nitze, the JCS, National Security Adviser McGeorge Bundy, and Special Assistant to the Secretary of State Adolf A. Berle. Presidential Assistant Schlesinger and Deputy Assistant Secretary of Defense William Bundy also played significant roles.[37]

Excluded were most of the government's Latin America specialists, both within the CIA's Directorate for Intelligence and the State Department. In State's Bureau of Inter-American Affairs, no one below Mann was brought in on the project. Nor was State's Bureau of Intelligence and Research (INR) involved. Within the military only a handful of officers other than the Joint Chiefs knew about the project. None of the Latin American specialists of the military intelligence services was informed.[38]

Other than the CIA planners, those reviewing the operation were almost all high-level officials who could give it only a fraction of their time. Moreover, secrecy made it difficult for them to gain a thorough grasp of the scheme. The CIA was reluctant to provide written documents. The planning documents it did share circulated briefly at White House meetings and were collected at the end of each session. The president and his advisers relied chiefly on oral briefings for a picture of the plan, missing in the process significant details. The White House, for instance, never understood clearly the exact sequence of air strikes the CIA proposed to conduct.[39]

In addition, the non-CIA officials reviewing the project were mostly generalists who knew little about Cuba or Latin America. It was hard for them to judge assumptions central to the plan, especially regarding the likelihood of uprisings and defections. They had to rely on the advocates' upbeat assessments. After the debacle, McGeorge Bundy ruefully observed that in the future the president "should have intelligence estimates presented to him by others than advocates."[40]

On February 17 Kennedy and his advisers met to review the plan. The president favored "mass infiltration" rather than an all-out assault. The meeting ended inconclusively. On March 11 the president and his advisers met again with the planners. Bissell observed that the Brigade, now numbering almost a thousand, would soon reach a peak of readiness and could not be held together beyond April. He warned that "time is against us." There was still "much active opposition in Cuba." The morale of the militia was poor and the effectiveness of regular forces very low. Nonetheless, the regime's authoritarian controls were increasingly effective. Bissell estimated that within six months it would probably be impossible to overthrow Castro without committing "a more sizeable organized military force than can be recruited from among the Cuban exiles."[41]

Bissell outlined several options for using the Brigade, including a night landing, after which it would move to the mountains to operate as guerrillas. He recommended against it, given the problems of landing at night and of resupplying such a large force. Another option was to land the force in an inaccessible area where it could build up, "protected by geography" from swift counterattack. He recommended against this as well because the remote site would limit the impact of the landing on the population. The CIA's preferred option was the Trinidad scenario: a large, surprise landing at daybreak, "detonating a major revolt." If this failed to occur, the exiles could take to the hills as guerrillas. "This course of action," Bissell argued, "has a better chance than any other of leading to the prompt overthrow of the Castro regime." If effectively used, Bissell concluded, the Brigade had a "good chance" of toppling Castro.[42]

Kennedy said that he expected "to authorize U.S. support for an appropriate number of patriotic Cubans to return to their homeland." Rejecting the Trinidad scenario as too "spectacular," he asked for alternatives that would "provide for a 'quiet' landing, preferably at night, without having the appearance of a World War II-type amphibious assault."[43] He also instructed that the Cuban exile groups in Miami be forged into a new coalition, which would serve as de facto Cuban government-in-exile.

Within days, the agency fashioned a new coalition of Cuban exile movements, merging the original Frente Revolucionario Democrático with more left-of-center groups. And three days after Kennedy rejected Trinidad, the CIA had three new proposals: a revision of the Trinidad concept, a combined airborne and amphibious assault in Oriente Province, and an amphibious landing on Zapata Peninsula, in a swamp known as the "Bay of Pigs."[44]

The Zapata concept, which quickly found favor in the White House, differed in several respects from Trinidad. Zapata called for a "quieter" night landing in the remote and sparsely inhabited Bay of Pigs. Once ashore, however, the exiles' basic mission would be the same: seize and hold an extended beachhead until Cubans began to revolt. The terrain would favor the invaders. Any counterattack would have to follow one of the only three roads that led into the otherwise impassable swamp. Having destroyed Castro's air force in a surprise

D-Day attack, the exiles' air wing, operating from a captured airfield at Zapata, would interdict movement along these roads and bomb strategic targets throughout the island.[45]

Ultimate success, however, still depended on the chain reaction in Cuba. As Rusk told the Taylor Board, the Brigade's "highly-trained men expected to get ashore and run into some militia units and beat the hell out of them. This would be the kind of a bloody nose that would get things moving." In the words of General Wheeler, "The basis for success . . . was that there would be a sizeable and early popular uprising." In a memorandum to the president written a few days before the invasion, Schlesinger explained that the operation could work "if the landing succeeds in setting off uprisings behind the line and in stimulating defections from Castro's militia." As Rusk observed, "It was believed that the uprising was utterly essential to success."[46]

In the original Trinidad concept, the planners had anticipated that much of Trinidad's population would rally to the Brigade as it came ashore. In Zapata, the CIA expected a slower popular response. Bissell counted on a "significant" reaction once the beachhead "had been held for three or four days." Eventual popular revolt within Cuba nonetheless remained the key to success.[47]

The CIA intended to support the landing in every way it could. In a scenario reminiscent of Guatemala, CIA propagandists would work to dishearten Castro loyalists and rally the population to the Brigade. Radio Swan and other CIA-controlled radios would try to convince Cubans that a wave of revolt was sweeping the island. The CIA would airdrop millions of leaflets calling for revolt. It planned to disrupt the communications of Castro's forces and suggest to them that the enemy was all around. Castro's microwave communication centers were key targets of the Brigade's planes. The CIA also planned a diversionary landing of 160 exiles in Oriente Province two days before the main invasion. As the Brigade landed at the Bay of Pigs, specially outfitted craft would approach other points along the coast, imitating the lights, sounds, and electronic signals of large invasion forces. The planners hoped that Castro would not know where to concentrate his troops and that his supporters would lose their nerve.[48]

Last, unbeknownst to all but a handful of colleagues, Bissell also had another weapon. At his instruction, a highly secret CIA team had been planning since mid-1960 to assassinate Castro. In one scheme, they considered poisoning his cigars. In a later effort, they enlisted Mafia "hit men." Although in the end these plots all failed, in early 1961 Bissell hoped "that Castro would be dead before the landing." To this day, it is unclear who outside the CIA knew of the plots. The Senate select committee that in 1975 investigated U.S. assassination plots against foreign leaders believed it "likely" that Dulles knew. It found, however, insufficient evidence to conclude that Kennedy and Eisenhower or their advisers knew of the schemes.[49]

The planners presented the Zapata concept and two alternative scenarios to the Joint Staff review team on March 14. The team reported to the JCS the next day that Zapata was the best of the three alternatives. But they regarded the original Trinidad scheme as still the best plan. On March 15 the chiefs met, endorsed these findings, and reported to McNamara that Zapata "has all the prerequisites necessary to successfully establish the [Brigade] in the objective area." They added, however, that landing in the remote Bay of Pigs might draw less of a response from the Cuban population. Calling Zapata the best of the three alternatives, they cautioned that none of these was "as feasible and likely to accomplish the objective as the basic para-military plan."[50]

The JCS meeting was surprisingly brief. As Attorney General Robert Kennedy noted during the Taylor Board's postmortem, "As I look at the records, I see that the original Zapata Plan plus the alternatives were considered by the JCS for twenty minutes."[51]

The CIA was buoyant about Zapata. On March 16, Bissell told the president it was "on balance more advantageous than the Trinidad Plan." Only few days earlier, Bissell had argued that a night landing posed "unacceptable military risks"; the Brigade "would run the risk of becoming completely disorganized and scattered." By March 16, however, he had overcome his concern about night operations. A few days before the invasion, Bissell assured Robert Kennedy that "the chances of success were about two out of three."[52]

As the planners pushed for their plan, they provided misleading assurances. In promoting the Trinidad plan, they had emphasized that the exiles were trained in unconventional warfare, and therefore could, in a mishap, continue to fight as guerrillas in the Escambrays, Cuba's traditional insurgent stronghold. With the change to Zapata, the landing site was eighty miles from the Escambrays. But the planners assured the White House that the Bay of Pigs was also good guerrilla terrain, and that the Brigade could retreat into Zapata's swamps and from there make it to the Escambrays. As Robert Kennedy later observed, Bissell stressed that "failure was almost impossible . . . even if the force was not successful in its initial objective of establishing a beachhead, the men could become guerrillas, and, therefore, couldn't be wiped out."[53] The Taylor Board concluded:

> In approving the operation, the President and senior officials had been greatly influenced by the understanding that the landing force could pass to guerrilla status, if unable to hold the beachhead. These officials were informed on many occasions that the Zapata area was guerrilla territory, and that the entire force, in an emergency, could operate as guerrillas. With this alternative to fall back on, the view was held that a sudden or disastrous defeat was most improbable.[54]

The assurances were misleading. Admittedly, the officers and some enlisted men had trained as guerrillas in 1960, but when the CIA decided on a conventional strike force, this training ceased. In the words of a CIA study done shortly after the invasion, following the shift to a strike force, "at no time did the Brigade . . . receive training to fight as a guerrilla force. To have attempted to conduct such training would have detracted from the purpose for which the Brigade was organized and would have been detrimental to morale." Shortly before the landing, the CIA did discuss with the Brigade leaders the possibility of operating as guerrillas in an emergency, but "little interest or enthusiasm was displayed by the Brigade personnel concerned for any aspect of the plan that involved retreat and defeat, to include this contingency for guerrilla operations plan."[55] In short, the bulk of the Brigade was not trained for and its leaders were uninterested in guerrilla action, which was not a serious option.

In addition, the Bay of Pigs was unsuitable for large-scale guerrilla operations. The terrain offered almost no water or game. In the words of the Taylor Board, "The guerrilla alternative as it had been described was not in fact available." Looking back, Bissell explained: "It was rather lightheartedly assumed by the CIA that the swampy regions around the Bay of Pigs, while utterly different geographically from the mountains near Trinidad, could support guerrilla operations. With hindsight, this assumption was highly questionable, and, in any event, was not carefully researched in the planning of the operation."[56]

As they pushed their plan, the planners also withheld crucial thoughts. They were disturbed by the restrictions on the operation, particularly the ban against using Americans in combat and the requirement of a "quiet" landing. In notes for an unpublished article he began in 1963, Dulles criticized the fallacy that the landing could be quiet "yet [spur] an uprising in Cuba and mass defections." "The very fact of a *quiet* landing," Dulles noted, "rendered both impossible. Revolt and defection required the utmost 'notice' to the people of Cuba." Yet the planners did not protest the restrictions Kennedy placed on the plan. As Dulles wrote:

> [We] never raised objection to repeated emphasis that the operation: a) must be carried through without any "combat" action by U.S.A. military forces b) must remain quiet [and] disavowable by U.S. gov't c) must be a quiet operation yet must rouse internal revolt vs Castro [and] create a center to which anti Castroites will defect.[57]

Intent on seeing the invasion proceed, the planners probably did not want to cause more doubts that might have led Kennedy, who already had serious misgivings, to cancel the operation altogether. In Dulles's words, "It was a sort of orphan child J.F.K. had adopted (from the Republicans)—he had no real love and affection for it. [He was] . . . only half sold on the vital necessity of what he was doing."[58] As far as the planners were concerned, a landing with unwelcome restrictions was no doubt better than no landing at all.

Moreover, the advocates were not convinced that the limits imposed by the president would necessarily hold. Under Eisenhower, the CIA had been accustomed to a president whose philosophy was "When you commit the flag, you commit it to win." Once a covert operation began, he could be counted on to authorize what was necessary for success. As Dulles noted, "I have seen a good many operations which started out like the B of P—insistence on complete secrecy, noninvolvement of the U.S.—initial reluctance to authorize supporting actions. This limitation tends to disappear as the needs of the operation become clarified." The CIA planners seem to have assumed that when the invasion of Cuba began, Kennedy would be no different, and would authorize the participation of U.S. forces in combat if required. Thus they had another reason not to "raise objections" to restrictions they deemed unwise.[59] As Dulles candidly wrote:

> [We] did not want to raise these issues—in an academic discussion—which might only harden the decision against the type of actions we required. We felt that when the chips were down—when the crisis arose in reality, any action required for success would be authorized rather than permit the enterprise to fail. . . . We believed that in a time of crisis we would gain what we might lose if we provoked an argument.[60]

Thus, while Kennedy insisted that the operation involve no Americans in a combat role, the CIA quietly assumed that he would eventually commit whatever was needed—including U.S. forces—to win.[61]

The White House formally reviewed the CIA's three alternatives on March 15. The president and his advisers continued the review the next day. Kennedy was adamant that the operation should involve nothing beyond the capabilities of exiles acting on their own, so as to not betray the U.S. hand. The White House found Zapata the best of the CIA alternatives. Kennedy, however, made changes "to reduce the noise level." He asked that the invasion fleet clear the area by dawn. On March 16 Kennedy allowed the CIA to proceed on the assumption that he would authorize the Zapata plan, yet reserved the right to cancel the operation up to twenty-four hours prior to landing. The invasion was set for April 5.[62]

In the next two weeks, the invasion date slipped to April 10, then to April 17—the actual day of the landing. During this period, Kennedy reviewed the project several more times. As one meeting followed the next, support within the administration for the operation proceeded to build. By mid-April, most of his advisers had come out in favor of the plan.

The White House and State Department officials were swayed by the planners' optimism and constant assurances. The venture also appealed to the anticommunist fervor of the administration's cold warriors. By 1961, the anticommunism of Special Assistant to the Secretary of State Adolf Berle was at an almost fanatical pitch. Berle was convinced that the Communists had a plan for world aggression. As he noted in his diary of March 1961, he expected that they would soon precipitate "a major climax over Latin America, like the climax when Communism sought to take over all of Europe in 1947." A few days later, he recorded why he supported the plan: "Sooner or later we are going to have to meet the Cuban question head on and it ceases to be a matter of diplomacy and is rapidly getting to be one of force. . . . I think we had best precipitate the climax. . . . we ought to have the battle on our ground instead of on theirs."[63]

Assistant Secretary Mann also shared the cold war spirit. He was skeptical of the Trinidad plan, "where everybody grabbed a musket and went out" when the Brigade came ashore. Mann doubted that popular support would materialize so quickly. He also worried that the invasion would violate the UN and OAS charters. But with the switch to Zapata, Mann grew more confident in a plan "which didn't depend initially on any help from the Cuban people themselves." After reviewing the legal theories of nonintervention, he also concluded that the invasion would be justified as self-defense because Cuba was becoming a Communist state that threatened U.S. security. By March, he was in favor of the plan.[64]

Secretary of Defense McNamara also came out in favor of the project. He had entered office intent on completely overhauling the Department of Defense. As he grappled with the task, he seemingly had little time for the Cuba plan. In fact, he apparently lost or overlooked at least two JCS reports on the project. When he did focus on the plan, he concluded that it had "a marginal probability of success." He nonetheless drew reassurance from the JCS. Like the other civilian decision makers, he assumed that since the chiefs did not oppose the plan, they approved it. McNamara was also encouraged by the belief in the guerrilla fallback. Moreover, he realized that "never again would we have a chance to overthrow Castro without utilizing Americans."[65]

Assistant Secretary of Defense Nitze and his deputy William Bundy likewise approved the plan. In early 1961, Nitze was handling nuclear test ban negotiations with the USSR and coping with the U.S. balance of payments crisis and crises in Laos and the Congo. As he later wrote, "I allowed my other concerns to crowd from my mind proper attention to this operation." He furthermore believed that the "moral right to try to stop the Communist menace from invading our hemisphere was not the issue. The Soviet Union had inserted itself in our backyard. . . . Like a spreading cancer, it should, if possible, be excised from the Americas." He was "uneasy," however, about the practical aspects of the plan after discussing it with General Lansdale. Nitze talked to William Bundy and to the planners about Lansdale's fears; they all disagreed. Nitze ended up backing the plan.[66]

William Bundy, a former CIA official, was inclined to trust the judgment of his former colleagues in the agency, who had a record of success. Like many others, he also believed that the JCS had approved the plan. He went along.[67]

William Bundy's brother McGeorge, originally skeptical of the operation, was impressed by the CIA's efforts to address the president's every concern. As he wrote to Kennedy before the first White House review of Zapata, "[The CIA has] done a remarkable job of reframing the landing plan so as to make it unspectacular and quiet, and plausibly Cuban. . . . I have been a skeptic about Bissell's operation, but now I think we are on the edge of a good answer." The changes did not dispel all of his doubts, but at the start of the new administration, he thought that as national security adviser, he should see that the president heard the views of all the players, not push his own views. McGeorge Bundy did not press the reservations he still had.[68]

A few advisers did oppose the plan. Based on his experience as an infantry colonel in World War II, Rusk thought that, militarily, the operation "didn't have the chance of a snowball in hell." He was skeptical about the likelihood of uprisings. Nor did he think an operation so large could be covert. He also believed that it would violate international law. But at the start of the new administration, Rusk did not think it was his role as secretary of state to pass judgment on the military aspects of the plan. He also believed that as secretary of state he should, in the words of biographer Warren I. Cohen, not "influence the debate, but preside over it," and only afterward give his views privately to the president. Well attuned to the nuances of power, he further realized that he had no power base of his own and did not yet have Kennedy's full confidence. Rusk was thus reluctant to speak out strongly against the plan in the White House meetings. Instead, he voiced his opposition in camera to the president.[69]

Schlesinger also opposed the project. Skeptical that the Cubans would rise, he feared the landing would trigger, instead, bloody civil war. He also worried that it would "dissipate all the extraordinary good will which has been rising toward the new Administration through the world." But Schlesinger was merely a junior adviser; the role the president intended for him was unclear and his power uncertain. He lacked the means and motivation to challenge the plan vigorously. He spoke against it in one or two private conversations with Kennedy and sent the president several memoranda opposing the operation. He was silent, however, in the White House meetings.[70]

The most outspoken opposition came from outside the executive branch. In January 1961, Senate staffer Pat Holt, tipped off by CIA contacts, concluded from bits of information he gathered right and left that an invasion was in the works. Holt told his boss, Senator J. William Fulbright, chairman of the Senate Foreign Relations Committee. They thought that the invasion would be a major mistake. They set forth their views in a memo the senator gave Kennedy in late March 1961. The venture, they argued, would be universally perceived as "a brainchild and puppet of the United States." It would violate U.S. treaty obligations, and would likely falter in the face of "formidable resistance" within Cuba. They advocated restraint, not belligerence, against Castro. "The Castro regime," they wrote, "is a thorn in the flesh, but it is not a dagger in the heart."[71]

Kennedy invited Fulbright to join him at an April 4 meeting on the operation. There Fulbright reiterated to the president and the assembled White House, State Department, CIA, and Defense Department officials his objections, with little effect. In the ensuing discussion, the bulk of the president's advisers, including McNamara, Berle, Mann, Nitze, and William Bundy, recommended going ahead. Only Rusk voiced some reservations.[72]

The president again met with key advisers on April 5, April 6, and April 12 to review the plan. Rusk eventually declared that the Zapata plan was as good as could be devised. Kennedy, while indicating that he wanted to use the force and authorizing continued planning for the execution of Zapata, asked what was the last date on which he could cancel the operation. The reply was April 16. The president made his final decision alone, giving the CIA the final go-ahead in a telephone call on the afternoon of the sixteenth, only hours before the Brigade started to land.[73]

Kennedy had little enthusiasm for the venture. A few days before the invasion, he told Schlesinger: "You know, I've reserved the right to stop this thing up to 24 hours before the landing. In the meantime, I'm trying to make some sense out of it." On the campaign trail, however, Kennedy had advocated strong support for Cuba's "freedom fighters." It was now difficult to call off a plan that matched his rhetoric, and that had the backing of no less a figure than Eisenhower himself. By canceling it, Kennedy would run the risk of appearing "soft" on communism—at a time when the memory of Senator Joseph P. McCarthy's savage attacks on the Truman administration were still fresh.[74]

Moreover, the invasion was forcefully advocated by the CIA, which enjoyed Kennedy's confidence and had a record of success. As Kennedy explained after the operation, Dulles had assured him: "Mr. President, I know you are doubtful about this, but I stood at this very desk and said to President Eisenhower about a similar operation in Guatemala 'I believe it will work.' and I say to you now, Mr. President, that the prospects for this plan are even better than our prospects were in Guatemala."[75] The JCS gave the impression that they fully supported the plan. The opinions of the "experts" carried great weight. As Kennedy subsequently observed, "If someone comes in to tell me this or that about the minimum wage bill, I have no hesitation in overruling them. But you always assume that the military and intelligence people have some secret skill not available to ordinary mortals." In addition, the president was convinced that the guerrilla escape route made the operation all but fail-safe.[76]

There were, of course, glaring flaws in the plan that, notwithstanding the blandishments of the experts and the belief in an escape hatch, should have caused Kennedy grave concern. Despite his wish to keep the operation quiet and covert, it was clear that it would be neither. Fourteen hundred exiles with tanks, artillery, an invasion fleet, and an air force could not stage a "quiet" landing, even in the backwater of the Bay of Pigs. Yet, turning a blind eye to the obvious, Kennedy convinced himself that by shifting the operation from a daylight assault at Trinidad to a night landing at Zapata, he had pared it down, in Schlesinger's words, from a "grandiose amphibious assault to a mass infiltration." As CIA Inspector General Kirpatrick, who conducted the agency's postmortem on the operation, later wrote, "President Kennedy seemed to think this was going to be some sort of mass infiltration that would perhaps, through some mystique, become quickly invisible."[77]

Nor was this the only instance of presidential self-delusion. By the spring of 1961 it was clear that the invasion plan was an open secret and that U.S. involvement would be assumed by all. The *New York Times* January 1961 report on the CIA trainees in Guatemala was but the first of many of press revelations about the project and the U.S. role therein. By March, several leading journalists had gained an accurate picture of the plan through their contacts in Miami. As Kennedy read their accounts in the *New York Times* and other papers on the eve the invasion, he exploded: "I can't believe what I'm reading! Castro doesn't need agents over here. All he has to do is read our papers."[78]

Ultimately, however, the president and his advisers wished this problem away, deluding themselves into thinking that the United States could mask its role. As Schlesinger subsequently wrote, by late March,

> obviously no one could believe any longer that the adventure would not be attributed to the United States—news stories described the recruitment effort in Miami every day—but somehow the idea took hold around the cabinet table that this would not much matter so long as United States soldiers did not take part in the actual fighting. If the operation were truly 'Cubanized,' it would hopefully appear as part of the traditional ebb and flow of revolution and counterrevolution in the Caribbean.[79]

Indeed, wishful thinking, in which Kennedy mistook his desires for reality, seems to have played a significant part in the decision to go ahead. Given his record of earlier successes, it is not altogether surprising that the new president allowed his hopes to color his judgment as he evaluated the plan. Up till then, Kennedy had enjoyed an almost unbroken string of victories in his political career, often against all odds. Emboldened, the president seems to have assumed that despite the difficulties of the Cuban venture, his luck would hold and he could not fail. Reflecting upon the episode, Schlesinger wrote:

> One further factor no doubt influenced him: the enormous confidence in his own luck. Everything had broken right for him since 1956. He had

won the nomination and the election against all the odds in the book. Everyone around him thought he had the Midas touch and could not lose. Despite himself, even this dispassionate and skeptical man may have been affected by the soaring euphoria of the new day.

Echoing these words, Theodore C. Sorensen, another close adviser, wrote: "For once John Kennedy permitted his hopes to overcome his doubts, and the possibilities of failure were never properly considered."[80]

Wishful thinking apparently affected other decision makers as well. Eager to see the operation succeed, senior officials reviewing the plan accepted many of the CIA's optimistic assertions on faith. In the words of Lieutenant General Fred M. Dean, one of the ranking Joint Staff officers who followed the CIA planning and preparation for the invasion, "Everybody was so hopeful, it seemed to me, that this operation would work that they tended to accept as opposed to really question information that was provided." William Bundy voiced a similar view: "I let feeling carry me along. I took what the agency said at face value, which I never did again. There was a lot of wishful thinking, hoping the operation would go because we wanted it to go."[81]

Buoyed by their previous successes, the senior CIA planners were likewise given to confusing hopes and reality. Having toppled the regimes of Mossadegh in Iran in 1953 and Arbenz in Guatemala the following year, senior CIA officials assumed that Castro was but another weak despot who would be no match for their craft. As one key CIA planner recalled: "There was the Guatemala precedent and we had euphoria." Reflecting upon the atmosphere that prevailed among many agency planners, he acknowledged: "We were guilty of wishful thinking. We did not like Castro, and we were convinced he had to go. There was the belief that as a result Castro could not stay in power if the U.S. put its hand to it."[82] These illusions would soon be drowned in the swamps of the Bay of Pigs.

The attack began when eight exile B-26 bombers, taking off from staging bases in Nicaragua, swept down on three of Cuba's major airfields. It was Saturday, April 15, at dawn. In the weeks leading to the invasion, the air strikes had been the subject of extended debate. As early as January 1961, CIA planners warned that "the Cuban Air Force and naval vessels capable of opposing our landing must be knocked out or neutralized before our amphibious shipping makes its final run into the beach. If this is not done, we will be courting disaster." Colonel Hawkins, the military commander of the Cuban project, repeatedly stressed that control of the air was vital for success.[83]

Originally, the planners wanted to destroy Castro's air force in a single, all-out D-Day strike, but the State Department objected that this would be too "spectacular." CIA and State compromised: a first wave of aircraft would stage limited strikes on Cuban airfields three days before the landing. The chief purpose of these strikes was political. While other exile aircraft bombed Cuba's airfields, one plane would make a staged "emergency" landing at Miami airport. The pilot would pretend to be a Cuban Air Force pilot who had defected, strafing his base as he left. This would suggest that Castro's pilots were turning against him and, it was hoped, would "support the fiction that the D-Day landing was receiving its air support from within Cuba." The CIA also hoped that the purported defection would encourage genuine defections from the Cuban Air Force. On D-Day, the Brigade's planes would stage an all-out attack on Castro's airfields, destroying the rest of his planes.[84]

From a diplomatic standpoint, the timing of the invasion could not have been worse. The United Nations General Assembly in New York was in session, scheduled to take up on April 17 Havana's complaint of U.S. "aggression and acts of intervention" against Cuba. The Saturday strikes set off a furor, triggering a chain of events that led to the cancellation of the D-Day strikes.

The new U.S. ambassador to the UN was former Illinois governor Adlai E. Stevenson, longtime standard-bearer of the Democratic Party's Left, and Kennedy's rival for the 1960 Democratic presidential nomination. The two had never been close. Following Kennedy's election, Stevenson aspired to be secretary of state. He accepted the UN post after Kennedy assured him that he would be a senior participant in the conduct of foreign affairs. As a condition for accepting, Stevenson had insisted that no important foreign policy decisions be made "without an opportunity to express my views." "When NSC considers foreign policy matters," he had declared to Kennedy, he "should have option to attend."[85]

Yet, as the White House grappled with the invasion plan throughout the first three months of 1961, Stevenson was left out of the debate. In April, Kennedy decided to advise him of the looming invasion. On April 8, CIA's Tracy Barnes briefed Stevenson and a few other State Department officials at the U.S. Mission to the UN (USUN) in New York. Schlesinger, delayed by another meeting, joined Barnes toward the end of the briefing. As one participant, State Department Assistant Secretary for International Organization Affairs Harlan Cleveland, later put it, the briefing was "evasive."[86]

According to Stevenson's notes, Barnes said that "discontented Cubans," training in Louisiana and Guatemala, were preparing to move against Castro. "Rich Cubans, Am[erican]s, and Canadians behind them." Barnes added that seventy-five American military trainers were in Guatemala on "private contracts"—"mercenaries," he called them, "hired by FRD [Frente Revolucionario Democrático]." The exiles' arms, he continued, were "all on market—Nothing from U.S." The venture, he asserted, would be "truly a *Cuban* operation." The scale and date of the landing were left unspecified; there was no mention of air strikes.[87]

After the invasion, Schlesinger regretted that the briefing had been "probably unduly vague." As Stevenson's deputy Francis T. Plimpton subsequently recalled: "I had the impression that we were going to send a few canoes across in the dead of night and gather up in the mountains, and, then, eventually, do something." Stevenson was unenthusiastic but did not object. He simply asked that the operation not take place until the General Assembly had adjourned. He was left, in Schlesinger's words, "with the impression that no action would take place during the UN discussion of the Cuban item." Meanwhile, the invasion was scheduled for April 17, the same day the item would be discussed.[88]

On April 15, the first air strike took place, destroying several of Castro's combat aircraft. Flying a Brigade B-26, an exile pilot landed in Miami the same morning and recited his cover story. The press spotted the lie. Reporters noticed that the B-26's guns had not been fired and that it had a metal nose, whereas Cuban B-26s had plexiglass fronts. In Miami's Cuban exile community, family and friends quickly recognized the pictures of the defector in the press. He was a former Cuban Air Force pilot who had fled Cuba months before.[89]

The same day, a beleaguered Stevenson strove to refute Cuba's charges that the United States was behind the attack. At the USSR's request, the UN's Political Committee called an emergency meeting that afternoon. Seeking to establish the facts of the raid, Assistant Secretary Cleveland called the State Department, which contacted the CIA. The latter stated that the bombing was the work of defectors. From Rusk's office, USUN received the statement Stevenson was to use: "Regarding the two aircraft which landed in Florida today, they were piloted by Cuban Air Force pilots. These pilots and certain other crew members have apparently defected." At the meeting, Stevenson dismissed Cuban accusations and read his text.[90]

Stevenson discovered the truth only the next day, as the CIA cover story fell apart. On Sunday, April 16, USUN officers were preparing for the UN General Assembly debate the next day. They planned to provide a flood of technical details about the defector's plane to prove that it was a Cuban aircraft that had taken off from Cuba. In the afternoon, however, they learned from Washington that it "wouldn't be worthwhile to pursue that line of inquiry any longer."[91]

Stevenson was appalled. His position in the upcoming debate had become untenable, and he had misled the UN, compromising his reputation for integrity, one of his great prides. He cabled Rusk:

> I had definite impression from Barnes when he was here that no action would be taken which could give us political difficulty during current UN debate. . . . I do not understand how we could let such attack take place two days before debate on Cuban issue in GA [General Assembly]. Nor can I understand if we could not prevent such outside attack from taking place at this time why I could not have been warned.[92]

Stevenson considered resigning. Besides cabling, he also phoned Rusk. According to former senator Barry M. Goldwater, Kennedy later told him that Stevenson had "threatened to stand up in the UN and tell the world we were behind this operation."[93] Kennedy was anxious to avoid a break with Stevenson, who commanded strong loyalties in the Democratic party. As these events were unfolding, the D-Day strikes again came under review.

The planners had presented the schedule of D-2 and D-Day strikes at a White House meeting of April 12. It is not clear, however, how much attention the White House paid. According to one participant, "The paper setting forth the air strikes was passed around at the April 12th meeting. . . . However, this document was only passed around at the meeting, read and considered by some, and collected after the meeting. It is doubtful if the President read it or understood the details." According to a CIA document prepared shortly after the invasion, "The fact that air attacks on D-day were planned was specifically mentioned by the Deputy Director (Plans) when he briefed the President on the contemplated operation."[94] In any event, as no one objected to the proposed schedule, the planners assumed it was approved.

While Stevenson was communicating with Washington, CIA Deputy Director Cabell checked with Rusk Sunday afternoon to confirm that the D-Day strike had White House approval. Rusk, concerned about the impact of the earlier raid, worried about the repercussions of a second strike. As he later explained, "Stevenson was catching hell at the UN. I did not think that this strike would do the job and be effective. It would compound the problems of Stevenson at the UN." Rusk called the president. As Robert Kennedy afterward told Hanson W. Baldwin of the *New York Times,* "Rusk communicated Stevenson's concern and his own to President about 'very adverse' effects on UN— Latin America." Explaining to Kennedy that the CIA planned to launch a second wave of strikes at dawn the next day, Rusk argued that this would be a mistake. Kennedy ordered the second wave canceled unless there were "overriding considerations."[95]

At CIA headquarters, the cancellation came as a devastating blow. Twelve Cuban Air Force planes had survived Friday's attack. Unless they were destroyed, they would wreak havoc on the invasion force, whose lumbering B-26s were no match for Cuba's nimbler Sea Fury fighters and armed jet trainers. Cabell and Bissell met with Rusk that evening at the State Department to appeal the cancellation. They later described the meeting in a memorandum for the Taylor Board:

> The Secretary informed us that there were political considerations preventing the planned air strikes before the beachhead airfield was in our hands and usable. The air strikes on D-2 had been allowed because of military considerations. Political requirements at the present time were overriding. The main consideration involved the situation at the United Nations. . . . Ambassador Stevenson had insisted essentially that the air strikes would make it absolutely impossible for the U.S. position to be sustained.[96]

Cabell and Bissell rejoined that it was too late to stop the landing and that "failure to make air strikes in the immediate beachhead area the first thing in the morning (D-Day) would clearly be disastrous." Cabell explained that the exiles would probably lose one or more ships. The Brigade would be "subjected to a heavier scale of air attack than would otherwise have been the case." But the most serious impact would be on the Brigade's ability to isolate the battlefield. Cabell told Rusk:

> The B-26s were being counted upon to attack approaching Cuban ground and Naval elements and close-in artillery and tanks. No fighter cover was being provided for the B-26s and they would thus face the prospect of serious attrition during these battlefield operations. The beachhead could then be overwhelmed by the superior surface attack which could be brought against it.[97]

Rusk concluded that the air strikes were important but not "vital" and reiterated that D-Day strikes against airfields and other targets outside the beachhead should not take place. He called Kennedy in the presence of two CIA officials. Summarizing their views, Rusk added: "I am still recommending, in view of what's going on in New York, that we cancel." Rusk offered Cabell the opportunity to speak to Kennedy, but the CIA deputy director declined. As he later explained: "Mr. Bissell and I were impressed with the extremely delicate situation with Ambassador Stevenson and the United Nations and the risk to the entire political position of the United States, and the firm position of the Secretary. We saw no point in my speaking personally to the President and so informed the Secretary." A few hours later, however, at 4:30 on the morning of the invasion, Cabell appealed to Kennedy to authorize direct U.S. Navy cover to protect the exile fleet as it withdrew from the beachhead. Kennedy refused.[98]

The cancellation of the second strike seriously weakened the plan. Moreover, the White House had made a major military decision without so much as consulting those best qualified to comment on the matter: the military. At no time on April 16, as the White House debated the wisdom of the second strike, did it consult the JCS. Lemnitzer learned of the cancellation when Wheeler and Gray awoke him during the night to convey the CIA's request for air cover. He thought that "pulling out the rug" like this was "almost criminal." He fully supported Cabell's request for U.S. air cover on D-Day. But he was not consulted on this either. Burke learned of the canceled air strike the next morning. He was "horrified."[99]

This was not the only problem to arise before the Brigade even landed. The final plan called for a diversionary landing in Oriente Province on the night of D-3 to D-2 to "draw Castro's forces to the east and confuse his command." Some 160 exiles on an old Cuban freighter, *La Playa,* arrived off Oriente on time, but the diversion never took place. The first night a reconnaissance team spotted militiamen along the shore. The exiles postponed the landing until the following night. On the second try, they aborted the operation and fled without informing anyone. The group's weak leadership seems mostly to blame.[100]

The main body of exiles waded ashore at Zapata on the night of April 16. No sooner had the advance units reached the beaches than fierce firefights broke out. By daybreak, a pitched battle was under way, which quickly reverberated in the halls of the UN, where Cuban and East Bloc delegates denounced U.S. "aggression." The fallacy that the United States could plausibly deny involvement, to which the White House and the CIA had clung for months, was cruelly exposed. Throughout the world, the operation was attributed to the United States.

The exiles, however, were in far more trouble than U.S. diplomats at the UN. The landing went wrong from the start. The CIA had told the exiles that Zapata was largely deserted and that they would land unnoticed. In fact, construction was under way day and night on a resort at Playa Giron (Blue Beach), one of the three beaches where the Brigade was supposed to land. As a reconnaissance team closed in on the shore, it found large sections of the beach awash in the glare of vapor lamps. It barely reached land before clashing with a militia patrol. Despite Kennedy's ban on U.S. participation in combat, the first invader to land and open fire was an American CIA paramilitary operative. Elsewhere along the coast, machine guns opened up on a landing ship. At Playa Larga (Red Beach), the second landing site, the exiles ran into the militia almost upon landing. The attackers found a microwave communications center, the equipment still warm. The alert had been given.[101]

Problems multiplied throughout the night. Many of the troops were supposed to cover the last few thousand feet to the shore in light fiberglass launches. The outboard motors of most boats malfunctioned. Several launches capsized. Soon, less than a quarter of the boats were usable for the twenty-minute trip to the beach. Making matters worse, the CIA planners had missed a strip of razor-sharp coral lying off Blue Beach. Some launches sank on the reefs. Others stopped short of the coral barrier, forcing the troops to wade through chest-deep water to reach the shore. The Brigade's large LCUs (landing craft utility), carrying tanks and heavy equipment, had to wait for high tide at dawn to reach the beach. Between the faulty launches and the reefs, the fleet failed to unload all of the troops and withdraw before daylight as planned. As morning broke, an entire battalion and most of the supplies had not yet been unloaded. Soon disaster struck.[102]

At dawn, several of Castro's remaining aircraft attacked the beaches and the invasion fleet still off shore. A Sea Fury hit the freighter *Houston*, laden with troops and equipment. The crippled ship ran aground. A few hours later, Castro's planes dealt an even worse blow, setting ablaze thousands of gallons of aviation gas on the *Rio Escondido*. The ship sank, taking with it the bulk of the Brigade's supplies and its communications trailer.[103]

The loss of the radio gear was severe: without it, the Brigade could not communicate with its B-26s. Meanwhile, communication between the beachhead command post and Brigade units was difficult because many of the soldiers' portable radios had been soaked as the men waded ashore. Later that morning, enemy aircraft shot down two B-26s flying air cover for the exiles. The invasion fleet's two other freighters, carrying most of the Brigade's remaining supplies, fled to the open seas. They did not turn back until U.S. warships stopped them, respectively one hundred and two hundred miles from Cuba.[104]

Castro, who had long anticipated an invasion, lost no time counter-attacking on the ground. He immediately dispatched half a dozen infantry and militia battalions to reinforce his forces at the scene. By afternoon, the reinforcements were engaging the exiles. Meantime, Castro's security forces rounded up suspected opponents throughout the island. Prisons were soon overflowing. In Havana alone, more than 200,000 people were herded into the city's sports stadium, theaters, and ballparks. By nightfall, most of those who might have been tempted to support the landing were in custody.[105]

Castro's quick, effective response surprised the CIA. The planners had assumed that the several landings and diversions would confuse him and that his forces would fight halfheartedly at best. Instead, he reacted decisively and his troops generally fought with determination. As the Taylor Board noted with understatement: "The effectiveness of the Castro military forces, as well as that of his police measures, was not entirely anticipated or foreseen." Some 20 years later, Bissell acknowledged more candidly that a "contributing cause of failure...was that Castro's ground forces moved more decisively, faster and in greater force than anyone had anticipated."[106]

Some Castrist units did falter, and some of the prisoners the exiles took offered to join the Brigade. A number of local residents also supported the invaders; a few took up arms alongside them. The Brigade also scored a few early successes. In the afternoon of D-Day, its artillery and planes decimated a militia column some nine hundred men strong. Yet widespread defections never occurred, and the bulk of Castro's troops fought on.[107]

Nor did the landing trigger unrest behind the lines. CIA's Radio Swan sought to create an atmosphere of civil war suggesting that Castro was losing control, and urged active resistance to the regime. But with most of Castro's opponents in jail or cowed by his crackdown, no one outside the beachhead stirred in favor of the Brigade. CIA psychological warfare had worked against Arbenz in 1954. It was ineffective, however, in Cuba, where Castro enjoyed far more control than Arbenz ever did in Guatemala. By the end of D-Day, Castro's vastly superior forces were pushing the exiles back.

As the operation foundered, officials in Washington found it very difficult to follow the situation on the ground. The loss of the signal equipment on the *Rio Escondido* and on the *Atlantico,* which fled on the morning of D-Day, severely limited the communications capability of the troops at the beachhead. Most of what Washington knew came from the despatches of the *Blagar,* an LCI (landing craft infantry) that served as Brigade flagship and was in radio contact with the Brigade commander ashore. In the wake of the air attacks on the morning of D-Day, an American CIA contract agent aboard had unilaterally taken over as commander of the invasion ships that had not sunk or fled. CIA computers automatically encoded all transmissions sent to the invasion force. Aboard the *Blagar,* the flood of incoming messages had to be decoded by hand. It often took hours to render Washington's cables in clear English.[108]

Decision makers in Washington were thus usually several hours behind. In the words of the Taylor Board, "The President and his advisors were generally in the dark about important matters as to the situation ashore." In an April 18 message to CINCLANT Commander Dennison and the Navy ships off Cuba, the JCS stated bluntly: "We are operating almost entirely in the dark. Forward assessment of situation as you see it." In a private memo dictated shortly after the debacle, Robert Kennedy noted: "It was complete lack of communication. Nobody was able to determine what was going on really there."[109]

Still, by the second day it was clear that the Brigade was losing. By then, Castro had arrayed tens of thousands of troops, with armor and heavy artillery, against the exiles. In a memo to the president on Tuesday, April 18, McGeorge Bundy reported somberly:

> The situation in Cuba is not a bit good. The Cuban armed forces are stronger, the popular response is weaker, and our tactical position is feebler than we had hoped. Tanks have done in one beachhead, and the position is precarious at the others.
>
> The CIA will press hard for further air help—this time by Navy cover to B-26s attacking the tanks. But I think we can expect other pleas in rapid crescendo.[110]

Indeed, by the evening of D+1, pleas for overt intervention had become almost frantic. The exiles fought bravely but were hopelessly outnumbered and outgunned. The sinking or flight of their ships left them with little ammunition other than what they had carried when they landed, which was fast running out. With Castro's fighters controlling the air, the exiles' B-26s could no longer provide the air support that had proven so effective against enemy counterattacks on the afternoon of D-Day. By the end of the second day, six B-26s and over a third of the Brigade's air crews had been lost. On the ground, the beachhead teetered on the verge of collapse.[111]

Shortly before midnight on Tuesday, April 18, the president called an emergency White House meeting. Among those attending were Vice President Johnson, Rusk, Robert Kennedy, Lemnitzer, Burke, McGeorge Bundy, Dulles, Schlesinger, and Bissell. Bissell and Burke urged the president to commit U.S. forces to prevent a disaster. Joint Staff Director Wheeler, who was also present, later recalled that "Bissell was tre-

mendously upset. In fact, he could hardly talk coherently at the outset."
Rusk strongly opposed direct U.S. intervention, arguing that the United
States had pledged not to attack Cuba and that "the President shouldn't
appear in the light of being a liar." Robert Kennedy stressed that the
White House simply did not have enough information to judge whether
air cover would make a difference. In his brother's words, "Jack was in
favor of giving [air support]." Earlier on, John Kennedy had said that
"he'd rather be called an aggressor than a bum."[112] According to
Wheeler, the president seemed close to granting Bissell's request:

> I got the impression from President Kennedy's reactions, facial remarks,
> and so on, that he was extremely desirous of doing something to correct
> the situation. . . . he said, well, perhaps we ought to put in the navy air off
> the carrier which was lying offshore. . . . He was quite insistent . . . that he
> wanted to do something. I had the very distinct impression that he was
> going to go ahead and do something. However, after a fairly brief discus-
> sion along these lines he went back into his own office with two or three of
> his advisors and later came out and said, no, he would not do this, about
> five or ten minutes later.[113]

Another participant, Lieutenant General Brent Breitweiser, likewise remembers that the president seemed swayed by the CIA's appeal, but finally decided against intervention after stepping out briefly with his
brother.[114]

Earlier that morning, Lemnitzer had suggested that the time had
come for the Brigade to take to the hills. He was surprised to hear Bissell reply that the unit was "not prepared to go guerrilla." Burke was
unwilling to abandon the Brigade to its fate. When the president returned to the room and said he would not commit U.S. forces because
he did not want the United States involved, Burke replied: "Mr. President, damn it, we are involved." As he later recalled,

> I asked: "Can I not send in an air strike?" "No." We had a long discussion
> on that. I said, "Can we send a few planes?" [He] said: "No, because they
> could be identified as United States." "Can we paint out their numbers or
> any of this?" "No." "Can we get something in there?" "No." Over and
> over—everything, "No." . . . "if you'll let me have two destroyers, we'll give
> gunfire support and we can hold that beachhead with two ships forever."
> "No." "One destroyer, Mr. President?" "No."[115]

Eventually, Kennedy relented. In a last-minute compromise, he authorized six unmarked Navy jets to provide an hour's cover, beginning
at 6:30 A.M. on April 19. They were not to engage ground targets but
to protect the exiles from air attack. The exiles' B-26s, otherwise hopelessly vulnerable to Castro's fighters, would use the cover to strike enemy forces threatening the beachhead. This bid to help the Brigade
proved futile, however. In a mix-up between the Navy and the CIA, the
B-26s arrived over the beachhead an hour before the jet cover was
scheduled to begin. Two B-26s were shot down and the others fled be-

fore the Navy planes reached the scene. Four more B-26 pilots had died, this time American contract pilots whom the CIA had thrown—without the White House's knowledge—into the battle.[116] The ban against Americans fighting with the Brigade again had been ignored.

Throughout, Washington often attempted to control the actions of U.S. forces in minute and sometimes unreasonable detail. As the Brigade steamed toward Cuba, U.S. Navy planes and ships were to protect it up to the Cuban coast. The Navy was told, however, to avoid "overt association." Navy ships were to keep "maximum practicable range" ahead of the exiles' ships. Navy aircraft "should not give the appearance of covering the ships of the Cuban Force." U.S. fighters were not to attack any hostile plane unless it "commences to fire on the Cuban Force ship(s) or if it opens its bomb bays and commences its bomb run." To Admiral Dennison, this made little sense. Waiting to be shot at to respond was, as he subsequently mused, "considerably late. My idea would be to intercept them well out and get them out of the area. If they wouldn't go, shoot them down. . . . When do you feel justified in shooting somebody who's threatening you? You don't wait till you see his fingers squeeze the trigger."[117]

Dennison soon received more surprising orders yet. He later recalled that when the exiles were reeling from Castro's counterattacks, he was ordered to set up a safe haven off Cuba for any Brigade ships that escaped. The order

> went into considerable detail. It was really a tactical order addressed to me as Commander-in-Chief. I wouldn't have sent the thing to a captain. It was not just what they wanted done but exactly how to do it, how many destroyers to use. I called up Lemnitzer . . . and said: "this is a strange one . . . the last paragraph in it says that the Joint Chiefs of Staff interpret this to mean, set up a safe haven. This is the first order I ever got from somebody who found it necessary to interpret his own orders."
>
> He said, "Where did you get this directive?" And I said, "I got it from you." He said, "Who do you think wrote it?" I said: "You did." He said: "No, I didn't. That order was written at 1600 Pennsylvania Avenue."
>
> I said, "Well, you can just tell 1600 Pennsylvania Avenue that I'm not going to do it that way. I'll do what they want done, but I'll use all the forces that I think are necessary. They don't know what's going on as much as I do."[118]

Dennison soon had other problems to face. When the enemy overran the beachhead on the afternoon of April 19, the White House ordered the Navy to patrol off the Bay of Pigs to pick up survivors. Implementing this, however, was a challenge. Dennison had been briefed on the invasion plan only once, in late 1960. Since, the scenario for the landing had changed "radically." Yet, in his words, he "had never had an opportunity to study the detailed plan nor the effect of successive changes. . . . This lack of information made intelligent planning for evacuation or for direct support . . . almost impossible." He did not know how many troops had gone ashore, where they had landed, or where they were likely to be. The Navy did its best to pluck stragglers from the beaches, ignoring orders from Washington that seemed especially unwise. Dennison was most dismayed by one "strange directive," authorizing the commander of a destroyer "to ground his ship if it will facilitate mission."[119]

At one point, the rescue barely avoided disaster. As the *La Playa,* with 160 Brigade members aboard, fled after the aborted diversionary landing in Oriente Province, it steamed into a formation of U.S. warships. The Navy knew nothing about the feint in Oriente, hundreds of miles from the Bay of Pigs. Encountering the freighter bristling with troops, a destroyer "dammed near opened fire on it, thinking it was the enemy."[120] At the last moment the Navy identified the ship.

By April 20, the Navy had picked up twenty-six survivors; Castro's forces had captured a thousand more. The exiles who took to the swamps were rounded up within days. The landing had ended in ignominy for the Brigade and its patron, the United States. Meanwhile, Castro's victory greatly enhanced his prestige at home and abroad. In a chance encounter with White House aide Richard N. Goodwin in Argentina four months after the invasion, Cuban minister Ernesto "Che" Guevara sarcastically said that "he wanted to thank us very much for the invasion—that it had been a great political victory for them—enabled them to consolidate—and transformed them from an aggrieved little country to an equal." The invasion also caused Cuba to draw even closer to the USSR. Worried that the United States might strike again, perhaps with U.S. forces, Castro brought Soviet small arms, artillery, armor, and, eventually, nuclear missiles into Cuba.[121]

In the United States, the debacle was greeted by stupefaction and angry recrimination. Publicly, Kennedy assumed full responsibility for the fiasco. Privately, the president and his advisers heaped blame on the CIA and the JCS. Robert Kennedy summarized the prevailing White House view in a conversation with Hanson Baldwin of the *New York Times,* which Baldwin recorded in his notes: "Other than mistakes made by CIA greatest mistakes made by military—Lemnitzer and Burke. Had responsibility of studying whole plan for more than a month. Did not give it the attention or study it deserved. President accepted their judgment as to whether it was militarily feasible." CIA personnel, for their part, insisted that the invasion would have had a good chance of success had Kennedy not canceled the D-Day air strikes.[122]

There is little doubt that the cancellation of the strike was a serious blow. As events proved, the invasion fleet was hopelessly vulnerable to attack by Castro's remaining planes. And without control of the skies, the Brigade's B-26s could not stop, as planned, Castro's forces as they counterattacked down the three narrow causeways leading to the beachhead. Nevertheless, even if the D-Day strikes had occurred and destroyed what was left of the Cuban Air Force, the Brigade's prospects still would have been bleak. Even if the B-26s had not been challenged in the air, they would have faced deadly ground fire. Castro dispatched large numbers of antiaircraft weapons to the beachhead, which his forces used effectively. These weapons would quickly have taken a deadly toll of the Brigade's seventeen B-26s.[123]

Moreover, barring direct U.S. intervention, the Brigade could have prevailed only if the invasion triggered large-scale defections and uprisings. Although the planners had convinced themselves that these were likely, reality was different. During the three days the beachhead lasted, the exiles fought well, inflicting far greater losses than they suffered. Yet despite Castro's forces' heavy losses, few Cubans defected. And for every Castrist fighter who fell, several others stepped forward to take his place. Meanwhile, Castro's internal crackdown left his domestic opponents powerless, preventing any significant popular reaction in support of the Brigade. Given the loyalty of Castro's forces and the impossibility of popular rebellion, the exiles could expect only defeat. For the invasion to succeed, conditions within Cuba would have had to be totally different from the situation that prevailed on the island in April 1961.

Kennedy's worst disaster, the Bay of Pigs, is also a paradigm of the problems that have beset U.S. strategic special operations of the past thirty years. All of the various shortcomings observers have decried in these operations plagued the Cuban invasion. U.S. intelligence was poor. The CIA mistakenly thought that the landing site was mostly deserted and that the exiles could land unnoticed. It missed the reefs at Blue Beach, which caused the landing to fall behind schedule—leaving the hapless invasion fleet still offshore when Castro's aircraft struck. U.S. intelligence badly underestimated the mettle and effectiveness of Castro's forces. The United States lacked trustworthy, capable, and well-informed agents on the ground in Cuba who could accurately gauge the morale and capabilities of Cuban forces, or even competently scout out the invasion site.

Interagency coordination and cooperation was totally inadequate. In their desire to maintain secrecy—and, more important, retain tight control—the planners were reluctant to share information with the military, even though the latter had a legitimate "need to know." In a classic breakdown of coordination, exile B-26s reached the beachhead before the Navy jets providing cover.

The president and his key advisers received inadequate, one-sided information and advice. The planners kept up a steady drumbeat of optimistic assurances. Meantime, they failed to mention unfavorable details, like the mutiny of the Brigade, and acted to stifle criticism, be it Lansdale's comments or the review of the planning and preparation proposed by CIA Inspector General Kirkpatrick. Keen on seeing the operation proceed and confident events would take on their own dynamic once the invasion began, the planners did not protest when the White House imposed restrictions that, in their view, weakened the plan. The thick curtain of secrecy that the planners maintained in Washington denied the White House the benefit of the views of experts from the CIA's analytical branch and the Department of State who did not have a vested interest in the plan. Among the handful of presidential advisers who knew about the operation, few gave it much attention and even fewer vigorously pressed the doubts they had. Moreover, the president, the planners, and key White House advisers engaged in wishful thinking, wishing away major flaws of the plan or convincing themselves that the Cubans would rise and that Castro was but another shaky despot who could never be the match of the United States.

Last, execution of the operation was flawed by repeated, inappropriate White House intervention. The president canceled the key D-Day air attack without soliciting the advice of his senior military experts. The White House tried to direct the movements of individual U.S. ships covering the invasion, even though it had only the dimmest notion of the situation at the scene. In short, the Bay of Pigs was a model of how not to plan, evaluate, and execute strategic special operations—a model from which the U.S. government failed to learn for two decades. The flaws that had marred the Cuban invasion were to be repeated again and again in strategic special operations that followed.

FOUR

Raid to an Empty Camp

Throughout the Vietnam war, the U.S. military went to extraordinary lengths to save its personnel from captivity. Time and again, rescue crews braved daunting odds to recover airmen who had been downed in enemy territory—often, North Vietnam itself. One of the most dramatic examples occurred during North Vietnam's 1972 invasion of South Vietnam. On April 2, 1972, Lieutenant Colonel Iceal E. Hambleton was shot down south of the demilitarized zone between North and South Vietnam. He parachuted to the ground, only to land in the path of three North Vietnamese divisions. For the next eight days, the Air Force conducted up to ninety strike sorties a day to keep the enemy away from his position and secure the area for a helicopter rescue mission.[1]

The United States lost four aircraft and eleven aviators trying to reach Hambleton. On the eighth day, he escaped by making his way to the Cam Lo River and swimming downstream out of the main enemy concentration. A Marine Corps rescue party picked him up after he had spent three nights floating down the river. During his ordeal, the U.S. military declared the seventeen-mile radius around his downed aircraft a "no fire zone," where air strikes and artillery fire were severely restricted. This covered most of the operations sector of South Vietnam's Third Army Division, which was left to fight off with almost no artillery or air support three enemy divisions with armor and heavy artillery.

The United States had good reason to worry about its servicemen falling into enemy hands. The fate of those captured by the North Viet-

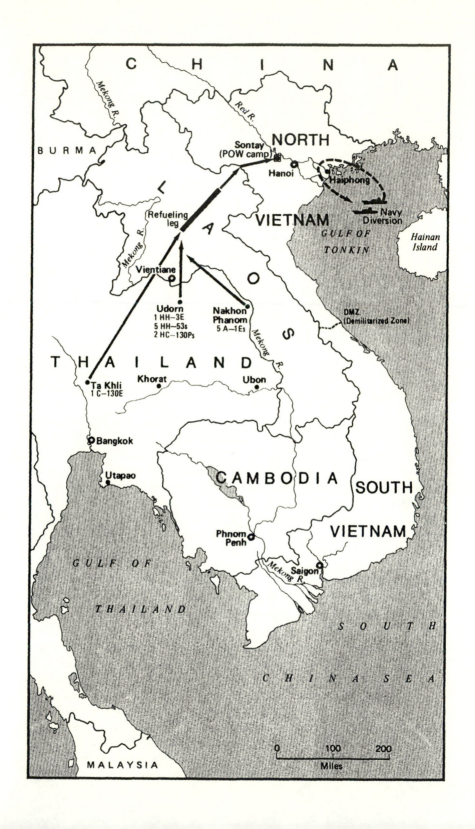

namese or the Vietcong was grim. Vietnamese Communists had little regard for the Geneva Convention on Prisoners of War (POWs). Communist captors routinely confined American POWs in sordid compounds, where they were fed insufficiently, denied proper medical care, and often tortured.[2]

By 1970 more than fourteen hundred U.S. servicemen were prisoners of war or missing in action (MIA) in Southeast Asia. Their fate was a major concern of the Department of Defense, which made intelligence collection on POWs and MIAs one of its highest intelligence priorities. Within the U.S. intelligence community, the whereabouts and welfare of POWs and MIAs was a top "Key Intelligence Question."[3]

The White House also worried about the POWs. President Richard M. Nixon, staunchly promilitary, had a personal interest in the plight of these men, some of whom, by 1970, had been imprisoned longer than any U.S. POW in World War II. The POWs and MIAs had also become a charged domestic issue. Spurred by the vocal "POW/MIA League of Families," tens of thousands of Americans were writing North Vietnam's government, demanding better treatment for the POWs. More than four hundred members of Congress had signed their own protest against conditions in North Vietnam's POW camps.[4]

As emotions over the POW issue rose, in mid-May 1970 Air Force intelligence experts made an unusual discovery. Examining aerial reconnaissance pictures taken over North Vietnam, they spotted evidence that as many as fifty POWs were held in a small compound at Sontay, some twenty-three miles northwest of Hanoi. More unusual yet, they were calling for help: aerial imagery of the camp showed that they had set out laundry to dry in a pattern spelling out the code letters for search and rescue. A quick review of the camp's location and defenses convinced the Air Force that a rescue mission was feasible. Senior Air Force officers shared their findings with Army Brigadier General Donald D. Blackburn, special assistant for counterinsurgency and special activities (SACSA) to the Chairman of the JCS.[5] SACSA handled the Pentagon's most sensitive "special operations."

The idea of a raid at Sontay, deep inside North Vietnam, immediately appealed to Blackburn. If successful, the operation would free fellow soldiers from their ordeal at the hands of the North Vietnamese. Blackburn, who had long been impatient with the restrictions on the U.S. war effort, saw other merits to the idea as well. Since President Lyndon B. Johnson had halted the bombing of North Vietnam in March 1968, U.S. forces had been forbidden from carrying the war to the North. An expert in unconventional warfare, Blackburn longed to stage commando raids against key North Vietnamese installations such as the Lang Chi hydroelectric dam. Built with Soviet assistance, it was nearing completion northwest of Hanoi, and would greatly increase North Vietnam's electrical output.[6]

In Blackburn's view, if the United States dealt a few crippling blows directly in the enemy's "back yard," Hanoi might become more flexible at the Paris peace talks between the United States and North Vietnam, then at a stalemate. So far, he had been unable to convince his superiors of the usefulness of commando strikes against the North. A raid that brought U.S. POWs home—and showed in the process how easily U.S. commandos could operate in North Vietnam—might make the JCS more receptive to some of the other operations he had in mind.[7]

Studying the data, Blackburn and his staff quickly concluded that a rescue was feasible. In early June, the SACSA director first mentioned the idea of a raid to the outgoing JCS Chairman, General Earle G. Wheeler. Wheeler was enthusiastic: "I don't see how *anyone* could say 'No' to this operation," he declared.[8] On June 5 Blackburn briefed the Joint Chiefs, recommending that SACSA study a possible rescue operation. The chiefs agreed.

On June 10 SACSA convened a thirteen-person feasibility study group drawn from the four services. Most came from the Army, Navy, and Air Force staffs at the Pentagon. Others came from the Defense Intelligence Agency (DIA), the Department of Defense's intelligence agency. They worked throughout June and early July. Although not formally part of the feasibility study group, the CIA was closely involved. Upon receiving JCS approval to conduct his study, Blackburn called on George A. Carver, CIA special assistant for Southeast Asian matters, and described his idea of a raid on Sontay. Carver pledged his office's full support.[9]

A month after the feasibility study group first convened, Blackburn presented its findings to the JCS. Admiral Thomas H. Moorer, who on July 2 had replaced Wheeler as Chairman, presided over the meeting.[10] Blackburn reported that since first spotting POW activity at Sontay, DIA had concluded there were as many as sixty-one prisoners at the camp. Aerial reconnaissance showed that the compound was relatively isolated, surrounded by paddies where helicopters could land. Blackburn presented the study group's proposal: landing at night, a small, heavily armed heliborne force would rush the camp, overpower the guards, and lift off with the POWs. The rescuers would have to move quickly because large numbers of North Vietnamese troops were garrisoned only miles away. Blackburn and the study group believed the rescuers could be in and out in minutes and were confident that the mission had a good chance of success.[11]

The new JCS Chairman was attracted to the proposal. Moorer thought a successful rescue mission would benefit all of the POWs in North Vietnam, not just those at Sontay. He later explained:

> I felt very strongly that if we could get some of the POWs back home and let them circulate it would enable us to explain about the torture [and other abuse the POWs suffered]. The American people, who had been whipped up by the press, which was getting much of its information from Hanoi... would then have understood. This would have made it much easier to even-

tually free the other POWs.... What I was hoping for was what took place after the Christmas 1972 bombing of North Vietnam. The boys would have come home after Sontay.[12]

Moorer also saw another virtue to the proposed operation: although its primary objective was to "free the boys," it would also "convey to the North Vietnamese a hard lesson," leaving them uncertain and apprehensive about what further action the United States might take. At the end of the meeting, the JCS approved the mission concept and instructed SACSA to begin detailed planning and training for possible execution of the raid.[13]

Blackburn immediately began selecting personnel for the mission. On August 8 the JCS created the special Joint Contingency Task Group (JCTG), which reported to SACSA, to handle planning and preparation of the operation. To head the task group, SACSA picked Brigadier General Leroy J. Manor, who commanded the Air Force's Special Operations Force (SOF) at Eglin Air Force Base in Florida. SOF was the Air Force's unconventional warfare unit that supported U.S. and allied special operations in Southeast Asia. To second Manor, Blackburn chose Colonel Arthur D. Simons, an Army Special Forces officer with extensive experience in unconventional warfare in Vietnam. Meanwhile, SACSA expanded the thirteen-person feasibility study group to a full-fledged planning staff of 38. It included Manors and Simons, most of the original feasibility study group, additional officers from the Pentagon and the field, and two CIA officials. Four members of the planning group participated in the raid.[14]

The planning group had access to the resources of the entire intelligence community, including the National Security Agency (NSA), which specialized in electronic (signals) intelligence, and the National Reconnaissance Agency, whose expertise was aerial and satellite reconnaissance. The planners also could task the Strategic Air Command's SR-71 Blackbird spyplanes and Buffalo Hunter observation drones, as well as the Tactical Air Command's reconnaissance jets. Finally, to ensure that the planners received the best intelligence possible, Blackburn was instrumental in convincing CIA Director Richard M. Helms, NSA Director Vice Admiral Noel A. Gayler, and DIA Director Lieutenant General Donald V. Bennett to put some of "their key people" in charge of intelligence gathering in support of the raid.[15]

Much of the intelligence flowing to the planning group was first-rate. The NSA identified blind spots in the North Vietnamese radar network the raiders could exploit to fly undetected to the POW camp. The planners also received excellent information on the nature and location of the antiaircraft defenses around Sontay, as well as on enemy reaction times. As Manor commented after the raid, "Military and national intelligence agency assessments of enemy capabilities and reaction... were highly accurate."[16]

The collection effort nevertheless suffered from a major drawback.

The intelligence community had to rely almost exclusively on technical means of collection because the United States had no clandestine agents in North Vietnam who could check the situation on the ground. There were limits to the amount and type of information obtainable by technical means. Many U.S. technical collection "assets" had to be used sparingly. If too many reconnaissance planes or drones overflew Sontay, the North Vietnamese would become aware of U.S. interest in the camp. Satellite or aerial imagery enabled U.S. photo interpreters to determine how many persons were in the prison courtyard on a given day, but the pictures were not detailed enough to show whether these persons were Caucasians or Vietnamese. And if the skies were overcast when the reconnaissance aircraft or satellite passed over the camp, the pictures showed nothing but clouds.[17]

The Air Force's Buffalo Hunter drones, capable of flying at treetop level, could snap pictures beneath cloud cover. Their cameras were also sensitive enough to capture the features of people on the ground. Yet these drones provided very little information on Sontay. In September and October 1970 the Air Force sent seven Buffalo Hunters over the camp. Two were shot down; another four malfunctioned.[18]

Finally, there was a serious limitation to all overhead imagery. As Secretary of Defense Melvin R. Laird noted after the raid, "We have not been able to develop a camera that sees through the roofs of buildings." While U.S. photo interpreters could monitor activity in the prison courtyard, they were unable to tell whether anyone occupied the buildings. When the POWs were moved out of Sontay on July 14, U.S. intelligence failed to notice. That summer, U.S. analysts observed a noticeable decrease in activity within the compound. They knew, however, that the North Vietnamese sometimes punished their captives by keeping them in their cells for extended periods. Despite the drop in activity, the interpreters assumed that the POWs were still at Sontay. Only in the last days before the raid did the intelligence community start questioning whether any POWs were still there.[19]

While U.S. intelligence was doing its best to collect information on the camp and North Vietnamese defenses, Manor and Simons organized the JCTG. The raid required "infinitely complex" flying[20] to evade the enemy's radar and air defenses, then the deadliest in the world. At Sontay itself, the raiding party would need split-second reflexes and exceptional *sang froid* to rescue the POWs before nearby garrisons reacted and reached the scene. Manors and Simons were determined to assemble the best personnel available. After almost a decade of U.S. military involvement in Vietnam, they had a large pool of seasoned troops from which to draw.

All of the task force members were volunteers. In Manor's words, the Air Force pilots were the "very best people available." Each helicopter pilot had on average over four thousand flying hours. Many of the Air Force crews were from the Special Operations Force at Eglin Air

Force Base. The ground force was just as impressive. Simons personally interviewed some five hundred volunteers at Fort Bragg, North Carolina, home of the Army Special Forces. He selected a hundred. Among them were Captain Richard J. Meadows, whom Simons later described as the "best captain" in the Army, and Lieutenant Colonel Elliot P. Snydor, whom Simons termed one of the Army's two or three "best combat colonels."[21] Almost all of the members of the JCTF had seen combat in Southeast Asia.

The JCS and SACSA granted Manor maximum freedom. As he later observed: "This was the only situation in thirty-six years in the military where I had complete authority to plan and execute a mission with a blank check." Manor used this freedom creatively. Early on, for instance, the planners decided that the Air Force's prop-driven A-1 Skyraider attack planes were best suited to provide close air support at the camp. Although slow, they were very maneuverable and could hit ground targets with great precision. The JCTG further determined that the best ordnance for the low-level bombing the A-1s would perform was the CBU-24 Rockeye bomb. The planners discovered, however, that the Air Force had never certified the Rockeye on the A-1. As Manor later noted, normally "it is a lengthy and involved procedure to get a new piece of equipment certified on an airplane, but in this case I thought we were justified in cutting some of the corners." Disregarding "accepted regulatory procedures," Manor took a shortcut to obtain "a real quick certification on the A-1s," much to the alarm of one of his subordinates, who warned: "I will do as you tell me, but someone is going to end up in jail." As Manor later put it: "But it worked real well. We were fortunate, of course, that there were no mishaps."[22]

While SACSA's planning group worked at the Pentagon refining the plan, the JCTG trained at Eglin Air Force Base. Its mission was exceedingly complex. The ground security force of fifty-six Special Forces personnel, led by Simons, would take off from Thailand in six assault helicopters and fly three and a half hours at night to Sontay. To escape radar detection, the force would hug the Laotian mountains, twisting and turning through mountain valleys. The flight path exploited the blind spots in the enemy's radar coverage, which occurred when the North Vietnamese radar dishes swung from one side to another. The ensuing flying required "a precisely timed movement from Thailand over Laos and into [North Vietnam] from the west." Two specially configured C-130 Combat Talons would lead the helicopters to their target. These guideplanes carried a forward-looking infrared system (FLIR) that enabled the aircrews to see the ground at night almost as clearly as by day. Five A-1 attack planes would accompany the Combat Talons and the helicopters to Sontay.[23]

To catch the North Vietnamese completely off guard, the raiders planned to reach Sontay at 2:00 A.M. on a Sunday morning. To achieve shock and surprise, one helicopter would land inside the prison itself, while the others touched down in the paddies outside the prison walls. While part of the ground force was overpowering the guards and securing the area, the rest would free the POWs. The rescue force had to be on the ground less than thirty minutes—the minimum time, the planners estimated, for enemy reinforcements to arrive.[24]

Landing a helicopter at night inside the tiny compound, surrounded by ten-foot walls and forty-foot trees, was a challenge. Because the HH-53s the bulk of the force would use were too big to land in the courtyard, the planners added a smaller HH-3, which could fit in the opening. Even the HH-3, however, would have barely two feet of clearance for its rotors. The planners therefore opted to crash land it inside the camp. The raiders would destroy the plane before leaving Sontay.[25]

Adding the HH-3 posed new problems. The HH-3, slower than the larger HH-53 or the C-130 Combat Talon, had a maximum speed of 105 knots, barely 5 or 6 knots above the C-130's stalling speed. To keep up with the Combat Talons, the HH-3 had to fly in "drafting position" behind the wing of one of the C-130s. In this way, the helicopter gained a few knots by riding the aerial wave that formed behind the C-130 as the air reestablished equilibrium after being compressed under the larger airplane's wing. To maintain this formation, however, the C-130s "had to mush along, noses high, at speeds not much above stalling." The technique would test the C-130 pilots' skill throughout the three-and-a-half-hour flight to the camp. The other pilots faced challenges of their own. Because the HH-53s' tanks did not carry enough fuel for the round trip to Sontay and back, they had to refuel from tanker aircraft over Laos. As one of the helicopter pilots commented afterward: "We'd refuel at nighttime. Have any of you ever seen how tough that is in a helicopter? Well, daytime is pretty easy. Nighttime with lights on is not too bad, but nighttime with no lights and no radio will damn near give you a heart attack."[26]

The Army and Air Force were not the only services involved in the mission. As the rescue party neared the camp, Navy planes from three carriers in the Tonkin Gulf would conduct a large-scale diversion over North Vietnam, east of Sontay. Because the United States had stopped bombing North Vietnam in 1968, the planes would simulate an attack on Hanoi and Haiphong, not conduct actual strikes. They would drop flares instead of bombs and use live fire only if attacked. By saturating the enemy radar and air defense network as the raiders approached the camp, the planners hoped to confuse the enemy and draw its attention from Sontay.[27]

The plan incorporated the traditional elements of a successful raid: speed, surprise, and violence of execution. Manor and the planners also included another element to enhance the chance of success: redundancy. They knew that if the raid failed, the United States was unlikely to have an occasion to try again. They determined to do all they could to prevent a "mission abort" due to equipment failure or loss. U.S. intelligence estimated that as many as a hundred POWs might be at Sontay. The raiders would need a minimum of three HH-53s to evacuate that many prisoners and the rescuers; the planners decided to use five HH-53s. Similarly, although the helicopters required only one Combat Talon to lead them to Sontay, the planners included two. Two A-1s were needed for close air support over Sontay; Manor and his group used five. The plan called for a RC-135 flying command post and an EC-121T airborne radar platform, orbiting outside of North Vietnam, to support the mission; Manor included a backup for each.[28]

The planners tried to anticipate everything that could go wrong. In military jargon, they extensively "what-iffed" the plan. The ground security force was divided into three groups, each with a separate task. According to the main plan, a fourteen-man assault group would crash land aboard the HH-3 into the courtyard and sweep the cell blocks. Simultaneously, the rest of the ground force, divided into a twenty-three-man support group and a twenty-man command group, would land outside the compound in two HH-53s. While the support group, led by Simons, was overpowering the guards, the command group would take up blocking positions around the camp. Manor and his staff, however, realized that one of the helicopters might have mechanical problems en route to Sontay and that the entire ground force might not reach the camp. The planners devised contingency plans in the event of a mishap. "Blue" Plan called for the command and support groups to carry out the mission by themselves if the assault force failed to reach the camp. Alternatively, the ground force would attack according to "Red" or "Green" plans if either the command or support group was lost.[29]

Manor and Simons also strove to meld the task force's Army troops and Air Force crews, who never had worked together before, into a highly cohesive team. At the outset, there was minor friction. Some in the Army resented the choice of Eglin as the training site. They doubted the Air Force crews would train as hard as necessary in the comfort of what, for many, was their home base. The issue made its way to "quarters where decisions were made," including, it appears, the immediate entourage of Air Force Chief of Staff General John D. Ryan. Eventually, all agreed that Eglin was the best choice because security was better there than at any alternative site.[30]

Far more significant was the fact that the Air Force had to execute a mission it had never performed before. Sontay would be the first time its helicopters had flown an assault mission. As one senior planner later observed, "It took the Air Force pilots some time to get adjusted to what was going on." The pilots, for instance, had to adjust to the different air-to-ground signal and communications procedures used by the Army. To overcome such problems, inherent to any joint operation, Manor "emphasized the importance of a completely joint and unified approach to every facet of this complex operation." As he subsequently recalled: "This was viewed as essential and was insisted upon throughout the planning, training, [and] employment."[31]

Within the JCTG, nine Army officers and enlisted personnel worked full-time organizing and controlling the training of the ground force. Four JCTG Air Force personnel directed the task group's air operations. Manor made sure the two groups met regularly to coordinate their activities. Similarly, Manor and Simons scheduled daily training meetings between the air crews and the ground force to ensure they all had the same understanding of the mission and of their respective roles. Actual joint training took place almost every night. The result was, in Manor's words, "a closely knit team which was essential to survival and extremely effective."[32]

Finally, Manor and Simons devised a grueling training regimen, complete with live fire, full rehearsals, and countless practice flights simulating the difficult flight to Sontay. By November 1970, the ground force had practiced every facet of the mission more than 170 times. The air crews had logged more than a thousand hours of flying. Cross-training was extensive, so that, in the words of one helicopter pilot, "every man in the helicopter would know each other guy's job." The JCTG commanders tried to prepare for every possible contingency. The pilots learned to fly into dense cloud cover at night and resume formation when they broke out. The crew of the second Combat Talon was prepared to replace the leading C-130 as the guideplane up to the moment the raiders reached Sontay. The Army force rehearsed the alternative attack plans extensively. Manor later observed, "As much effort went into planning and training for emergencies and unforeseen circumstances as was expended in the planned concept."[33]

The project was extremely closely held. As JCS Chairman Moorer later recalled, other than the SACSA planners, a few intelligence analysts, and key members of the JCTG, fewer than fifty people knew that the United States was preparing a rescue mission. Of this number, half had merely partial knowledge of the project. Even within the JCTG, very few knew they were training for a raid into North Vietnam. The others, who had simply volunteered for an unspecified "special mission of the highest importance," were left wondering where they would eventually deploy.[34]

During the summer and fall preceding the raid, the JCS received several briefings on the project. According to Admiral Harry D. Train, then executive assistant to JCS Chairman Moorer, the other chiefs let Moorer "take the lead." As Train later explained: "Blackburn, Simons and the others dealt directly with the Chairman of the JCS; the other members of the [JCS] were kept informed." Moorer monitored the operation as closely as he could. In his own words, he was "as close to the operation as you could get." Nor did he rely merely on information from SACSA. He also conferred directly with Simons and others in the

JCTG, asking them if they had ideas for improving the plan. In addition, Moorer personally "what-iffed [the operation] to quite a degree." Within the Pentagon, Lieutenant General John W. Vogt, director of the Joint Staff, also followed the project closely.[35]

A meticulous organizer, Manor strove to ensure that the planners overlooked no detail. He recommended that besides the JCS's periodic review of the project, the Pentagon hold a full-scale "murder board" review of SACSA's final plan; a group of officers with no prior association with the mission would probe the plan systematically for weaknesses. But fearful of leaks, Manor's superiors decided to keep those aware of the plan to a minimum and declined to hold a murder board.[36]

It is not clear when the White House first learned of the plan. Secretary of Defense Laird was briefed on the proposal on June 8, 1970, and then again on July 17—a week after SACSA's feasibility study group reported that a rescue mission had a good chance of success. In both cases, Laird authorized continued planning but made no commitment that the mission would actually proceed. It is not clear whether, following either briefing, he discussed the proposed raid with the president. Laird has disclosed, however, that he consulted with Nixon in August, before authorizing actual training of a force for the mission.[37]

In any event, by September 1970, the White House was closely involved. On September 14, Manor reported to the JCS that the JCTG would be ready to deploy to Southeast Asia early the next month. He recommended that the mission be authorized, and proposed an execution date of October 21, 1970. On September 24, the JCTG director briefed Laird and CIA Director Richard M. Helms, again recommending that the mission take place in October. Manor later stated, "The Secretary deferred his approval pending word from higher authority." Three days later, Laird and Moorer presented the plan to Nixon, then on an official visit to Western Europe. The briefing took place aboard the U.S.S. *Springfield,* the flagship of the U.S. Sixth Fleet in the Mediterranean. Nixon "said that he 'approved' the rescue—in principle," but that before deciding when it should take place, he wanted Assistant for National Security Affairs Henry A. Kissinger fully informed. On October 8, Blackburn, Manor, and Simons briefed Kissinger and his deputy, Major General Alexander M. Haig, at the White House.[38]

The president and his national security advisers were impressed with the proposal. JCS Chairman Moorer later recalled, "The White House was enthusiastic about the plan." Looking back, his former assistant Admiral Train echoed: "I think it is fair to say the White House...leapt on the opportunity of Sontay, [thinking] this is great." According to Manor, Kissinger "enthusiastically received the plan." At the end of his October 8 briefing, Kissinger congratulated the planners for an "original and imaginative" proposal. Encouraging the White House's enthusiasm was the military's own confidence in the plan. In Moorer's words, the JCS "were absolutely confident that the troops could go in and out without losing any of them." Blackburn assured Kissinger of a "95% confidence factor that the assault group could execute the mission without loss."[39]

The president and his advisers nonetheless realized that the raid could backfire. Kissinger worried that if the operation failed, it might create more POWs. Nixon remained shaken by the antiwar demonstrations that had swept the country after the U.S. invasion of Cambodia earlier that year. During one White House discussion about the proposed raid on Sontay, Nixon noted that he could not afford any more "near-riots." Recalling the march on Washington antiwar activists had staged to protest the Cambodia incursion, the president mused: "Christ, they surrounded the White House, remember? This time they will probably knock down the gates and I'll have a thousand incoherent hippies urinating on the Oval Office rug. That's just what they'd do."[40]

As Nixon weighed authorizing the mission, he consulted the senior U.S. negotiators at the Paris peace talks, Ambassador David K. Bruce and his deputy, Philip C. Habib. Following his briefing on the *Springfield,* Nixon asked the two men to meet him in Ireland. Without mentioning the proposed mission, he asked about the prospects for a negotiated release of the POWs. The diplomats' assessment was "bleak." Meanwhile, Kissinger discreetly sought a second opinion about the raid. Immediately after his October 8 briefing, Kissinger privately consulted Joint Staff Director Vogt, who had accompanied the briefing team. A member of the Washington Special Action Group (WSAG), a high-level interagency crisis-management group chaired by Kissinger, Vogt had worked extensively with Kissinger. "John," Kissinger asked, "I want your evaluation, not just theirs. The operation is risky. Can we do it? Will we be embarrassed?" Vogt assured Kissinger that the U.S. military could "do it with a high degree of professionalism."[41]

It was the proposed execution date of October 21, however, that seems to have concerned the White House the most. Unbeknownst to the JCS or the planners, in the fall of 1970 Nixon and Kissinger were working secretly to restore diplomatic relations with the People's Republic of China. President Yahya Khan of Pakistan was scheduled to meet Nixon on October 25 at the White House. Khan would visit China shortly thereafter and Nixon wanted him to deliver a written message to the Chinese. The United States, the text said, regarded a Sino-U.S. rapprochement as essential, and offered to send a high-level secret emissary to Beijing. The White House asked the JCS whether the rescue mission could be delayed a month. Informed that the next launch window would be around November 21, the president decided to let the proposed October "execute" day slip by.[42]

Although Nixon and his national security advisers worried about the timing of the raid and the risk of failure, the White House's review of the operation was less than thorough. Kissinger's October 8 briefing by Manor and Simons lasted less than thirty minutes, at the end of which Kissinger concluded that the two commanders were "most impressive." More significantly, the White House appears to have accepted with little questioning the military's optimism about the operation. Had the president or his advisers asked about the U.S. record in POW rescue operations, they might have had second thoughts. The U.S. military had not conducted a successful POW rescue since the Civil War. The experience in Southeast Asia had been particularly bleak. Between 1966 and 1970, U.S. forces had mounted forty-five raids in Cambodia, Laos, and South Vietnam to rescue American POWs, and had freed one. He died shortly after of injuries his captors—who apparently had been forewarned of the operation—inflicted moments before he was rescued.[43]

More surprising yet, the White House seems to have accepted on faith the military's assurances that Sontay was an active POW camp. The president and his advisers listened, impressed, as the JCS Chairman told them there were some seventy Americans in the camp. Of this number, Moorer continued, DIA had tentatively identified sixty-one by name.[44] Remarking in his memoirs that U.S. forces found not one POW there, Kissinger notes acidly that "we knew the risk of casualties, but none of the briefings that led to the decision to proceed had ever mentioned the possibility that the camp might be empty." But if the military did not mention this at the time, the White House never asked about it, either. One senior military official was struck by the White House's failure to raise this basic question. Upon leaving Kissinger's briefing on October 8, the official mused that "there had been something odd about the meeting. Henry Kissinger had not even asked how sure they were that there were any prisoners in Son Tay."[45]

The White House gave the final go-ahead on November 18. Days earlier, the rescue force had deployed to forward bases in Southeast Asia. The number of senior policymakers involved in the final decision was very small. On November 18, Moorer gave the president, in company of CIA Director Helms, Kissinger and his deputy, Haig, Secretary of Defense Laird, and Secretary of State William P. Rogers, a last briefing. Nixon was enthusiastic. As one participant later recalled, the president was "lapping it up 'like an eight-year-old at his first cowboy movie.' " Moorer explained that the launch window was November 21–22. When he mentioned that the mission would be canceled if there was any sign that the enemy was aware of the objective, Nixon protested: "Damn, Tom, let's not let *that* happen. I want this to *go*." The president asked a few questions; there was some discussion of the costs of failure. Nixon then closed the meeting, indicating that he would make his final decision shortly. Later that day, Helms, Kissinger, Laird, and Moorer met at the Pentagon to discuss the plan further. The president kept in contact by secure phone, and at the end of the day authorized the raid. Execution was set for Sunday, November 21.[46]

The decision reflected the White House's deep and growing concern over the POWs. Prospects for their negotiated release seemed dim.

Meanwhile, the United States had recently received alarming information about their treatment. On November 13, North Vietnam had made known the names of six POWs who, the North Vietnamese asserted, had died in captivity. Hanoi had previously released names of Americans who had been killed in action over North Vietnam, but this was the first indication that U.S. servicemen were dying in captivity. The Pentagon was alarmed about the circumstances of several of these deaths.[47]

One officer on the latest list was Air Force Major Wilmer N. Grubb, who had been downed over North Vietnam in January 1966. The following month, Hanoi had released pictures of him in captivity, in which he appeared in good health. Upon releasing the November 13 list, however, the North Vietnamese indicated that Grubb had died on February 4, 1966, of "injuries sustained in his plane crash." According to this date, he had died days before Hanoi had released the pictures of him. Also on the list was Air Force Major Edwin L. Atterbury. As Benjamin F. Schemmer writes in his book on Sontay, *The Raid:*

> The DIA had learned that he had escaped early in 1969 in "fairly robust health," but was recaptured soon after he got "over the fence." Yet, the DIA also knew, Ed Atterbury had never been seen or heard from again by a fellow POW. North Vietnam would only report that he "died in captivity" on May 18, 1969.[48]

Explaining after the operation why he had been in favor of the raid, Secretary Laird noted that he "could not ignore the fact that our men were dying in captivity." During Moorer's briefing, Nixon had exclaimed: "How many more POWs will we find out are dead if we wait much longer?" The administration hoped not only to rescue the prisoners at Sontay but also to send a message to all U.S. POWs. As Laird stated:

> I think that one of the things that convinced me more than anything else to recommend to the President that this operation go forward was my discussions with several of the prisoners who were released [by Hanoi earlier]....
> I ... heard their concern that we in the United States had forgotten them.
> In order to maintain oneself for 5, 4, 3 years, there must be hope, and according to these men many of our prisoners of war were losing their hope and their faith. I felt that this was important to their survival.[49]

As Moorer later recalled, he "wanted not only to rescue the prisoners, but also impart to the North Vietnamese a message." The White House shared this desire. Following the raid, a senior administration official confided to a press contact that the president had authorized the mission not only to free the POWs but also for "transcendent reasons."[50] The administration presumably saw the raid as a way of indicating that the United States could inflict punishment, even without resuming bombing of the North, if North Vietnam did not become more flexible at the stalemated peace talks.

As the "execute" date drew close, however, some in the intelligence community began to doubt there were any POWs at Sontay. From June 6 to early October 1970, U.S. photo interpreters studying imagery of the camp noted a steady decrease in courtyard activity. The least activity was on October 3, when imagery from a high altitude SR-71 reconnaissance plane showed the courtyard overrun by weeds. The analysts concluded, however, that the Vietnamese probably were punishing the POWs by keeping them in their cells.[51]

But in the second half of November the United States obtained fresh intelligence, this time from a well-placed North Vietnamese, which forced the experts to reconsider their conclusion. The source was a senior official of North Vietnam's "Enemy Proselyting Office," which supervised the detention of U.S. POWs. A few days before Nixon gave his final go-ahead, the Vietnamese provided a foreign diplomat in Hanoi, who had befriended him, a coded list of U.S. POWs in the North and where they were held. The diplomat, who worked closely with U.S. intelligence, passed this on to his U.S contacts.[52]

The list quickly reached Washington, where it was decoded by November 19. Sontay was not on the list, which indicated that most of the POWs were at a camp at Dong Hoi the intelligence community had not heard of before. Checking their latest overhead imagery, DIA photo interpreters noticed that the old army barracks at Dong Hoi recently had been enlarged. The North Vietnamese also had built new walls dividing the barracks into smaller compounds, and soldiers were manning the guard towers, previously in disuse.[53]

Working through the night, DIA analysts reviewed all of the data on Sontay. Imagery taken on November 3 and 13 showed that activity at the compound had picked up again. As JCS Chairman Moorer later recalled, the pictures showed smoke rising from the chimneys and active footpaths. General Blackburn similarly recalls that, up to the end, there was evidence of a vegetable garden growing in the courtyard. In *The Raid*, Benjamin Schemmer relates that on the morning of November 20, DIA Director Bennett reported to Moorer with two stacks of photos and cables. Holding a stack in each hand, Bennett said: "I've got this much that says 'They've been moved'. . . . And I've got this much that says 'They're still there.' " As General Vogt later observed: "In the last 18 hours before the operation Bennett had serious doubts. But he would not commit himself. Nor would others in the intelligence community. There was not enough concrete data to say yes or no."[54]

Others involved in the operation, however, recall that the final intelligence estimates were more specific—and pessimistic. According to Secretary Laird's military assistant, Brigadier General Robert Pursely, DIA told Laird and him before the operation that "the chance that prisoners were still at the camp was, at best, 10 or 15 percent. Last-minute reconnaissance overflights had been unable to find evidence that the camp was still in use." Moorer's assistant, Admiral Train, likewise remembers that the last-minute intelligence reports were bleak: "Twelve hours before the raid we had fairly high confidence it was empty. The photography showed the grass had not been walked on in 10 days. On the basis of the photographic evidence alone we knew that it was empty." Train, accompanied by one of DIA's foremost photo analysts, personally briefed Laird on the significance of the latest photo reconnaissance.[55]

According to Admiral Moorer, when some in the intelligence community began to have doubts about the presence of POWs at Sontay, the White House was duly informed. As he observed, the administration "received all of the information [on the camp] that was available in Washington." Admiral Train concurs that Nixon and Kissinger were informed of the results of the latest photo reconnaissance.[56] The Pentagon urged the White House to proceed nonetheless. As Moorer later explained: "I argued more strongly than all the others that we should go in and conduct the rescue mission. . . . We had some doubts the POWs were there, but the forces were poised to go and there was some possibility the POWs were still there."[57]

The senior military officials associated with the plan all shared this view. As Joint Staff Director General Vogt later observed, "It was now or never." The operation was ready to go, and the chances of mounting another rescue bid if it was canceled were slim. It would be "criminal," he thought, to call off the raid: "What if some of the POWs were still there?" "Every one in the decision loop," he recalled, "still wanted to go." The White House quickly agreed with the military's recommendation. With the raid due to launch in hours, the administration was not interested in doubts. As Admiral Train later put it, "They didn't want to know."[58]

While the Washington players grappled with the latest intelligence from Sontay, Manor and his force faced problems of their own. Manor and the JCTG deployed to Southeast Asia between November 10 and 16. The chain of command for the mission was unusual. The JCTG received logistical support from local U.S. forces, but, in contrast to standard procedure for U.S. military units deploying abroad, did not come under the authority of the local U.S. theater commander. Instead, Manor continued to report directly to the JCS. The Sontay raid was the first U.S. military operation of any scale, other than reconnaissance operations, that came under the direct command of the Joint Chiefs of Staff.[59] The National Military Command Center (NMCC) in the Pentagon could communicate almost instantaneously with Manor, who would direct the operation from a command post in Danang, South Vietnam. The elaborate radio network Manor had set up for the operation would enable him to communicate directly with the raiders at every stage of the mission. Reports from Sontay could thus be relayed to Washington within minutes.

Despite these excellent communications, the JCS avoided "micromanaging" the operation. Before the JCTG deployed to Southeast Asia,

Moorer made clear to Manor that, as "on scene commander," he was free to run the mission without interference. Moorer said he reserved only the right to cancel the operation on the basis of intelligence or other information. "I've given you a job to do," Moorer added. "You're liable now to get a bunch of requests for reports or information on one thing after the other. Ignore them."[60]

Manor used his discretion to make two crucial changes. The first was to advance the mission by a day. The launch date of November 21 had been chosen as one of the few days that would offer the raiders the specific weather conditions they required. Weather was crucial to success: the pilots needed a fairly clear night, with no more than four-tenths cloud cover and clouds no lower than five thousand feet, to find their way to and operate at Sontay. Lighting was also important. The raid could not take place by full moon, which would have silhouetted the raiding force against the sky. Yet the pilots needed some moonlight for navigation, which at times would be at treetop level. The pilots could not refuel in flight if there was strong wind. Nor could the carriers in the Tonkin Gulf launch diversionary strikes if there were more than moderate seas.[61]

With the help of his weather officer, Manor had determined that there were only two "windows" in late 1970 that promised to offer the optimum combination of clear skies, adequate moonlight, and moderate wind and seas. One was between October 21 and 25, the other between November 21 and 25. Researching meteorological data for the previous five years for the region, the weather officer had estimated there was a 97 percent chance of clear skies over North Vietnam in October and November. But the weather in Indochina in the fall of 1970 was highly unusual. Whereas October and November usually bring dry weather to the region, October and November 1970 ushered in the worst storms Laos and Vietnam had experienced in years. As Manor noted in his after-action report, "Roughly five years worth of typhoons, based upon climatic norms, moved into the area during the two months." The raiders arrived in Southeast Asia on the heels of a typhoon that left North Vietnam and the mountains of Laos blanketed in rain and clouds. The weather had not cleared by November 19, when Manor learned that a new typhoon, Patsy, was forecast to reach the target area by the evening of November 21—the night the mission was supposed to take place. Patsy was expected to bring with it several more days of inclement weather.[62]

Manor also learned, however, that the weather might improve for a maximum of twenty-four hours on November 20. Photoreconnaissance conducted late in the afternoon of the twentieth confirmed that the weather was starting to clear. The JCTG commander faced a dilemma: either launch the mission under "marginal" weather conditions on the evening of the twentieth or wait days, possibly weeks, for better weather. Before leaving the United States, Manor had received authority to advance the mission date if conditions so required. Taking a chance, he set the mission for the twentieth.[63]

Manor also used his authority to make another change. Concerned about the enemy surface-to-air-missile (SAM) sites around Sontay, he decided at the last minute to add a flight of four F-105 Wild Weasels to the mission. The Weasels carried electronic warfare equipment and radar-guided Shrike missiles for SAM suppression. They would circle above Sontay while the commandos raided the camp and attack any SAM radar that locked onto a U.S. aircraft.[64]

The JCTG commander briefed the task force on the objective on the afternoon of November 19. The men greeted the news of their destination with "wild applause." The raiders' helicopters lifted off from the Royal Thai Air Force Base in Udorn, Thailand, shortly before 11:00 P.M. on November 20. Over Laos, they ran into thick cloud cover that all but precluded visual contact. The pilots, however, had practiced for this and quickly resumed formation when they broke out of the clouds. The tactical intelligence on enemy air defenses was excellent. The raiders flew undetected down the Red River valley, one of the most heavily defended valleys in history, all the way to Sontay.[65]

As they approached Sontay from the west, Navy jets swung into action from the east. In Manor's words, "They did an absolutely outstanding job and the timing was perfect." The diversion, aimed at creating the impression that a large force was attacking Hanoi and Haiphong, threw the enemy's air defenses into confusion. Seconds before the raiders reached the camp, however, an emergency light flashed on the instrument panel of the lead helicopter, signaling a possible transmission failure. In helicopters, such failures are often catastrophic: the transmission can disintegrate in seconds, causing a crash. The lead helicopter had a vital mission to perform. Flying at treetop level, it was to sweep over the camp, raking the guard towers and barracks with its miniguns, each spewing four thousand rounds a minute. Following this softening of the compound, the HH-3 would crash land inside. The lead helicopter pilots gambled that the warning light was malfunctioning and pressed on. The gamble proved right; the aircraft kept flying. Instants later, however, another emergency arose.[66]

Four hundred yards south of the prison camp lay a walled compound similar in size and appearance to the POW camp. U.S. analysts had concluded that it was a secondary school. Amidst the confusion caused by the fire of the lead HH-53's miniguns and illumination flares dropped by the C-130s, the helicopter carrying Simons's support group landed at this "school" by mistake. It was a lucky mistake: the "school" was actually a barracks full of armed troops. Startled, they fought back. In a brief but fierce firefight, Simons's team killed scores of enemy and set the barracks ablaze. Thanks to the pilots' error, the raiders were able to eliminate a major—and completely unanticipated—threat to the mission.[67]

The firefight did not slow down the mission. The planners had anticipated that the entire force might not reach the objective and devised appropriate contingency plans. With Simons's men busy at the "school," the rest of the force implemented "Blue Plan," which called for the assault and command groups to take the camp by themselves. Switching without difficulty to a scenario that they had practiced countless times, they swept through the camp. The extensive training paid off in other ways as well. The helicopter crews and the ground forces formed a cohesive and effective team. Moments after leaving the support group at the "school," the pilots of Simons's aircraft realized that they had inserted the commandos at the wrong place. Without hesitation, and despite the heavy fire on the ground, the pilots swung back to the "school," where Simons's group scrambled back onto the aircraft. Nine minutes after they had landed at the wrong objective, Simons and his men linked up with the rest of the force at the prison compound. There the assault group broke the bad news to Simons: there were no POWs at the camp.[68]

After mopping up the last pockets of enemy resistance in and around the camp, the raiders withdrew to the landing zone outside the compound. Twenty minutes into the raid, they spotted several enemy trucks a few hundred feet away, headed in their direction. Fire from the raiders' antitank weapons stopped the convoy in its tracks. The A-1s strafed the vehicles and, twenty-seven minutes after ground operations had begun, the last raider was airborne again. The entire force made it back safely to Thailand.[69]

Of the four strategic special operations examined in this study, Sontay came closest to success. Tactically, the raid, brilliantly planned and executed, was a masterly accomplishment. Penetrating deep inside some of the most heavily defended airspaces in history, the United States caught the North Vietnamese by surprise on the outskirts of their own capital. The raiders inflicted heavy losses while sustaining minimal casualties: one raider broke his ankle, another sustained a minor gunshot wound.

When measured against its larger objectives, however, the raid was a disappointment. It did, in an unexpected way, have a positive impact on the POWs. After the operation, the North Vietnamese, fearing the United States might try again, regrouped all of the POWs, until then dispersed throughout the country, in one location in downtown Hanoi. The morale and bargaining power of the POWs, now a single, large group, increased significantly and their treatment improved. Nonetheless, the raid fell short of its key stated objective, freeing a group of POWs, and thus ranks as a failure.

The raid did succeed, however, as the military and probably the White House hoped it would, in serving notice to the North Vietnamese that they were vulnerable to U.S. military pressure other than bombing. After the raid North Vietnam showed a greater appreciation of its vulnerability to commando attacks, boosting its internal defenses, including the recall of some units that had been fighting outside the country.[70] There is no evidence, however, that proving U.S. raiders could operate in Hanoi's "back yard" had any effect beyond prompting North Vietnam to bolster security at home. It had no visible impact on North Vietnam's policy toward South Vietnam, where the war dragged on for years. The United States would end up mining North Vietnam's ports in 1972 and conducting the intense bombing campaign of Christmas 1972, when U.S. B-52s pummeled North Vietnam for twelve days, before the United States and North Vietnam finally signed the Paris Peace Agreement.

The Sontay raid, moreover, was marred by some of the same problems that plagued the Bay of Pigs, and, once again, resulted in failure for the United States. The intelligence the United States collected by technical means—overhead imagery, analysis of the enemy's electronic transmissions and signals—was often first-rate. The planners had excellent imagery showing the camp and its surrounding in minute detail and superb intelligence on North Vietnam's air defenses, which enabled the raiders to reach Sontay undetected. But there were also important intelligence gaps. U.S. intelligence completely missed the presence of a large enemy force at the nearby "secondary school." Had Simons's group not fortuitously neutralized this force by landing there by mistake, this garrison would have posed a deadly threat as the raiders withdrew from Sontay. Likewise, U.S. intelligence did not realize until the last minute that the POWs might have been moved, and never could determine for sure whether there were any POWs left at Sontay. Once again, U.S. intelligence was inadequate, due in large part to the lack of qualified agents on the ground who could gather information technical intelligence could not provide.

In the Sontay raid, interagency coordination in Washington was smooth. The planners enlisted from the start the full cooperation of the various parts of the intelligence community, which shared the military's intense desire to help the POWs and supported the raid without reserve. In the field, interagency coordination ended up being superb, largely because the planners had the time—and acumen—to hone the rescue force, fashioned out of disparate parts, into a tightly knit team. It took time and effort to achieve this, however. When the U.S. military began planning the mission, it did not have a helicopter force skilled in ferrying ground troops for long-range assaults. Had the planners tried to launch the mission shortly after the POWs were first spotted, they would have had to rely on a far less cohesive force.

Just as had been the case in the Bay of Pigs, the information and advice the president received left something to be desired. As in the Cuban operation, the White House heard chiefly from the advocates—Chairman Moorer and the planners, who were left to evaluate the soundness of their plan essentially by themselves. No one outside the

JCS and the planners examined the plan in extensive detail. Moreover, the president's advisers failed to ask key, basic questions, such as how certain it was that there were POWs in the camp, or what made the military so confident it could execute the raid successfully, given its record in POW rescue missions. In part, the president himself may have been responsible for dissuading his advisers from asking too many hard questions by not concealing his enthusiasm for the plan. The fact that the raid went as well as it did is attributable to the exceptional quality of the personnel who planned and executed it, not the quality of review to which the White House and the Pentagon submitted the plan.

FIVE

Last Fiasco in Indochina

In May 1975, barely two years after the last U.S. combat forces had left Vietnam, U.S. servicemen were again fighting in Southeast Asia. As dawn broke over Cambodia on the morning of May 15, U.S. Marines assaulted the small Cambodian island of Koh Tang, twenty miles off the Cambodian coast. The United States had struck to recover the crew of the U.S. merchant ship *Mayaguez*, seized three days earlier by forces of Cambodia's new Communist regime. Before the day was over, the United States had recovered the ship and crew, triggering a wave of jubilation throughout the country. After years of bitter war that had led to deep divisions at home and defeat abroad, the nation finally enjoyed a victory, won for a popular cause.

As time has passed, however, and more become known about the details of the crisis, a more sober assessment is in order. The U.S. military has opened its archives on the affair and key decision makers in the event are increasingly willing to talk. From these sources has emerged a less inspiring picture—one of hasty embrace of confrontation and the launching of an improvised, flawed operation that narrowly avoided defeat.[1]

On May 12, 1975, President Gerald R. Ford's 8:00 A.M. intelligence briefing contained unusual news: a U.S. merchant ship, the *Mayaguez*, had just radioed that it was being seized by Cambodian naval units.[2] When the incident occurred, the *Mayaguez* had been sailing in waters the United States considered international sea lanes but that the Cambodians claimed as territorial waters. The *Mayaguez*'s radio soon fell

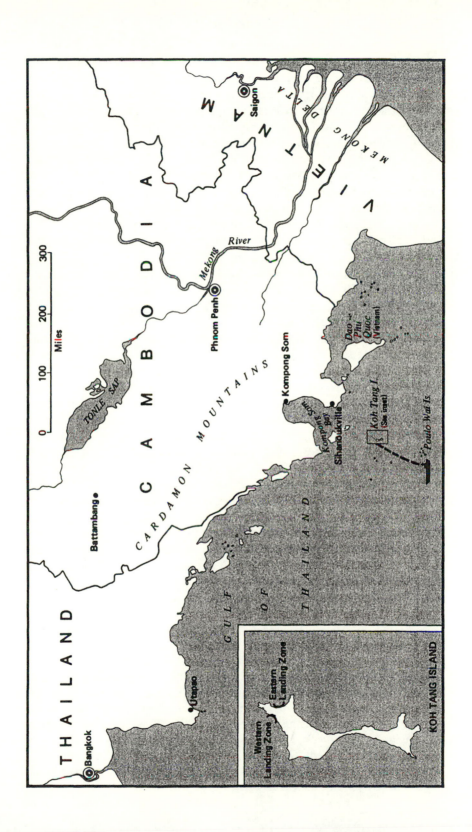

silent. Authorities in Washington did not know the freighter's exact location nor what had happened to its forty-man crew.

Thus began the most dramatic foreign policy crisis of the Ford
administration. At noon that day, the president convened the first of the
four National Security Council (NSC) meetings he would hold on the
crisis. Attending were those whose opinion Ford would consult repeatedly during the next three days: Vice President Nelson A. Rockefeller;
Secretary of State and Assistant for National Security Affairs Henry A.
Kissinger; Secretary of Defense James R. Schlesinger; the acting Chairman of the Joint Chiefs of Staff, General David C. Jones; Director of
Central Intelligence William E. Colby; Assistant to the President Donald H. Rumsfeld; and the deputy assistant for national security affairs,
Lieutenant General Brent Scowcroft.[3]

The incident came at a dark time for the United States. Despite the
expenditure of billions of dollars and the loss of more than 58,000
American lives, U.S. policy in Southeast Asia had met with tragic failure. A few weeks earlier, the Cambodian and South Vietnamese allies of
the United States had fallen to Communist forces. As a senior administration official later recalled, the mood at the top of the administration
was "a brooding sense of defeat." Speaking that spring of Congress's
failure to send last-minute assistance to prop up the Cambodian and
South Vietnamese regimes and their subsequent defeat, Ford mused:
"At the last minute of the last quarter we don't make that special effort,
and now we are faced with this human tragedy. It just makes me sick
every day I hear about it, read about it, and see it."[4] Anger at the new
Communist regimes in Indochina ran high.

U.S. policymakers were also gravely concerned about the country's
image. They feared that, having witnessed the collapse of two close U.S.
allies, friends and foes alike would conclude that the United States had
lost the will to defend its vital interests. The administration was anxious
to counteract the impression that the United States had become a "helpless giant."[5] In early May 1975, this concern was especially keen; Ford
was about to meet his major Western European counterparts at a
NATO conference in Belgium, where the issue of U.S. credibility was
likely to arise. Similarly, Secretary of State Kissinger was preparing to
meet Soviet Foreign Minister Andrei Gromyko. Moreover, ever since
the fall of South Vietnam, North Korea had been increasingly belligerent toward South Korea. The administration was in a combative mood.
Speaking to reporters shortly after the fall of Indochina, Kissinger stated
bluntly that the United States "must carry out some act somewhere in
the world which shows its determination to continue to be a world
power." Singapore's Prime Minister Lee Kuan Yew, on a state visit to
Washington the week before the *Mayaguez* crisis, summarized the
administration's mood: "They are looking for a crisis," he observed.[6]

Two other factors also influenced U.S. decision makers' perceptions.
One was the painful memory of the North Koreans' 1969 capture of the

Navy intelligence ship U.S.S. *Pueblo*. Eleven months of arduous negotiations had ensued. To recover the crew, the United States ultimately had to express "regrets" for the *Pueblo*'s activities. The ship itself was never returned. The Ford administration was determined to prevent another such humiliation.[7] Finally, Ford's domestic fortunes also subtly influenced, no doubt, White House perceptions. Following President Richard Nixon's 1974 resignation over the Watergate scandal, Ford was the country's first unelected vice president to have become president. With the 1976 presidential election little more than a year away, his popularity was at an all-time low and his leadership increasingly questioned. In the view of one senior official, from the onset Ford "was not unconcerned with the effect of the crisis on his popularity."[8]

Administration officials reacted angrily to the seizure of the *Mayaguez*. As one senior administration official recalled, the reaction in the NSC was "outraged astonishment that cheeky little beggars in a third rate country had taken a crack at the U.S." The Chief of Naval Operations, Admiral James L. Holloway, later described the government's reaction in similar terms: "There was an almost universal feeling that one too many feathers had been plucked from the eagle's tail and that we could not allow such harassment from a rinky-dink country. From the President down, there was a great concern to act." Still another participant recalled that from the beginning "there wasn't a dove in the place."[9]

Some were particularly forceful in calling for a decisive response. According to inside accounts, at the first NSC meeting Kissinger argued that unfortunately the lives of the *Mayaguez*'s crew had to be "a secondary consideration."[10] The stakes, he explained, far exceeded humanitarian concerns. This was the occasion for the United States to restore its credibility by an exercise of military might. "At some point," Kissinger continued, "the United States must draw the line. This is not our idea of the best such situation. It is not our choice. But we must act upon it now, and act firmly."[11]

Ford shared the determination to act. But he also was seriously concerned about the welfare of the crew. By the end of the first NSC meeting, he opted for a dual approach. The United States would try to contact the new Cambodian authorities, with which it had no diplomatic relations, to demand the immediate and unconditional release of the ship and crew. Simultaneously, the Pentagon would prepare a series of military options for use if diplomacy failed.[12]

Notwithstanding Ford's concern about the crew, hostility toward Cambodia and the administration's bellicose mood influenced White House decisions and attitudes from the start. Based on the information available in Washington, it was impossible to determine whether the ship's capture was the individual act of a local commander or the considered decision of Cambodia's new government. Very quickly, however, the White House started treating the incident as a deliberate provocation by the new regime. As a senior White House adviser later observed: "We decided, while we had no way of knowing, that we had to assume it was [a central government decision.] In either case, our actions had to be the same."[13]

As the crisis wore on, the thought that the incident might have occurred without the approval of the top Cambodian leadership seems to have vanished altogether. David H. Kennerly, a photographer and Ford intimate who was snapping pictures at the last NSC meeting before the assault, was so stunned by the discussion that he spoke up. As Ford recounts in his memoirs:

> "Has anyone considered," he asked, "that this might be the act of a local Cambodian commander who...might not have gotten his orders from Phnom Penh? If that's what has happened, you know, you can blow the whole place away and it's not gonna make any difference. Everyone here has been talking about Cambodia as if it were a traditional government. Like France. We have trouble with France, we just pick up the telephone and call. We know who to talk to. But I was in Cambodia just two weeks ago, and it's not that kind of government at all. We don't even know who the leadership is. Has anyone considered that?"[14]

Apparently the president and the NSC had not entertained the thought for some time. In his memoirs, Ford recalls that he welcomed Kennerly's advice, which represented a fresh view.[15]

In fact, there were indications that the new Cambodian authorities had no desire for a confrontation with the United States and that the incident could well have been the act of a local commander. During the last days of Cambodia's pro-Western Lon Nol regime, Prince Norodom Sihanouk, chief spokesman for Cambodia's insurgent Patriotic Front, had sent a message to Mike Mansfield, chairman of the Senate Foreign Relations Committee. The telegram, which Mansfield had passed on to the White House, revealed the front's fear that U.S. forces might return to Cambodia. Writing on the eve of Phnom Penh's fall, Sihanouk stressed that the insurgents were poised to take the city. The only reason that the front was waiting, Sihanouk explained, was that it "did not want to give President Ford the pretext he so dearly wanted to unleash American armed forces." Sihanouk appealed to Congress to end U.S. aid to the Lon Nol regime and withdraw U.S. advisers, lest the White House use the safety of U.S. personnel "as a pretext to launch a new, massive invasion of our small country."[16] Such statements gave reason to wonder whether the Patriotic Front, still consolidating its grip on power, had chosen to invite U.S. retaliation by capturing a U.S. merchant ship. Yet the White House almost immediately treated the incident as a deliberate act of the new regime.

Hostility toward Cambodia and concern for the U.S. image—and perhaps that of the president as well—also seem to have influenced the importance and visibility the administration gave to the incident. Even if the ship's capture was a clear policy decision of the new regime, this was not automatically of major concern. The detention of U.S. ships operating in waters another nation claimed as its own was not new. By one account, between 1952 and 1975 a hundred U.S. ships had been seized by Ecuador alone; Ecuadoran forces had shot at, beaten, and imprisoned U.S. crews. The United States typically had treated these as minor incidents, responding with quiet diplomacy.[17] Clearly, the capture of a U.S. ship by a radical, anti-U.S. Southeast Asian regime following the recent U.S. defeat was far more serious. Yet sensitive as it was, it need not have been immediately—and publicly—treated as a major crisis.

The White House, however, did just that. Right after the first NSC meeting, White House Press Secretary Ron H. Nessen announced the ship's capture to the press. He reported somberly that Ford had termed the seizure "an act of piracy" and "instructed the State Department to demand the immediate release of the ship. Failure to do so," Nessen warned, "would have the most serious consequences."[18] The public ultimatum conveyed to the world that the United States still took seriously any challenge to its interests. It also gave the American people the sense the White House was firmly in charge. If, however, the Cambodians had had any desire to release the ship quietly, the statement made it more difficult to do so without losing face. With the public dramatization of the crisis, chances for a peaceful solution likely decreased.

Given, of course, its mistrust of Cambodia's revolutionary regime, the administration placed little stock in diplomacy. Participants in the NSC meetings recall that although the executive made a good-faith attempt to solve the crisis diplomatically, it held little hope that diplomacy would prevail. As one senior adviser later observed: "We did pursue diplomacy through all avenues that we saw possible. [But] I don't think that we believed there was a great chance the *Mayaguez* would be turned back because we sent a diplomatic protest. There wasn't much pressure to hold back the military and give diplomacy more time." Admiral Holloway likewise recalled: "The President was reluctant to use force unless he had to. He would have liked to come to the conclusion that diplomacy would lead to the crew's release, but I think we all concluded there were limited chances that negotiation would result in their release."[19] Momentum toward a dramatic confrontation thus quickly began to build. It would proceed unabated, until barely two days later the attack on Cambodia began.

The Department of State faced serious difficulties exploring a diplomatic solution. The United States had no diplomatic relations with the new regime. Other than Beijing, the new Cambodian government had very few diplomatic missions abroad. In the past, the United States occasionally had communicated with the Cambodian leftists through the People's Republic of China. The White House therefore sought the assistance of the Chinese. After the first NSC meeting broke up shortly before 1:00 P.M. on May 12, the head of China's diplomatic mission to the United States was called to the Department of State at 4:30 that afternoon. But when Deputy Secretary of State Robert S. Ingersoll presented Chinese Ambassador Huan Chen with a message for the Cambodians, demanding the release of the ship, the Chinese representative declined to accept it.[20]

While the State Department was seeking to contact the Cambodians, the far-flung military strength of the United States was being mobilized to deal with the crisis—only to encounter problems of its own. The Department of Defense's central command post, the National Military Command Center (NMCC) in the Pentagon, was first in Washington to learn of the capture of the *Mayaguez*. Soon after receiving the news around 5:00 A.M. on May 12, the NMCC ordered Thailand-based U.S. planes to locate the ship. They did not, however, take off until 9:30 A.M.; by then it was nighttime in the Gulf of Thailand.* The aircraft located several boats in the area where the *Mayaguez* was known to have been last but could not identify the ships in the dark. Not until 9:12 P.M. on the evening of May 12—after dawn had broken in the Gulf of Thailand—did Navy pilots identify the *Mayaguez* at anchor off the Cambodian islands of Poulo Wai.[21]

During these hours, the planners of the JCS in Washington, the U.S. Commander in Chief, Pacific (CinCPaC) in Hawaii, and the U.S. Support Activities Group (USSAG) at Nakhon Phanom in Thailand—the central U.S. command in that country—frantically reviewed military options. The crisis hardly could have occurred at a worse time. Only weeks before, the bulk of U.S. combat units in Southeast Asia had evacuated the last Americans from South Vietnam as it was being overrun by the North Vietnamese. The units were scattered at sea, sailing toward U.S. bases in the region. On the afternoon of May 12, the NMCC ordered several warships, including the aircraft carrier U.S.S. *Coral Sea,* the escort destroyer U.S.S. *Harold E. Holt,* and the guided-missile destroyer U.S.S. *Henry B. Wilson,* to proceed immediately to the scene. But the earliest the nearest ship, the *Holt,* could reach the area was noon on May 14. In the interval, once the *Mayaguez's* exact location was known, U.S. aircraft kept it under constant watch.[22]

By the morning of May 13, the crisis was the center of White House attention. The NSC met twice that day. As the crisis wore on, Washington decision makers grew increasingly frustrated with diplomatic efforts. After Ambassador Chen declined to accept a message for the Cambodians, the White House decided to use U.S. diplomats in China. Shortly after midnight on May 13, officials of the U.S. liaison office in Beijing left diplomatic notes at China's Ministry of Foreign Affairs and the local Cambodian diplomatic mission. Both messages reiterated the demand for the immediate and unconditional release of the ship

---

* Gulf of Thailand time was eleven hours ahead of Washington time. Unless indicated otherwise, all times in this study are Washington time.

and its crew. Throughout May 13, neither the Chinese nor the Cambodians acknowledged with a response having received a message.[23]

The White House was not alone in its frustration. U.S. popular opinion was incensed by the seizure of the ship; congressional sentiment also was running high. On the afternoon of May 13, White House staffers informed key members of Congress that the United States insisted on the immediate release of the *Mayaguez* and was sending warships to the scene. Those contacted overwhelmingly favored a forceful approach. House Majority Leader Thomas "Tip" O'Neill summed up Congress's mood: "Those bastards, we can't let them get away with this. They'll harass us forever." Upon learning of the movement of U.S. warships, Congressman Robert Mitchell commented approvingly: "That's the least we can do. I'm for doing more. We can't let these birds horse us around." Congressman El Cederberg was as militant: "[We] can't allow it to happen... we must do what it takes to get the ship back." Most senators echoed this stance. Senate majority leader Robert Byrd applauded Ford's initial steps, adding that the president "should give them [a] deadline and then go in and get them." Senator Strom Thurmond opined: "They are testing us. President must be firm. Public will back him 100%." James Eastland, president pro tempore of the Senate, was the most hawkish of all: "Blow the hell out of them," he urged.[24] Before the day was done, his wish would be gratified.

While U.S. diplomatic efforts elicited little response, military events moved at a quickening pace. On the evening of May 12, U.S. planes radioed that the *Mayaguez* was under way from Poulo Wai. The freighter soon dropped anchor off the nearby Cambodian islet of Koh Tang. Upon instructions from the White House, Navy fighters fired rockets fore and aft of the *Mayaguez* to discourage further movement of the ship.[25] The Cambodians apparently understood the message; the ship remained at this mooring for the rest of the crisis.

Between 6:00 and 9:00 A.M. on May 13, night settled over the Gulf of Thailand. AC-130 Spectre gunships began a vigil over the ship. Scanning the darkness with low-light vision devices and infrared sensors, they observed significant movement of people from the *Mayaguez* to smaller Cambodian boats, which proceeded to Koh Tang, where some passengers disembarked. But the planes could not tell whether those going ashore were the *Mayaguez*'s crew or the captors. The military concluded, however, that the crew probably had been transferred to Koh Tang.[26]

Aware that the president might launch a rescue operation at any moment, the Pentagon scrambled to ready an appropriate force. In the morning of the thirteenth, the JCS ordered the movement of U.S. Air Force Air Police and heavy helicopters from outlying bases to the U.S. Air Force base at Utapao, Thailand, the U.S. installation closest to Koh Tang. By that afternoon, units from the Third Marine Amphibious Force (III MAF) were also on their way to Utapao from bases in the

Philippines and Okinawa. By then, tragedy had already struck. A helicopter carrying twenty-three air police and crew members had crashed
en route to Utapao, killing all aboard. They were the first casualties of
the *Mayaguez* affair.[27]

Before the night ended, more casualties, this time Cambodian, followed. The White House was increasingly concerned that the captives
might be transferred to the mainland, some twenty miles north of Koh
Tang. The president and his advisers feared that the crew would be
"swallowed up" by the Asian landmass and disappear from sight.[28]
Thus, upon instructions from the Oval Office, at 7:00 P.M. on May 13
the JCS ordered U.S. aircraft to prevent any movement of boats to or
from the vicinity of Koh Tang. U.S. planes dropped ordnance in front
of three small surface craft headed from the island to the mainland, forcing them to turn back. Shortly thereafter, one boat resumed its course
toward the Cambodian coast, despite repeated warning shots from the
jets.[29]

The White House was in close touch with the drama unfolding at
Koh Tang. Throughout the crisis, communication between U.S. forces
in the field and Washington was nearly instantaneous. An Airborne Battlefield Command and Control Center (ABCCC)—a specially configured
C-130 transport plane—orbited near Koh Tang, monitoring the communications of U.S. combat units and relaying their messages to
USSAG headquarters. From there, messages flashed within seconds to
the NMCC, itself linked by secure phone to the White House.[30]

At 8:10 P.M., Deputy Assistant for National Security Affairs Scowcroft called Ford at the White House. A brief dialogue ensued:

> S: Three little boats have taken off toward the northeast. One boat has
> been sunk. The second has turned back and the third is continuing at
> full speed. If they can't stop it any other way, we have no choice but to
> destroy it.
>
> F: I think we have no choice. . . . If we don't do it, it is an indication of
> some considerable weakness.
>
> S: No question about it.
>
> F: I think we should just give it to them.
>
> S: To show them we mean business.
>
> F: I am glad they got the first two. I think we ought to take the action on
> the third one.[31]

At 8:20 P.M., the boat was sunk. U.S. planes, however, noticed a
fourth boat, with dozens of people aboard, headed for the mainland. By
then it was day again in the Gulf of Thailand, and one plane spotted
what appeared to be "possible Caucasians huddled in the bow." U.S.
fighters swooped over the craft, firing across its bow and dropping tear
gas on deck. The pilots could not confirm any Caucasians were aboard.
The boat briefly changed course, then resumed sailing toward the
mainland.[32]

Shortly before 10:00 P.M. the Pentagon called Scowcroft, describing the situation and explaining that one of the pilots thought he could disable the boat by hitting it in the rear. The Pentagon wondered if the White House wanted to try to disable it "and possibly sink the boat." Scowcroft again called Ford, explaining the sighting of a boat on which "there may be some Caucasians," adding that "the pilot thinks he can stop it without sinking it."

F: Well, I don't think we have any choice.

S: If they get the Americans to the mainland they have hostages and . . .

F: We have to predicate all these actions on the possibility of losing Americans.

S: I will have them ask the pilot to do his best to stop it without sinking it.

F: I think that is right.[33]

Scowcroft ordered the Pentagon to "have the pilot . . . disable it and not sink it."[34] According to key players familiar with the episode, the order to disable the boat disturbed senior Pentagon officials, who feared such action could imperil members of the *Mayaguez* crew who might be on board. These officials reportedly withheld the order to shoot until it was too late for the planes to act. Military records show that U.S. planes fired warning shots in front of the craft and blanketed it with tear gas, but did not shoot at it. At about 11:30 P.M. on May 13, the boat reached the mainland port of Kompong Som. After the crisis it was discovered that all of the *Mayaguez* crewmembers had been aboard.[35]

Shortly after midnight on May 14, the military received blanket permission to sink any boat attempting to leave or reach Koh Tang. Within minutes, U.S. planes sank three more Cambodian craft. The pilots had orders to check each target carefully before firing, to determine whether any Americans were aboard. But the speed of the planes made it nearly impossible to ascertain who was on deck, and it was impossible to tell who might be below deck. Nonetheless, by the first hours of May 14, four Cambodian craft had been destroyed. Before the crisis ended, another three boats were sunk.[36]

On the third day, events moved steadily toward a violent climax. On the morning of May 14, the Chinese returned the message left the previous day at their Ministry of Foreign Affairs, stating that the Cambodians had refused to accept it. Throughout the day, Washington waited in vain for a response to the message U.S. officials had left at the Cambodian mission in Beijing. Shortly after 1:00 P.M. on May 14, the U.S. Mission to the United Nations delivered a letter to UN Secretary General Kurt Waldheim, requesting his assistance.[37] This was a short-lived and desultory diplomatic attempt, however; before the afternoon was over, Ford ordered U.S. troops into combat to recover the *Mayaguez* and its crew.

The president ordered the operation during the fourth and last NSC

meeting of the crisis. Convening on the afternoon of May 14 at 3:45
P.M., the participants reviewed the events of the previous days, noting
the lack of Cambodian response to U.S. diplomatic efforts. As in the
previous NSC meetings, the discussion was open and wide-ranging. In
a postcrisis interview, Ford described how he conducted NSC discussions: "I liked to hear the discussions on the various points of view. I
don't mind contention. At some meetings the discussion got very frank.
. . . I don't think anyone was inhibited because I was there."[38]

The NSC discussed the captors' apparent efforts to move the crew
and debated where the Americans were most likely to be held. The decision makers reviewed the unconfirmed sighting of "possible Caucasians" on the boat that had docked at Kompong Som the night before.
They also learned that intercepted Cambodian broadcasts indicated that
perhaps some of the crew had been moved to the mainland. Weighing
the evidence, Ford and his advisers concluded that some Americans
might have been on the boat that had run the U.S. blockade. The NSC
members nonetheless assumed that some captives, at least, remained on
the *Mayaguez* or Koh Tang.[39] At the previous NSC meeting late in the
evening of May 13, the acting JCS Chairman, General David C. Jones,
had outlined a series of military options. These included landings on the
Mayaguez and Koh Tang island to recover the crew, tactical or B-52 air
strikes against Kompong Som and other Cambodian targets, the mining
of Kompong Som's harbor, and the capture of the city by an amphibious force of Marines.[40]

Listening to Jones review these options on May 14, the president
and his advisers agreed on the need to solve the crisis by force. The ensuing discussion dealt chiefly with the scale and timing of the operation
to be undertaken. Once again, Kissinger was the most vocal advocate of
force. Believing that nothing less than the entire U.S. position in Asia
was at stake, he urged the president to send a clear signal of U.S. resolve. Backed by Vice President Rockefeller, Kissinger advocated both a
mission to recover the crew and B-52 strikes against the Cambodian
mainland.[41]

While agreeing with the need to recover the crew by force, Schlesinger was, in Ford's words, "far less eager to use *Mayaguez* as an example for Asia and the world." Seconded by both the Chairman of the
Joint Chiefs of Staff, General George S. Brown, just returned from a
trip abroad, and General Jones, Schlesinger urged greater restraint. Using B-52 strategic bombers against Cambodia, he argued, would be
overreacting.[42] Jones voiced a note of caution about the rescue. Explaining that U.S. troops were poised to take the *Mayaguez* and Koh Tang,
he observed that by waiting another twenty-four hours, U.S. forces
would be better prepared. Command and control would be more firmly
in place, giving the mission a better chance of success.[43]

After some additional debate, at 4:45 P.M. Ford gave his orders.
The Marine Corps and Air Force units standing by at Utapao were to

execute the rescue mission at once. Nor would the Cambodian mainland be spared; recoiling from the use of B-52s, Ford instructed that carrier-based jets attack key military targets in and around Kompong Som, once the landing at Koh Tang had begun.[44]

For the first time since the U.S. withdrawal from Vietnam, U.S. forces were being sent into combat. Underpinning this decision was a variety of concerns, one of which was the safety of the crew. Since the takeover of Cambodia by the Khmer Rouge revolutionary forces in April 1975, alarming accounts of atrocities had been reaching the West. As President Ford noted in an interview shortly after the crisis: "We were dealing with a government that, by its recent actions, had shown a very abnormal attitude toward its own people and I could imagine how they might treat Americans. . . . the longer they were in the hands of the Cambodians, the more likely they would be mistreated, killed, or used as hostages.[45]

Clearly, however, other considerations were at least as important in the decision to go ahead. There was no indication that the crew faced an imminent threat. As Admiral Harry D. Train, then Director of the Joint Staff, later recalled: "We thought that if the Cambodians had wanted to kill the crew, they would have already done it. Since they hadn't, we believed that they were keeping the crew to seek a political objective."[46]

The decision to use force seems to have been largely motivated by the fear that the crew would be moved to the mainland. The president and his advisers were alarmed by the apparent efforts to move the crew. The NSC members believed that if the prisoners reached the Cambodian coast, the United States would quickly lose track of them. The fate of the crew would then rest entirely in the Cambodians' hands. As a key White House adviser subsequently recalled: "The overwhelming desire was to move quickly and try and get the crew from moving outside of our physical capability. If this happened, we would have been incapable of a rescue. We wanted to move quickly, so [our action] could be surgical, instead of a blunderbuss or [our being reduced to] impotence."[47]

There were several reasons for the keen desire to keep the crew from the mainland. The NSC members worried about the hardships the men might suffer during prolonged imprisonment in Cambodia. The White House was further alarmed by the prospect of another *Pueblo* affair, in which the United States would again be unable to recover the crew short of lengthy negotiations.[48]

Ford, in particular, was adamant that the United States should not endure another such affront. Shortly after the recovery of the *Mayaguez*, he conceded in an interview with journalist Roy Rowan the influence of the 1969 precedent on his handling of the crisis. The *Pueblo*, he explained, "was sort of a benchmark from which we could proceed." In an interview with journalist Hugh Sidey, Ford left no doubt that one of his key concerns was avoiding another *Pueblo*. When Sidey asked if Ford had been "dead set against the notion of having them taken in as hostages and then negotiated over for months," the president replied unequivocally: "Yes. That was one thing I was absolutely going to avoid." In a separate interview, Scowcroft observed: "We were trying to . . . prevent the ship and especially the crew from being spirited away somewhere, where we'd certainly lose the possibility of rescuing them, and then be subject to the kind of humiliations that we were with the *Pueblo* and appear powerless."[49]

The desire to show U.S. resolve and seek vengeance on Cambodia also influenced the decision to use force. After the operation, Ford acknowledged his concern about appearing decisive: "Subjectively, I was having thoughts like this: if I had done nothing, the consequences would be very, very bad, not only in failing to meet that problem, but the implications on a broader international scale. Something was required. I felt it would be best to try diplomacy first and, if that failed, to take strong, decisive action—as opposed to the incremental use of force—even though the odds might be against us. It was far better than doing nothing."[50]

The air strikes against Cambodia had little to do with recovering the crew. Ford stated at the time that they were necessary to keep Cambodian forces from interfering as U.S. Marines recovered the freighter and landed on Koh Tang. A few hours after deciding at the fourth NSC meeting to launch the mission, Ford convened the congressional leadership at the White House for a briefing on the operation. The congressmen and senators broadly agreed with the decisions to land on the island and recover the *Mayaguez*. Several, however, including Senate Majority Leader Mike Mansfield and Assistant Majority Leader Robert Byrd, strongly opposed strikes against the mainland. Noting that there were an estimated 2,400 Khmer Rouge troops at the mainland bases of Kompong Som and Ream, Ford replied, "I would never forgive myself if the Marines had been attacked by 2400 Cambodians." The president repeated this explanation after the operation.[51]

In fact, the mainland forces most likely to threaten U.S. troops were the fast patrol boats at Kompong Som. They could have reached Koh Tang swiftly, where their heavy machine guns would have posed a serious threat to the helicopters conducting the Marines' landings.[52] These boats were not, however, the targets of the mainland strikes. U.S. planes attacked marginal military installations, striking Kompong Som airport, where there were fewer than a dozen dilapidated planes. It is unlikely these antiquated, prop-driven aircraft could have left the ground. If they had, they would have been hopelessly outclassed by U.S. jets. U.S. warplanes also attacked a railroad marshaling yard, naval barracks, warehouses, and an inactive refinery. The administration asserted that the latter could have supplied fuel to the Cambodian forces. In fact, the refinery had been inoperative for years; U.S. military planners had long since removed it from the list of Cambodian military targets.[53] In short, tactical considerations had little to do with the choice of targets, which reflected a desire for political effect and the intent to inflict maximum punishment.

Additional facts point up the punitive and demonstrative nature of the strikes against the mainland. Up to the last minute, the administration contemplated B-52 strikes. As the NSC gathered for its final meeting on the afternoon of May 14, twelve B-52s were ready for takeoff at Guam, poised to strike at the harbor and airfield of Kompong Som.[54] After considerable internal debate, at the last moment the White House decided against B-52 raids and opted for bombing by Navy fighter bombers, which could pass for tactical strikes. Nonetheless, the NSC's willingness to contemplate B-52 raids for so long suggests that a major reason for attacking the mainland was to deliver a crushing and spectacular blow. Indeed, an internal White House planning document of May 13 on military options against Cambodia noted that the benefits of bombing the mainland would be to "convince the Cambodian Government of our resolve" and to "serve as a potent warning to other would-be aggressors."[55]

With the passing of time, key participants have been explicit about the real purpose of the mainland strikes. Secretary of Defense James Schlesinger has written: "The purpose of the engagement of U.S. military forces was simply to extract our people from Cambodia—and to provide a lesson for the Cambodians and the others." Scowcroft was even blunter: "Frankly, we argued the strikes on the mainland as militarily justified and theoretically, of course, we struck targets that could have aided them [the Cambodians] in the operation. In fact it was a demonstration—a punitive strike."[56]

Clearly, concern for the captives was but one of the motives behind the decision to use force. In fact, there is considerable evidence that notwithstanding the president's early concern about the crew, in the end other considerations became paramount. As the crisis wore on, antagonism against Cambodia, fear of another humiliation, and the wish to set an example apparently became so strong that they ultimately generated untrammeled enthusiasm for a forceful response—to the exclusion of the original concern about the welfare of the crew.

The White House disregarded evidence suggesting that the incident could be solved peacefully. It soon became apparent that the capture of the ship was not an isolated incident meant solely to provoke the United States. The Oval Office quickly discovered that, upon seizing power, the new Cambodian regime had unilaterally extended Cambodia's territorial waters to ninety miles off its coast. Less than two weeks before the *Mayaguez* incident, Cambodian gunboats had tried to stop a South Korean freighter sailing off the Cambodian coast. The day they took the *Mayaguez,* they also tried to seize a Swedish merchant ship in the same shipping lanes. A few days earlier, Cambodian patrol boats had captured several Thai fishing boats and a Panamanian freighter. The

Cambodians released the Panamanians within hours; the Thai were freed soon after. But the White House dismissed such indications that the *Mayaguez* incident might be peacefully resolved. Within the first twenty-four hours Ford had concluded that "there was of necessity going to be a confrontation."[57]

Similarly, the White House rapidly concluded that the Cambodians' failure to respond to the diplomatic messages delivered in Beijing meant that they were not interested in a peaceful solution. Conceivably, Phnom Penh's silence was the result of poor communication and confusion in a country in revolutionary turmoil. The White House apparently discounted this possibility, however, even though U.S. monitoring of Cambodian communications revealed that the authorities in Phnom Penh were having difficulty following the situation off the Cambodian coast.[58]

Finally, the administration paid little attention to intelligence suggesting that the People's Republic of China was seeking a peaceful solution and hopeful its efforts would succeed. In the morning of May 14, the U.S. embassy in Tehran reported hearing from a Pakistani diplomat that the Chinese, embarrassed by the *Mayaguez* incident, were using their influence with Cambodia and expected the ship to be released soon. The Pakistanis had learned this from a high-level Chinese source. But the State Department concluded that the report was of "questionable validity," and the White House paid no attention to it.[59] Hours after the report reached Washington, the president ordered the attack on Koh Tang and the mainland.

The administration ended up displaying an almost unthinking preference for the language of force. The NSC members ignored or downplayed negative implications of the military plan. The rescue mission entailed considerable risks for the crew. Even assuming that the operation was fully successful—an uncertain proposition at best—the most the Marines could do was rescue the Americans who were on the *Mayaguez* or Koh Tang. Any captives on the mainland—and it was likely at least some were there—could have been in even greater jeopardy after the operation. The reaction of the captors to an assault on Koh Tang was unpredictable, and their brutality could well have increased. There is no evidence, however, that the NSC paid much attention to the fate of the Americans who might be left behind.

The Oval Office seems similarly to have downplayed the danger the operation would pose to any captives on the freighter or Koh Tang. The rescue mission was anything but sophisticated. The plan called for a company of Marines to land at dawn on tiny Koh Tang—about three miles long and barely a mile across at its maximum width—and broadcast by loudspeaker an ultimatum demanding the immediate release of the crew. If the Cambodians failed to comply, the Marines were to storm their positions and sweep the island, supported as needed by air strikes.[60] Had this occurred, the prisoners' chances of being hit by crossfire, not to mention any air strikes on an island barely a mile across, would have been great. In addition, U.S. forces had little idea of the location of the enemy on the island and an even vaguer sense of where the crew might be held. The plan failed to meet the basic requirement of any successful rescue mission: neutralization of the captors as soon as the rescuers arrive, before the captors can harm their prisoners.[61] There was a good chance that when the Marines attacked Koh Tang, frightened or furious Cambodian fighters would kill whatever crew members were at hand.

The ship's recovery would also be hazardous for any Americans aboard. A second force of Marines some fifty men strong would land by helicopter on the helicopter platform of the U.S.S. *Holt,* which would close in on the *Mayaguez* on the afternoon of May 14. As the main force of Marines landed on Koh Tang, U.S. warplanes were to blanket the *Mayaguez* with tear gas. The *Holt* would pull up to the ship and the Marines, reenacting a maneuver they had last performed in the nineteenth century, would clamber over the gunwhales and recapture it.[62] The *Holt*'s approach to the *Mayaguez,* of course, would be anything but swift. As the recovery of the ship began to unfold, the Cambodians on board would have ample time to retaliate against captives in their custody.

The NSC members never seemed to appreciate how much of a threat the operation posed to the crew. In an interview shortly after the operation, Ford explained that he had anticipated some casualties among the crew: "I must say that I assumed—not happily, but I assumed that we would be most fortunate if we got everybody back without loss of life. . . . The possibility [was] that we would lose some. How many, I couldn't tell."[63] In fact, the rescue scheme had a good chance of killing most or all of the crew.

Most Washington decision makers seem to have simply wished away such glaring deficiencies in the plan. The president and his advisers downplayed the possibility that the Cambodians might seek vengeance on the captives as the rescue began. Looking back, CIA Director Colby observed: "[We realized that the crew might get hurt], but thought that if you can move hard and fast enough, you can overcome this problem." Chief of Naval Operations Holloway similarly recalled: "The mission was fraught with potential for outcomes that were not . . . good." However, "we thought we knew how those people might be thinking. . . . Our conviction was that by being tough as hell, by showing the Cambodians that we meant business, the chances were better than even that they would understand this force and would deliver [the crew] alive." Another JCS officer closely involved with the operation recalled that the plan rested on a prevailing belief: "We Americans almost always think that the enemy won't kill its prisoners."[64] In the enthusiasm to proceed, Washington decision makers seem to have explained away the grave dangers the mission entailed for the crew.

The executive seems to have been equally quick to dismiss the high risks the mission entailed for U.S. forces. The plan called for Marines from Okinawa to conduct a heliborne assault with Air Force rescue helicopters based in Thailand. Under the best of circumstances, the difficulty of conducting a successful operation with units that have never worked together, drawn from services that rarely train together, is great. As Admiral Train subsequently mused: "I always think it's the ninth wonder of the world that we put Marines in Air Force helicopters and got a successful operation."[65]

In addition, what the force was supposed to accomplish would have been perilous even for a cohesive combat team. According to DIA estimates, the enemy on Koh Tang numbered up to two hundred Khmer Rouge regular troops, with mortars, recoilless rifles, and heavy machine guns. The intelligence estimates of CINCPAC and USSAG, also widely disseminated in Washington, were only slightly lower.[66] Against this potentially powerful force, the United States was sending in a first wave of 175 Marines in eight helicopters. The latter, moreover, are highly vulnerable to heavy weapons ground fire. Yet, in an effort to limit the threat to any Americans captive on Koh Tang, the Washington planners decided against any heavy, prelanding bombing or shelling to soften up the landing zones. Finally, the first wave of Marines would have to wait until the helicopters flew back to Utapao and then returned to Koh Tang—a round trip of close to four hours—before receiving reinforcements. According to standard military doctrine, a successful assault requires clear superiority over the defenders.[67] In the case of the *Mayaguez* operation, however, the military and civilian decision makers were willing to proceed against very unfavorable odds.

The Pentagon's enthusiasm for the rescue mission, despite the high risks involved, stemmed from various causes. The military had just mounted a highly successful evacuation in a hostile environment, taking all Americans out of Cambodia and South Vietnam as the two pro-Western regimes fell. The Pentagon's mood was one of "can do." The memory of the Vietnam debacle was also painfully fresh; many senior officers were eager to strike back at their former foes. Looking back, Secretary of Defense Schlesinger recalled that as the Communists overran Indochina, the dominant feeling in the U.S. military was "We can't let those bastards get away with *this*." According to Brigadier General Anderson W. Atkinson, then a senior Joint Staff officer closely involved with the planning, there was at the time "a lot of talk, after Vietnam, of getting our manhood back."[68] Moreover, as a senior administration official observed, "I think [the military men] were influenced by the same broader considerations as the civilians. I don't think that they were neutral. The NSC conveyed the impression that we needed to do something."[69]

Not all in the military, however, downplayed the risks involved. USSAG commander Lieutenant General John J. Burns and his chief of staff, Major General Earl J. Archer, had "reservations" about undertaking the rescue with such a limited force, thinking the operation would be "touchy."[70] But the messages from Washington suggested such thoughts were unwelcome. Speaking to military investigators conducting a postmortem of the operation, senior officers in Thailand recalled that Washington seemed intent on launching the rescue mission no matter what. Archer noted: "Based upon discussions and guidance from Washington, the intelligence estimates were not going to have an impact on any of the decisions to execute the operation." The commander of the 17th U.S. Air Force Division (17AD), Brigadier General Walter H. Baxter, who was closely involved in the planning at Utapao, observed: "I guess it was immaterial to find out [new information about the enemy on Koh Tang] because the Marines were going to be ordered in any way."[71]

Back in Washington, at least one key military official had misgivings. General David C. Jones, who was acting JCS Chairman for much of the first two days of the crisis while General Brown was in Canada, was concerned about the intelligence on Koh Tang. Jones worried about the uncertainty regarding the odds the Marines would face.[72] But from the start of the crisis, NSC members had been dissatisfied with his handling of the situation and relied more on the advice of Chief of Naval Operations James L. Holloway. Jones may have felt inhibited at expressing too many doubts, although at the last NSC meeting he did emphasize the advantage of waiting another day. Most military decision makers in Washington, however, seemed quick to dismiss the odds the Marines might face. As one senior military official observed, the other chiefs were eager to proceed without delay. As the official noted: "I think Jones wasn't sure of how to act, but he may have been the only one. I believe the chiefs didn't think about [delaying the operation] a lot. I think there was an agreement on the need to act fast." Another senior JCS official recalled: "My recollection is that the operation did not appear to be overly risky. I don't recall great wringing of hands on the part of members of the Joint Staff. . . . We felt this had a good chance of success."[73]

The White House similarly discounted the high risks the Marines were likely to incur. Admittedly, it submitted the military proposal and assessments to limited review.[74] The president and his advisers were nonetheless familiar with the general outline of the mission. The NSC was conversant enough with the details of the planning to veto as impractical one early JCS proposal, which called for U.S. helicopters to hover above the *Mayaguez* while Marines rappelled to the deck. The White House, moreover, received the estimates of at least one hundred well-armed Cambodian troops on the island. Presumably, it also saw the DIA estimates putting the enemy force as high as two hundred. One White House planning document noted that "it is estimated that it may take approximately 1,000 Marines to secure island. With high confidence could be considerably less but intelligence information quite sketchy."[75] Nor could the White House have ignored how many Marines the Pentagon planned to use. Yet the White House embraced the JCS's optimistic view.

Had the White House delayed the operation twenty-four hours, the chances of success would have dramatically increased. By the afternoon of May 15 local time (morning, Washington time) the carrier U.S.S. *Coral Sea* would have reached Koh Tang. The Marines could have used its deck the next morning to stage the assault, reducing the interval between assault waves to minutes rather than hours. The number of men and helicopters available for the landing would have greatly increased. The carrier U.S.S. *Hancock,* with a dozen Marine Corps helicopters and two companies of Marines aboard, was steaming as fast as possible to the scene. In the first hours of May 16 local time (afternoon of May 15 in Washington), it would have been close enough to fly its helicopters to the *Coral Sea* in time for the attack. Meantime, by May 15 the U.S buildup around Koh Tang would have been such that the United States could have enforced a tight blockade around the *Mayaguez* and the island until the rescue began.[76] By the third day of the crisis, however, the administration had decided it could no longer wait.

In short, as the crisis wore on, senior decision makers seem to have been overtaken by unbridled enthusiasm for a military response. The White House disregarded indications that there might be a solution short of force. It seems to have wished away the major risks the military plan posed to the captives and rescuers alike, rushing ahead with a mission that faced daunting odds.

Indeed, it appears that the desire to strike an exemplary blow rapidly reached such a pitch that the White House decided on a military rescue less than thirty-six hours after the crisis began, and came close to authorizing a mission even more hazardous than what actually took place. Apparently, the president almost sent troops in action nearly a full day before the landing ultimately occurred.

The White House ordered the Marines into action at 4:45 P.M. on Wednesday, May 14, some two and a half days after it first learned of the seizure of the ship. But Ford had decided much earlier to solve the crisis by force. According to Robert C. McFarlane, then an aide to Scowcroft, Ford approved "the basic concept of an armed assault" on the *Mayaguez* and Koh Tang at the third NSC meeting, on late Tuesday, May 13. Thereafter, the basic question was no longer whether but only when the rescue operation would take place. Other reliable reports indicate that the White House opted for a military solution even earlier. Shortly after the operation, White House aides confided to contacts in the press that by the morning of May 13, barely twenty-four hours into the crisis, the president had already decided to recover the captives by force. According to these sources, "it was . . . Tuesday morning when

Ford actually became convinced he would have no choice but to use force to obtain the release of the *Mayaguez* and its crew.[77]

Other informed sources later also recalled that the White House decided very early to use force. In the words of Admiral Train: "I think that in the first 24 to 36 hours we decided to go in...[in fact] closer to the first 24 hours." The commander of the U.S. Seventh Fleet in the Pacific, Vice Admiral George P. Steele, recalls being startled to receive signs, only hours after the seizure of the *Mayaguez,* "that we were going to go to battle stations on this thing." Steele received within "six or eight hours" of the outbreak of the crisis a call from Admiral Maurice F. Weisner, Commander in Chief of the U.S. Pacific Fleet (CinCPacFlt), warning: "They're going to do something big here. And you better get ready for it."[78] At the latest, the White House decided for a rescue a day and a half into the crisis; more likely, it embraced a military solution within twenty-four hours.

There is also evidence that the White House came close to sending troops into action a full day before the rescue mission took place. By the afternoon of May 13, the military had assembled one hundred air police at Utapao. The chief mission of the U.S. Air Force Air Police is to provide security at Air Force bases; its suitability for the rescue was questionable, but it was the closest force at hand. USSAG's original plan, approved by the JCS, was to land the air police directly on the *Mayaguez* at 7:00 P.M. on May 13, at daybreak in the Gulf of Thailand.[79]

It appears that this operation was canceled only at the last minute, when Marines from the Philippines began to arrive at Utapao. According to military records, the original "planning focused on boarding and seizure of the *Mayaguez* with an AF security police helo assault at first light on the 14th [approximately 7:00 P.M. Washington time on May 13].... All was in readiness at 0400 hours [May 13, 5:00 P.M. in Washington] for execution."[80] The commander of the 17th U.S. Air Force Division (17AD), Brigadier General Walter H. Baxter, who was closely involved in the planning at Utapao, commented shortly after the operation:

> The Mayaguez was captured and we observed it from a distance. The next thing we saw it from airplanes. We did a quick action search launch and decided to hurry up there to board the Mayaguez next morning [May 14, Gulf of Thailand time; evening of May 13, Washington time]. We did a lot of things in a short period of time. We had a 12-hour lead time. Get helicopters, get landing nets and board the Mayaguez. We got the word "Hold" when we were ready to launch....Released the security police forces and substituted the Marines.[81]

Colonel R. B. Janca, 17AD vice commander, who was in charge of preparing the air police launch, likewise stated: "Finally about 140400G [5:00 P.M., May 13, Washington time], the C-141 [transport plane carrying the first Marines] landed just before the Security Police were to launch." Asked about these indications that the mission almost occurred on the second day, Admiral Train later observed: "We were going to use the first people who got into position. We were close to going in with the air police, but as we looked at the alternatives it became apparent that the air police were lightly armed."[82] These ill-suited forces thus narrowly avoided action on the afternoon of the thirteenth, thirty-six hours after the crisis began.

Even after canceling the air police mission, however, the White House's sense of urgency did not abate. On the evening of May 13 the executive again came close to launching a rescue, almost twenty-four hours before the assault actually took place. As soon as the first Marines disembarked at Utapao, they were ordered to prepare for the capture of the *Mayaguez*. The third NSC meeting of the crisis was then under way. The minutes of this as well as the other NSC meetings remain classified. There is reason to think, however, that by the end of the third meeting the White House was on the verge of sending in the Marines without further delay.

The third NSC meeting ended at 12:30 A.M. on May 14. At 12:55 A.M.—twenty-five minutes after the meeting ended—the Marines and helicopter crews at Utapao were ordered to their aircraft in anticipation of an immediate launch. Although the precise chain of events that led to these actions remains unclear, it seems that the White House came close to launching the assault that night. Ultimately, however, the Marines were released for rest at 3:00 A.M. on May 14. But in subsequent interviews, senior officials emphasized that the only reason the executive waited until the evening of May 14 was that the military was not fully ready before. According to Admiral Train, the only factor determining the timing of the operation was "the build-up speed of the Marine and Air Force units." A senior administration official closely involved in the crisis put it bluntly: "We launched the operation at the earliest possible moment. As a matter of fact, when the first planes left the carrier [*Coral Sea*, to bomb the mainland], the carrier was still out of range of the returning planes."[83]

In conclusion, the administration's handling of the *Mayaguez* fell short of cool, careful deliberation. When the ship was seized, the administration reacted with deep anger. From the start, there was strong sentiment among the president's advisers to lash back and set an example. Ford's original reaction was more reserved; at the outset he also showed strong concern about the safety of the crew, and his first decision was to explore military as well as diplomatic responses. But as the crisis wore on, the urge to retaliate and restore U.S. prestige gained sway. By the time the Marines took off for Koh Tang, the crew's welfare had become merely one consideration among many others. Ultimately, the fear of another national humiliation, the urge to punish Cambodia, and the wish to show U.S. resolve seem to have generated almost blind enthusiasm for a forceful response. The president and his advisers ignored evidence suggesting that the crisis might be peacefully resolved. They overlooked the glaring weaknesses of a plan that could kill much or all of the crew and many rescuers. The White House rapidly became so taken with the language of force that it decided on a rescue mission barely twenty-four hours into the crisis and launched it at the earliest possible moment. The United States would pay a price for haste.

SIX

There Are No Snakes on Koh Tang

Planning and directing the *Mayaguez* operation fell to the closest U.S. military headquarters, the U.S. Support Activities Group/7AF (USSAG) in Nakhon Phanom, Thailand. Technically a joint command, it included representatives from the four services. In fact, it was predominantly an Air Force command, headed by an Air Force officer, Lieutenant General John J. Burns. In the three years prior to the capture of the *Mayaguez*, USSAG's main mission had been to provide air and logistical support to the South Vietnamese and Cambodian allies of the United States. In April 1975, USSAG had been heavily involved in the successful large-scale evacuation of Americans from Cambodia and from South Vietnam as the two countries fell to Communist forces.[1] Now USSAG faced a new challenge. Almost overnight, it was to organize the disparate U.S. units at hand into an integrated force and conduct one of the most difficult military operations of all: a combat rescue mission.

Within hours of receiving these orders, Burns sent one of his senior subordinates, Brigadier General Walter H. Baxter, commander of the 17th Air Division, to Utapao. Baxter was to act as Burns's deputy and oversee the Marines and helicopter units as they worked on the Koh Tang landing and the recapture of the *Mayaguez*. At Utapao were HH-53 helicopters from the 3rd Aerospace Rescue and Recovery Group (3d ARRGp) and CH-53s from the 21st Special Operations Squadron (21st SOS) that had flown in from their bases at Korat and Nakhon Phanom in Thailand. They would provide the helicopter airlift for the operation. Marines from Battalion Landing Team (BLT) 2/9 of the 3d Marine

Amphibious Force (III MAF) and a reinforced company from III MAF's 1st Battalion flew in from their bases respectively in Okinawa and the Philippines on May 14.[2]

USSAG reviewed the planning proposals that came out of Utapao. It also planned the complex sequence of actions required to support the capture of the island and the recovery of the ship. USSAG worked out the necessary communication nets, set up reconnaissance flights, and arranged naval gunfire as well as tactical air support for the rescue mission. USSAG was also in charge of blockading Koh Tang. USSAG planners had to choreograph a complicated aerial ballet of flying command posts, reconnaissance planes, fighter jets and tankers to refuel them, and search-and-rescue aircraft for any crews downed at sea.[3]

Both USSAG and the forces at Utapao received continuous guidance from higher commands. Recognizing the stake the White House had in a successful rescue, Burns anticipated that Washington would control the operation tightly. To simplify the chain of command, he proposed that during the crisis USSAG report directly to the JCS through the Pentagon's National Military Command Center. In an early message, USSAG explained: "The international implications of this operation make restraint imperative. Complete command and control must be maintained by COMMUSSAG/7AF [Commander, USSAG], who will be acting upon direction from the National Military Command Center." But CinCPac, the unified regional command in Hawaii with overall control of all U.S. forces in Asia, was not about to relinquish its authority over a subordinate command. With JCS acquiescence, CinCPac vigorously reasserted control over the U.S. headquarters in Thailand. In reply to USSAG, CinCPac pointedly noted: "Command and control will be maintained by CINCPAC, who will be acting under direction from JCS (NMCC)."[4] In theory, then, USSAG was to plan and execute the rescue under the supervision of CinCPac, which reported to Washington. The NMCC, however, could communicate directly with Nakhon Phanom. In practice, the U.S. headquarters in Thailand answered simultaneously to the commands in Hawaii and the Pentagon, which both provided a steady stream of orders, advice, and information.[5] The final plan was a composite of inputs from USSAG, CinCPac, and Washington.

USSAG faced special problems preparing the mission. At its heyday in the early 1970s, it had been a major headquarters, with a staff of over five hundred, but USSAG dwindled as U.S. involvement in Vietnam diminished. By 1975, the United States had decided to dismantle the command altogether. When the *Mayaguez* crisis erupted, USSAG had been scheduled to close down the next month; since mid-1974 personnel who had left at the end of their tours had not been replaced. Planning the rescue fell to an organization less than half its former size and no longer functioning at peak efficiency. Making matters worse were the pressures of time. Merely fifty-six hours elapsed from the time Nakhon

Phanom was instructed to prepare for a rescue to the departure of the Marines for Koh Tang.[6] Burns's original order was to be ready for a rescue within twenty-four hours, though the timetable later slipped. Thorough planning under these circumstances was difficult.

USSAG faced additional difficulties of a different sort. It was up to the White House, acting upon the advice of the JCS, to decide on the military action to take against Cambodia. The NMCC and CinCPac provided USSAG general guidance and reviewed its tactical planning to ensure that its preparations conformed with the president's decisions. Soon, however, higher headquarters went far beyond such broad command and control. CinCPac and the NMCC began to follow and direct USSAG's activities in minute detail, ultimately hampering its ability to carry out its mission.

CinCPac's and the NMCC's thirst for information was unquenchable. They demanded that USSAG report almost continuously, and in extraordinary detail, on its planning as well as on the smallest developments in the Gulf of Thailand. USSAG chief of staff General Archer later described these demands as "crushing." "I sat there with my hand glued to the telephone," he recalled.[7] One USSAG staffer noted bitterly in his end-of-tour report:

> The constant request for detailed information to be furnished higher headquarters was a definite hindrance to both the Mayaguez and TV/FW operation. A secure conference line was opened for this purpose and remained open for the duration of each operation. This not only required extra personnel to man the circuits, but also unnecessarily divided the attention of the 7AF battle staff. Much effort was expended in answering questions concerning the most minute detail. I certainly realize that the Mayaguez and TV/FW were of national importance and had the highest level interest; however, this is little justification for the headquarters to require tail numbers and call sign of each aircraft.[8]

Washington and Hawaii often insisted that Burns or one of his immediate deputies personally answer their queries.[9] USSAG's senior officers were repeatedly distracted from planning the details of the rescue mission.

The planners at Nakhon Phanom and Utapao staggered under the avalanche of information from Washington and Hawaii. The volume of messages sent by CinCPac and the Pentagon was overwhelming. As III MAF commander Major General Carl W. Hoffman, who was monitoring the traffic between the U.S. forces in Thailand and higher commands, later observed: "I became a zombie just trying to keep track [of all of the messages].[10]

Moreover, part of the information flowing to Thailand was redundant or even worthless. As the crisis wore on, the temptation to become involved apparently became irresistible to some in Washington and Hawaii, who sought a role by forwarding whatever information chanced to be at hand. Colonel John M. Johnson, commander of the Marines who deployed to Utapao, later spoke with barely contained anger about some of the information he received. Because the nearest secure phone line was at some distance from his command post at Utapao, every time he received a call from the NMCC or from CinCPac, he had to stop what he was doing, find a vehicle, and drive to the base communications center. One time Johnson made the trip to hear a major general in Washington announce that he had located an American petroleum engineer who had once been on Koh Tang. Johnson listened dumbfounded to the information the general had gleaned: "The prevailing winds are from the south-southeast... there are no snakes on the island. ... The vegetation is not so dense as to require machete like clearing." Johnson snapped after the operation: "In many cases these calls, although they may have been highly beneficial to higher authorities, simply interfered with any efforts on our part to effectively carry out the planning for the task that faced us."[11]

Often, senior officers in Washington and Hawaii decided on matters of the smallest operational detail, ignoring the traditional prerogatives of the commander in the field. Early in the crisis, III MAF commander Hoffman was amazed when he saw the orders from higher headquarters sending Marines from the Philippines and Okinawa to Utapao. The message designated a specific rifle company by name to execute the recovery of the *Mayaguez*.[12] No one, however, had asked the commanders of the battalion the company belonged to which company they thought could do the job best.

Officers in the Pentagon or Hawaii calibrated the minutiae of operations unfolding thousands of miles away. Not surprisingly, they were often unaware of key aspects of the situation in the field, and their commands were sometimes singularly ill-advised. As the destroyer *Holt* steamed toward Koh Tang, a general in the NMCC, which had established a special voice link with the ship, asked the skipper how fast he was going. He reported that the *Holt* was proceeding at 80 percent power. The general brusquely replied, "Well, we want you to get there as fast as you can. Let's make full power," and terminated the call before the skipper could say more. What the officer in the NMCC did not realize was that 1052-class destroyers like the *Holt* were prone to engine trouble. Furthermore, because of its role in the evacuations of Cambodia and South Vietnam, the *Holt* had received next to no upkeep for months. The ship was in such poor condition that Vice Admiral George P. Steele, commander of the Seventh Fleet, "didn't know whether he was going to break down."[13] Steele and his staff calculated that a full-power run would bring the *Holt* on station about an hour earlier than originally scheduled, or about 4:00 A.M. on May 15, local time. By then it would still be night. Since the *Holt*'s role in the rescue mission did not begin until dawn, the gain in time would make no difference. Meanwhile, to gain an hour, the *Holt* would run a good chance of breakdown that could leave it dead in the water. It took Steele, who vigorously protested the NMCC order, "ten hours before we could get that ship slowed down a little bit."[14]

As the crisis wore on, Nakhon Phanom received increasingly detailed instructions on the conduct of operations in the Gulf of Thailand. Having ordered USSAG to prevent any movement of the *Mayaguez* from its anchorage off Koh Tang, higher commands spelled out exactly how to do so, leaving USSAG no discretion in the matter. USSAG's planes were to monitor the temperature of the ship's smokestack for any sign that its engines had started. If the ship moved, U.S. planes were to drop five-hundred-pound bombs in front of its bow. If it did not stop, the planes should open fire with 2.75-inch rockets. If this failed, they were to use 20-mm canon.[15]

By imposing excessive reporting requirements, inundating the planners with a flood of at times useless information, and trying to direct local actions in the smallest detail, the Pentagon and CinCPac greatly complicated USSAG's task. But Nakhon Phanom's greatest challenge, perhaps, was to put together a joint operation on such short notice. Since World War II, the U.S. military has often had problems with operations where several services are involved. In the *Mayaguez* operation, such difficulties expanded almost geometrically.

Serious problems of interservice coordination plagued planning and preparation of the rescue mission in both Nakhon Phanom and Utapao. As an official postmortem later observed, a "break-down in command arrangements appeared to have occurred when the operation was changed from uni-service (AF) to joint, with the introduction of USMC [Marine Corps] units."[16] Cooperation between the Marine Corps and the Air Force was uneven at best. The problem was especially acute at Utapao, where no one effectively coordinated the efforts of the different services and forces. General Baxter had been sent to Utapao to oversee the units of the Marine Corps and Air Force that would execute the operation. But as the postmortem commented, Baxter's "exact duties were vague and not defined to key participants." As a result, the command arrangement proved "inadequate." The various units and services at Utapao ended up working largely on their own.[17]

A Marine Corps after-action report captured the confusion at Utapao: "Present in the CP [command post] during the day were various USAF officers, although it was unclear to [BLT] 2/9 as to exactly who they were or what their relationship to the [Marines] was.... A meeting was held at which the final plan was formulated. Present were ... several USAF officers, including a Brigadier General [Baxter] whose exact role was unknown to 2/9 personnel." Commenting on the situation at Utapao in a postoperation interview, Lieutenant Colonel Randall W. Austin, commander of the troops who landed on Koh Tang, observed: "I was never sure who everyone was." An Air Force colonel present later recalled that "preparations at Utapao lacked coordination and leadership. No one seemed to be in charge. Everybody appeared only interested in their thing."[18]

Flawed interservice coordination also marred the dissemination of intelligence. Air Force reconnaissance planes quickly took excellent pictures of Koh Tang. These pictures, however, did not reach the Marine Corps until shortly before the operation. For most of the planning the Marines did not have as much as map of the island. They relied mostly on a few shots of Koh Tang, taken from six thousand feet with a handheld camera by a Marine Corps officer who made a visual reconnaissance of the island on an Army aircraft. The Marine planners at Utapao received the snapshots twelve hours before the attack.[19]

Similarly, the Marines never received crucial information the Air Force acquired on enemy forces and defenses at Koh Tang. In the two days leading up to the rescue mission, Air Force planes frequently overflew the island, often drawing antiaircraft fire. USSAG received no fewer than eleven reports of antiaircraft fire from Koh Tang. Several reports identified the position of antiaircraft weapons on the island. One AC-130 gunship, using sophisticated scanning devices, located at least three gun emplacements on a key beach where the Marines planned to land. None of this got to the Marines. A CinCPac postmortem on the operation laconically observed: "No apparent threat advisories were issued on the small arms, automatic weapons and AAA [antiaircraft artillery] threats from Koh Tang Island."[20]

The Air Force also failed to pass on to the Marines vital information on the enemy's strength. During the crisis Nakhon Phanom received several force estimates from IPAC, CinCPac's intelligence branch. The first report put the Cambodian presence on the island at no more than twenty military personnel. Subsequent IPAC messages, however, estimated there were perhaps a hundred well-armed troops on Koh Tang. USSAG's own estimates variously put the strength of the island's garrison at anywhere from one to three hundred regular troops. USSAG forwarded these reports to the U.S. Air Force 307 Strategic Wing at Utapao. But USSAG neither gave the information to the Marines who were to assault Koh Tang nor instructed the 307 Strategic Wing to do so.[21] A tragically absurd situation thus prevailed.

The only official estimate of enemy forces the Marines at Utapao received was IPAC's original estimate of some twenty Cambodian troops. To augment this meager intelligence, the Marines interviewed Cambodian refugees at Utapao who had recently been on Koh Tang. A former Cambodian naval officer estimated there were no more than twenty-five Cambodians on the island.[22] The Marines had the illusion they would face only token resistance on Koh Tang. Meanwhile, snarled in red tape in an Air Force command post a few hundred yards away, was accurate information on the powerful enemy they would actually face.

It is, of course, not certain that, even if the Marines had received ac-

curate information on Koh Tang, the operation would have been different. The White House seemed intent on sending in the Marines, no
matter what. Still, had the Marine Corps commanders realized the size
and power of the enemy defense, they would have argued strongly for
changes to the plan. As one of the ranking Marines at Utapao later observed: "Had we known of an intelligence estimate of about 100 KC
[Khmer Communist], we would have tried to change the plans. It
would have been suicide to go in against that size force without preparatory strikes." After the operation, Austin emphasized that had he been
aware of IPAC's and USSAG's revised estimates, he would have "fought
harder" for "preparatory fires on the landing zones." As it turned out,
the Marines walked into a lethal trap totally unawares.[23]

Poor interservice cooperation had further ramifications yet. Air
Force planners seem to have repeatedly ignored specific needs and concerns of the Marines. USSAG had on hand sophisticated reconnaissance
aircraft with photographic equipment that could identify Cambodian
fortifications on Koh Tang. But although USSAG launched numerous
reconnaissance flights during the crisis, it made no effort to reconnoiter
the defenses on the island. As a postoperation study observed: "A slic-
ing run using a nose oblique camera may have revealed defensive positions and additional buildings near the LZs [landing zones]." But "no
apparent VR [visual reconnaissance] missions were fragged [ordered] or
flown in order to identify Cambodian defenses on Koh Tang Island."[24]

A few hours before taking off for Koh Tang, the Marines developed
the pictures taken during their reconnaissance flight over the island.
Looking at the photographs, Air Force officers at Utapao noticed what
they thought were possible antiaircraft positions. The Marines asked the
Air Force how it would handle this threat to their insertion. Lieutenant
Colonel Austin later described their response: "It was somewhat unclear
what they were going to do about it. (They said they were 'going to
look at it in the morning.')." Air Force officers stated that "these possible positions were to be evaluated on scene at first light and hit by CAS
[close air support] strikes if deemed appropriate."[25] But the fighters over
Koh Tang never checked out, let alone attacked, the suspected gun sites
before the helicopters arrived. There is no record of Air Force commanders in Nakhon Phanom or Utapao pointing out to the CAS pilots
covering the landing these possible gun emplacements.[26] The helicopters
met a devastating barrage of fire as they began to land on Koh Tang.

The Marines had no more success with their request for slow-flying
OV-10 observation planes. The Marines knew from experience in Vietnam the limitations of jet fighters in a ground-support role. With their
high speed and high fuel consumption, which gives them limited loiter-
ing time over targets, jet fighters can have difficulty gaining a clear picture of the situation on the ground. Colonel Johnson asked that piston-
driven OV-10 Broncos be on hand at Koh Tang. These slow-flying
planes typically serve as forward air controllers (FACs), pinpointing en-

emy targets and directing air or artillery strikes. Within the Air Force, however, there is much resistance to the idea that light propeller aircraft can outperform jet fighters in a tactical support role. Not surprisingly, USSAG considered its F-4 and A-7 jets well suited for the job; no OV-10s were at hand when the Marines landed at Koh Tang.[27]

The rescue mission suffered from another flaw with potentially devastating consequences. While USSAG struggled to keep its planning secret, well-informed Washington officials liberally shared their knowledge of the plan. Hours before the rescue began, Washington journalists, learning that the operation was likely to take place, broadcast the news to the world. Soon after the last NSC meeting on the afternoon of May 14, one broadcast journalist reported on ABC that "the latest NSC meeting has set the stage for a major military initiative when daylight hours reach the Gulf of Thailand." Another ABC journalist revealed that "officials said the most likely strategy to recover the Mayaguez would include simultaneous Marine landings on the Mayaguez deck and on Koh Tang Island." Quoting "Pentagon sources," an NBC broadcast journalist reported that "a helicopter operation 'is in the works'. . . . The operation is imminent—hours away . . . —but will depend on decisions made at the White House."[28]

Government sources and the media gave advance notice of the U.S. military's next move. Given the turmoil in Cambodia, it is debatable whether this ever came to the attention of its military. Nonetheless, the outline and timing of a highly sensitive and supposedly secret U.S. operation were made public even as the White House was authorizing the mission. And it remains that when U.S. helicopters approached Koh Tang, the enemy was ready.

Ford called the final NSC meeting of the crisis at 4:00 P.M. on May 14. Forty-five minutes later, he gave the order to execute. The plan seemed simple: eleven Air Force CH and HH-53 helicopters loaded with Marines were to proceed from Utapao to Koh Tang. Eight would land on the island while the other three unloaded their passengers onto the *Holt*, which would then proceed to the *Mayaguez*. For the Air Force crews and Marines who were to execute the mission, however, the operation became a twelve-hour ordeal that barely avoided disaster.

The execute order reached Utapao within minutes. It was then almost 4:00 A.M. on May 15, Gulf of Thailand time.* The helicopters stood on the tarmac, flight crews at the ready, the Marine Corps assault force, commanded by Lieutenant Colonel Austin, waiting silently alongside. As soon as the order was received, the troops filed on board the aircraft, which lifted off one after another into the night. Within thirty minutes, the last helicopter was on its way.[29]

The airwaves crackled with activity as USSAG fed higher com-

---

* All times that follow are Gulf of Thailand time unless noted otherwise.

mands' voracious appetite for information. The helicopter flight time from Utapao to Koh Tang was almost two hours. CinCPac required that Burns, who had been working on the operation almost nonstop since the start of the crisis, provide a running phone commentary of the uneventful flight. "Keep the info coming," CinCPac demanded. As the helicopters neared the island, its demands became increasingly strident: "Essential that you volunteer info on the operation immediately." Soon CinCPac was insisting that USSAG read "when received" over the secure phone the situation reports from the *Holt,* provide the "landing times of helos as soon as they land," and give an exact count of the tactical aircraft over Koh Tang.[30] CinCPac, thousands of miles away, began controlling the operation down to the smallest detail.

As dawn broke over the Gulf of Thailand, the helicopters quickly closed in on their objectives. The boarding party successfully disembarked onto the *Holt,* but the Marines headed for Koh Tang met fierce resistance. As the first helicopter touched down, the Cambodians unleashed a withering barrage of automatic, machine-gun and rocket-propelled-grenade fire. In an early manifestation of the poor coordination that plagued operations throughout the day, the helicopters had no air cover as they approached the island. A heavily armed AC-130 gunship, ideally suited for this role, had been orbiting Koh Tang earlier that morning. The gunship left minutes before the helicopters arrived. Meanwhile, the fighters tasked with protecting the landing were refueling from an airborne tanker when the helicopter assault began. The incoming craft were all but defenseless in the face of devastating enemy fire.[31]

The helicopters were supposed to land simultaneously at two locations on Koh Tang. Two were to insert on a narrow western beach, while the six others touched down on a larger, eastern beach on the opposite side of the island. The planners anticipated that within minutes 180 Marines would be on Koh Tang. Intense enemy fire played havoc with these plans. The first four helicopters attempted to land at about 6:00 A.M. Within ten minutes, enemy gunners shot one down and caused another to crash land on the east beach. A third helicopter ditched at sea moments after unloading troops on the west beach. The fourth was so badly hit that it could not land and limped back to Thailand. By 6:15, fourteen Americans were dead, and on each beach a handful of survivors were fighting for their lives.[32]

At this point, Air Force unfamiliarity with heliborne assaults compounded the difficulties of an insertion that threatened to become a disaster. A principle of Marine Corps helicopter assaults is that once an insertion has begun and an aircraft is shot down, the other helicopters "go in by the light of the burning plane." Once the first troops are on the ground, the buildup must proceed at any cost, lest they be overrun. But when the first Air Force helicopters took hits over Koh Tang, most pilots in the following aircraft instinctively aborted their landing runs, awaiting further instructions. The pilots failed to realize that their maneuver left a force of barely fifty Marines and downed airmen stranded on Koh Tang, desperately fighting off counterattacks from a force at least four times that size.[33]

As the morning wore on, the attackers rallied. By 6:30 A.M., Air Force fighters began pounding suspected Cambodian positions and the remaining helicopters again attempted to offload their troops. Braving a hail of bullets, grenades, and mortar rounds, four helicopters landed in the next hour and a half another eighty Marines on the west side of the island. In the process, three planes were damaged so badly they were grounded for repairs when they made it back to Utapao, and remained unusable for the rest of the operation. By 10:00 A.M., twenty-five Marines and airmen had established a defensive perimeter at the eastern landing zone and some sixty Marines were fighting on the west beach. Also on the west side, more than a thousand yards south, another pocket of twenty-nine Marines had dug in. To its dismay, this small group, which included Marine Corps commander Austin, was inserted outside the designated western landing zone. More than a thousand yards of dense jungle separated Austin's group from the west beach.[34]

Throughout the morning the Marines' position was precarious. Facing them was a large, well-entrenched force that fought stubbornly. Meanwhile, the Marines had persistent problems coordinating with the planes above. Part of the problem was that they had lost in the helicopter crashes most of their UHF (ultra high frequency) radios, which they habitually use to communicate with air support, and were left chiefly with VHF (very high frequency) radios, which they normally rely on only to communicate between ground units. As they used VHF to communicate both among themselves and with the planes above, the radio frequencies became saturated to the point that they were barely usable.[35]

Adding to the confusion, orbiting one hundred miles north of Koh Tang was an Air Force Airborne Command and Communications Center (ABCCC) crammed with communications and tracking gear. The ABCCC, code-named Cricket, was in direct radio contact with Nakhon Phanom as well as with the Air Force, Navy, and Marine Corps units executing the rescue mission, and served as USSAG's on-scene representative. The flying command post was supposed to control the movements of the various units on or around Koh Tang and to direct air and naval support,[36] but in the first hours of the operation, Cricket's picture of the situation was at best confused.

USSAG's battle plan called for the helicopters to land at two places on the island, but in preoperation briefings Cricket's staff officers were told of only one designated landing zone. Cricket was startled when it received messages from Marine Corps units on different parts of Koh Tang. Moreover, Cricket never had been given the radio call signs of the various Marine Corps units forming the ground assault force. The ABCCC was at a loss to determine exactly who was calling from where. As a subsequent military report on the operation observed: "It ... appears there was a breakdown in the central coordinating function, especially in the first hour or two of the Koh Tang assault and extending intermittently into the day."[37] For hours, Cricket could not guide with any precision the fighters providing air cover, which were left to carry out supporting strikes as best they could.

Given their speed, the fighters had difficulty identifying Marine Corps positions on the island. Making matters worse was their fast turnover. Until the arrival of OV-10 observation planes in the afternoon, at all times one jet acted as on-scene commander of the tactical aircraft over Koh Tang, directing the bombing and strafing runs of the other fighters. But given the jets' high fuel consumption, each on-scene commander could assume this role only briefly. Throughout the rescue operation, there were no fewer than fourteen tactical aircraft commanders over Koh Tang. Between 5:30 and 6:30 A.M., when the first helicopter landings occurred, the on-scene commander changed four times. Shortly after the operation, a downed helicopter pilot who was with the Marines on the east beach voiced his frustration with the jets: "It seemed like nobody was briefing the guy who was coming in next [on] what was going on. [We] had to brief every flight that showed up . . . had to brief every one of those guys on our position. By that time they had enough to make two passes and had to leave because they had to hit the tanker again."[38]

Cricket's reports and transcripts of message traffic over Koh Tang record the fighter pilots' confusion. Two hours after the operation had begun, they were describing the situation as confused and reporting that they were having "trouble ID'ing [identifying] targets." Cricket observed that there still was "no accurate determination of GSF [ground security force] locations." After the operation it was "the universal opinion among the chopper crews" that the jets were too fast to provide adequate support without a slower-flying forward air controller to direct them.[39] Although during the day the jets sometimes relieved the pressure on the Marines, their performance was uneven. Not until the arrival of the first OV-10 Broncos, which USSAG belatedly sent when it understood the seriousness of the situation, did the air crews gain an accurate picture of the Marines' positions.[40] With the Broncos taking over in late afternoon as forward air controllers, the close air support became far more effective.

Despite the shortcomings of the air support, from dawn to noon fewer than 120 servicemen, dispersed in three separate groups, fought off a far larger force.[41] The Marines belonged to the III MAF's Ready Reaction Force, stationed in Okinawa. At the outbreak of the crisis, III MAF's most seasoned troops were at sea, returning from the evacuation of South Vietnam. The role of Ready Reaction Force had fallen to a battalion of greener recruits. Apart from some officers and NCOs, they were seeing combat for the first time.[42]

The two pockets of Marines on the west of the island rapidly established radio contact. To Austin, it was clear that they had to link up as soon as possible. As the larger group on the west beach started pushing southward, however, it ran into stiff resistance, took several casualties, and pulled back. Austin and his men, meantime, were pushing northward. His group, consisting mostly of radio operators and members of a heavy mortar section, had only a handful of rifles. They nonetheless pressed forward, flushing out the enemy from several defensive positions. By midmorning, the force on the west beach, reinforced by a score of Marines from helicopters that had finally managed to land, resumed fighting its way south. The two groups linked up by 12:30 P.M.[43]

While the Marines fought at Koh Tang, other operations against Cambodia proceeded essentially unopposed. After receiving its contingent of troops, the *Holt* drew alongside the *Mayaguez* and the Marines clambered aboard. By 8:10 A.M., the *Holt* reported that a thorough search had revealed no Americans or Cambodians aboard.[44]

Meanwhile, Navy air strikes against the Cambodian mainland were under way. A few minutes before 6:00 A.M., as the first helicopters approached Koh Tang, five flights of attack aircraft launched from the *Coral Sea* and headed toward the Cambodian port of Kompong Som. Less than half an hour later, Cambodian Minister of Information and Propaganda Hu Nim began a nineteen-minute statement on Cambodian radio. Hu Nim asserted that "U.S. Imperialism has repeatedly and successively carried out intelligence and espionage activities to conduct subversive, provocative acts against the newly liberated New Cambodia." This was why, he continued, Cambodian forces had detained the *Mayaguez,* which he called a "CIA spy ship." Hu Nim concluded, however, with the promise to release the ship: "Our [revolutionary government] will order the Mayaguez to withdraw from Cambodian territorial waters and will warn it against further espionage or provocative activities. This applies to the Mayaguez or any other ships, like the ship flying the Panama flag which we released on 9 May 1975."[45]

U.S. listening services flashed a translation to Washington within minutes. The president briefly conferred with Secretary Kissinger and at 7:30 A.M. instructed that the fighters headed for Cambodia withhold their ordnance. Appalled by the cancellation of an operation under way, the JCS protested to Secretary of Defense Schlesinger, who urged the president to rescind the order. A few minutes before 8:00 A.M. Ford ordered that the operations against the mainland proceed as originally planned. Shortly before 10:00 A.M., the first bombs fell on Ream airfield near Kompong Som.[46]

After the rescue, Ford said he proceeded with the bombings because the Cambodian broadcast did not promise specifically to release the crew. According to the president, "They made no mention of the crew, and thus I decided that the operation should proceed as planned since we had received no indication assuring the safety of the crew. Nor was it clear that this local broadcast had any official standing in Phnom Penh." It is, however, hard to imagine how the Cambodians could propose to "order the Mayaguez to withdraw . . . and warn it against further espionage or provocative activities" unless they were speaking of both the ship and its crew. In its own rhetoric, the administration drew no fine distinctions between ship and crew. In its ultimatum of May 12, the White House called for the "immediate release of the ship"—without perceiving a need to add that the United States also wanted to recover the crew.[47]

Minutes after Hu Nim's speech reached Washington, CinCPac intercepted a message from an unknown Cambodian radio station saying: "Let the Americans go. We do not want to become prisoners ourselves." Shortly before the first jets began pounding the mainland, a Navy observation plane noticed a small boat, flying a white flag and carrying what appeared to be "about thirty Caucasians." The destroyer U.S.S. *Wilson,* recently arrived on scene, headed for the craft. At 10:15 A.M. the *Wilson* reported that it had intercepted the boat and found the entire *Mayaguez* crew alive and well on board. The Cambodians had decided to release them at about 6:30 that morning—at almost the same time the Marines began landing on Koh Tang—and had let the crew set out in a small fishing vessel.[48]

The White House was immediately informed that the crew was safe in U.S. hands. It nonetheless decided to continue bombing the mainland. According to Press Secretary Nessen, when the White House learned that the crew was safe, Scowcroft asked was there "any reason for the Pentagon not to disengage?" "No," reportedly replied Kissinger, "but tell them to bomb the mainland. . . . Let's look ferocious! Otherwise they will attack us as the ship leaves." At 10:44 A.M., Schlesinger informed the JCS Chairman that the wave from the *Coral Sea* should "strike as planned."[49]

The White House ordered that further military actions on Koh Tang should aim at extracting the Marines without additional casualties. The JCS advised CinCPac Commander in Chief Admiral Noel A.M. Gayler "that there was no commitment to keep the Marines on the island or to capture it," and requested that CinCPac prepare to evacuate the troops.[50] But disengaging was a harrowing affair. The release of the crew offered no relief to the servicemen on Koh Tang; throughout the morning their position remained precarious and enemy pressure was unremitting. For the first six hours the troops in the west beach landing zone assessed their situation as "critical." After the operation, the Marines described the combat that morning as intense and close; "grenade dueling was the rule rather than the exception."[51]

Problems of interservice coordination and micromanagement continued as the day progressed. USSAG never told Austin of the recovery of the crew—despite its relevance for troops whose mission was to search the island for the crew. Instead, minutes after learning that the *Wilson* had recovered them, USSAG ordered Cricket not to mention withdrawal to the force on Koh Tang. Meanwhile, higher headquarters' micromanagement and demands for information continued unabated. General Burns later recalled that as soon as the first helicopter crashed, and before he could even evaluate the situation, he received calls demanding, "You've got helicopters down. What are you going to do about it?"[52]

From CinCPac, in particular, came a steady drumbeat of demands for battle reports and casualty counts. Callers from Hawaii would speak only to USSAG's senior officers; CinCPac upbraided Burns for not answering a call in person and allowing a duty officer to respond instead. "Imperative we have someone with authority on phone," CinCPac commanded.[53]

All too often, CinCPac tried to direct actions of various units on or around Koh Tang. From Hawaii, CinCPac ordered movements of ships off the island, even deciding when the *Wilson* should provide supporting fire to the Marines. At times CinCPac tried to control the tactics of individual helicopters above the island and of the Marines on the ground. For Colonel Johnson, the overall commander of the Marine Corps force conducting the mission, who followed the mission from Utapao, the involvement of senior commands reached ludicrous levels. He commented after the operation: "I have seen a lot of 'squad leader in the sky' operations in my day, but this one beats anything that I have ever seen. Although from my level we could not ascertain exactly who was doing what to whom, where, when, and how, it certainly appeared that the lowest level of command was being exercised at least at Hawaii and perhaps even farther back in Washington."[54]

Unfortunately, the picture of events on which CinCPac and the NMCC based their tactical decisions left much to be desired. It was hard enough for USSAG, in touch with Cricket and many of the naval and air units in action at Koh Tang, to follow accurately the rapidly changing tactical scene. It was even more difficult for decision makers in Hawaii and Washington. The NMCC and CinCPac were in radio contact with some of the ships at the island. The higher commands received most of the combat information, however, through a series of relays. The units on and around Koh Tang typically communicated with Cricket, which reported to USSAG. Nakhon Phanom passed on the information to CinCPac and the NMCC. At each step, chances for distortion of the original message proliferated.

By placing an enormous burden of reporting on USSAG, the NMCC and CinCPac increased the chance they would receive inaccurate accounts. Faced with relentless demands for information, USSAG was under pressure to pass on whatever was at hand, even when it did not fully understand developments itself. One senior member of USSAG's battle staff warned shortly after the operation, that such pressure was "counterproductive" and could result in "misleading details being forwarded" just to respond to higher headquarters' demands."[55]

The information flowing to CinCPac and the NMCC was of uneven quality and sometimes conveyed an inaccurate picture. This caused misunderstandings that led Washington and Hawaii to issue flawed tactical orders. When CinCPac first ordered the *Wilson* to begin naval gunfire support for the Marines, the island was miles out of reach of the destroyer's five-inch gun. It took the *Wilson* a full hour's sailing to get close enough to open fire.[56]

Late in the morning, another ill-advised CinCPac order threatened to have catastrophic consequences. According to the original plan, after landing the first wave of troops, the helicopters were to fly back to Utapao, take on more Marines, and return to Koh Tang. But when the helicopters returned to base after unloading the first wave on the island, USSAG found that they had taken so many hits that only three were still safe to fly. U.S. Air Force units in Thailand supplied another two helicopters. By midmorning, a second wave of five helicopters, carrying more than 120 Marine reinforcements, was under way.[57]

As the flight neared Koh Tang, the JCS issued the order, following the recovery of the *Mayaguez* and its crew, to "concentrate efforts on withdrawal of Marines from the island." It was then shortly after 11:00 A.M., and throughout the morning the Marines repeatedly had called for reinforcements, anxiously asking Cricket when they would arrive. The Marines described their situation as critical and said they were in danger of being overrun. Somehow, however, CinCPac had received information that the Marines were "in no imminent danger," with "the opposition forced back." Instructed by Washington to concentrate on withdrawing, CinCPac ordered USSAG to recall the second helicopter wave.[58]

General Burns realized, however, how badly the Marines needed reinforcements and pressed CinCPac to change its order. Colonel Johnson, who was monitoring communications between USSAG and Cricket, also protested up the chain of command. A Marine Corps general in Hawaii joined the protest. A few minutes later CinCPac rescinded its order, and the helicopters proceeded with their original mission.[59]

The five aircraft arrived over Koh Tang shortly before noon. In the next half hour, despite extremely heavy enemy fire, some coming only fifty yards from the landing zone, all but one helicopter inserted its troops on the west beach. This last aircraft was badly damaged trying to land and limped back, without offloading its passengers, to Thailand, where it made an emergency landing. By 12:30 P.M., another one hundred Marines had joined the servicemen on Koh Tang.[60]

As the helicopters unloaded their troops, Austin's command group linked up with the main Marine Corps force in the western landing zone. Only then did Austin learn from the reinforcements that the *Mayaguez* crew had been rescued hours before. With more than two hundred men on the west beach, the main U.S. position had become fairly secure. But the twenty-five servicemen on the east beach were as exposed as ever. In the early afternoon, two helicopters attempted to rescue them, only to be driven away by enemy fire. One crippled helicopter limped on a single engine to the carrier *Coral Sea,* which had recently arrived in the vicinity of Koh Tang.[61]

Enemy pressure continued throughout the afternoon. Meanwhile, USSAG, CinCPac, and the NMCC held a series of conference calls on how to extract the troops. As time passed, their concern mounted steadily. Although the force on the west beach was large enough to survive the night, they feared that the position on the east beach would be overrun when night fell. But given the aircraft losses incurred earlier, for most of the afternoon USSAG had only three flyable helicopters—far too few to evacuate the men on Koh Tang. Moreover, two of these aircraft spent much of the afternoon ferrying to Thailand the casualties they had taken off the island after landing reinforcements. From 2:30 to 5:00 P.M., only one helicopter was available at Koh Tang.[62]

At approximately 4:30 that afternoon, U.S. commanders decided on an almost desperate extraction bid. With JCS concurrence, CinCPac ordered the small motor launches of the destroyers *Holt* and *Wilson* to draw as close to the island as possible. The Marines were to "swim/push [their] wounded [a] few feet to [the] boats." At about the same time that CinCPac gave this order, two OV-10 Broncos arrived at Koh Tang and began directing fighter strikes against the island. Armed with machine guns and rockets, the Broncos also hit enemy positions. From then on, the effectiveness of the air strikes greatly increased.[63]

Shortly thereafter, the number of helicopters at Koh Tang rose again. Following emergency repairs, at 5:00 P.M. the damaged helicopter on the *Coral Sea* was airborne again. In the next half hour, the two helicopters that had taken wounded to Thailand returned to Koh Tang, accompanied by a third aircraft that had been grounded after the morning landings. Working feverishly, mechanics at Nakhon Phanom had returned it to service. With more helicopters available and improving close air support, CinCPac decided at the last minute on an evacuation by air rather than by small boat.[64]

Just after 6:00 P.M., the OV-10s directed a concerted effort to extract the twenty-five men on the east beach. Protected by one OV-10 and two helicopters, a third helicopter landed on the beach while the Marines and airmen dashed to it. The Bronco flew repeatedly over the beach, strafing enemy positions in the treeline. Drawing heavy enemy fire, the helicopter lifted off, a Marine dangling from an outside a machine gun mount. He was pulled in as the aircraft reached an altitude of two hundred feet. Almost at the same time, the OV-10 silenced a heavy machine gun that had opened up on the helicopter as it took off. The twenty-five troops on the east beach had made it out alive.[65]

Despite the improved air support, problems of interservice coordination continued. Throughout the operation several specially outfitted C-130 aircraft had been orbiting the island. Each plane carried a pallet-mounted, fifteen-thousand-pound BLU-82 bomb, the largest nonnuclear bomb in the U.S. arsenal. The Marines had asked that they not be used without first informing the ground commander. Upon instructions from CinCPac, shortly after 6:00 P.M. a C-130 dropped a BLU-82 on the southern part of the island.[66] No one had warned the Marines, who saw a C-130 make a low pass and jettison a pallet, which billowed gently to the ground at the end of a parachute. They assumed this was an airdrop of supplies they had requested earlier. They learned otherwise when the bomb landed eight hundred yards away, leveling an area the size of a football field. After the operation, Colonel Johnson observed:

> It seemed to me throughout the hours leading up to the execution of the operation, that someone, somewhere was bound and determined we were going to throw those big mothers all around for some reason or another. ...I had reiterated time and time again that they should not be employed without the knowledge of the ground support force commander on the ground, without complete knowledge of where the forces on the ground were disposed, and preferably only on the request of the ground security force commander.[67]

More problems followed. A helicopter evacuation at night, under fire, is one of the most hazardous military operations of all. This is precisely what the Air Force undertook after evacuating the east beach. Shortly after dusk, the helicopters made a run for the west beach. They showed up without warning; no one had told the Marines on the west beach that their evacuation was about to begin.[68]

Austin had been in radio contact with Cricket throughout the afternoon. He knew that headquarters was contemplating evacuating all U.S. troops that evening rather than waiting until the next day. But the Marines were never told which evacuation scenario had been adopted. As the Marine Corps after-action report notes:

> Throughout the late afternoon, there were indications that extraction plans were being developed.... CO [Commanding Officer] 2/9 was not informed exactly as to what was being discussed but he was asked at various times if (a) Small boats from the USN [U.S. Navy] ships are feasible? (Answer: yes, if available) (b) Could the extraction be done entirely from the eastern side? (No, not without a massive assault across the island) (c) Could a helicopter extraction be done at night? (Yes, although difficult, it was going to be dificult and heavily opposed whenever it was done).
>
> No word was ever received on what was finally decided, or when it was going to be done.... At approximately 1800 one helicopter ... com-

pleted the extraction of the small group on the eastern side. Shortly thereafter, several additional helos appeared on the horizon and it was obvious that a helo extraction of the main force was *on.*[69]

By then, however, Austin had concluded that "probably we were going to spend the night" on the island. Although "amazed" that the extraction had begun, the Marines on west beach had little time to ponder their surprise. By then it was dark, and they had to mark the landing zone with flashlights. As noted in the Marine Corps after-action report, when the first helicopters landed, "a heavy fire fight, with exchange of grenades, erupted along the entire front." As Austin later recalled, it was "about the heaviest exchange of small arms that occurred during the entire day." In the words of a subsequent Marine Corps report, "During this period of time confusion existed in and about the beach area."[70]

Under the best of circumstances, the west beach landing zone could hold no more than two helicopters at once. But with visibility at the darkened beach poor, the aircraft landed one at a time. U.S. servicemen displayed conspicuous gallantry. Despite withering fire, the helicopter crews, some of whom had been flying almost nonstop for fourteen hours, pressed on. At one point, an OV-10 pilot made repeated low passes over the landing zone with his landing lights on, guiding the helicopters in and drawing away enemy fire.[71]

Nonetheless, the operation barely escaped disaster. As the first helicopter approached the beach and met a hail of automatic weapons fire, the aircraft's gunners raked the area with Gatling-gun fire. As the Marine Corps after-action report observed: "This fire was unfortunately directed into the landing-zone and across the entire front, miraculously and narrowly missing the Marines." Minutes later the next two helicopters almost collided at the landing zone. As the pilot of the second helicopter was taking on Marines, he realized that another aircraft was about to land on top of him. Startled, he flashed on his lights, attracting at the last minute the attention of the incoming helicopter, which broke off its approach.[72]

Not all of the confusion was in the air. Although the aircraft arrived without warning, the Marines had contingency plans for a helicopter evacuation. As the first Marines boarded the planes, the others fell back on the landing zone, reducing their perimeter of defense. As they pulled back, the Cambodians closed in aggressively. As successive helicopters lifted off with more troops, the Marines' position became increasingly precarious.

By 7:30 P.M. a mere seventy-one Americans, badly outnumbered by a tenacious foe, remained on the island. Radioing that they "need[ed] to get out within 15 minutes, or [they wouldn't] get out," they urged the aircraft to "go for broke."[73] With an AC-130 gunship and an OV-10 laying down a curtain of machine-gun, cannon, and rocket fire, two helicopters made it to the west beach for the final extraction. By then, the cohesion of the Marines at the landing zone seems to have become frayed.

The first of the two helicopters evacuated some forty more Marines. Not all were inside the plane. As it lifted off, another Marine left the island dangling from an outside gun mount. He was pulled in when the aircraft was one hundred feet above water. At about 8:00 P.M., the last aircraft landed on the island and twenty-seven Marines scrambled inside. Moments before the plane lifted off, one of the helicopter's gunners dashed onto the beach, looking for stragglers. At the treeline he found another two Marines. The pilot of this helicopter noted after the operation, "These two Marines would have been left behind if TSGT [Task Sergeant] Fisk had not gone to look for them."[74] Commenting later on the harrowing evacuation, a senior Marine Corps general observed that the last Marines dove into the helicopter "as into a truck driving away." "I'm surprised any of them got out alive," he mused.[75]

Not all of the Marines did make it out. As the helicopters offloaded the troops on the *Holt* and the *Coral Sea,* the Marines soon realized that three men had been left behind. According to III MAF commander Major General Hoffman, there was a "groundswell sentiment among the Marines to go back in" and look for their missing comrades. The Marines first received permission to return to the island. As 7th Fleet Commander Vice Admiral Steele later recalled: "There was an order issued to go back and see if anyone had been left alive." Steele recalls that the order was almost immediately rescinded, however. The three missing Marines were subsequently declared "Missing In Action"; their exact fate remains unknown. According to General Burns, USSAG intercepted shortly after the operation a transmission from the Cambodians on Koh Tang reporting that they had suffered "55 killed and 70 casualties."[76]

The recovery of the *Mayaguez* and its crew caused a wave of jubilation in the United States. Unaware that the Cambodians had been prepared to release the ship and crew before the Marines ever landed on Koh Tang, U.S. public opinion deemed the operation a major success. Congressman Carroll Hubbard of Kentucky summed up the mood, commenting: "It's good to win one for a change." Abroad, reactions were mixed. Although some close allies approved the action, the President's Daily News Summary of May 16, 1975, termed the international reaction "largely critical." The Indian press called the United States a "cheat and a bully"; the Chinese termed the operation "an outright act of piracy"; and the Hong Kong–based *Far Eastern Economic Review* commented acidly that "the only diplomacy of consequence in the dispute was that of the gunboat."[77]

Undoubtedly, the United States had projected an image of resolve, offsetting to a small extent the humiliation of the Vietnamese debacle. The operation was a strategic signal that may have had a sobering effect on foes of the United States in Asia, helping, perhaps, restrain the

North Koreans, who had been increasingly belligerent toward South Korea.

Yet, despite its possible strategic merits, the operation was a tactical fiasco. Eighteen Americans were lost and another forty-nine were wounded, landing at the wrong place to rescue prisoners whom the Cambodians were about to set free. Moreover, many of the flaws apparent in earlier strategic special operations marred the *Mayaguez* operation. Unlike the intelligence in the Bay of Pigs and Sontay episodes, the intelligence the senior U.S. civilian and military leadership received in this crisis was generally good. The White House knew well before sending in the Marines that some or all of the crew might not be on the island.[78] DIA and CinCPac estimated correctly the enemy forces on Koh Tang—even though, in one of the operation's many breakdowns in interservice coordination, these accurate estimates never reached the Marines. Despite the sometimes heroic individual performance of Air Force personnel at Koh Tang, overall Air Force support for the Marines was poor. Besides neglecting to pass on key intelligence, the Air Force never conducted preassault strikes against suspected enemy gun emplacements and disregarded the Marines' requests for OV-10s. During the operation, the helicopter pilots' unfamiliarity with helicopter assaults and the fighters' difficulties in providing effective close-air support compounded the Marines' problems. USSAG never told the Marines of the recovery of the crew. Nor were the Marines warned about the BLU-82 or informed about the final scenario for evacuating the island.

Back in Washington, senior civilian and military leaders, eager to retaliate against Cambodia and prove U.S. resolve, apparently wished away key shortcomings of the plan. They glossed over the highly unfavorable odds the Marines faced and the grave dangers the rescue posed for the crew. The Marines were rushed into action, when waiting an additional day would have meant a much greater chance of success. Finally, despite their limited understanding of the tactical situation at Koh Tang, decision makers thousands of miles away sought to direct in detail the execution of the mission, at times with near-catastrophic consequences. CinCPac made key tactical decisions without informing, let alone consulting, the Marine Corps commander on the island. The upshot was an operation that narrowly avoided disaster. As one Pentagon general observed shortly after the operation: "We were lucky all of the Marines did not get killed." One of the most sobering comments came from 7th Fleet commander Vice Admiral Steele, as he mused on the price of haste: "I just feel those men died in vain....It was just a terrible rush to get it done."[79]

SEVEN

Hostages of the Ayatollah

On November 4, 1979, a mob of islamic fundamentalist militants over-ran the U.S. embassy in the Iranian capital of Tehran, seizing sixty-three diplomats and embassy personnel. Thus began the Iranian hostage crisis, a 444-day ordeal that was to be the Carter administration's most serious foreign policy crisis. Iran had been in turmoil since early 1978, when is-lamic militants had taken to the streets in protest against Iran's ruler, Mohammed Reza Shah. Hostility to the shah had been building up in Iran for years, and the demonstrations triggered a ground swell of pro-test that swept the country, drawing millions into the streets.

As antigovernment demonstrations continued throughout 1978, the crowds grew ever larger and more violent. By early 1979, it was clear that most Iranians had turned against the shah and that the security forces, the mainstay of his regime, were crumbling. Aware that he had lost control, the shah fled into exile on January 16, 1979. A few days later, Ayatollah Ruhollah Khomeini, the spiritual leader of the islam-ic activists who had spearheaded the protests, returned from exile in France to a triumphal welcome in Tehran.[1]

For the next eighteen months, a bitter power struggle unfolded in the islamic theocratic state that replaced the shah's regime, as islamic "moderates" and radicals vied for the soul of the revolution. The mod-erates—chiefly Western-educated, middle-class Iranians who hoped to create a liberal, democratic state within an islamic framework—held at the outset key positions in the new regime. In February 1979, Kho-meini chose for prime minister Mehdi Bazargan, a French-trained scientist

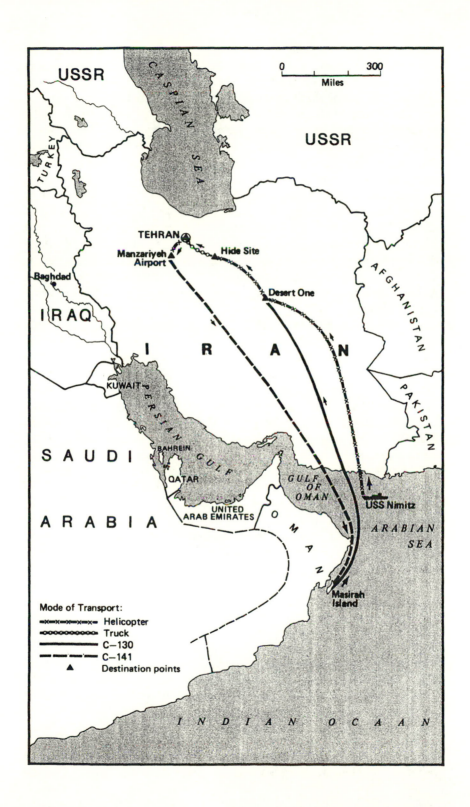

and thinker whose writings sought to conciliate modern science and islamic thought. Another key "moderate" was Abolhassan Bani-Sadr, a Western-educated intellectual and Khomeini associate who early in the new regime occupied a succession of important ministerial positions.

The moderates faced implacable hostility from islamic radicals, many of them regrouped in the Islamic Republican Party (IRP), who enjoyed wide support among the *ulema,* Iran's numerous and influential clerics; the traditional merchants of the bazaar; and the urban masses. The radicals, who controlled many of the lower echelons of government, worked ceaselessly to bring down their moderate rivals and impose their vision of a rigidly islamic state that would purge Iran of foreign influences. The militants who seized the embassy on November 4 were part of this power struggle. Ostensibly, they had acted to protest the U.S. decision to allow the cancer-stricken shah to enter the United States on October 22 for treatment. But they also wanted to embarrass Prime Minister Bazargan and his government, whom they accused of betraying the islamic revolution.[2]

In the hours following the embassy takeover, it became clear that many of Iran's new leaders sympathized with the militants and that the Iranian government was in no hurry to seek the hostages' release. The administration geared up for a crisis. On November 5, the White House's foreign policy coordinating committee, the Special Coordinating Committee (SCC)—including Vice President Walter F. Mondale; National Security Adviser Zbigniew Brzezinski; Secretary of Defense Harold Brown; Secretary of State Cyrus R. Vance; Secretary of the Treasury G. William Miller; Attorney General Benjamin R. Civiletti; the JCS chairman, General David C. Jones; the director of the Central Intelligence Agency, Admiral Stansfield Turner; and White House Chief of Staff Hamilton Jordan—held the first of its many meetings on the hostage crisis. The next day, Carter chaired the first NSC meeting on the hostage-taking. At the State Department, the special Iran Working Group began functioning round the clock. The Pentagon examined possible military responses, including a rescue mission.

The White House and the military quickly determined that the location of the hostages, in the midst of a large, hostile city hundreds of miles from the closest U.S. base, made a rescue extremely difficult. Most of the hostages were held in the embassy compound. The U.S. chargé d'affaires, Bruce L. Laingen, and two of his colleagues were at the foreign ministry in Tehran, where they had been on a call when the militants overran the embassy. Taken hostage at the same time as the personnel at the embassy, Laingen and his colleagues would remain at the ministry throughout their detention.

By November 6, the president had concluded that the United States should seek the release of the hostages through diplomatic means. At the NSC meeting that day, Carter stated flatly that he did not want to solve the problem by military force. He decided to send former U.S. attorney general Ramsay Clark, accompanied by the chief counsel for the Senate Select Committee on Intelligence, William G. Miller, to Iran, to attempt to secure the hostages' release. Clark, a longtime critic of the shah, had met Khomeini while the latter was in exile in France, and had voiced support for Iran's islamic revolution. Clark enjoyed the respect of several of Iran's new leaders, and the White House hoped he could meet with Khomeini. Miller had spent several years in Iran with the State Department.[3] Speaking to his close advisers on November 9, Carter made clear that he viewed military action as a last resort. "The problem with all of the military options," he observed, "is that we could use them and feel good for a few hours—until we found out that they had killed our people. And once we start killing people in Iran, where will it end?"[4] Carter, however, ordered the Pentagon to continue contingency planning for military responses, including a rescue mission, which could be used if attempts to reach a peaceful solution failed.

Clark's mission aborted when the Iranian authorities refused to let him enter Iran. For the next five months, the administration pursued every conceivable diplomatic means of freeing the hostages. The crisis became a humiliating ordeal, as month after month the United States found itself powerless to obtain their release. Their plight dominated the news and became an obsession for the White House. Carter later wrote:

> The safety and well-being of the American hostages became a constant concern for me, no matter what other duties I was performing as President. I would walk in the White House gardens early in the morning and lie awake at night, trying to think of additional steps I could take to gain their freedom without sacrificing the honor and security of our nation.[5]

The frustration of the American public and of U.S. officials alike grew steadily as the crisis dragged on with no end in sight. Carter was exasperated within days. On November 7, he told Jordan why he had banned a pro-Khomeini rally in front of the White House by Iranian students in the United States: he feared clashes with counterdemonstrators that might prompt the Iranians to retaliate against the hostages. He then added:

> I may have to sit here and bite my lip and show restraint and look impotent, but I am not going to have those bastards humiliating our country in front of the White House. . . . if I wasn't President, I'd be out on the streets myself and would probably take a swing at any Khomeini demonstrator I could get my hands on.[6]

Carter's frustration would keep growing as the crisis festered month after month.

The United States quickly slapped economic sanctions upon Iran. In November it banned the import of Iranian crude and froze Iranian assets in U.S. banks worldwide. It pressed its allies to adopt sanctions of their own. In the first weeks of the crisis, the United States also used a variety of intermediaries, both Iranian and other, to try to negotiate secretly the hostages' release. The most promising intermediaries turned out to be two private foreign nationals who enjoyed close ties to the Iranian leadership, and with whom the United States made contact in January 1980. Christian Bourguet, a French lawyer, and Hector Villalon, an Argentinian businessman living in Paris, represented the government of Iran in various legal matters, including its efforts to extradite the shah, who in December had left the United States for Panama. Bourguet and Villalon enjoyed the confidence of Sadegh Ghotbzadeh, then a close adviser to Khomeini, and to Bani-Sadr. Ghotbzadeh and Bani-Sadr authorized Bourguet and Villalon in writing to represent Iran in discussions with the United States on the hostages. As the crisis dragged on, the other secret negotiating tracks proved, one after the other, to be dead ends. By early 1980, the only remaining track was with Bourguet and Villalon.[7]

By late January 1980, U.S. officials had agreed with the two intermediaries on a scenario that, they assured, had the assent of Khomeini and Iran's Revolutionary Council, the highest government body in the new Iranian regime. Under the scenario, Iran would request that the United Nations send a special commission to Iran to look into Iranian grievances against the shah. The commission would also visit the hostages. Once the commission had heard Iran's complaints and seen the hostages, the militants at the embassy would turn the latter over to the Iranian government. The commission would then present its findings on Iran's grievances to the UN and Iran would free the hostages. In February, Bourguet and Villalon arranged a secret meeting in Europe between a senior Iranian official and White House Chief of Staff Jordan. By then Ghotbzadeh had become Iran's foreign minister. Meanwhile, in January Bani-Sadr had been elected president of Iran. The Iranian official assured Jordan that the scenario enjoyed the support of Iran's leaders and the Revolutionary Council.[8]

By mid-February the UN commission had been formed and briefed on the scenario. It arrived a few days later in Tehran, but the plan quickly unraveled. Although Ghotbzadeh and Bani-Sadr were anxious to implement it, they were thwarted by the militants at the embassy and their allies in the government. The militants stalled when Ghotbzadeh urged them to let the commission see the hostages. When Ghotbzadeh announced on March 6 that the Iranian government intended to assume custody of the hostages, the militants, backed by some of Iran's most powerful clerics, resisted the transfer.

A tug-of-war ensued between Bani-Sadr and Ghotbzadeh, on the one hand, and the militants and their supporters on the other. The Revolutionary Council asked Khomeini, who wielded ultimate authority in Iran, to arbitrate. On March 10 Khomeini declared that he would ask the militants to let the commission members see the hostages if the commission first made public its findings on "the crimes committed by the ousted shah and the interferences by the aggressive United States." The commission members, who had come to Tehran expecting that Iran would adhere to the original scenario, felt manipulated and left.[9]

The collapse of the scenario laboriously negotiated with Bourguet and Villalon—and through them, the United States thought, with the government of Iran—was, in Carter's words, a "bitter disappointment." In late March, Carter wrote a personal letter to Bani-Sadr, warning that unless the Iranian government assumed custody of the hostages by March 31, 1980, the United States would take "additional non-belligerent measures."[10] The United States also let Iran know through friendly countries that it was prepared to impose harsher sanctions, including, perhaps, closing Iran's seaports. Bani-Sadr quickly replied through Bourguet and Villalon that his government would take control of the hostages by April 1. Ghotbzadeh sent word that Bani-Sadr was about to announce publicly that the Revolutionary Council had approved the transfer of the hostages to the government's control.[11]

At about 5:30 A.M., Washington time, on April 1, the White House received the translation of key portions of a speech Bani-Sadr had delivered that day in Tehran. He had stated that the Iranian government would take control of the hostages if the United States officially announced it would not spread "propaganda" or make "provocative" statements about the hostages until the formation of Iran's new parliament. Bani-Sadr also called upon the United States to recognize the right of the Iranian parliament, or Majlis, to deal with the hostage question. The Majlis was to convene in a few weeks. In late February Khomeini had declared that the Majlis should determine the hostages' fate.[12]

Carter convened a news conference at 7:20 A.M. that day, calling Bani-Sadr's statements "a positive step." Carter said that in the hope these positive developments would continue, he had decided not to implement additional sanctions he had been considering imposing on Iran. The media broadcast his statements as the polls were opening in the Wisconsin presidential primaries, where Carter was running. The president had decided to seek reelection and was pursuing, in the face of a strong challenge by Massachusetts Senator Edward M. Kennedy, the democratic nomination for the 1980 presidential election. Carter's optimism was to prove short-lived. Later that day, it was apparent that Bani-Sadr's opponents once again had managed to block the hostage transfer.[13] Unable to break the deadlock, Bani-Sadr appealed to Khomeini. The ayatollah ultimately determined that the hostages should stay in the militants' custody.

January through April was a particularly unnerving period for U.S. officials grappling with the crisis. Several times they had thought a negotiated settlement was in sight, only to have their hopes dashed because of factional fighting in Iran. Reflecting on the UN commission's visit to Tehran, White House Chief of Staff Jordan later wrote:

> We were on a roller coaster...one hour we would get positive news sto-
> ries, and the next they would be contradicted by discouraging cables from
> Bourguet and Villalon via the Swiss; then, several hours later, upbeat mes-
> sages would come from Bourguet and Villalon, and in the meantime the
> news reports would be negative.[14]

Carter's wife Rosalynn recalls in her memoirs the strain of this period:
"Our lives became a seesaw of emotions as scheme after scheme fell
apart." In his own account of the crisis, CIA Director Turner recalls
meeting with Carter the day after the UN commission left Tehran. "I
had never seen him show such signs of stress," Turner writes.[15]

Baffled by the turmoil in Iran and the inability to reach agreement
with Tehran, Carter rapidly became convinced of the irrationality of the
Iranian leadership. In early January he commented to Jordan that the
seizure of the hostages "was an inhumane act committed by a bunch of
radicals and condoned by a crazy old man." A few months later, he told
a group of senior advisers that the United States was "dealing with a
crazy group." Writing years later about Khomeini's role in the failure of
the UN commission's visit, Carter concluded that the ayatollah had been
"apparently deranged."[16] The intractable crisis and those responsible for
it filled Carter with anger. As Rosalynn Carter later wrote: "We were
usually quiet watching the [television] news from Iran, but I could always tell by the grim set in his chin and the vein that throbbed in his
temple that Jimmy was filled with anger and revulsion as he watched the
terrorists."[17]

By spring the president faced mounting pressure to solve the crisis.
Looking back on the hostage drama, National Security Adviser Brzezinski wrote:

> Perhaps surprisingly, there was never any explicit discussion of the relation-
> ship between what we might have to do in Iran and domestic politics; nei-
> ther the President nor his political advisers ever discussed with me the
> question of whether one or another of our Iranian options would have a
> better or a worse domestic political effect.[18]

Nonetheless, the White House was keenly aware of Senator Kennedy's
stiff challenge for the Democratic nomination. Though Carter and his
domestic advisers may not have mentioned it in White House meetings,
they fully realized the impact the crisis could have on the election. One
of Jordan's first thoughts upon learning of the seizure of the hostages
was "This could mean war with Iran. And what would it do to the campaign?"[19] In December 1979, Carter, convinced there could be no solution as long as the shah remained in the United States, sent Jordan to
ask Panamanian strongman Omar Torrijos to take the shah. Torrijos
readily agreed. Jordan, who had befriended Torrijos during the negotiations for the 1978 Panama Canal treaty, reportedly confided to him
that Carter's reelection might hinge on the outcome of the crisis.[20]

By April 1980 the administration and the American public were increasingly impatient with the stalemate in Iran. On March 25 the president met at the White House with Bourguet, then on a brief visit to the United States. The president openly vented his exasperation. Describing the hostages as pawns in a domestic power struggle between revolutionary Iran's contending factions, Bourguet termed the situation very frustrating. Carter's response was immediate.

> Frustrating? Look at the spot *I'm* in. I am the President of a great country. Fifty-three people look to me for support week after week and month after month while we watch this comic opera in Tehran. Neither Bani-Sadr nor Khomeini has the courage to take the hostages away from the terrorists. I would like to continue to be patient, but it is very difficult for us to do so.[21]

Carter's exasperation was widely shared in the White House. On April 4, Gary Sick, an NSC staffer deeply involved in the crisis, wrote in a memo to NSC Deputy Director David Aaron: "The hawks are flying. I had two unsolicited suggestions [from other White House staffers] for a blockade of Iran before breakfast this morning." Secretary of State Vance has recalled that by late March "within the White House there was growing impatience with the diplomatic approach. Increasingly, I heard calls for 'doing something' to restore our national honor. Carter himself was losing faith that the strategy worked out in November and December could produce positive results."[22]

The American people were equally exasperated. In the early days of the crisis, the U.S. public rallied around the president and responded approvingly to the restraint he displayed in dealing with Iran. As the crisis wore on, however, the public's impatience grew steadily and its support for Carter eroded. By late 1979, the percentage of those approving the president's handling of the crisis had dropped from 75 to 61 percent; a Gallup Poll noted "the growing impatience with the lack of movement." By early April 1980, Carter's approval rating had, according to Gallup, plummeted to 40 percent. The White House was keenly aware of the public mood. In late February, Brzezinski recorded in his journal that "pressure from the public and from Congress for more direct action against Iran was building." During a NSC meeting of March 18, as Brzezinski recalls in his memoirs, Carter commented that "the American people were getting sick of the situation...and he was sick of it as well."[23]

The White House probably felt the pressure to "do something" even more keenly after the March 25 primaries in Connecticut and New York. Carter trailed Kennedy in both states. In Chief of Staff Jordan's words, these were "shocking defeats." Carter's chief pollster, Patrick Caddell, concluded that the electorate had delivered a "protest vote."[24] Given the failure of diplomacy, the White House's mounting frustration and conviction that the Iranian leaders were irrational fanatics, and rising domestic pressure to solve the crisis, military options were bound to seem increasingly attractive. In his memoirs, Jordan recalls his thoughts after he was first briefed in March 1980 on the planning for a rescue:

> After months of waiting and hoping, negotiating and failing, here was a way to go in and snatch our people up and have the whole damn thing over! Not to mention what it would do for the President and the nation. It would prove to the columnists and our political opponents that Carter was not an indecisive Chief Executive who was afraid to act. It would bolster a world community that was increasingly skeptical about American power. A daring mission would right the great wrong done to our country and our citizens.[25]

Since the start of the crisis, the military had been working in great secrecy on a rescue mission. A very small group of administration officials, comprising Brzezinski and his deputy David Aaron; Brzezinski's military assistant, Brigadier General William E. Odom; Defense Secretary Brown, State Department Deputy Secretary Warren Christopher; and CIA Director Turner, met regularly with JCS chairman General Jones and his senior assistant, Lieutenant General John S. Pustay, to review the planning for the mission. Very few others in the administration knew such planning was under way.[26]

Within the military, the operation was equally closely held. The JCS formed the *ad hoc,* secret Joint Task Force (JTF), which reported directly to the Joint Chiefs of Staff, to plan and prepare the mission. Few beyond the Joint Chiefs, Generals Pustay and Odom, and the JTF knew about it. The JTF commander (COMJTF), Army Major General James B. Vaught, had a distinguished combat record and considerable experience in paratroop and ranger operations. Colonel James H. Kyle, an Air Force officer with a background in special air operations, was formally designated deputy JTF commander and commander of the task force's air wing. Colonel Charlie A. Beckwith, commander of the Army's elite Delta Force, commanded the JTF's ground component, whose main role would be to storm the embassy in Tehran and free the hostages.[27]

As is often the case in *ad hoc* organizations, the JTF's chain of command was less than clear. In late November 1979 the JCS assigned Major General Philip C. Gast, an Air Force officer who until early had headed 1979 the U.S. Military Assistance and Advisory Group (MAAG) in Iran, as "consultant" to the JTF. Gast's primary role was to lend his expertise on Iran. Early on, however, he became deeply involved in supervising the JTF's helicopter training. Colonel Kyle, nominally the overall commander of the JTF's air component, essentially limited himself to the command and supervision of the C-130 aircraft assigned to the force.[28]

The JTF's chain of command became murkier yet as Marine Corps Colonel Charles H. Pitman became involved. Pitman, by training a helicopter pilot, was at the time an assistant to JCS Chairman Jones. Although Pitman was not formally part of the JTF, Jones's senior assistant, General Pustay, directed Pitman to review all planning and training involving the JTF helicopter force. For months, Gast's and Pitman's respective roles were unclear. The members of the Special Operations Review Group, which conducted the Pentagon's inquiry into the Iran rescue mission fiasco, noted in their postmortem, "Rescue Mission Report":

> [In November–December 1979], it was implied that [Colonel Pitman] was in charge of the helicopter force during the preparation phase, and he believed this to be so. However, COMJTF may have thought differently, and it was evident throughout the first two months of training that much (if not all) of the COMJTF direction of effort concerning helicopter preparation and special mission capability training was done through [General Gast] who was thought to be the consultant on Iran. In mid-January 1980, the role of [Pitman] had evolved into that of overall helicopter force leader, since no other designation had been made, and, at his request, he began to attend the COMJTF planning meetings.[29]

Complicating matters further, the helicopter detachment assigned to the JTF had a designated commander, Marine Corps Lieutenant Colonel Edward R. Seiffert. Seiffert devoted himself to the daily management of the unit, ensuring that it acquired the flying skills required for the mission. The overall result, however, was a confused chain of command. In the words of the Special Operations Review Group, "*Command and control was excellent at the upper echelons, but became more tenuous and fragile at intermediate levels.* Command relationships below the Commander, JTF, were not clearly emphasized in some cases and were susceptible to misunderstandings under pressure."[30]

The personnel who would execute the mission came from a variety of backgrounds. Delta Force, the Army's elite counterterrorist unit, had the job of freeing the fifty hostages at the embassy compound, while a smaller thirteen-man team of specially trained Army Special Forces would free Laingen and his two colleagues at the foreign ministry. On their way in and out of Iran, the raiders had to stop at two airstrips deep inside the country, where Army Rangers would provide protection. The Pentagon assigned to the JTF an *ad hoc* helicopter force, whose composition shifted during the preparation of the mission. Ultimately, the helicopter force ended up composed chiefly of Marines, with a few members from other services. The Air Force provided C-130 and C-141 transport planes and AC-130 gunships to support the operation. Most came from the Air Force's 8th Special Operations Squadron, stationed at Hurlburt Air Force Base, Florida. The bulk of the units involved in the rescue mission had never worked together before.

Finding the right pilots for the helicopters, which would take off for the mission from an aircraft carrier in the Gulf of Oman, was a challenge. After researching the capabilities of the helicopters in the U.S. inventory, the planners opted for the RH-53 Sea Stallion, the Navy version of the H-53, the largest U.S. troop-carrying helicopter. Normally used for minesweeping, the Sea Stallion is, apart from a few technical modifications, essentially the same as the CH-53 and HH-53 the Marine Corps and Air Force use to ferry troops and heavy equipment. The Sea Stallion, however, has folding rotor blades so it can fit below a carrier's deck. The RH-53, which has a range of up to 750 miles, also carries a greater payload than the CH-53 and HH-53. RH-53s, moreover, commonly operate off carriers; their presence in the Gulf would not arouse the suspicion of hostile intelligence services—particularly of the Soviets, whose intelligence ships routinely shadowed U.S. carriers.[31]

At the outset, the planners intended to use Navy helicopter pilots and crew chiefs, assisted by Marine Corps copilots and gunners. The Navy pilots were to contribute their skill in carrier operations, the Marines their experience in heliborne assaults. Within weeks, however, it became clear that most of the Navy pilots, trained in a far different mission, had problems adapting to the flying required for a long-range, low-altitude troop insertion and extraction. Most of them were soon replaced by Marines, although a few Air Force and Navy officers were among the helicopter crews who eventually attempted the rescue mission.[32]

A number of the helicopter pilots were excellent fliers. According to JTF commander General Vaught, the least experienced had more than fifteen hundred hours of flying time; some had logged over five thousand hours. As he later recalled, at one point the Army sent the JTF two of its "best heavy helicopter pilots." After training for a few days with the pilots the JTF had already assembled, the Army fliers acknowledged that they were not as good at doing what the mission required and asked to return to their units. Others, however, were less impressed. Looking back, Lieutenant Colonel Seiffert observed: "I knew this group of pilots was not the very best of stick and rudder men we had." Major Logan Fitch, the Delta Force officer who was to lead the assault on the embassy, was more outspoken yet. "God, it was a nightmare," he recalled. "It was a zoo. You've got people who are milk-run aviators, and all of a sudden you throw them into damn night flying . . . I've been in some pretty hairy places, and I've never been more scared than I was riding around in the back of those helicopters."[33]

Most of the pilots, in particular, had little or no background in the specialized flying the operation required. They would have to cover hundreds of miles at night, sometimes at treetop level to avoid detection, using special night-vision devices. As the authors of the "Rescue Mission Report" noted, the JTF helicopter pilots had limited experience in key aspects of the flying involved: "The crews had received only limited training [in the specialized PINS navigational systems used for the mission] and expressed low confidence in the equipment and their ability to employ it."[34]

There were, however, almost two hundred Air Force pilots available who were familiar with the CH-53 and experienced in long-range or special-operations-type flying. The Special Operations Review Group emphasized that

> these USAF pilots, more experienced in the mission profiles envisioned for the rescue operation, would have probably progressed more rapidly than pilots proficient in the basic weapons system but trained in a markedly different role.... Mastering a new, difficult, and complex mission requires a pilot to acquire and hone new skills and, more importantly, a new mindset. Transitioning from an HH- or CH-53 to an RH-53 requires only learning a few new flight parameters and slightly altering already established procedures, something every experienced pilot has done several times.[35]

Rescuing more than fifty hostages deep inside hostile territory was a daunting task. The plan was complex and would unfold over two days. The mission would begin as eight helicopters lifted off at nightfall from a carrier in the Gulf of Oman. The pilots, whose helicopters could not reach Tehran without refueling and lacked aerial refueling capability, would fly six hundred miles at night, part of the time twisting through mountain valleys, until they reached their first rendezvous point. In early versions of the plan, this was a small military airfield fifteen miles outside Nain, a town some two hundred miles southeast of Tehran. That first night, Army Rangers would seize the airfield, where fuel-bearing C-130s would then land and refuel the helicopters as they flew in. To keep the local garrison from giving the alert, the Rangers would hold the airfield until the raiders stormed the embassy in Tehran the following night.

The Nain scenario, however, presented a significant risk of compromise. By March 1980, the planners had located a more secure rendezvous site to replace Nain. Dubbed Desert One, it was a remote, flat stretch in the Dasht-E-Kavir desert, 260 miles southeast of Tehran. The helicopters would rendezvous there the first night with six C-130 transport planes that would be carrying fuel; Delta Force, the team who would assault the foreign ministry; a few Iranian exiles who had volunteered to help with the mission; and a detachment of Rangers who, with Delta Force, would secure Desert One. The helicopters would refuel and take on Delta Force, the Special Forces, and the exiles.

The C-130s and the Rangers were to leave Iranian airspace by daybreak, while the helicopters would proceed to a hideaway fifty miles southeast of Tehran: a *wadi*, or dry river bed, in the hills outside the city of Garmsar. Discharging the raiders, the helicopters would continue to an equally remote spot a few miles away. Both the raiders and the helicopters had to be in place before daybreak. The men and aircraft, the latter concealed under camouflaged netting, would remain in hiding until the next evening.[36]

At nightfall on the second day, several members of a team of U.S. clandestine operators, infiltrated into Iran ahead of the main rescue force, would meet the raiders at the wadi. The agents, accompanied by the exiles and some Delta Force members, would proceed to a warehouse on the outskirts of Tehran containing six prepositioned civilian trucks. The group was to drive the trucks back to the hideaway, pick up the remaining raiders, and return to Tehran. Most of the raiders would hide in the back of the trucks while the exiles and a few Americans drove. Once in Tehran, the thirteen Special Forces would head for the lightly guarded foreign ministry, while Delta Force, almost one hundred men strong, would proceed to the embassy, which was protected by dozens of armed militants. The raiders were to storm the foreign ministry and the embassy between 11:00 P.M. and midnight.[37]

The assault on the embassy was expected to take about forty-five minutes. While the raiders freed the hostages, the helicopters would leave their hiding site and begin orbiting north of Tehran. When called via radio, one helicopter would pick up the special forces and the three U.S. diplomats in an empty lot near the foreign ministry. The other helicopters would pick up the remaining hostages and their rescuers at the embassy, or, if this was infeasible, at a stadium across the street. Two AC-130 gunships would be overhead to provide covering machine-gun and cannon fire as necessary.[38]

The helicopters would fly to Manzariyeh, code named Desert Two, an airstrip thirty-five miles south of Tehran, occupied by a small Iranian air force detachment. As the rescue in Tehran was under way, a Ranger force was to fly in aboard Air Force C-141s and seize the strip. Upon reaching Manzariyeh, the hostages and rescuers would fly off with the Rangers on the C-141s, leaving the helicopters behind. The operation was expected to last a total of about forty hours.[39]

Good intelligence was critical to success. The raiders needed as much information as possible on the location of the hostages and security at the compound, security practices, checkpoints on the road from the wadi to Tehran, the location and strength of army and police units near the embassy, and the like. When the JTF planners began looking for ways of collecting this intelligence, they discovered that the CIA's case officers in Iran were all being held hostage by the Iranians. Within days of the hostage-taking, however, the CIA infiltrated replacement case officers into Tehran to take control of its agents there. The Department of Defense later infiltrated several agents of its own, all active duty or retired military personnel, to gather intelligence.[40]

Looking back on the mission, CIA Director Turner has stated that "the operational support of the CIA to Delta Force was superb in every respect. It was as fine an accomplishment as I have seen in more than 30 years of service." "The intelligence given to Delta Force," he maintained, "was fully accurate and more than adequate to do the job." He acknowledged, however, that it was not until January 1980 that the CIA had become "reasonably sure" that all of the hostages were in the embassy compound, and was able to provide vital information on defenses at the embassy and the best way of infiltrating Delta Force into Tehran. This, he conceded, had taken "too long."[41]

Others, however, believe that the collection, analysis, and dissemination of intelligence for the mission left much to be desired. In the early stages of the planning, communication between the intelligence community and Delta Force's intelligence analysts was not without problems. Beckwith later recalled:

> Nearly every agency that sent us material used a different system. A report would come in stating that the source was "untested." [Delta's] intelligence guys needed more than that. Was the source reliable on any basis? Another report might read: "An untested source received through an unofficial contact..." What does "unofficial contact" mean? Was the contact reliable or unreliable in the past?[42]

The Special Operations Review Group leveled a different criticism, commenting that

> certain elements of the Intelligence Community seemed slow in harnessing themselves initially for the tasks at hand....
> The [Review] group believes that Intelligence Community assets and resources could have been pulled together more quickly and effectively than was actually the case.[43]

JTF and other military sources were harsher yet. In the words of General Vaught:

> Intelligence from all sources was inadequate from the start and never became responsive...I had to develop an [intelligence] net, because the [CIA] did not, would not, or could not, provide sufficient agents to go in country and get the information we needed....The preponderance of the agents in the field sent to facilitate the operation and acquire information were military....They were doing a job the Agency [CIA] should have done.[44]

One action officer complained:

> We had a zillion shots of the roof of the embassy and they were each magnified a hundred times. We could tell you about the tiles; we could tell you about the grass, and how many cars were parked there. Anything you wanted to know about the external aspects of that embassy we could tell you in infinite detail. We couldn't tell you shit about what was going on inside that building. That's where humans come in.[45]

After the operation, a former assistant chief of staff for intelligence mused: "The CIA couldn't deliver support to the military. The intelligence the Agency provided was virtually useless in operational terms—the military needed peripheral on-the-ground intelligence, which the Agency didn't have the capability to provide."[46] Moreover, General Vaught maintained, when the military found qualified clandestine agents to send into Tehran, the CIA was "not overly helpful" in providing the identity papers they needed. The CIA, he explained, "said they were concerned that we were asking these people to go in and get captured."[47]

Shortly before the operation, the CIA had an intelligence windfall. A Pakistani cook who had been employed at the embassy in Tehran and had continued to work there after the hostage seizure left Iran in April 1980. Seated next to him on the plane out was a CIA agent. The cook identified precisely where in the sprawling twenty-seven-acre compound the hostages were kept. They were all in the chancery. Delta Force's job became simpler. Instead of having to search fourteen embassy buildings, they could concentrate on the chancery. The planners, however, viewed this last-minute intelligence bonanza with some suspicion: "I didn't necessarily believe [the cook's information] that much," Vaught later said. "He was an untested source, a last-minute flash in the pan." Hence, Vaught decided not to pare down the size of the rescue force.[48]

Although good intelligence was critical to success, secrecy was just as important. If forewarned, the Iranians could ambush the raiders, causing a military and foreign policy disaster. The Pentagon spared no effort to prevent leaks. It was successful: there never was any indication that the Iranians or any other hostile intelligence service had wind a rescue mission was afoot.[49] In the interests of security, however, the planners took steps that impaired the raiders' readiness.

The planners enforced rigid compartmentalization. Most of the experts in the intelligence community the JTF tapped for information never knew about the planned mission. As the Special Operations Review Group noted, "Some of these officers felt that their initial effectiveness may have been impaired somewhat by not being told more about the true nature of the operation from the beginning."[50]

Extreme compartmentalization had other negative consequences as well. Military pilots typically meet face to face with the weather specialists who provide the weather data for a mission. To enhance security, however, the JTF decided that JTF meteorologists would pass the weather data on to an intelligence liaison officer, who would brief the pilots. As it turned out, the helicopter and C-130 pilots were never told about the suspended dust storms that occur in Iran at certain times of the year—even though the JTF meteorologists had identified the storms as a possible flying hazard. When the helicopter pilots encountered hundreds of miles of suspended dust over Iran, it came to them as a total surprise.

The Special Operations Review Group criticized the compartmentalization between pilots and meteorologists. While acknowledging that face-to-face meetings would not have guaranteed that the pilots grasped the problem of the dust storms, it observed that "the interplay of meteorologist and operator is the process that most often surfaces the questions that need to be answered." The review group doubted that face-to-face briefings would have compromised security, and concluded that "direct interface between mission pilots and air weather officers would have increased the likelihood of foreknowledge of the suspended dust phenomenon."[51]

To minimize the risk of leaks, there were no full-scale rehearsals of the mission. Elements of the JTF did rehearse together the different stages of the operation, but the largest exercise involved only four helicopters and two C-130 transports, whereas the plan called for eight helicopters and four C-130s at Desert One. As a result, the rescuers were not fully prepared for what awaited them. In the words of the review group, "As [Desert One] filled up with C-130s, more than had been exercised at a western United States training area, it took on new and larger dimensions than had been experienced."[52]

The helicopter and transport plane crews did not meet before or after rehearsals to critique the exercises. As the review group later noted, better coordination among the elements of the rescue force during training would have "enhanced force readiness."[53] The rescue force was less than a fully cohesive team—unlike the raiders who had conducted the daring Sontay mission a decade earlier.

The planners also tried to reduce the risk of detection by keeping the force lean. This weighed heavily in the decision to use only eight helicopters. Helicopters are more susceptible to mechanical breakdowns than fixed-wing aircraft and more vulnerable to ground fire. Accordingly, the rule of thumb in heliborne combat operations is to include a backup for each helicopter required for a mission.

The planners, however, proceeded differently. They exhaustively researched the technical data on the RH-53 to determine its frequency of breakdowns, then did a mathematical risk analysis to determine the optimum number of helicopters. This first came out at four. It later rose to six, then seven, as the size of the rescue force increased and temperatures in Iran rose between November, when planning began, and April, when the mission took place.[54] (The airlift capability of helicopters decreases as air temperature goes up.) Days before the raid, the planners added an eighth helicopter. Eight helicopters meant two backup aircraft because the planners ultimately determined that the raiders had to leave Desert One with at least six helicopters to complete the rest of the operation. As it turned out, they had to abort the mission at Desert One when only five of the helicopters that reached the site were still safe to fly.

The review group criticized the use of only eight helicopters, noting that

> an unconstrained planner would more than likely have initially required at least 10 helicopters under JTF combat rules, 11 under the most likely case, and up to 12 using peacetime historical data.... aside from [operational security], no operational or logistic factor prohibited launching 11 from [the carrier] NIMITZ and continuing beyond the halfway point to Desert One with 10 helicopters....

In retrospect, it appears that on balance an increase in the helicopter force was warranted.[55]

Admiral James L. Holloway, chairman of the Special Operations Review Group, later described the planners' calculations as a "thick book of higher math." He blamed the use of only eight helicopters on the planners' "preoccupation with systems analysis, which is not a substitute for good, honest judgement." Complex as the calculations were, they were not relevant to the problem at hand. They were based on the record of the RH-53's performance under normal operating conditions—usually towing minesweeping equipment at sea level—a far cry from flying 900 hundred miles in desert heat, 6,000 pounds overweight, at altitudes ranging from treetop level to 4,000 feet.[56]

Careful planning and preparation are key to success in all military operations, and even more so in special operations, where one mistake can jeopardize the mission. Not all JTF members, however, were as thorough as possible. In his memoirs, Beckwith recalls that more than a month before the mission some of his men began to tire of practicing.

> The rehearsal scheduled for that afternoon was out at the range where the operators had laid out and built an area to the embassy compound's scale. . . . Red, White, and Blue Elements had ridden out to the range in trucks, gone over the wall, taken down the embassy mock-up, withdrawn to another area representing the soccer stadium, and there, lined up into helicopter loads. Delta had run this exercise a hundred times at least. It had become drudgery. In mid-March, people began to say, "Aw shit, not again!"[57]

This reaction is surprising on the part of personnel charged with such a difficult and sensitive mission. Presumably, every exercise was an opportunity to hone their skills and increase the chances of success.

Some planners showed a lack of thoroughness of their own. They paid insufficient attention, in particular, to command and control. Eight RH-53 helicopters and six C-130 transport planes, piloted by Marine Corps, Navy, and Air Force crews and carrying a collection of Rangers, Delta Force commandos, and Special Forces would land at Desert One. Many would meet there for the first time. Communications between the various elements of the rescue force were likely to be difficult, especially at night, with twenty-four RH-53 and twenty-four C-130 engines roaring and kicking up the desert dust. Yet, as the Special Operations Review Group subsequently noted,

> the plan for this desert rendezvous was soft. There was no identifiable command post for the on-scene commander; a staff and runners were not anticipated; backup rescue radios were not available until the third C-130 arrived; and, lastly, key personnel and those with critical functions were not identified for ease of recognition.[58]

The planners were confident the pilots would enjoy good visibility over Iran, which would allow them to see the terrain they were overflying through their night-vision goggles,[59] instead of flying entirely by instruments. The planners realized, of course, that bad weather, including suspended dust storms, could occur along the route, but they believed that the probability of encountering clear skies over the flight path on any given day was reasonably high. They further believed that the JTF meteorologists could predict poor weather over Iran, making it unlikely the raiders would run into unexpected bad weather. As Colonel Kyle, commander of the JTF's C-130 element, later observed, the JTF had "unwavering confidence" in its weather experts' ability to "forecast the en route weather accurately so that we could cancel the launch if inclement conditions were present."[60]

These assumptions were based on the meteorologists' study of available historical weather data for Iran and the accuracy with which they predicted Iranian weather in the first few months of 1980. By placing such stock in the weather experts, however, the planners overlooked that they were working from poor records. The raiders' flight path covered vast stretches of desert for which there were few historical weather data. Nor were there any operational weather stations providing current data. Meanwhile, satellite imagery could not pick up low-level clouds under a higher-altitude cloud bank. Nor did it reveal much about nighttime weather.[61]

Still, the planners were so confident about the weather that they did not equip the helicopters with sophisticated navigational aids such as Forward Looking Infrared (FLIR) or Terrain Following Radar (TFR), which facilitate navigation in foul weather. They also ruled out the use of a "pathfinder" guideplane to lead the helicopters to Desert One. Pathfinders—often C-130s with advanced navigational gear—fly ahead of aircraft with less sophisticated equipment to guide them to the objective in bad weather or across unfamiliar terrain. C-130 guideplanes had led U.S. helicopters to the POW camp in the Sontay raid. When the helicopters en route to Desert One encountered dust storms the meteorologists had failed to predict, the poor visibility caused one aircraft to turn back and the others to arrive hours late.[62]

In addition, the planners did not pay enough attention to the mechanical problems most likely to happen during the mission and to the procedures to follow if they occurred. Helicopters of the H-53 family sometimes develop hairline cracks in their rotor blade spars. A cracked spar can eventually result in rotor blade failure, causing a crash. By 1980, there had been thirty-one incidents of cracks in CH-53 and HH-53 spars, causing three crashes. H-53 pilots use the "Blade Inspection Method," or BIM, to detect possible cracks. The BIM records any pressure loss in the spars, which are filled with pressurized nitrogen. A drop in pressure may be due to a leaky filler valve, to a defective spar seal, or to a crack.[63]

Standard peacetime operating procedures require pilots to land as soon as possible when the BIM cockpit indicator goes off and check the second indicator attached to the rotors. If both indicators show a loss of pressure, the aircraft is grounded until the rotor system is repaired. These procedures, appropriate under normal conditions, are overly cautious in combat operations. The Navy version of the H-53, the RH-53, had entered service in 1973. Between then and 1980, forty-three BIM indications had occurred on RH-53s, but none of these nitrogen leaks was due to a cracked spar. As the Special Operations Review Group observed, "In 38,216 RH-53D flying hours (229,296 blade-hours) logged through December 1979 not one crack has been found in an RH-53D rotor blade spar." All of the confirmed cracks in H-53s spars had been on Marine Corps and Air Force H-53s, which have titanium blades. RH-53 have aluminum blades.[64]

Furthermore, the manufacturer's studies showed that a H-53 helicopter flying at 120 knots—the average speed of the helicopters during the mission—could fly approximately twenty-seven hours with a cracked spar before the spar disintegrated.[65] Under combat conditions, an RH-53 can still fly, despite a BIM.

The planners, however, did not research the implications of a BIM—even though they occurred twice on JTF helicopters in training—and tell the crews it was reasonably safe to keep flying if it occurred. When the BIM warning light flashed on one of the helicopters en route to Desert One, the pilots immediately landed. The second indicator also showed a pressure loss. Unable to repair the aircraft in the field, the crew abandoned it. The review group observed that "a BIM indication was a likely occurrence on the mission and had been experienced in training. BIM indications and other likely malfunctions should have been identified and researched in detail and information provided aircrews as part of their mission preparation."[66]

In another display of less than thorough planning, the JTF apparently never prepared a final written plan for the operation. The review group commented:

> To the best of the review group's knowledge, no final plan for the rescue operations was ever published prior to mission execution. A written plan to supplement oral briefings to the Joint Chiefs of Staff would have provided them a document to study and review in the privacy of their own offices, which might have sharpened their understanding of details and led to more incisive questions in subsequent discussions.[67]

Such questions would have been welcome because there seems to have been a measure of wishful thinking in the planning and preparation. Wishful thinking apparently colored some JTF members' assessment of the force's readiness. Beckwith, for example, had misgivings about the helicopter pilots and crews. In his memoirs, he notes that the pilots did not have "their hearts and souls" in learning to use the specialized PINS navigational aids installed in the helicopters.[68] He also worried about the helicopter gunners, some of whom had commented in training that they planned to "open up" with their guns when they lifted off from Tehran—not, in Beckwith's view, a good idea when there might still be friendly troops on the ground.[69] But Beckwith apparently wished the problem away. As he later wrote: "On the other hand, everyone wanted to have confidence in these leathernecks. If not them, who? If not now, when? The Marines got the benefit of the doubt."[70]

The planners likewise assumed rather lightly that the risk of detection of the rescue force before it reached the embassy was manageable. In fact, the likelihood of compromise at Desert One was significant. Because the helicopters had to refuel en route to Tehran, the rescue force needed access to a secluded landing site, at a reasonable distance from the capital, where fuel-bearing C-130s could land. After careful review, the planners settled on the remote Dasht-E-Kavir Desert One site. Running through this site, however, was a road connecting two midsize Iranian cities that travelers often used at night to escape the daytime heat. There was a good chance that passersby would stumble across the rescue force during the nighttime refueling. When CIA agents landed clandestinely at the strip a few nights before the raid to take soil samples and plant remote-control landing beacons, four vehicles drove by while they were on the ground.[71]

The planners devised a scenario to deal with such contingencies. Upon landing at Desert One, two roadblock teams, each with a Farsi speaker, would take up position along the road. Impersonating Iranian soldiers, they would turn back any Iranians who happened by, pretexting that Iranian Army maneuvers were under way. If this subterfuge failed, the Iranians would be spirited out of Iran aboard the C-130s once refueling operations had ended, to be freed when the rescue mission was over. The Iranians' vehicles would be disabled, to give the impression that they had broken down.[72] The ruse assumed, however, that by daybreak Iranian authorities would not have noticed the travelers' disappearance and begun a vigorous search, which would have likely uncovered signs of the raiders' passage at Desert One. As the review group noted, the raiders stood a good chance of having to abandon a helicopter or other equipment at the site. "The vehicles and helicopter abandoned along the road would more than likely draw attention to the C-130 wheel ruts," the review group wrote. This could have alerted the Iranians, hours before the assault on the embassy, to the presence of Americans in Iran. The review group concluded that, although there was no alternative to landing at Desert One, the plan "probably carried more risk that the JTF had assessed."[73]

The planners likewise seemed to have downplayed the difficulty of entering and leaving Tehran. The plan called for more than 120 U.S. commandos and clandestine agents to drive on the second night in six covered civilian trucks from the hideaway near Garmsar into Tehran. The planners knew there was at least one permanent checkpoint along the way, and that there was also a risk of mobile checkpoints. They anticipated, however, that the guards probably would not look into the trucks. If they did, the plan called for the raiders to seize them and take them along.[74] In early 1980, however, Tehran was the capital of a country still in the throes of a violent revolution. Tension between Iran and Iraq, which would soon lead to war, was also escalating. Iranian security forces were likely to be reasonably vigilant. Whether the raiders could have made it into Tehran as easily as expected is unclear.

The planners were equally sanguine about the prospects of making it out of Tehran. The Iranian Army maintained an armored cavalry unit in the city, with tanks, armored personnel carriers, and self-propelled antiaircraft cannons. Part of the unit was stationed a few blocks from the embassy. The Iranian police also had armored vehicles equipped with heavy machine guns. U.S. intelligence estimated that it would take up to ninety minutes for the cavalry unit to react in strength. The intelligence community could not tell, however, where the police kept its armored vehicles or what their reaction time might be.[75] Even a few armored vehicles with machine guns could have posed a deadly threat to the helicopters. The planners, however, assumed that Iranian armor would not react in time, and that if it somehow did, the AC-130 gunships flying above Tehran could neutralize the threat. But although the gunships were heavily armed flying artillery platforms, they were themselves vulnerable to the self-propelled ZSU-23 antiaircraft guns, a deadly rapid-fire, radar-guided antiaircraft cannon.

There were, furthermore, thousands of revolutionary guards, militia, and other security personnel with automatic weapons in Tehran. The raiders would need at least forty-five minutes and perhaps more to secure the embassy and rescue the hostages. There would be considerable shooting that was bound to attract attention. Chances were good that by the time the helicopters arrived, a number of armed Iranians would have assembled in the neighborhood. Unarmored helicopters like the RH-53 are quite vulnerable to light-arms fire. Whereas the AC-130 gunships might have had a reasonable chance of spotting and neutralizing armored vehicles, they would have been far less effective, even with their sophisticated night-vision devices, in spotting and eliminating the dozens of snipers who could have positioned themselves in the buildings around the embassy. The helicopter evacuation could have become highly risky, especially if the aircraft had been unable to touch down on the compound and were forced to land in the stadium across the street—a difficult task, especially at night, which the pilots had never rehearsed.[76] If enough armed Iranians made it to the embassy before the raiders left, the extraction could have become extremely hazardous.

In summary, planning and preparation of the mission were flawed. The JTF's chain of command was confused. Although most members of the rescue force had never worked together before, there was no full-scale rehearsal. The choice of the helicopter pilots and the decision to use only eight helicopters were questionable. Extreme compartmentalization may have prevented the aircrews from receiving key information. The planners were less than thorough in thinking through the requirements of command and control and in anticipating problems that could arise. Some apparently wished away shortcomings of the rescue force. The planners downplayed the risk of detection at Desert One, as well as the difficulties of getting into and out of Tehran. Yet, when General Vaught briefed President Carter and his close advisers on the plan in early April 1980, days before the execution of the mission, he assured the White House there was a "damn good chance of success."[77]

EIGHT

The Helicopters That Couldn't

On March 22, 1980, President Carter received his first full briefing on planning for a rescue mission as he spent the weekend at the presidential retreat at Camp David. By then the hostage crisis had dragged on for more than five months. From then on, in the words of National Security Adviser Brzezinski, "the rescue option began to take on a kind of inevitability."[1] With Carter at the briefing were Vice President Mondale, Secretary of Defense Brown, Secretary of State Vance, CIA Director Turner, JCS Chairman Jones, Brzezinski and his deputy Aaron, and White House Press Secretary Jody Powell. For several hours General Jones presented the plan, which he described as "exceptionally complex." In contrast, however, to the skepticism the JCS had evidenced in November 1979 about the possibility of rescuing the hostages, Jones was positive about the rescue plan. After months of planning and training, the military was confident it had finally developed a workable plan and a force that could execute it.[2]

Carter found the plans Jones described at Camp David "much more feasible than those presented at the outset of the ordeal." He authorized the CIA to land a small plane covertly at Desert One, where its crew would both verify that the ground was firm enough for the raiders' aircraft and plant remote control landing lights.[3] The president stated, however, that he had not yet decided to authorize the rescue. He wanted to give negotiations another ninety days, he explained, before considering a rescue mission. Jones pointed out that by then the nights in Iran would have become too short to conduct the operation in two days. The mission would take an additional night, greatly increasing the risk of compromise. Vance opposed military action unless the hostages were harmed, stressing that it could endanger the hostages and push Iran into the Soviets' arms. As Brzezinski later recalled, Carter asked "with some impatience" whether Vance was prepared to wait until the end of the year while the hostages languished in captivity.[4]

In the next few days prospects of a negotiated settlement became more remote than ever. On April 1 the Iranian radicals definitively foiled Bani-Sadr's plan to take custody of the hostages. On April 3, Bani-Sadr indicated that, in Jordan's words, he was "washing his hands of the entire matter and the fate of the hostages rests with the Ayatollah." At this point Carter all but gave up on negotiations. As he told Jordan on April 3,

> the only people in the world who think we're going to get out people back soon are you and your French friends. The people in Iran may want to solve this thing, but they don't have the courage to do it. And we look foolish. I go out and announce the plan, and forty-eight hours later it's falling apart. . . .
>
> You've done the best you've could. But it just hasn't worked and I don't think it's going to work.[5]

On April 7, Carter convened the NSC at the White House. Stating that he was totally exasperated, he explained that the situation had changed markedly in the preceding week. Negotiations with Iran had reached an impasse. As CIA Director Turner later recalled, the United States, Carter opined, "had leaned over backward with the Iranians, to the point of being inept." The country, Carter continued, was close to the point where it would have to act forcefully. He said he had decided to break diplomatic relations with Iran, and ordered White House Counsel Lloyd Cutler to draft legislation allowing the seizure of the Iranian assets in the United States, which had been frozen at the start of the crisis.[6]

The discussion then shifted to military options. Carter said he was willing to consider the mining of Iranian ports but not a rescue mission, which, in his view, would probably cost some of the hostages their lives. Most of those present, however, favored the rescue mission. Secretary of Defense Brown and General Jones, concerned that mining might prompt Iran to seek minesweeping assistance from the USSR, spoke in favor of the rescue mission. So did Turner, who believed it would be months before mining had much effect on Iran. Mondale and Brzezinski likewise supported the rescue option. State Department Deputy Secretary Warren Christopher urged sticking with diplomatic pressure. The meeting broke up without Carter's having indicated whether he had been swayed by the arguments in favor of the mission.[7]

Brzezinski fully shared the president's disillusionment with the secret negotiations. On April 10 he sent Carter a memorandum arguing,

In my view, a carefully planned and boldly executed rescue operation represents the only realistic prospect that the hostages—any of them—will be freed in the foreseeable future. Our policy of restraint has won us well-deserved understanding throughout the world, but it has run out. It is time for us to act. Now.[8]

On April 11, Carter reconvened the NSC. Mondale, Brown, Brzezinski, Jones, Turner, Jordan, and Powell joined the president in the cabinet room. Christopher stood in for Vance, away on a short vacation. Carter, stating that the likelihood of the hostages' speedy release was remote and that the time had come for action, asked Brown and Jones to present the rescue plan. Carter then polled his advisers for their views.[9]

Christopher spoke first, emphasizing that he had not discussed the plan with Vance and could not speak for him. Christopher argued that there remained nonbelligerent options to explore before using force, such as blacklisting Iranian shipping and organizing an international telecommunications embargo. Brown dismissed these options as unimpressive. He reviewed the military options, concluding that a blockade would push Iran closer to the USSR and recommending the rescue mission instead. Mondale and Brzezinski agreed. Brzezinski urged that the mission begin without delay because the rescuers had to operate at night, and nights in Iran were growing shorter. Jordan, Powell, and Turner also favored the mission.

The president noted that the captors had recently made new threats against the hostages. Although he could not see what the United States might have done differently, he continued, the country had been "disgraced" by the handling of the crisis. Stating that the nation's honor was at stake, Carter ordered the military to launch the raid as soon as possible. Jones indicated this was April 24. The day after this meeting, Jordan, fearing that he had sounded only lukewarm in favor of the raid, wrote the president a memo putting himself "squarely on the side of the mission."[10]

One key adviser did not share the prevailing view. When Vance returned to Washington on April 14, he was, in his own words, "stunned and angry that such a momentous decision had been made in my absence." The next day, he privately expressed his strong objections to Carter. The hostages were, in Vance's view, in no immediate danger. Meanwhile, he worried, the operation was so complex it could easily fail. Even if it succeeded, he feared that a number of hostages would almost certainly be killed. Moreover, the raid could trigger an anti-American backlash throughout the Islamic world and push Iran closer to the USSR. Iran might also seize new hostages among Americans, many of them newsmen, still in Iran. Vance further believed that with the imminent election of the Majlis, Iran might soon have a more stable government capable of negotiating seriously.[11]

Carter offered Vance a chance to share his views with those who had considered the rescue mission on April 11. The group reconvened at the White House on April 15. A grim-faced president explained that Vance strongly opposed the mission and asked him to explain. Vance's views, in Jordan's words, met with "awkward silence." Vance later recalled, "No one supported my position." Brzezinski argued that the time had come to "lance the boil through a rescue mission." Addressing Vance, Carter said that his greatest fear was that the crisis could lead to a direct confrontation with the Soviets. "The chances of that," Carter explained, "are much greater if we exercise any of the other military options—a punitive air strike, mining the harbors, or a blockade—than if we go in, rescue our people, and get out." Carter added that his decision was unchanged. There was no further discussion of the merits of the mission.[12]

The group gathered with Carter at the White House on the evening of April 16 to meet with the mission's senior planners and leaders. Also present were Vance, Christopher, and Deputy Secretary of Defense W. Graham Claytor. JCS Chairman Jones introduced JTF commander General Vaught, General Gast, and Delta Force commander Beckwith. For the next two and a half hours, the JTF officials detailed the operation step by step. They assured that it had a "good chance of success." Vaught warned, however, that if anything went wrong, the odds would range "between zero and one hundred percent, and the two figures could be close together." Asked about the likelihood of casualties, Vaught warned that it was impossible to give a precise estimate. He ventured, however, that two or three hostages and several rescuers might be injured.[13] Beckwith explained that Delta Force planned to "take the guards out." When Christopher queried whether this meant they would be shot in the shoulder or the like, Beckwith was clear: "We're going to shoot each of them twice, right between the eyes." Beckwith stressed that he and his men were eager to undertake the mission: "We want to do it and think we can," he said.[14] Carter was impressed. As he recalled in his memoirs, "In their meticulous description of every facet of the operation, I received satisfactory answers to all my many questions."[15]

Mindful of the problems caused when the White House intervened in the execution of the Bay of Pigs invasion, Carter stressed that he would not interfere with the conduct of the raid. The chain of command for the operation, he explained, ran from him to the secretary of defense to the JCS Chairman to the JTF commander. No one else should be involved. The president said he would appreciate, however, being kept informed of the progress of the mission.[16]

At no point did anyone ask the planners to quantify what they meant by a "good chance of success." Had they, they might have been surprised. Looking back, Colonel Beckwith mused:

> The probability of success was about 50 percent at the outset.... The probability of success and risks of these types of operation are extremely high. On the other hand, the cost in manpower and equipment was not very high; therefore, I recommended we undertake the operation. This is a fact in special operations.... I don't know if the White House and the JCS realized that there was less than a 50 percent chance.... But I had twenty-three years' experience in special operations. I knew.[17]

Reflecting upon the White House discussions about the plan, Brzezinski noted:

> [When the chances for success were raised], we did not ask for quantification. We saw all the different aspects of the plan and the plan in toto had a high probability of success.... If any senior military person had said to the president that there was only a 50-50 chance, he would not have gone for it. If I had known it I would not have pressed for it.[18]

In his own recollections about the operation, another senior White House official echoed this point. Stating that the chances for success were never quantified, he added that he nonetheless assumed they were in the order of 60 to 70 percent. Had he imagined the risks were higher, he would have had serious misgivings.[19]

In fact, although the senior civilian decision makers discussed the mission at length on March 22, April 11, April 15, and April 16, asking the military many questions, they could not in a few hours examine every facet of the plan—especially because, as in the case of the Bay of Pigs, there were no written documents to consult after the briefings.[20] Moreover, most of the civilians lacked the military expertise to critique the plan in depth. Of the civilians involved, only Carter and Turner, both former Navy officers, had significant military expertise, although neither had a special-operations background. In the last analysis, the civilians had to rely on the Pentagon for an exhaustive critique of the plan, but the only military experts who reviewed the plan in full detail were the JTF planners. Had other personnel, more detached from the mission, scrutinized the JTF's work, they probably would have spotted some of its shortcomings. The operation, however, was so tightly held that, as the Special Operations Review Group later observed, the plan was never rigorously evaluated "by qualified, independent observers short of the Joint Chiefs of Staff themselves."[21]

The JCS lacked the time to examine every facet of the planning and preparations. The chiefs, as a group, received only three briefings on the mission. For security reasons, they could not ask their staffs to help them evaluate the plan. As the review group noted, the JCS "were acting in essence as their own action officers and were denying themselves the staffing support they normally enjoy when reviewing plans of a less sensitive nature."[22] After the operation, Army Chief of Staff General Edward C. Meyer and Marine Corps Commandant General Robert H. Barrow both acknowledged that "they had not asked all the hard questions they should have." The chiefs apparently assumed—without ever checking—that the mission had been thoroughly rehearsed. "Somehow we had it in our heads," Barrow explained, "that this thing had what one would call a full dress rehearsal." In their eagerness to find a way out of the crisis, some of the chiefs—like certain JTF planners—may have also wished problems away. In the early days of the crisis, when the Pentagon had first considered a rescue mission, Barrow had told Defense Secretary Brown that "any thought of having any kind of a rescue was simply impossible, if not crazy." A few months later, Barrow assented to the JTF's highly risky plan. He subsequently explained that as the crisis wore on and pressures grew, "you tended to be more willing to take a risk. National emotions tended to displace earlier caution."[23]

In short, no one other than the planners themselves conducted an exhaustive and skeptical review of the plan, checking every detail and probing every assumption. Thus the White House never learned about the shortcomings in the organization, preparation, and training of the JTF. Nor did the civilians fully appreciate the optimism underlying the planners' judgments about the ease of reaching Tehran undetected and withdrawing without unacceptable losses.

From April 17 on, Brzezinski, Brown, Turner, and Jones followed mission preparations daily, consulting often with Carter. Meanwhile, the JTF deployed to Egypt, then to its main staging point, the Omani island of Masirah in the Gulf of Aden. On April 18, Jordan, pursuing his secret diplomacy, met again with his senior Iranian government contact in Europe. The latter opined that it would be "months and months" before Iran released the hostages. Jordan immediately relayed this gloomy assessment to the president. On April 19 the State Department received a message that the senior U.S. hostage, Chargé Laingen, had managed to forward through the Swiss ambassador in Tehran. Laingen urged that the United States take strong action against Iran. As Carter writes in his memoirs, "These two reports from Iran—one from a spokesman within the government and the other from the head of the American diplomatic team—confirmed my resolve to proceed with the rescue."[24]

On April 23, the president received an intelligence briefing on Iran based on the latest information from all U.S. government sources. The intelligence community concluded that Iran was unlikely to release the hostages for months and that circumstances were favorable for a rescue bid. The same day, CIA Director Turner reiterated his support for the mission, telling Carter, "I agreed with the plan because it was the right thing for the country; otherwise, we would not get the hostages out for a considerable time. Second, I felt the plan was workable." As Turner later wrote in his account of the rescue mission: "Although this would be a high-risk operation, I believed the Iranians were disorganized and there was a good chance of our pulling off the series of complex actions involved without their being able to react decisively."[25]

Many factors no doubt influenced the president's decision to launch the raid. One was the anger, frustration, and humiliation Carter and his advisers felt after trying for so long to negotiate an end to the crisis. As the president told the NSC, he believed that the United States had been humiliated and that its national honor was at stake. Furthermore, when the radicals derailed Bani-Sadr's efforts to take over the hostages, Carter gave up hope that negotiations could free them in the foreseeable future. Carter also faced mounting public pressure to "do something" about the hostages. Such pressure, which no doubt weighed heavily in an election year, especially against the backdrop of his slide in the polls and the New York and Connecticut primary defeats, may have subtly influenced the president. CIA Director Turner later recalled:

> The hostages had been dominating American foreign policy for 156 days. Every evening we winced when [CBS News television anchor] Walter Cronkite signed off with yet a higher number of days. Although no one raised it in the NSC, a recent Gallup Poll showed that approval of the President's handling of the crisis had fallen to 40 percent, down from 75 percent in November and 61 percent in January. The public expected something more than having its expectations alternately raised and dashed.[26]

Another factor seems to have been the White House's growing concern for the hostages' safety. As Deputy Secretary of Defense W. Graham Claytor later observed, "All along we had a feeling of threat to the physical well-being of the hostages in a dangerous, unpredictable situation." Looking back, Brzezinski made the same point: "The threat to the hostages was considered real. We had information from overt as well as covert sources that some might be tried and executed. We also thought that maybe not all of the hostages were alive."[27]

In his memoirs, Carter states that this loomed large in the decision to go ahead. He suggests that by April the threat to the hostages had intensified because Iraq had begun threatening to invade Iran and the Iranians were convinced the United States was behind the threat. Citing his diary entry of April 10, 1980, where he had noted, "The Iranian terrorists are making all kinds of crazy threats to kill the American hostages if they are invaded by Iraq—whom they identify as an American puppet," Carter writes: "We could no longer afford to depend on diplomacy." Whether there was a genuine threat to the hostages, however, is a matter of debate. In November, the United States had sent word to the highest levels of the Iranian government that any harm to the hostages would trigger retaliation. The Iranians apparently got the message. Visiting the hostages in mid-April, the International Red Cross found no evidence they were in physical danger or ill health.[28] The president and key advisers, however, seemed convinced that the threat to the hostages was growing. Faced then, as they saw it, with the choice of waiting helplessly until Iran released—or perhaps harmed—the hostages, adopting additional and probably ineffectual nonbelligerent sanctions, or taking steps such as mining that could further radicalize Iran, the rescue mission seemed, in Jordan's words, "the best of a lousy set of options."[29]

Last, just as wishful thinking apparently colored the judgment of some military planners and decision makers, it may also have affected some civilian policymakers' assessment of the rescue option. In his memoirs, Jordan notes that by the spring of 1980 he was so frustrated that, upon learning about the rescue option, he was "excited by the prospect of a bold and successful resolution of the crisis." Eager for a solution, he found it difficult to focus on the possible drawbacks of the operation. Jordan has described the thoughts that raced through his mind during his first briefing on the plan:

> *It will be a great coup for the Pentagon if the mission succeeds—and Carter's ass if it fails.* But I couldn't even contemplate failure.... [I] couldn't get my mind off the helicopters lifting off from the embassy grounds with the hostages. I wanted desperately for this Godforsaken crisis to be over and done with.[30]

Given the White House's exasperation with the crisis, Jordan may not have been the only one unwilling to contemplate the possibility of failure.

At 6:00 P.M.* on April 24, the first C-130s carrying Delta Force, the Special Forces team, and a Ranger security group took off from Masirah for Iran. An hour later, eight RH-53 helicopters lifted off from the carrier U.S.S. *Nimitz* in the Gulf of Oman. Flying in formation, they veered eastward and began the six-hundred-mile flight to Desert One. Barely half an hour after the lead C-130 took off, the first incident occurred. As the C-130 approached the Iranian coast, its crew realized that the planners had miscalculated the launch time. The plan called for the plane to cross the Strait of Hormuz and enter Iranian airspace under cover of darkness. It was still daylight, however, as the plane neared the coast. The crew spotted five or six commercial ships in the waters below. The plane quickly adjusted course to avoid flying near them.[31]

Two hours into the mission, another incident occurred: the BIM warning light flashed aboard helicopter number 6, Dash Six. The crew immediately landed on the desert floor. Checking the rotors, they confirmed a loss of nitrogen. They abandoned the aircraft and boarded another helicopter, Dash Eight, which had seen Dash Six land and landed alongside.[32] Because the planners had never checked the implications of a BIM, the pilots did not realize Dash Six could have flown for at least another twenty hours—more than enough to finish the mission.

Some three hours into the raid, the helicopters encountered the suspended dust the meteorologists had failed to predict. The pilots were

---

* All the times that follow are local (Iran) time.

totally unprepared for what ensued. The fine dust taxed their flying skills to the utmost; in the words of one pilot, it was like "flying in a bowl of milk." A highly experienced Air Force helicopter pilot called it "the worst flying that I have ever done. . . . I never saw anything for the next three hours." The pilots broke out of one dust storm only to enter another, which extended almost all the way to Desert One. For the next two hours, they flew by instruments, at altitudes averaging one hundred feet, and sometimes as low as twenty-five feet. Their night-vision goggles made matters even worse. After half an hour's use, they caused disorientation, vertigo, and splitting headaches. The Air Force helicopter pilot observed: "I kept getting vertigo. . . . The guy I was flying with was constantly getting vertigo also."[33] Unable to maintain formation, the helicopters proceeded separately toward Desert One. The C-130 pilots, in contrast, had little difficulty. Their planes carried the FLIR (infrared) system, which provides an accurate picture of the terrain ahead, regardless of the weather.

Compounding the helicopter pilots' predicament was their mistaken belief that they had to fly low to evade radar detection. In fact, the planners had determined that the only significant radar threat came from radar stations along the Iranian coast; inside Iran, the threat was negligible. This information, however, never reached the helicopter crews. The latter did hear, however, that the CIA reconnaissance plane that had flown to Desert One before the raid had picked up radar signals as it left the site. After looking into the matter, JTF experts had concluded that these signals were, in all likelihood, from U.S. ships in the Persian Gulf, not from Iranian radar. But the helicopter pilots never were told about this either. They thus assumed, based on the report from the CIA reconnaissance flight, that they had to stick close to the ground all the way to Tehran. The C-130 pilots, better informed, crossed the coast at low level, then flew the rest of the way to Desert One at altitudes between one and three thousand feet. Had the helicopter pilots known it was safe to do the same, they could have simply flown above the dust clouds.[34]

Four hours into the mission, several essential flight instruments, including the gyroscope, failed aboard Dash Five, which was still in the second dust cloud. In *Best Laid Plans,* David Martin and John Walcott graphically describe the helicopter pilot's predicament:

> Davis's gyroscope had overheated and failed. Unable to see any landmarks or to use the artificial horizon provided by the gyroscope, Davis became disoriented in the swirling dust. . . . At one point, the helicopter slipped into a 40-degree bank and nearly crashed. Davis descended to 75 feet but still could not see anything on the ground to help him regain his bearings. He still had 110 miles to go to Desert One and a 9,000 foot mountain ahead. He couldn't climb over it without the risk of exposing himself to Iranian radar. He couldn't go around it because his electronic navigation aids weren't working.[35]

The pilot opted to head back to the *Nimitz*—unaware that if he pressed ahead, he had only twenty-five more minutes to fly before exiting the dust. The lead C-130, which had already reached Desert One, could have passed this on and confirmed that visibility at the site was good. But the C-130 had no secure communications with the helicopters, and the planners had determined that the aircraft would keep nonsecure radio communications to a minimum. Dash Five's pilot later stated that he would have kept on going had he known that weather at Desert One was good.[36] Similarly, if the planners had added a pathfinder aircraft to the force, the helicopters would not have been hindered by the dust and Dash Five could have continued.

At 10:00 P.M. on April 24, the lead C-130, carrying Colonel Kyle, commander of the C-130 force, and Beckwith arrived over Desert One. The plane used a remote control device to activate the landing lights the CIA team had planted during its March flight to the site. The C-130 crew spotted with their FLIR system a truck traveling down the road running past the landing strip. The pilot circled the area until it drove by. As soon as the plane landed, Rangers and Delta Force members, some riding small motorcycles brought aboard the C-130, fanned out and set up roadblocks. They had been on the ground only a few minutes when a bus came down the road. They shot out its tires and captured the forty-four occupants, most of them women and children. Soon after a fuel truck, followed by a smaller pickup, came along. A Ranger blasted the fuel truck with a light antitank weapon, setting it ablaze. Its driver ran to the pickup, which sped away. A raider tried to follow it, but his motorcycle was slow to start and the pickup disappeared into the night. Flames from the blaze shot hundreds of feet into the night sky.[37]

Kyle, the on-scene commander, was in direct radio contact with JTF commander Vaught, who monitored the operation from a special command post at Wadi Kena, in Egypt. Kyle described the incidents to Vaught, who relayed the information to the Pentagon's National Military Command Center, which, in turn, passed it on to the White House. Brown and Brzezinski reviewed the situation and decided that the mission could proceed. As Brzezinski later explained:

> Since it was pitch dark, we had no reason to believe that the Iranians who got away knew that something major was afoot, especially since the region was known for various incidents of smuggling. And as to the bus passengers, we felt confident that we could simply evacuate them. Brown and I agreed there was no basis for aborting the operation.[38]

Brown and Brzezinski informed the president of the incidents at Desert One and of their assessment. After consulting with Mondale and JCS Chairman Jones, Carter agreed that the mission should proceed. As the White House saw it, the fuel truck and pickup "appeared to be driven by smugglers. . . . It was highly unlikely that they would go to the

police. In fact, Colonel Beckwith believed they thought our team was
Iranian police."[39] The White House was gambling that even though the
raiders had blown up a fuel truck, let witnesses escape, and were about
to spirit away some forty civilians, Iranian authorities would not realize
for at least another twenty-four hours that a hostile force was operating
in Iran. The review group concluded that these incidents had seriously
increased the risk of discovery.

> The intrusion of the Iranian vehicles at Desert One significantly increased
> the chances of the Iranians' identifying the intent and timing of the opera-
> tion. Although there was a workable plan to handle the bus passengers, the
> burned-out truck, empty bus, and abandoned heavy-lift helicopter near a
> well-traveled road could have resulted in early discovery by Iranian
> authorities.[40]

As it turned out, the White House did not have to worry long whether
its gamble was correct. A new mishap soon caused the abort of the mission at Desert One.

Shortly after the destruction of the fuel truck, the five other C-130s
landed. Two promptly departed after unloading troops and equipment.
The other C-130s, including three tankers with fuel for the helicopters,
remained at the site, their sixteen turboprop engines running. The helicopters were scheduled to arrive at Desert One in formation, thirty minutes after the last C-130s, but the dust had played havoc with the plan.
The helicopters straggled in one by one between an hour and an hour
and a half late. The flight leader, who was supposed to arrive first, was
last to land. Another planning shortcoming quickly emerged: there were
inadequate contingency plans for the case where the flight leader arrived
late. As the review group observed, "The lack of effective command and
control became evident when the helicopter flight leader did not arrive
first at Desert One as scheduled. There was no way to quickly find out
or locate who was in charge."[41]

Several helicopter pilots arrived badly shaken. One told Beckwith
outright that if they had any sense, the raiders would abandon the helicopters in the desert and all leave Iran in the C-130s. Another urged
that "some very careful consideration ought to be given to calling off
this operation. You have no idea what I've been through.... I'm really
not sure we can make it."[42] The helicopter pilots had experienced bad
surprises up to the moment they landed. Instead of finding the firm surface they expected, they ran into soft sand that made their landing particularly difficult. One pilot later recalled:

> The dust was really thick. More than 6 inches where we were programmed
> to land. Our checks...had not predicted that amount of sand, due to
> storms. We dug in and nearly went over. I had to leap frog the aircraft. Go
> up for about five seconds, then come down, then back up, and down. Fi-
> nally we got to a hard enough place and were near the fuel line and that
> was it. You couldn't ground taxi.[43]

As the number of C-130s and helicopters at the landing site grew, the insufficiencies in the planning and preparation became painfully apparent. Having never conducted a full rehearsal, the raiders were not fully prepared for the complexity of the loading and refueling operations involving eight transport planes and six helicopters. The Air Force pilots returning from Desert One stated that "they had seen immediately that the operation had taken on complexities which had not been envisioned during the training stage." The roar of sixteen C-130 and eighteen RH-53 engines was deafening, and the propellers and rotors kicked up a blizzard of dust. As the review group observed, "Personnel moving about Desert One were shadowy, somewhat fuzzy figures, barely recognizable."[44]

Making matters worse, several senior officers wore no insignias of rank. Nor did other key personnel wear readily recognizable identification signs. Colonel Kyle, the on-scene commander, had no fixed, easily identifiable command post where he could be readily found. There was no clear second in command. Confusion ensued. Some helicopter pilots later stated that "in some cases, they did not know or recognize the authority of those giving orders at Desert One." Adding to the confusion, many of the Air Force, Marine Corps, and Army units did not have radios enabling them to talk to one another. Kyle, in particular, had no radio communications with Delta Force commander Beckwith, the C-130 and helicopter pilots, and the rangers providing security at Desert One. Kyle wrote after the operation, "We never seemed to know what the roadblock team was doing."[45]

Six helicopters eventually arrived—the minimum the planners had deemed necessary to proceed to Tehran. Only five, however, were still safe to fly. Two hours from the *Nimitz,* the hydraulic system of Dash Two had begun malfunctioning. Inspecting the aircraft at Desert One, the crew found that a hydraulic pump had failed. Because repairing the hydraulic system of a helicopter is a major task, they had not taken spare pumps. Even if they had, they could not have completed repairs by dawn.[46]

The failure of the pump left only one of the aircraft's two hydraulic systems functioning. Flying helicopters without backup hydraulics is hazardous; should the remaining hydraulic system fail, the controls lock up, causing a crash. Moreover, the heavier the load the helicopter is carrying, the greater the chance of overtaxing the remaining hydraulic system and causing a lock. Lieutenant Colonel Edward R. Seiffert, the helicopter flight leader, determined that Dash Two should fly no further.[47]

The rising tension at Desert One took a toll on interservice relations that had been shaky from the start. When Seiffert arrived, Beckwith jumped aboard his aircraft to request permission for his men to board. Seiffert, engrossed with the other helicopter pilots, paid no attention to him for several minutes. Beckwith, who, in his own words, was getting "pissed," "rapped" Seiffert's helmet with his hand. The exchange grew stormy: Seiffert's copilot was, as Kyle later wrote, soon "out of his seat and about to confront Beckwith" before Seiffert calmed him down. When Kyle boarded the helicopter moments later, Seiffert's first words were "It's nice to talk to somebody who's still in control of his faculties and can calmly discuss the situation." Later, Beckwith greeted the news that Dash Two could no longer fly with words to the effect that the helicopter pilots "finally found an excuse to quit."[48]

Kyle reported to Vaught that only five helicopters were flyable. This was relayed to the president, who asked for Beckwith's assessment. Beckwith judged it would be imprudent to proceed with fewer than the minimum number of helicopters the planners had deemed necessary for the mission. In his memoirs, he describes why he thought it unwise to proceed with only five: "These helicopters can only carry so much weight. To get to the hide-site I need to lighten their loads. This means I gotta leave behind eighteen to twenty men. Everyone's doing two jobs as it is, some of them three.... Which twenty would I leave?" Carter agreed and instructed to abort the mission.[49] For all their elaborate calculations, the planners had underestimated the number of helicopters needed.[50]

Upon receiving the order to abort, Kyle decided that the flyable helicopters would return to the *Nimitz* and the C-130s, with the Rangers and the rest of the raiders, would fly back to Masirah. As the force prepared to withdraw, it was clear that it was less than a cohesive team. In his published account of the mission, Beckwith relates,

> I went from one C-130 to another, working out in my mind the number of men who had to be put on board each one. I also wanted to make sure none of the C-130 pilots took off on their own. "Hey, don't leave here on your own initiative. We gotta get Delta on board."
>
> I grabbed one pilot by the arm and shouted over the noise of his engines, "For God's sake, don't leave."[51]

Later, when asked what had prompted him to make such a plea, Beckwith said candidly: "I didn't know all of the plane pilots, what they would or would not do."[52]

At this point, tragedy struck. The C-130s had been on the ground, engines running, far longer than anticipated. One had to take off within minutes in order to have enough fuel to make it back to base. Dash Three, positioned in the C-130's way, prepared to hover out of its path. Martin and Walcott describe the scene:

> Until now, Schaefer [pilot of Dash Three] had relied on the refueling hoses—black snakes against the white desert floor—to tell him where he was in the maelstrom of dust that was Desert One. But now the hoses were stored aboard the C-130s, and the only thing Schaefer could see was the black-clad figure of a sergeant from the Air Force control team who was standing between Dash Three and Lewis's C-130. Schaefer lifted off and

turned 10 degrees to the left, keeping his eyes fixed on the sergeant. But the sergeant backed away from the 100-mile-per-hour blast of Schaefer's rotors. What Schaefer thought was a stationary object was now moving: Schaefer believed he was drifting left when in fact the sergeant was moving right. Reacting to the optical illusion, Schaefer banked back to the right and flew into Hal Lewis's C-130.[53]

The two aircraft exploded in a ball of fire, killing eight crewmen and injuring several others. The heat was so intense that no one could approach the burning aircraft. The situation became even more dangerous as the fire detonated the ammunition aboard the two planes. As one helicopter pilot later recalled:

> It took only three minutes to disintegrate both airplanes.... You could see the rotors burning and folding back like straws in the intense heat.... We pushed our craft for power and tried to get away from the burning 53 and 130, because their rounds were cooking off. You could see the tracers flying all over the place and bouncing off the other aircraft.[54]

Flying shrapnel from the exploding aircraft and ammunition set off by the fire disabled at least one and possibly more of the remaining helicopters. It was now close to 3:00 A.M. and daybreak was fast approaching. Several C-130s were very low on fuel. Kyle decided to abandon the helicopters and evacuate the entire rescue force without further delay aboard the remaining C-130s. He chose not to destroy the helicopters before abandoning them, fearing that more exploding aircraft would increase the danger to the raiders and the C-130s. He asked General Vaught instead to send an air strike to destroy the helicopters once the raiders left Desert One.[55]

Poor communication and coordination, which had marred earlier operations at Desert One, complicated the last stage of the evacuation. As the review group noted, "Instructions to evacuate helicopters and board the C-130s had to be questioned to determine the identity of those giving the orders to establish their proper authority."[56]

The flight out was hair-raising. Air Force ground controllers at Desert One, who had placed temporary lights on the desert floor to mark the takeoff strip, inadvertently traced a path that cut across the road running through the desert site. On takeoff, two C-130s plowed straight through the sandy shoulder of the road, narrowly avoiding a crash. One participant later recalled:

> We got on the last 130. We were overweight. Everything went out the back door, motorcycles, machine guns, etc.... He began taxiing and I really didn't think we were going to get off of the ground.... [We] hit a ditch in the ramp. I thought the wheels had been ripped off. We were laying on the floors on top of each other.... We were thrown into the air and then the aircraft came up and hit me, vice my going back down. That's when I thought "Here we go, the next time we hit, we're going to dig in." But we just kept bounding and bouncing and finally we went up and stayed.[57]

The turmoil at Desert One did not escape the attention of the Iranian authorities for long. As the C-130s were making it back from the site, the United States picked up intelligence that Tehran was aware that some sort of incident had occurred in the area of Desert One.[58]

The air strike Kyle had requested against the helicopters never took place. Apparently, Vaught and his staff and senior authorities in Washington feared that it would endanger any raiders who might be left behind, as well as the passengers of the Iranian bus. There was also a risk that Iranian fighters might challenge U.S. planes conducting the strike, raising the confrontation to a new and dangerously high level. The upshot, however, was that the CIA and military secret agents waiting in Tehran found themselves in jeopardy. Unbeknownst to Kyle when he ordered the evacuation from Desert One, the Marines had left in the helicopters classified material on the Tehran portion of the raid. This included the location of the warehouse with the trucks the raiders were supposed to use and other information betraying the presence of the U.S. agents. Ultimately, they all slipped out of Iran, although some had to use "ingenious methods" to escape.[59]

Those associated with the mission often blame its problems on plain bad luck. As Carter noted in his diary the morning the mission failed, "The cancellation of our mission was caused by a strange series of mishaps—almost completely unpredictable. The operation itself was well planned. The men were well trained. We had every possibility of success." When asked what was the ultimate cause of failure, Deputy National Security Adviser Aaron replied ironically: "Allah's will."[60]

In reality, the fiasco cannot be attributed merely to ill luck or an untoward providence. The planners accumulated mistakes that helped bring about failure. They used too few helicopters in an operation that would push the aircraft to the outer limits of performance. They neglected to research the implications of mechanical problems that might occur and brief the pilots accordingly. Overconfident about the weather, they did not assign a pathfinder to the mission. They failed to anticipate the problems of command and control likely to occur at Desert One. They lacked a contingency plan for assaulting the embassy with less than the full complement of ninety-three Delta Force members who had embarked on the mission. The raiders were thus unprepared to continue with only five helicopters. The Sontay planners, in contrast, had prepared and extensively rehearsed contingency plans to raid the POW camp even if they lost a third or more of the ground force en route. One can only wonder what other mistakes were made in planning for the rest of the mission, which would have come to light—possibly with disastrous consequences—had it proceeded past Desert One.

Moreover, many of the familiar problems that had marred earlier strategic special operations surfaced again in the Iran raid, gravely weakening it. Once again, U.S. intelligence left much to be desired. Following the seizure of the embassy, there were no U.S. agents in country who could gather information for a rescue mission. Although the United States infiltrated new agents, it took two months before its intelligence could identify with any degree of certainty where all of the hostages were located or provide basic information on access routes into Tehran or the defenses at the embassy.

Interagency and interservice cooperation was a source of problems from start to finish. At the outset, part of the intelligence community seemed slow to gear up in support of a rescue. Although this later improved, the JTF was never satisfied with the support it received from the CIA. Interservice coordination was hardly better. It was not until February 1980—three months after the seizure of the embassy—that the U.S. military had fashioned from disparate Air Force, Army, Marine Corps, and Navy elements a force with the minimum skill and cohesion to attempt a rescue. It never became a well-knit team, however. Delta Force mistrusted the Marine Corps helicopter crews, some of whom reciprocated in kind. Beckwith was unsure of some of the C-130 pilots. Most of the members of the rescue force barely knew one another. The result was confusion and friction at Desert One.

As in previous strategic special operations, the president received inadequate information and advice. To preserve secrecy, other than the planners themselves, only a handful of senior civilian decision makers and the JCS reviewed the plan. But the civilians lacked the time and expertise to critique it thoroughly. The JCS had the expertise, but lacked—or did not take—the time. The JTF's optimistic assessments and many planning shortcomings went unchallenged. Noting the absence of any in-depth, independent review of the plan by anyone other than the JCS, the review group opined that had such a review occurred, "some of the issues now being addressed by the review group might have arisen in sharper focus during the actual planning phase." This, the review group continued, could have made "a critical contribution to ultimate mission accomplishment."[61]

The president's advisers, moreover, failed to ask a key question. Just as no one in the run-up to the Bay of Pigs thought to ask the JCS exactly what they meant by "fair chance" of success, no one in the Iranian episode asked the planners to be more specific about their estimates of "good chance" of success. Last, wishful thinking may have played a part in the Iran fiasco, contributing to the optimistic view the planners, senior military officials, and White House held of the plan.

Ironically, the White House had learned one lesson from the Bay of Pigs. It wisely decided not to interfere with the execution of the Iran raid once it was under way. Unfortunately, the other lessons of the Bay of Pigs and subsequent strategic special operations had gone unlearned. Once again, there was a bitter price to pay.

NINE

Why We Failed

Of the four strategic special operations examined in this study, Sontay came the closest to success. Brilliantly executed, in the end the raid was nonetheless a failure because it did not achieve its chief objective, the recovery of U.S. POWs. The Bay of Pigs and the Iran rescue mission were disasters that exacted a high price in human life and U.S. prestige. The *Mayaguez* operation was similarly a fiasco, although the fortuitous recovery of the ship's crew obscured the fact that eighteen Americans died landing at the wrong location to rescue prisoners the Cambodians had already decided to free. Moreover, close examination of these episodes confirms that, as hypothesized at the outset of this study, recurrent problems have plagued U.S. strategic special operations. Faulty intelligence, poor interagency and interservice cooperation and coordination, provision of inadequate advice to decision makers, wishful thinking, and overcontrol of mission execution by officials far removed from the theater of operations have repeatedly jeopardized the ability of the United States to conduct such missions successfully.

Recurrent Problems

Inadequate Intelligence

The first recurrent problem is inadequate intelligence on the objective and enemy forces defending it. U.S. intelligence has manifest strengths; some of the intelligence provided to the planners of the special operations examined in this study was first-rate. In both the Sontay and Iran missions, U.S. experts provided accurate and highly detailed information on enemy air defenses, allowing U.S. aircraft to fly deep into enemy territory undetected. In the Sontay raid, this intelligence enabled the raiders to fly to the outskirts of Hanoi through what was then the densest air defense network in the world.

The United States excels at collecting intelligence through technical means such as overhead photography (imagery intelligence, or IMINT) and the monitoring of electronic transmissions (signals intelligence, or SIGINT), which provided the information on North Vietnam and Iran's air defenses. But although technical means of collection can reveal the size, equipment, and disposition of enemy forces, they have clear limitations. Overhead imagery is of limited or no use against targets that are carefully concealed—or, as in the case of Sontay, indoors. Moreover, whereas IMINT and SIGINT are useful to assess an enemy's capabilities, they offer only limited insight into thoughts and attitudes, particularly intentions and motivation, which are key determinants of how the enemy will perform in combat. Much of the intelligence of this type must be acquired by agents in direct contact with enemy forces or those close to them.

The collection of intelligence by human agents, known as human intelligence or HUMINT, can fill in many of the gaps in the knowledge gained by technical collection. The United States, however, traditionally has been weaker at HUMINT than at technical intelligence (TECHINT) gathering. This was manifest in the Bay of Pigs as well as the Sontay and Iran raids. One of the key assumptions behind the Bay of Pigs plan was that Castro's were poor fighting forces unlikely to offer much resistance. The planners believed and told the White House that the Brigade, better trained and equipped than Castro's forces, would rout the first Cuban units it encountered, triggering a wave of uprisings.

The assumption that an initial Brigade victory would spark a chain reaction of uprisings was, of course, fallacious. Had the planners or the White House looked, they would have found considerable intelligence indicating as much. By early 1961, U.S. agents operating in Cuba or debriefing the Cuban refugees streaming into Miami had gathered considerable evidence that Castro's security forces exerted increasingly tight control over the population. By January 1961, the intelligence community had concluded that Castro had, in all likelihood, more than made up for the decline in popular support for his regime by the effective security apparatus he had set up throughout the island.

The assumption that the Brigade would win the first battle against Castro's forces was just as flawed. Underpinning this belief was the planners' conviction that the morale and combat effectiveness of Cuba's regular armed forces and militia were low—a view the U.S. intelligence community shared. In a Special National Intelligence Estimate of December 1960, the intelligence community concluded that the overall combat efficiency of Castro's militia was poor, and that it would take as much as a year before even parts of it became an effective fighting force. The report called the Cuban Air Force's combat effectiveness "virtually nil," the Navy's poor, and the Army's low.[1]

As events demonstrated, this seriously underestimated Castro's forces. His army and militia doggedly pushed the exiles back into the sea, while his tiny air force devastated the invasion fleet. CIA Deputy Director for Plans Bissell later acknowledged that one of the causes of defeat was that Castro's troops "moved more decisively, faster and in greater force" than anticipated.[2] Only human intelligence could provide a full picture of the motivation and effectiveness of Castro's forces, and in this instance U.S. HUMINT had been wrong.

Inadequate human intelligence was again a problem almost a decade later in the Sontay operation. The intelligence community, using technical means of collection, was superb at pinpointing the weaknesses of North Vietnam's air defenses, but it could not tell for sure whether there were still any POWs at Sontay—or who occupied the compound near the camp, which U.S. photo analysts mistakenly assumed was a school. Good human intelligence could have filled in these gaps: effective clandestine agents in the area could have given eyewitness accounts of who was in and around the target.

Throughout the Vietnam war, however, U.S. attempts to build a covert network inside North Vietnam had met with scant success. Both the CIA and U.S. armed forces sent specially trained Vietnamese agents, known as Controlled American Sources, or CAS, to gather information inside North Vietnam. Most of the CIA's efforts failed dismally. Of the several hundred Vietnamese it infiltrated into the North, including North Vietnamese defectors who had gone to work for the CIA, almost all were killed or captured. For a time agents inserted by the armed forces, an operation SACSA handled, did better. When President Johnson halted the bombing of North Vietnam in 1968, however, he also forbade any missions to resupply the CAS in North Vietnam. Forty-five agents in the North were abandoned; some were caught, others surrendered or starved to death.[3]

After taking office in 1969, President Nixon lifted partially the ban on CAS insertion and resupply. Not surprisingly, however, volunteers for CAS missions had become rare. According to Lieutenant General Donald V. Bennett, who then headed the Defense Intelligence Agency, about two months before the operation the United States finally did manage to insert a lone agent in the Sontay area, but he found out "nothing."[4] With a better agent network inside North Vietnam, the United States might have been more successful gathering the information about Sontay that it required but that technical means could not provide.

Human intelligence was also a problem in Iran. Shortly after the embassy takeover, when Colonel Beckwith asked about U.S. covert agents operating in Tehran, he was dismayed to learn that there were none. The United States had to infiltrate several CIA and military covert agents into Iran to gather information on the precise location of the hostages in the embassy compound; the size, composition, weapons, and routines of the guard force; and a myriad of other details the planners desperately needed to know and that technical means could not provide. It was not until late December 1979, nearly two months after the embassy takeover, that these agents provided enough information to allow the planners to devise a detailed ground-assault plan.[5]

In time, other agents followed and the intelligence picture improved markedly. Almost to the end, however, there were significant gaps in the planners' knowledge. U.S. intelligence did not know for sure where in the sprawling compound the hostages were held until it debriefed the Pakistani cook who had worked there until April 1980. The information he provided about their whereabouts reached the rescuers literally on the eve of the mission. With a better local intelligence network, the planners could have obtained vital information they needed without waiting for weeks or even months.[6]

There are diverse reasons for the problems experienced gathering human intelligence for these operations. In part, these problems reflect unique circumstances prevailing at the time of some of these missions. Abandoning dozens of clandestine agents in North Vietnam a year and a half before the Sontay raid had decimated the U.S. covert network in the country and had made rebuilding it difficult. The weak U.S. intelligence network in Iran in the late 1970s partially reflected the U.S. decision, taken when the shah seemed firmly in power, to rely chiefly on his secret police for intelligence on Iran's domestic politics.[7]

The intelligence shortcomings in these special operations are also attributable to larger problems of U.S. intelligence. For most of the past three decades, the United States has, according to students of the U.S. intelligence community, placed far greater emphasis on technical intelligence gathering than on collection by human agents. TECHINT spending has generally outstripped HUMINT spending by a ratio of about seven to one. TECHINT received the lion's share of resources for a variety of reasons. It was invaluable, in particular, in tracking the size and deployment of the former Soviet Union's nuclear and conventional forces, a paramount U.S. concern during the cold war. As Loch K. Johnson, a prominent student of U.S. intelligence, has written, TECHINT thus "has revolutionized the collection task—and has made the world an infinitely safer place to live." Moreover, as Johnson notes, hardware produces pictures and other hard evidence whose value is easier to assess than that of reports by spies. The loyalty of hardware is never suspect.[8]

TECHINT has traditionally been the favorite of the U.S intelligence community for other reasons as well. As one senior military intelligence officer has put it:

It's a lot easier to control a satellite. It is a great responsibility to send a person to do something at a great risk. He might be caught and that could be embarrassing. Something like a satellite, miles above the earth, is never going to be captured. It certainly isn't going to confess. . . .

But when you have all these people running around all over the world lifting up rocks, and opening up filing cabinets, somebody is liable to get caught. That's risk. That's responsibility. And it's dangerous. A lot of high-tech, high-vis, big time, billions of dollars on electronic gear. . . . It's all low risk—zero-risk—and looks great, briefs great.[9]

As a result, the network of U.S. operatives in many parts of the world is often quite thin. When its forces invaded Grenada in late 1983, the United States did not have a single covert agent on the island—even though it had been concerned for months about the Grenada's leftward drift and its growing ties to Cuba. Nor was recruiting Grenadan agents unusually difficult; New York City harbors the largest concentration of Grenadans outside Grenada.[10]

Further constraining U.S. HUMINT collection is the cover U.S. intelligence officers typically enjoy abroad. According to students of the U.S. intelligence community, they usually operate overseas under "light" or "official" cover, passing themselves off as officials from other U.S. government agencies. Few are under "deep" cover, posing as private Americans unconnected to the U.S. government. Students of U.S. intelligence point out that although official cover is safer—formal association with the government provides a degree of protection—the gain in safety is at the expense of operational effectiveness. Official cover can restrict the circles in which an intelligence officer can move—and his or her ability to recruit and supervise local agents.[11] And when U.S. officials can no longer operate openly in a foreign country—as occurred when the United States broke relations with Cuba in early 1961 and the embassy in Tehran was overrun in late 1979—collection capabilities suffer accordingly.

Poor Coordination

A second recurrent problem in strategic special operations is poor coordination, which has marred both preparation and execution of these operations. Problems of coordination have varied. Lack of compatible equipment has been one source of difficulties; in the Iran rescue mission, many of the Air Force, Marine Corps, and Army units at Desert One did not have radios allowing them to talk to one another.

A major problem in interagency and interservice cooperation has been getting one agency or service to be fully alert and responsive to the needs of another. Information sharing in the Bay of Pigs was grossly inadequate. The CIA never told the Navy's Commander in Chief for the Atlantic, Admiral Dennison, whose units would escort the exiles to Cuba, how many men were in the exile force nor precisely where they would land. When the Navy was ordered to pick up Brigade survivors, this lack of basic information severely hampered its efforts. When a fleeing exile ship the Navy had never been told about sailed into the path of U.S. warships, they mistook the troop-laden cargo for an enemy vessel and almost sank it.

In the *Mayaguez* operation, the U.S. Air Force in Thailand never passed on to the Marines intelligence estimates showing that as many as three hundred regular Khmer Rouge troops were on Koh Tang. The Air Force never used the full range of sophisticated aerial reconnaissance aircraft at its disposal to reconnoiter in detail the enemy defenses that the Marines would encounter. The Air Force likewise failed pass on to the Marines what information it did gather on enemy gun emplacements while overflying the island. The slow-flying, heavily armed flying gunship that was orbiting over Koh Tang, by far the best aircraft to provide air support for the Marines, left the island as they arrived. Most of the aircraft that provided close air support were jets that flew too fast to gain an accurate picture of the situation on the ground, instead of the slower, better-suited propeller-driven planes that the Marines had requested. Ignorance of the Marines' needs continued throughout the day, as the Air Force commanders failed to tell the Marines about the recovery of the *Mayaguez*'s crew or warn them about the drop of the BLU-82 bomb. Similarly, the official postmortem on the Iran rescue mission suggested that the responsiveness of the intelligence community to the needs of the rescue-mission planners left somewhat to be desired. As the report noted, "Certain elements of the Intelligence Community seemed slow in harnessing themselves initially for the tasks at hand."[12]

In addition, the personnel who have come together to plan and execute strategic operations have had difficulties understanding one another's standard operating procedures. In the Sontay operation, it took time for the Air Force helicopter pilots, who had never conducted a heliborne assault, to get used to Army procedures for helicopter combat insertions. In the *Mayaguez* operation, Air Force helicopter pilots' unfamiliarity with helicopter assaults led several of them to break off their insertions when the first helicopters were shot down, leaving a handful of Marines on the island in the face of near-overwhelming odds. In the Iran rescue mission, the Delta Force planners were reportedly confused by the designations the intelligence agencies used in their reports to indicate the reliability of their sources.

Outright confusion and mutual mistrust have also marred the preparation and execution of strategic special operations. In the frantic planning for the *Mayaguez* operation, coordination between the services seems to have broken down. At times the planners from one service did not even understand the roles planners from the other services were supposed to play. The Air Force flying command post at Koh Tang did not know the call signs of the Marine Corps units on the island. For hours, it was at a loss to understand the tactical situation on the ground. At

Desert One, some of the raiders were unsure of the authority of those giving orders and unclear about who was in charge. Delta Force mistrusted the Marine Corps pilots and Colonel Beckwith was unsure of the Air Force aviators.

The reasons for these problems of interagency and interservice coordination are several. In the most extreme case, the Bay of Pigs, the CIA did not want to cooperate, and withheld key information to maximize control over the operation and influence policymakers' decisions. In the other cases, the lack of coordination was not deliberate but an unintended outcome of prevailing mentalities and practices.

Part of the problem is bureaucratic parochialism, or the natural tendency of organizational units to focus chiefly on their own primary missions and entailed needs and practices.[13] As a result, individual military services often pay limited attention to the needs of other services with which they are periodically called upon to work and to the requirements of smooth interaction. This helps explain why at Desert One many of the Army, Air Force, and Marine Corps units lacked radios allowing them to talk to one another. Bureaucratic parochialism also helps understand why part of the intelligence community may have been slow to support the Iran rescue mission, and why the Air Force never passed on key intelligence to the Marines. It also helps understand why Air Force commanders in the Mayaguez operation opted to use fast-flying jets—the Air Force's preferred aircraft for ground support—for ground strikes, and why they did not inform the Marines about the recovery of the crew or the use of BLU-82s.

A major reason for coordination problems encountered in these operations has been the practice of relying on *ad hoc* organizations and collections of disparate units to plan and execute the missions. In most instances, the United States set up special task forces instead of using existing commands to plan these operations. In each case, the United States brought together from different services or agencies forces that had never operated together before. The drawbacks of this approach are several. It makes it harder for those entrusted with the mission to enlist the assistance of other organizational units, both within and outside the military because *ad hoc* task forces lack regular, long-standing ties to these organizations. Had the planning of the Iran raid been conducted by a permanent organization with close, ongoing ties to the intelligence community rather than to an *ad hoc* group lacking a network of lateral contacts, the planners might have secured the intelligence community's full support faster.

Ad hoc organizations and forces also compound the problems caused by different standard operating procedures. Again, had the Iran rescue mission planners enjoyed long-term, well-established relationships with the intelligence community, they would have been less puzzled by the some of the intelligence reports they received. Units from different services that have never worked together will inevitably experience problems with discrepant procedures and routines, particularly when some units assume roles they have never performed before. In the Sontay and *Mayaguez* operations, the Air Force conducted heliborne assaults, not a standard Air Force mission. With time and proper training, units from different services will master one another's routines; in the thorough rehearsing for the Sontay mission, Air Force pilots learned to insert Army troops in a combat zone. In the *Mayaguez* operation, however, there was no time for rehearsals. Despite the pilots' bravery, their unfamiliarity with heliborne assault techniques increased the difficulty of the operation.

Another drawback of using *ad hoc* collections of forces, even if they are from the same service, is the difficulty of forging them into a cohesive team. It takes more to achieve teamwork than familiarizing each element with the routines and procedures of the others. A combat force truly functions as a team only when each member knows the strengths and weaknesses of the others, understands their thinking, reacts as they do in similar situations, and fully trusts them. Disparate elements can eventually become a team, but only after training together extensively, with special emphasis on unit cohesion. This happened in the Sontay rescue mission, after months of grueling training that constantly stressed teamwork. As a result, when the unexpected occurred and part of the raiding force landed at the wrong place, triggering a fierce firefight, the raiders reacted with cool cohesion and deadly effectiveness. In contrast, despite months of training, the Iran rescue force never became a team. When disaster struck at Desert One and the rescuers hastily withdrew, the Delta Force commander found himself pleading with a C-130 pilot not to leave before all of the troops were aboard.

Complete teamwork is essential in strategic special operations. The stakes are very high, there typically can be only one try, and the raiders, often operating deep inside enemy territory, normally cannot expect reinforcements in an emergency. They must prevail through speed, shock, surprise, and superior skill. Given the high odds, attempting such operations with anything less than a totally cohesive force is courting disaster.[14]

Excessive secrecy also impedes effective coordination in strategic special operations. In their zeal to preserve operational security, the planners of the Iran raid never held a full-scale rehearsal. They also practiced rigid compartmentalization, limiting contacts between elements of the force. Cohesion suffered: many raiders met for the first time at Desert One. Coordination problems further increase as the number of services or of units from the same service involved in an operation grows. The complexity of the Iran rescue mission, which involved Air Force C-130s crews, Air Force special operations "Combat Controllers" to direct aircraft on the ground, Marine Corps and Navy helicopter pilots, Delta Force, Army Special Forces and Rangers, and CIA and DOD clandestine agents vastly increased the problems of coordination.

Provision of Faulty Information to the National Leadership

Another recurrent problem in strategic special operations is that the president, who gives the final go-ahead, has often received faulty information on proposed missions. In the worst case, the Bay of Pigs, the CIA gave the president and his senior advisers false information, assuring them throughout the planning that there was a "guerrilla option," and suggesting that the operation therefore could not fail. If the invasion faltered, the CIA assured, the exiles could withdraw to the Escambray Mountains and keep fighting as guerrillas. Although this might have been true had the exiles landed at Trinidad, the guerrilla option ceased to exist when the invasion site shifted to the Bay of Pigs.

This provision of deliberately misleading information, was, fortunately, an exceptional occurrence. Much more common has been the provision of one-sided information: the president hears about the strengths of a proposed plan and of those who will execute it but fails to hear about important weaknesses or drawbacks of the operation. In the Bay of Pigs, Kennedy was told repeatedly about the Brigade's superb morale, but the agency kept quiet when the exiles mutinied in their training camp in Guatemala. In the Sontay raid, the planners never mentioned the historically abysmal rate of success of U.S. POW rescue missions. In the *Mayaguez* operation, senior military advisers in Washington apparently said little about the high risks the proposed assault on Koh Tang posed to the Marines and to the *Mayaguez*'s crew. In the Iran rescue mission, the White House never learned about the Joint Task Force's confused chain of command, the lack of thoroughness of the planning, the shortcomings in the training, or the lingering mistrust between Delta Force and the Marines.

A key reason that presidents have received one-sided information is the way most of these operations have been planned and prepared. In the Bay of Pigs, the Sontay raid, and the Iran rescue mission, planning and preparation fell to restricted groups of CIA or military personnel operating in utmost secrecy, with very little outside scrutiny. Other than the planners themselves, very few outside the Joint Chiefs of Staff and a handful of senior administration decision makers ever reviewed the plans and training.[15]

The Joint Chiefs of Staff had military expertise—although very few of them had any background in special operations—but lacked either the time or inclination to examine the planners' work in exhaustive detail. In the Bay of Pigs, Army Chairman General Decker, Air Force Chairman General White, and Marine Corps Commandant General Shoup devoted limited attention to the operation, whereas Admiral Burke and Joint Chairman General Lemnitzer, aided by Brigadier General Gray of the JCS staff, were more involved. In the Sontay operation, JCS Chairman Admiral Moorer followed preparations closely, the other chiefs far less so. In the Iran rescue mission, the chiefs, as a group, received only three briefings on the operation, although JCS Chairman General Jones and Army Chairman General Meyer individually devoted considerable time to the plan.[16] Consumed, however, by twelve-to-fourteen-hour work-days, none of the chiefs or their close assistants had the time to examine every facet of the military planning and training. And in the Bay of Pigs, where ultimate success depended on the reaction the invasion would trigger inside Cuba, none of the chiefs knew enough about Cuba to evaluate the claim that the landing would trigger uprisings and defections.

Most of the other senior officials involved in the Cuban invasion or the Sontay and Iran missions were civilians who lacked both the expertise and the time to examine thoroughly the planning and preparation. The few with military expertise, like CIA Director Turner or National Security Adviser Brzezinski's military assistant Brigadier General Odom, typically faced too many competing claims on their time to check every detail and question every assumption. Nor could they free themselves long enough to proceed to the field and probe thoroughly into the forces' training, readiness, and morale. Moreover, in the Bay of Pigs, apart from Assistant Secretary of State Mann, none of the senior administration officials involved knew much about Cuba. Yet only painstaking scrutiny, conducted by persons with relevant technical and country expertise, can uncover all of the weaknesses of a plan. In the Bay of Pigs and the Sontay and Iran raids, only the planners themselves were in a position to conduct this scrutiny.

The flaws of this arrangement are obvious. Planners have a personal stake in their plan. No matter how hard they try to stay objective, even first-rate planners are liable to overlook deficiencies in their product. Furthermore, some planners in these operations were less than first-rate. Thus shortcomings in the planning and preparation for the Bay of Pigs and the Iran rescue mission went unnoticed. The CIA, for instance, overlooked that by placing in a single van on the *Rio Escondido* all the Brigade's radios for communicating with its air wing, any mishap to the ship could cut off the ground force from its air support. When Castro's planes sank the freighter early in the invasion, the exiles lost contact with their aircraft. The leaders of the Joint Task Force preparing the Iran mission never realized the weaknesses of their arrangements for command and control and the confusion that could ensue. Overoptimistic about the chances of encountering clear skies over Iran, they neglected to equip the helicopters with advanced navigational gear or provide pathfinder aircraft that would have helped the helicopter pilots cope with the suspended dust clouds.

Moreover, planners are unlikely to call to the attention of the JCS or the White House flaws they perceive but cannot correct. Military officers have a strong sense of "can do" and are often reluctant to emphasize problems with a mission they have received. As Secretary of State Vance noted wryly shortly before the failed Iran rescue bid: "Generals will rarely tell you they can't do something."[17] This is especially true when the commanding officer intensely interested in the operation is the commander in chief. Thus, Marine Corps Commandant Barrow, who in late 1979 had opined that "any thought of having any kind of rescue was simply impossible, if not crazy," found himself fully agreeing in April 1980 with the highly risky hostage rescue plan. As he subsequently explained, "A year later, with the pressures . . . that were everywhere, you tended to be more willing to take a risk." In some cases, planners sense in their superiors such a strong desire to proceed with the mission that they feel negative information would be unwelcome. In the *Mayaguez* operation, senior commanders at USSAG headquarters had misgivings about a hasty assault on Koh Tang, but the tone of the messages from Washington intimated that doubts would be poorly received. As one senior USSAG officer, Brigadier General Baxter, commented after the operation, "It was immaterial to find out [new information about the enemy at Koh Tang] because the Marines were going to be ordered in anyway."[18]

In addition, enthusiastic planners eager to see a mission proceed sometimes suppress negative information about their plan. In the Bay of Pigs, the CIA discouraged dissent within the agency and strove to mute outside criticism. CIA Director Dulles personally appealed to Brigadier General Lansdale, an old friend, to stop criticizing the scheme. The CIA kept quiet about the Brigade's morale problems. They extolled the superior training the exiles had received but never mentioned that the landing force would include troops with little or no training at all. Well aware that Kennedy's attempts to render the operation "quiet" weakened the plan by reducing the likelihood of rebellion and defection in Cuba, the CIA nonetheless said nothing. In short, because of oversight, caution, or overenthusiasm, planners are unlikely to point out the weaknesses of a proposed operation. If the only others reviewing it are senior JCS and administration officials who lack the time and often expertise for an exhaustive review, the president may never learn of important shortcomings of the plan.

This is not, however, the only reason that presidents have received one-sided information. In several cases, although the JCS or senior White House advisers perceived weaknesses in a proposed plan, they failed to emphasize them strongly in discussions with the president.

In the Bay of Pigs, despite the limited time the JCS devoted to the plan, they noted major flaws in the CIA's tactical and logistical planning. The chiefs' criticism of these deficiencies was muted. They reserved some of their shrillest criticisms for the CIA proposal to use Guantánamo Bay as a fallback position for the exiles, which would have directly threatened the military's interests. Meanwhile, Secretary of State Rusk was skeptical about the plan, convinced it violated international law, could not remain covert, and that the expected uprisings would never materialize. Yet Rusk raised no strong doubts during the planning meetings, preferring to express his opposition to the president privately. Presidential Special Assistant Schlesinger also opposed the Cuban venture, convinced, in particular, that the promised uprisings would never materialize and that the invasion would lead to protracted civil war. But Schlesinger also dissented cautiously. He raised doubts in a few private conversations with the president or in memoranda to him but never spoke up in White House meetings. In the *Mayaguez* operation, while acting Chairman of the JCS General Jones worried about poor intelligence on enemy forces and the resistance the Marines might face, he never voiced forceful reservations.

In some instances, the advisers' reticence reflects bureaucratic parochialism. In the Bay of Pigs, the Joint Chiefs muted their criticism in large part because it was a CIA, not a military, plan and did not affect vital military interests. In Schlesinger's case, the motivation was bureaucratic prudence. Unsure of his role and standing in the new administration, he did not feel he could openly challenge the more senior officials who favored the plan. Rusk's reluctance to speak up in meetings stemmed in part from his concept of his role. He believed the secretary of state should stay above the fray in large meetings and offer his views to the president privately. But part of Rusk's reluctance reflected the prudence of a savvy bureaucratic player who knew that his power base in the new administration was still uncertain.

In other cases, presidents themselves may have unwittingly encouraged their senior advisers to still their doubts. Once the chief executive expresses a preference for a course of action, it takes strong advisers to object. The temptation for most is to fall in line and loyally support what they perceive as the president's choice. As former White House assistant George Reedy has written:

> The first strong observations to attract the favor of the president become subconsciously the thoughts of everyone in the room. The focus of attention shifts from a testing of all concepts to a groping for means of overcoming the difficulties. A thesis which could not survive an undergraduate seminar in a liberal-arts college becomes accepted doctrine, and the only question is not *whether* it should be done but *how* it should be done.[19]

In White House discussions on the Sontay mission and the *Mayaguez* operation, each president quickly made clear his preference to proceed with the operation. Nixon approved the Sontay raid in principle at the close of the first briefing the military gave him on the mission. By the end of the first twenty-four hours of the *Mayaguez* crisis, it was clear that Ford favored launching a rescue mission at the earliest possible opportunity—a preference that may well have inspired General Jones to downplay his misgivings.

Another reason reason that presidents receive faulty information is that they often fail to ask the right questions. In the White House briefings leading up to the Sontay raid, the president and his advisers never asked the military officers how they knew that American POWs were still at the camp. In the Bay of Pigs, the White House never asked the JCS for figures to illustrate what they meant when they said that the plan had a fair chance of success. The White House, buoyed by CIA assurances that the chances of success were about two out of three, might have been shocked to learn that for Brigadier General Gray and the JCS team that studied the plan, fair chance meant the odds were 30 to 70. As Rusk later mused:

> I failed President Kennedy by not insisting that he ask a question that he did not ask. He should have turned to our Joint Chiefs of Staff and said to them: "Now gentlemen, I may want to do this with U.S. forces, so you tell me what you would need. . . ." By the time the Joint Chiefs had come in with their sustained and prolonged bombing, their several divisions, a massive fleet, and their big air force, it would have become obvious to the President that that little brigade didn't have a chance at all.[20]

In the White House meetings leading up to the Iran rescue mission, Carter and his senior advisers never asked the military planners to quantify what they meant by good chance of success. National Security Adviser Brzezinski assumed this meant a high probability of success. The White House never realized that in the mind of one chief planner, the probability of success was about 50 percent. According to Brzezinski, had a senior military official said there was only a 50-50 chance, the president would not have approved the mission.

Wishful Thinking

Wishful thinking appears to be another recurrent problem in strategic special operations. For policymakers, strategic special operations offer the possibility of settling cheaply and at a single stroke major foreign policy problems that often seem otherwise nearly insoluble, such as the Iran hostage crisis. Planners, moreover, may have high personal or organizational stakes in seeing a proposed operation work, as was the case with the CIA in the Bay of Pigs. Hence, for policymakers and planners alike, strategic special operations often hold considerable appeal. The desire to see them succeed can result in wishful thinking, in which emotions color perceptions and judgments, leading planners and decision makers to mistake wishes for reality.[21] CIA Deputy Director Bissell and other senior officials closely involved in the Bay of Pigs have conceded that swayed by their hopes the invasion would succeed, they let wishful thinking affect their judgments. Two of President Kennedy's White House advisers, Arthur Schlesinger and Theodore Sorensen, have suggested it colored the president's thinking as well. Sorensen wrote, looking back, "For once John Kennedy permitted his hopes to overcome his doubts, and the possibilities of failure were never properly considered."[22]

Although the evidence is still limited, wishful thinking seems to have played a role in other strategic special operations as well. Recalling his first briefing on the Iran rescue mission, White House Chief of Staff Jordan writes how "I couldn't even contemplate failure.... I wanted desperately for this Godforsaken crisis to be over and done with."[23]

Wishful thinking in strategic special operations appears to have taken several forms. In some cases planners or decision makers have designed or evaluated these missions, making assumptions that had limited basis in fact but that spoke to their hopes of seeing the operations succeed. The most egregious case was the Bay of Pigs, where the planners assumed that a strong showing by the exiles would prompt anti-Castro Cubans to rise, whereas the bulk of U.S. intelligence showed that Castro's regime was tightening its grip steadily. In the Iran rescue mission, the planners lightly assumed that if they whisked out of Iran the passersby who were liable to stumble across the commandos at Desert One, Iranian authorities were unlikely to search for the missing persons and uncover evidence of the raiders' presence in Iran. The planners likewise downplayed the difficulties of infiltrating some hundred commandos into Tehran, then withdrawing them, along with fifty hostages, by helicopter, at night, in an unfamiliar city swarming with armed enemies, following a gun battle with the guards at the embassy compound.

Another form of wishful thinking, which often accompanies the first, is the rejection of information that runs counter to the planners' or decision makers' hopes for success. In the Bay of Pigs, Kennedy and his key advisers clung to the belief that the U.S. government could hide its hand in the invasion, even as the U.S. press was publishing detailed accounts of the invasion preparations in Miami and Guatemala. In the Iran rescue mission, the Delta Force commander was worried about the attitude and performance of the helicopter crews. Yet, despite the key role they would play in the mission, Beckwith ultimately wished the problem away.

Finally, the blind desire to see a proposed operation go ahead and succeed can foster a third and most extreme form of wishful thinking. Then occurs what may be called, to borrow Samuel T. Coleridge's expression, coined to designate less dangerous flights of fancy, the "willing suspension of disbelief."[24] At this point, planners or decision makers, taken with a course of action, cease to analyze it carefully and simply ignore or gloss over its drawbacks. Henry Kissinger has described how this occurred in the Nixon White House, as it examined the plan for what ultimately turned out to be the South Vietnamese Army's disastrous 1971 foray against the Ho Chi Minh trail in Laos: "We allowed ourselves to be carried away by the daring conception ... by the memory of the success in Cambodia, and by the prospect of a decisive turn. Energies were soon absorbed not in careful analysis but in the interdepartmental maneuvering through which the Nixon Administration made its decisions."[25]

Such wishful thinking seems to have occurred in the *Mayaguez* episode. Within barely twenty-four hours, the Ford administration, smarting from the humiliation of recent debacles in Cambodia and South Vietnam, chose to recover the crew by force. Lacking, however, was a hard-nosed evaluation of the rescue plan. In its enthusiasm for a rescue mission, the administration seems to have wished away the plan's many deficiencies. It disregarded the fact that the Cambodians might execute the captives when the Marines assaulted Koh Tang, brushed aside the major risks the attack posed to the Marines, and ignored the danger that a violent assault might kill the crew as well as their captors.[26]

Inappropriate Intervention in Mission Execution

A final recurrent problem in strategic special operations is inappropriate intervention by the White House and higher military headquarters in the operations as they unfold. Because of the high visibility of these missions and the stakes involved, the White House and the senior U.S. military leadership, including the JCS, follow their execution very closely. In the Sontay, *Mayaguez,* and Iran rescue missions, the National Military Command Center (NMCC) in the Pentagon maintained voice contact as the operations proceeded with the mission commanders, Brigadier General Manor in South Vietnam, Lieutenant General Burns in Thailand, and Major General Vaught in his command post in Egypt. In the *Mayaguez* operation, the NMCC and CinCPac, the military command responsible for all U.S. forces in Asia, could communicate directly with some of the units involved in the action at Koh Tang. In the Bay of Pigs, the poor communication link between the exiles at the beachhead and CIA headquarters made it far more difficult to follow events on the ground. As Robert Kennedy noted after the invasion, "Nobody was able to determine what was going on really there."[27] The White House and the Pentagon monitored the situation as closely as they could but to no avail.

During the Bay of Pigs and the *Mayaguez* episodes, the White House and senior military headquarters intervened in the operations as they were under way. In the Bay of Pigs, the White House canceled the planned D-day strike against Castro's airfields moments before the exiles' bombers took off. Later it sought to direct the movements of individual Navy ships trying to rescue Brigade survivors. In the *Mayaguez* operation, the Pentagon and CinCPac gave tactical instructions on executing the operation to the overall operation commander in Thailand, Lieutenant General Burns, and several of the units directly engaged in the fighting.

As eighteenth-century Prussian strategist Carl von Clausewitz observed, war is a "continuation of political intercourse, carried on with other means."[28] The president may rightfully intervene in an ongoing operation if he perceives that U.S. political interests require it. Kennedy was duly exercising his authority as chief executive and commander in chief in canceling the D-day strike. The way he did it, however, was wrong.

Success in warfare requires specialized knowledge and skills. The president should not alter an operation under way without first consulting his senior military advisers, who have this expertise, about the implications of the changes. Kennedy, however, canceled the D-day strike without consulting either the CIA or the military. Within hours, CIA Deputy Director Cabell and Deputy Director for Plans Bissell called on Secretary of State Rusk to protest the decision, outlining in measured terms the grave risks it entailed; Rusk conveyed these objections to the president. But Kennedy never solicited the views of the JCS, who, more senior than Cabell or Bissell, might have been more emphatic about the potentially catastrophic consequences of the decision for the Brigade. Lemnitzer stated after the invasion that, if consulted, he would have strongly opposed the cancellation. When, a few hours before the landing, Joint Staff officers informed him of Kennedy's decision, Lemnitzer considered the decision "absolutely reprehensible, almost criminal."[29] It is unclear that Kennedy fully understood the military implications of his decision until Castro's remaining airplanes decimated the exiles' fleet.

Moreover, the White House or senior military authorities should intervene in strategic special operations under way only to make changes required by high-level U.S. political interests or by an altered military situation of which the commandos are not aware. The Pentagon, for instance, might call back a force proceeding toward its objective if U.S. intelligence discovers that the enemy has detected the raiders and that the vital element of surprise is lost. The White House and higher military authorities must resist, however, the temptation, made possible by instantaneous modern communications, to substitute themselves for the on-scene commander and try to direct, from thousands of miles away, the tactical execution of the operation on the ground. The local commander's understanding of the tactical situation is inevitably better than that of the White House or some remote military headquarters.

The bulk of the information that the White House and higher military headquarters receive on operations under way comes from the commanders and units conducting the action. Yet, even when Washington or overseas commands can communicate directly with the forces engaged, these distant headquarters will always have an incomplete picture of the tactical situation. Commanders in combat lack the time for minute-by-minute descriptions of unfolding events. Nor can they, in brief radio communications, convey the full complexity of what they face, which in many cases they may sense intuitively more than they understand.

Furthermore, information flowing to the White House and higher military commands may be not only incomplete but wrong as well. In many cases, information proceeds from the units in the field to higher commands through a series of relays. In the *Mayaguez* operation, much of the information that flowed to Washington went from the Marines on Koh Tang to the orbiting command and control post, which relayed it to USSAG in Thailand and CinCPac in Hawaii, which in turn passed it on to Washington. At each relay point, those passing on the information may unwittingly misinterpret incoming messages and pass on distorted information. In addition, higher headquarters typically have a voracious appetite for information and frequently demand more reports. Lower commands thus may forward on whatever is at hand, even if they themselves do not fully understand the situation on the ground. As one of the senior officers of USSAG's battle staff noted after the *Mayaguez* operation: "[Higher headquarters'] desire for detailed information is counterproductive at best and can result in misleading details being forwarded just to satisfy the requirement."[30]

Attempts by the White House or higher commands to direct the tactical execution of operations run the risk of being based on incomplete and possibly erroneous information. The result can be highly misguided orders. In the *Mayaguez* operation, CinCPac, because of a wrong understanding of the tactical situation, gave a number of orders ranging from farcical to near-tragic. At one point, CinCPac called off the insertion of a second wave of troops on Koh Tang while the first wave of Marines, badly outnumbered, were fighting for their lives. Fortunately, following protests by USSAG's General Burns and other senior officers who realized the Marines' desperate straits, CinCPac rescinded the order.

Overcontrol by higher commands has other negative consequences as well. The requirement for mission commanders to report constantly distracts them from their primary task of running a successful mission. Second-guessing by Washington or other higher commands also inhibits mission commanders' initiative. Former Army chief of staff General Bruce Palmer has observed: "Success in such ventures comes only to the bold, and the bold must be left to their own intuition, judgments, and decisions."[31]

In summary, recurrent problems have marred strategic special operations, from the Bay of Pigs to the Iran raid, and have been a chief cause of their dismal outcomes. The two most common flaws in these episodes were poor coordination and provision of inadequate information to the White House. Poor coordination was arguably the most serious problem of the Iran raid and a major problem in the Bay of Pigs and the *Mayaguez* operations. It also affected early preparations for the Sontay raid—although in this last case the planners and mission commanders eventually overcame the problem. The provision of inadequate information to the president was the gravest shortcoming of the Bay of Pigs invasion, a serious weakness of the Iran mission, and a problem in the *Mayaguez* operation. It also was a flaw in the Sontay mission, whose plans received insufficient review. Inadequate intelligence was the major cause of the failure at Sontay, an important contributor to the Bay of Pigs debacle, and a significant handicap in preparing the Iran raid. Wishful thinking was perhaps the worst flaw of the *Mayaguez* episode. It also was a serious problem in the Bay of Pigs and may have marred decision making in the Iranian mission as well. Inappropriate intervention in mission execution occurred in the Bay of Pigs and the *Mayaguez* operations. Not surprisingly, the operation that came closest to success, Sontay, displayed the fewest of these recurrent flaws.

Addressing the Problems of Strategic Special Operations

The United States has conducted five strategic special operations in the past thirty years. Although the end of the cold war has caused the threat of global nuclear Armageddon to recede, the international environment is still far from benign. There remain states and groups, such as terrorists, hostile to U.S. interests and willing to challenge them by force. In this context, it is likely that U.S. leaders will, at some point, again face a situation where strategic special operations seem an attractive option. To prevent a recurrence of the problems that plagued the planning, preparation, evaluation, and execution of previous operations, changes in organizations, procedures, and mind-sets are in order. Some of these changes have, in fact, been under way for the past decade, as U.S. civilian and military leaders, dismayed by the country's poor record in strategic special operations, have sought to come to grips with the problem. More progress, however, is necessary.

Organizational Changes

U.S. intelligence agencies must continue to enhance their collection of human intelligence, particularly in the Third World, where threats to U.S. interests, notably terrorism and hostage-taking, will likely grow in coming years. In the early 1980s, the U.S. intelligence community became increasingly aware that HUMINT collection was inadequate. Under Director of Central Intelligence William J. Casey, the CIA aggressively sought to upgrade its HUMINT capabilities, increasing its personnel by a third and hiring hundreds of additional agents to collect human intelligence overseas. By the mid-1980s, the CIA reportedly had come close to worldwide coverage, devoting a share of its resources to almost every country in the world. The number of its agents in the Third World was up considerably.[32]

The military also has sought to enhance its HUMINT capabilities. In 1980 the Army, unhappy with CIA performance in the Iran hostage crisis and the intelligence community's overall ability to provide the specialized intelligence the military required, quietly created the Intelligence Support Agency (ISA) for covert HUMINT collection. Since its creation, ISA has been shrouded in secrecy, although in the mid-1980s some of its members' illegal doings attracted congressional and media attention. The most secret unit in the Army, it operates as a branch of the Defense Intelligence Agency. Officially, the Pentagon does not acknowledge it exists.[33]

Despite these efforts, there are still obvious shortcomings in U.S. HUMINT capabilities. The 1983 invasion of Grenada caught the CIA without a single agent on the island. U.S. estimates of the number of Cuban troops on Grenada proved wrong. Although a stated reason for the invasion was the rescue of American students, who, the administration believed, were endangered by the anarchy on the island, the United States did not know where many of them were. U.S. forces took three days to locate and reach some four hundred students living on the western half of the island.[34]

During the 1989 U.S. invasion of Panama, Panamanian strongman General Manuel Antonio Noriega evaded for days U.S. intelligence agents and armed forces seeking to capture him. Information on key Panamanian military units and objectives was also spotty, contributing to the high casualties U.S. Navy special operations forces (Sea-Air-Land teams, or SEALs) suffered during a raid on Panama's Paitilla Airport. After the invasion, one of the most senior officers overseeing U.S. special operations forces, Major General Hugh L. Cox, acknowledged that "again, as in the Grenada operation, the human intelligence factor that can contribute to mission success was not what it should have been or perhaps even could have been, and we need to do a better job for the future in that particular area."[35] These HUMINT shortcomings occurred even though there has been a large, permanent U.S. presence in Panama—including thousands of U.S. troops—for nearly a century.

In the Persian Gulf war, U.S. intelligence scored important successes. It kept close tabs, for instance, on the location of Iraq's armed forces and the equipment they fielded. But it also had serious gaps, particularly in areas where the best information comes from HUMINT. It failed, for example, to predict accurately the Iraqi forces' strength and willingness to fight. Commenting shortly after the war on U.S. intelligence in the conflict, General Carl W. Stiner, commander of the U.S. military's Special Operations Command, observed, "We had outstanding overhead systems.... But the United States—and this is no secret—is weak in the area of HUMINT intelligence." One frustrated Air Force officer reportedly exclaimed during the campaign that he would willingly trade all the overhead imagery for a reliable agent on the ground.[36]

The United States must continue to build up its human intelligence capabilities, and, with the end of the cold war, focus them more on Third World targets, from where threats to U.S. security increasingly are likely to come. Simultaneously, however, the executive and legislative branches both must exercise careful oversight of such intelligence activities. This is particularly true of units such as the Intelligence Support Activity, which, in its early years, operated with limited control by the top military leadership and none by Congress. Only careful oversight can ensure that overzealous operatives do not engage in unsanctioned covert operations or otherwise venture beyond the pale of the law.[37]

In addition, the history of strategic special operations in the past thirty years makes clear that relying on *ad hoc* groups and forces to plan and carry out these missions invites problems and, ultimately, failure. What the United States needs—and finally achieved in the past few years—is a permanent organization dedicated to preparing for and, as required, conducting special operations, and that also controls the forces required to execute them.

The advantages of such a standing organization are several. It is able to develop close, permanent ties to other organizations, notably the intelligence agencies, whose support is vital in special operations. By training together regularly, the forces it controls can achieve the cohesion and teamwork indispensable for success. A standing special operations organization, with a permanent cadre of specially trained forces also makes it possible, in a crisis, to devise more quickly an effective special operations response. In the Sontay and Iran missions, where the United States had first to assemble *ad hoc* planning groups and train appropriate forces, it took respectively four and three months to develop comprehensive rescue plans and the forces capable of executing them. A standing organization also ensures that when a strategic special operation is necessary, those available to do the job are steeped in the mind-set needed for successful operations. Success in special operations requires, besides proficient and cohesive forces, personnel who are bold, self-reliant, flexible and good at improvising, and adept at using and exploiting deception and surprise. This is a combination of traits that many otherwise well-trained and capable military personnel do not necessarily have.[38]

The United States has slowly fashioned such an organization. Shaken by the fiasco in Iran and spurred by the Special Operations Review Group that investigated it, which recommended creating a counterterrorist joint task force with a permanent staff and forces,[39] in 1982 the Department of Defense created the Joint Special Operations Command (JSOC). The Pentagon described JSOC as a "joint headquarters designed to study special operations requirements and techniques of all services to ensure standardization." It also was charged with planning and executing special operations. It directly controlled a limited number of U.S. special forces units, chiefly the Army's Delta Force, whose primary mission is antiterrorism, and SEAL team 6, an antiterrorist unit drawn from the elite Navy SEALs.[40]

JSOC's performance, however, was disappointing in Grenada, where most of the half dozen special operations it ran failed.[41] In early

1984 the Department of Defense created an additional special operations body, the Joint Special Operations Agency (JSOA). JSOA was an advisory body, which, according to its charter, advised "the JCS in all matters pertaining to special operations." Although it lacked control over specific forces, it developed special operations strategies and suggested ways of improving coordination between special operations units, most of which remained scattered under the operational control of their respective parent services, the Army, Navy, and Air Force.[42] By the mid-1980s these units included the Army's Delta Force, Rangers, Special Forces (popularly known as Green Berets), and Task Force 160, which provided helicopter and light aviation support to other Army special operations forces; the Navy's SEALs; and the Air Force's First Special Operations Wing. Concurrently with the creation of JSOC and JSOA, the Reagan administration embarked on a program of "revitalization" of U.S. special forces. Between 1981 and 1987, spending on these forces rose from $440 million to $1.1 billion a year. Their active-duty personnel went from 11,600 to more than 15,000.[43] Yet despite these changes, the problems of coordination posed by these widely dispersed special operations forces continued to worry many. As Noel C. Koch, then a deputy assistant secretary of defense with responsibility for special operations, observed in 1986: "Talk to anybody in the [special operations] community and ask them, 'What keeps you up at night?' They tell you it's command and control."[44]

That year Congress legislated a sweeping reform of U.S. special operations. For several years a small group in Congress, including senators William S. Cohen and Sam Nunn and congressmen Dan Daniel, Earl Hutto, and John R. Kasich, had studied the problems of U.S. special operations. Among their chief concerns were the fragmentation of the command of special operations forces and what they viewed as the services' halfhearted commitment to improving these forces—even though the administration viewed the upgrading of special operations forces as a priority. The group noted with dismay, for example, that five years after the failed Iran rescue mission, the military had the same number of special-operations-capable C-130 transport aircraft and even fewer long-range special-operations helicopters than at the time of Desert One.[45]

Convinced that the services would not take special operations reform seriously unless compelled to, the congressional reformers persuaded Congress to pass the Cohen-Nunn amendment to the Fiscal Year 1987 National Defense Authorization Bill. The amendment, and companion legislation adopted in 1987 and 1988, created a unified special operations command, the U.S. Special Operations Command (USSOCOM), headed by a four-star general officer reporting directly to the Chairman of the Joint Chiefs of Staff. USSOCOM has operational command of all special operations forces based in the continental United States, which for the first time come under a single commander. USSOCOM is responsible for organizing, training, and equipping special operations forces and providing combat-ready special operations elements to the military's regional commanders in chief (CINCs). USSOCOM also plans and executes special operations itself when so directed by the president or the secretary of defense.[46]

Additional USSOCOM duties include devising special operations strategy, doctrine, and tactics; developing and acquiring specialized equipment for special operations; and monitoring the promotions and careers of special operations personnel throughout the military. USSOCOM also prepares for the secretary of defense's approval the U.S. military's special operations budget. To increase further the attention special operations forces receive in the Pentagon, Congress also created the post of assistant secretary of defense for special operations and low intensity conflict (or, in the Pentagon's shorthand, ASD-SOLIC). This position gave special operations forces a high-level civilian advocate in the Pentagon bureaucracy, who, along with USSOCOM's Commander in Chief (USCINCSOC), can bring their needs and concerns to the secretary of defense's attention.[47]

The Pentagon's implementation of the legislation was hesitant at first. USSOCOM was formally established at MacDill Air Force Base in Florida in April 1987. But the Department of Defense waited more than a year to nominate an assistant secretary of defense for special operations, and originally assigned him limited staff. In the face of continued pressure from Congress, however, the Pentagon, in the words of Assistant Secretary of Defense Richard L. Armitage, got "the message."[48]

USSOCOM has become a major military command, controlling some 46,000 active and reserve special operations forces. Besides its headquarters staff, it maintains four component commands: the U.S. Army Special Operations Command, the Naval Special Warfare Command, the Air Force Special Operations Command, and the Joint Special Operations Command (JSOC). According to USSOCOM, JSOC "concentrates on joint special operations tactics and techniques." USSOCOM's forces train extensively, both with one another and with conventional forces of the armed services. With USSOCOM, the United States finally has an organization that can overcome many of the problems of coordination that have plagued U.S. strategic special operations of the past thirty years. In addition, thanks to the greater visibility USSOCOM and the ASD-SOLIC have given to special operations and to Congress's continued support for its practitioners, special operations funding remains high. The budget for U.S. special operations forces for Fiscal Year (FY) 1992 was $3.11 billion, up from $2.54 billion in FY1991; the budget request for FY1993 is $2.96 million. At a time when, with the end of the cold war, the rest of the military is shrinking, U.S. special operations forces are expected to expand slightly, with the addition of additional Army Special Forces units and Navy SEAL platoons.[49]

Though USSOCOM is only a few years old, it already has had a positive effect on U.S. special operations capabilities. Since USSOCOM's creation, the United States has been engaged in two conflicts: the Panama invasion and the Persian Gulf war. In both cases the special operations forces USSOCOM provided to the regional U.S. commands saw extensive action. In Panama, some 4,100 U.S. special operations personnel and 71 special operations aircraft, operating under the control of the U.S. Southern Command (SOUTHCOM), participated in Operation Just Cause. Although they did not conduct strategic special operations, they supported conventional forces by conducting reconnaissance and securing key objectives. Delta Force also rescued from a Panamanian prison an American held on spying charges. Although there were mishaps, the bulk of these missions were successful. In contrast to the strategic special operations of the past three decades, in particular in Just Cause, coordination among special operations forces and between these forces and conventional forces was excellent.[50]

Special operations forces saw even more action in the Persian Gulf war. Besides conducting a strategic special operation—helping track down the mobile Scud missiles Iraq was launching against Israel, threatening to drag it into the war—they undertook many other missions in support of Central Command's (CENTCOM) conventional forces. A flight of Air Force special operations helicopters opened the air war. On the first night of the coalition's aerial bombing campaign, MH-53 Pave Low helicopters, which specialize in the penetration of hostile airspace, led the Army attack helicopters that destroyed key Iraqi radar stations, opening a corridor for coalition jets to use on their raids into Iraq. Special forces conducted reconnaissance deep into Iraq. They helped divert Iraq's attention from the main thrust of the coalition's land offensive by simulating amphibious landings along the Kuwaiti coast. They rescued downed pilots in hostile territory. Although many details of these operations are classified, again the majority were successful, and apparently largely free of the problems of coordination that were such a problem in the past. Following the reform and revitalization efforts of recent years, U.S. special operations forces have become a well-integrated and well-honed military tool.[51]

Procedural Changes

Procedural changes are also needed to avoid some of the problems that have plagued strategic special operations in the past. Simply put, review and evaluation of proposed strategic special operations must be more thorough. Neither the Joint Chiefs of Staff nor the president should accept at face value planners' assertions and recommendations. Given the stakes involved, the Joint Chiefs should make every effort to review proposed plans as extensively they can. As noted earlier, however, it is not realistic to expect either the Joint Chiefs or the White House to review in detail every aspect of planning and preparation. Thus, when the planners believe they have a workable plan and the forces capable of executing it, a separate group of experts should review the project exhaustively.

This group would consist of experts with extensive special operations background and, as appropriate, regional expertise. To ensure that they have no personal stake in the operation, they should not have been associated with the earlier planning. They should be freed from other duties to devote themselves to this review, and instructed to probe as thoroughly and report back as candidly as possible. They would have authority to scrutinize every aspect of the preparations, from the concept of the plan to the training, motivation, and readiness of the forces that are to execute it. Time allowing, as part of this review the group would observe training in the field and spend time with the troops involved. The group's report would go to both the JCS and the White House.

The members of this group could come from USSOCOM personnel who are not part of the planning group, Joint Staff personnel with a special operations background, or a combination of both. To enhance its independence and objectivity, the group could include members of the Special Operations Policy Advisory Group (SOPAG). Formed shortly after the Iran rescue mission fiasco and upon the recommendation of the 1980 Special Operations Review Group, SOPAG comprises retired senior military personnel with considerable special operations background. They have an ongoing interest in special operations and maintain active security clearances. Although they advise the JCS on a range of special operations issues, the Special Operations Review Group saw the group's main purpose as the review of "highly classified special operations planning to provide an independent assessment function, which might otherwise be lacking due to the absence of the echelons of Service staff planners who normally review and critique JCS planning of a less sensitive nature."[52] The participation of SOPAG members, who, being retired, have little to lose by outspokenness, could help ensure a fully candid review.

In the past, the United States has paid a high price because special operations schemes contained flaws that never came to the attention of the senior military and civilian leadership. In the future, these leaders should spare no effort to obtain the most thorough and objective assessment possible of proposed operations.[53]

In addition, the president should make clear to his senior military advisers that he expects candid assessments from them as well. Until he makes up his mind about a proposed operation, he should avoid, to keep White House debates as frank as possible, giving any indication that he is inclined to favor or oppose the scheme. Once an operation is under way, the White House and senior military authorities should not intervene except when overriding political interests require it, or when

Washington receives key information the on-scene commander lacks. Efforts to micromanage the mission from afar will weaken the operation, heighten the risks run by U.S. troops, and increase the chance of failure. In the past decade, the White House and the Pentagon, aware of the problems caused by overcontrol of operations in the field, have stepped back from the micromanagement of military operations that characterized, for instance, the Vietnam War. In Grenada, Panama, and the Persian Gulf war, they avoided interfering in the local commanders' execution of military operations. But with today's instantaneous communications and the flood of information that satellites and other technical means of collection provide to Washington decision makers—fostering the impression they know as much as the commander on the spot—the temptation to intervene will always exist. Future Washington decision makers must exercise the same restraint as recent ones.[54]

Mind-set Changes

If the United States is to improve its ability to use special operations effectively and wisely, changes in mind-set are also in order. One problem is the suspicion of special operations that lingers among U.S. conventional armed forces. The United States has a long tradition of special operations, which includes the exploits of Francis Marion, the South Carolina "Swamp Fox" of the Revolutionary War; John Singleton Mosby and his Confederate raiders in the Civil War; and Merrill's Marauders in World War II. Yet, though Americans often have been skilled special operations practitioners, much of the U.S. military establishment has traditionally been skeptical of such warfare and those who practice it. As Brigadier General Blackburn, the driving force behind the Sontay raid, once remarked, "Special Forces have always been the bastards of the Army."[55]

The reasons for the conventional military's mistrust of special operations forces are, in part, historical. Special operations forces alienated many conventional officers in Vietnam by the image they often cultivated, as one officer recalled, the "Rambo mentality—the sun-shades, the Rolex watches" and by what some regarded as a privileged lifestyle. In the words of the same officer, "In Vietnam, some of the guys were living in lush camps in the mountains with TV, hot and cold running water and choppers delivering beer and steak. The rest of the Army became quite angry and decided to get rid of them when they got the chance. They got the chance after Vietnam." A number of those who, as junior officers, resented special operations forces in Vietnam are in the upper ranks of the U.S. military today.[56] In addition, for most of the cold war, the U.S. military's main focus was on deterring nuclear aggression and preparing for a major conventional war in Europe. The emphasis was on large weapons systems and heavy units. Special operations forces, deemed peripheral to these missions, held little appeal for most of the military.[57]

But the most enduring reason for the conventional military officers' frequent mistrust of special forces is the latter's elitist nature. Special operations units require above-average personnel, and tend to drain a disproportionately high share of the military's better enlisted men and noncommissioned officers. The result, in the words of former army chief of staff General Bruce Palmer, is that "when you form too many of them, you drain off too much 'cream' from the rest of the Army."[58]

Moreover, a common belief among many conventional officers is that special operations do not require unique skills. In this view, a well-trained force adept at classic military missions can handle unconventional operations just as ably. President Kennedy's personal military counselor, General Maxwell D. Taylor, epitomized this view when commenting on Kennedy's insistence that the U.S. military give more emphasis to counterinsurgency. Taylor downplayed counterinsurgency as "just a form of small war, a guerrilla operation in which we have a long record against the Indians. Any well trained organization can shift the tempo to that which might be required in this kind of situation."[59] Many in the military continue to believe that soldiers good at conventional warfare can easily "shift the tempo" to conventional warfare, be it counterinsurgency or special operations.

This skepticism of the elitist nature of special forces runs deep. As one member of the Special Operations Advisory Group (SOPAG), retired Army chief of staff General Edward C. Meyer, testified to Congress shortly after USSOCOM's creation: "The creation of [USSOCOM] is likely to create schisms within the military itself. Within the Army, for example, in visits out to [the Army Command and General Staff College at] Fort Leavenworth, one of the members of SOPAG received a very clear signal that the average Army officer believes that the Army is going to create a group of elitists."[60]

This mistrust of special operations manifests itself in several ways. One illustration is the services' unenthusiastic efforts in the early 1980s to implement the administration's agenda of revitalizing special operations forces. Despite the greater resources allocated to special operations forces during this period, their readiness remained problematic, in part because the services failed to provide them all of the equipment they needed. Between 1980 and 1985 over half of U.S. special operations units earned readiness ratings of no better than "marginally ready." In a December 1985 training exercise, all eleven of the Air Force's 1st Special Operations Wing aircraft—its AC-130 gunships, special operations MC-130 transport planes, and HH-53 helicopters—had mechanical problems, forcing cancellation of the exercise.[61] In 1986, the number of aircraft outfitted for special operations was the same as in 1980, far below what military estimates showed were needed. Many of these aircraft were more than 20 years old. Yet in 1985 the Air Force's Military

AirLift Command (MAC) placed the improvement of special forces air-lift fifty-ninth on its list of priorities. MAC's fifty-third and fifty-fourth priorities were travel by senior Air Force personnel; its sixtieth priority was modernization of the aircraft that had been used to spread the de-foliant "Agent Orange" during the Vietnam war.[62] Following consider-able pressure from the Pentagon's civilian leadership and Congress, the military has since addressed most of these problems. The readiness of special operations forces now compares favorably to that of conven-tional forces, and a multibillion-dollar program to improve special op-erations airlift is under way.[63]

Still, the services' commitment to special operations forces remains less than enthusiastic, as evidenced by the hesitancy with which they first implemented the Cohen-Nunn amendment—prompting some in Congress to speak of "malicious implementation." This problem too has been solved since, but the services' ambivalence about special operations endures. In the late 1980s, when Secretary of Defense Frank C. Carlucci directed the Department of Defense to reduce its budget by 10 percent, the services' initial response was to recommend a 33 percent cut for special operations forces. Moreover, if special operations forces enjoy budget increases or suffer only modest cuts when the rest of the military must cut back markedly, resentment of this privileged status may build.[64]

On the other hand, special operations forces' successes in support of conventional forces in Panama and the Persian Gulf may increase the mainstream military's appreciation of its special forces peers. The latter will also enhance their chances of overcoming suspicions by carefully avoiding the arrogant aloofness that often characterized U.S. special forces in the past. More attention to special operations in the curricula of the services' academies and advanced schools also will help foster a better understanding of their usefulness. Ending the lingering suspicion of special forces that runs through much of the conventional military es-tablishment, however, will take time.

Until this happens, this mistrust can hamper U.S. special operations capabilities in several ways. It can discourage qualified personnel from pursuing special operations careers, diminishing the pool of top talent available to special operations forces. It can breed rivalries affecting the quality of cooperation between special and conventional forces. Most important, it means that the military establishment, if left to its own de-vices, is unlikely to provide special operations forces all of the support, especially financial, that they require. Until the conventional forces that dominate the military fully accept the importance of special operations forces, Congress and the executive must stay vigilant to ensure that spe-cial operations forces receive the support they need.

Another mind-set should also change among the military and civil-ian leadership alike: their readiness to embrace strategic special opera-tions when U.S. interests are challenged abroad. In the past thirty years, the United States has launched no fewer than five such operations. No other countries save Israel, locked in a bitter struggle with its foes, and France, prone to use special operations to preserve its interests in its former African colonies, have been so inclined to exercise this option over the same period.

One reason that the United States has exerted this option so readily is that, as a superpower, its interests span the globe. The price of this global reach is that U.S. interests are challenged overseas more often than those of other nations. Another reason is no doubt the far-flung military establishment the United States maintained for decades to wage the cold war. This worldwide military presence made it easier to dispatch U.S. forces in surgical actions to protect U.S. interests abroad. Yet another reason is strategic special operations' inherent appeal. They promise to solve—if they succeed—cheaply and at a single stroke apparently intractable foreign policy problems. For policymakers wrestling with a challenge for which there seems to be no other solution, this can be a powerful lure.

But this only partially explains why the United States has launched such operations repeatedly. After all, until recently the Soviet Union also had global interests, a military apparatus that extended far beyond its borders, and its share of international challenges that must have left more than one Kremlin decision maker wishing for fast, clean solutions. Yet strategic special operations never became a fixture of Soviet foreign policy.

Part of the reason that the United States has repeatedly embarked on these operations may have to do with American culture and national style.[65] Combativeness is a strong cultural trait of American society, in which the use of force to achieve societal or individual objectives is a deep-rooted tradition. European immigrants to this country used force extensively against the native inhabitants to gain control of the land. Today, the nation's infatuation with personal weapons and the dismaying frequency with which they are used, not to mention the pervasive violence on television and movie screens, is evidence that the use of force in pursuit of key interests remains deeply embedded in American social mores.

As the United States became a regional, then world power, Americans were naturally prone to carry beyond their borders the pugnacity that marked their dealings amongst themselves. Constraining this impulse, however, was the moralistic streak that permeates American society. The first European settlers to this country sought to create a society morally superior to those from which they came. War between nations was part of the corruption of the Old World that they sought to leave behind. Americans thus shunned the Clausewitzian view, so widespread on the Old Continent, that war was merely a continuation of politics by other means—an acceptable recourse. They regarded war among nations as inherently evil. For Americans, the only circumstance under which

U.S. involvement in armed conflict abroad became acceptable was a "just" war meant to chastize and reform a disruptive, morally deficient foe.[66]

The United States soon reconciled, however, its inherent pugnacity and its moral strictures about overseas military action. Americans were quick to cast their foreign foes as morally bankrupt and to regard accordingly U.S. military interventions abroad as noble ventures. In the first half of the century, besides participating in two world wars, the United States fought repeatedly overseas, including in the Philippines, China, Mexico, the Soviet Union, Santo Domingo, Nicaragua, and Haiti. In each case, the United States saw itself as upholding essential human values against benighted or evil foes. In the four decades of the cold war, in which communism became the primary, although not exclusive, morally deficient foe, overseas U.S. military action continued apace. Besides fighting in Korea and Vietnam, U.S. armed forces conducted several strategic special operations, skirmished in Lebanon and against Libya, and intervened in the Dominican Republic, Grenada, and Panama. In short, a combination of natural brashness and moral crusading makes the United States prone to flex its military muscle abroad. To a degree, the repeated use of strategic special operations is but one manifestation of this propensity to use force to advance U.S. foreign policy goals.

Other American cultural traits may also help explain the U.S. readiness to engage in strategic special operations. Americans are doers, accustomed to mastering through ingenuity and hard work challenges, be they conquering a continent or setting a man on the moon.[67] They find it difficult to accept that there are problems they cannot overcome. Americans are also impatient, keen on solving problems fast. These traits may make them particularly susceptible to the lure of strategic special operations. Challenges such as Castro's revolution or the holding of fifty hostages in Iran, which month after month defied resolution by conventional diplomacy, were especially galling for the can-do, impatient American mind. In such cases, with no other recourse in sight, Americans more than others may be open to the appeal of strategic special operations, which offer the prospect of a solution—and a quick one at that.

There may be yet another reason for the appeal of strategic special operations to Americans. These operations speak to a basic American cultural myth. Americans are fascinated by the hero figure who, alone or with a few like companions, handily overcomes far more numerous foes, despite overwhelming odds, because he or she is braver, tougher, smarter, and inspired by a just cause. From the real-life Daniel Boone to the celluloid heroes of Hollywood, these are cherished figures of American popular culture. Strategic special operations, where real-life heroes, acting for their country, defy a much larger foe, counting on superior skill and daring to prevail, embody this heroic ideal. U.S. decision makers, culturally predisposed to admire such exploits, thus may find themselves insidiously attracted to proposed strategic special operations.

The proclivity of the United States to engage in strategic special operations is dangerous. The cold fact is that special operations seek maximum results with a mimimum of means, in the process pushing men and machines to the limit. As Clausewitz observed, "War is the realm of chance. No other human activity gives it greater scope: no other has such incessant and varied dealings with this intruder." His dictum applies even more to special operations than to conventional combat.[68] No matter how good the planning and the forces, special operations are inherently high-risk operations, more vulnerable than any other kind of combat to the vicissitudes of chance. Military and civilian decision makers considering resorting to strategic special operations should remember their historically high failure rate: in World War II, three in four of all British and U.S. special operations conducted in the European theater failed.[69]

U.S. decision makers should guard carefully against letting the deceptive appeal of strategic special operations undermine sober and realistic judgment. They must see these ventures for what they are. At best, they are well-prepared, well-rehearsed, high-risk gambles, wherein the dangers of failure and significant damage to U.S. prestige are great. Strategic special operations should be the option of the last resort, when lives and key U.S. national interests are at stake, and no other acceptable option is at hand.

Of the four strategic special operations examined in this study, only one arguably met this description: Sontay. U.S. POWs, held in abysmal conditions, were dying. Meanwhile, no other option, short of surrendering to North Vietnamese demands, was at hand. None of the other strategic special operations, however, was as justified. In the *Mayaguez* operation, the welfare of the crew was a real concern—although not necessarily in the short term—and U.S. credibility in the region conceivably was at stake. Waiting only twenty-four hours, however, would have given diplomacy a greater chance to succeed. Had it failed, the extra time would have allowed the military to mount a far more effective operation than the near-disaster that took place. Neither the Cuban nor Iranian episodes was a critical threat to U.S. interests, even though there was little chance of reaching an accommodation with either country soon. In Cuba, there was no threat to American lives. In Iran, the captors had occasionally threatened to harm the hostages, but the captors' actual treatment of the prisoners indicated that they were in fact anxious not to have any hostages die in captivity.

In short, only one of these operations was fully justified when it was launched. The others caused loss of life and national humiliation the United States should have been spared. In the future, U.S. decision makers should be specially vigilant to ensure that strategic special operations are used only as they should be used: as truly operations of the last resort.

Notes

Preface

1. Paul L. Kesaris, ed., *Operation ZAPATA: The "Ultrasensitive" Report and Testimony of the Board of Inquiry on the Bay of Pigs* (Frederick, MD, 1981), 181; Special Operations Review Group, "Rescue Mission Report," Department of Defense, Washington, DC, August 1980, 21.

2. On Guatemala, see Richard H. Immerman, *The CIA in Guatemala: The Foreign Policy of Intervention* (Austin, TX, 1982), and Stephen Schlesinger and Stephen Kinzer, *Bitter Fruit: The Untold Story of the American Coup in Guatemala* (Garden City, NY, 1982). On "Dragon Rouge," see Fred E. Wagoner, *Dragon Rouge: The Rescue of Hostages in the Congo* (Washington, DC, 1980). On "Eastern Exit," see Barton Gellman, "Amid Winds of War, Daring U.S. Rescue Got Little Notice," *Washington Post,* January 5, 1992, and Adam B. Siegel, "Lessons Learned From Operation EASTERN EXIT," *Marine Corps Gazette* 76 (June 1992): 74–81.

Chapter 1

1. Good accounts of the Bay of Pigs include Arthur M. Schlesinger, Jr., *A Thousand Days: John F. Kennedy in the White House* (Boston, 1965), 223–297; Peter Wyden, *Bay of Pigs: The Untold Story* (New York, 1979); and Trumbull Higgins, *The Perfect Failure: Kennedy, Eisenhower and the CIA at the Bay of Pigs* (New York, 1987).

2. The best work on Sontay is Benjamin F. Schemmer, *The Raid* (New York, 1976). On the *Mayaguez,* see Richard G. Head, Frisco W. Short, and Robert C. McFarlane, *Crisis Resolution: Presidential Decision Making in the May-*

aguez and Korean Confrontations (Boulder, CO, 1978), and Christopher Jon Lamb, *Belief Systems and Decision Making in the Mayaguez Crisis* (Gainesville, FL, 1988). On the Iran rescue mission, see Charlie A. Beckwith and Donald Knox, *Delta Force* (New York, 1983); Paul B. Ryan, *The Iranian Rescue Mission: Why It Failed* (Annapolis, 1985); James H. Kyle, *The Guts to Try* (New York, 1990); and Stansfield Turner, *Terrorism and Democracy* (Boston, 1991).

3. Strategic special operations are a subset of special operations. A good definition of special operations is "Small-scale, clandestine, covert or overt operations of an unorthodox and frequently high-risk nature, undertaken to achieve significant political or military objectives in support of foreign policy. Special operations are characterized by either simplicity or complexity, by subtlety and imagination, by the discriminate use of violence, and by oversight at the highest level. Military and nonmilitary resources, including intelligence assets, may be used in concert." Maurice Tugwell and David Charters, "Special Operations and the Threats to United States Interests in the 1980s," in Frank R. Barnett, B. Hugh Tovar, and Richard H. Shultz, eds., *Special Operations in US Strategy* (Washington, DC, 1984), 35.

The unconventional application of force differentiates strategic special operations from limited but conventional military strikes in support of major U.S. foreign policy objectives, like the 1986 air strike against Libya. The Bay of Pigs was unconventional in using a force of exiles to stage an amphibious landing with shoestring resources: a small fleet of mostly rickety cargo ships and a score of World War II–vintage bombers. The Sontay, *Mayaguez,* and Iran missions were unconventional in that their main object was the recovery of prisoners, not the neutralization or destruction of enemy forces or objectives.

4. On the operation against the Scuds, see Benjamin F. Schemmer, "Special Ops Teams Found 29 Scuds Ready to Barrage Israel 24 Hours Before Cease-Fire," *Armed Forces Journal International* 128 (July 1991): 36; and Douglas Waller, "Secret Warriors," *Newsweek,* June 17, 1991, 28. See the preface for more on the selection of the case studies for this work.

5. Richard M. Bissell, Jr., "Reflections on the Bay of Pigs Bay: OPERATION ZAPATA" (book review), *Strategic Review* 12 (Winter 1984): 69.

6. Beckwith and Knox, *Delta Force,* 295.

7. See, for example, Richard A. Gabriel, *Military Incompetence: Why the American Military Doesn't Win* (New York, 1985).

8. Quoted in Arthur M. Schlesinger, Jr., *Robert Kennedy and His Times* (Boston, 1978), 447.

9. Henry A. Kissinger, *White House Years* (Boston, 1979), 982.

10. Schlesinger, *A Thousand Days,* 259.

11. Bissell, "Reflections," 67.

12. Beckwith and Knox, *Delta Force,* 237.

Chapter 2

1. Senate Committee on Foreign Relations, *Events in United States–Cuban Relations: A Chronology, 1957–1963* (Washington, DC, 1963), 3–9.

2. Christian Herter, "Current Basic United States Policy Toward Cuba," November 5, 1959, Box 4, White House Office, Office of the Staff Secretary, International Series (hereafter WHO/OSS/IS), "Cuba (1) [59]," Dwight D. Eisenhower Presidential Library, Abilene, KS (hereafter DDEL).

3. On Guatemala, see Richard H. Immerman, *The CIA in Guatemala: The Foreign Policy of Intervention* (Austin, TX, 1982), and Stephen Schlesinger and Stephen Kinzer, *Bitter Fruit: The Untold Story of the American Coup in Guatemala* (Garden City, NY, 1982).

4. Herter, "Current Basic United States Policy Toward Cuba."

5. Senate Select Committee to Study Government Operations with respect to Intelligence Activities, *Alleged Assassination Plots Involving Foreign Leaders* (New York, 1976), 92–93. The Special Group comprised the president's assistant for national security affairs, the director of central intelligence, the deputy secretary of defense, and the under secretary of state for political affairs.

6. "Memorandum of Conference with the President," January 25, 1960, Box 47, Ann Whitman File, Dwight D. Eisenhower Diary Series (hereafter AWF/DDES), "Staff notes Jan 60 (1)"; Christian Herter to John W. Heselton, March 21, 1960, Box 8, Christian A. Herter Papers (hereafter CAHP), "Chronological file, Mar 60 (2)," DDEL.

7. Gordon Gray Oral History (hereafter OH) DDEL, 27.

8. "A Program of Covert Action against the Castro Regime," March 15, 1960, Declassified Documents Reference System (hereafter DDRS), 1989/000015; Paul L. Kesaris, ed., *Operation ZAPATA: The "Ultrasensitive" Report and Testimony of the Board of Inquiry on the Bay of Pigs* (Frederick, MD, 1981), 3–5 (*ZAPATA* reproduces key parts of the 1961 postmortem by a White House appointed board composed of retired General Maxwell D. Taylor, Chief of Naval Operations Admiral Arleigh A. Burke, CIA Director Allen W. Dulles, and Attorney General Robert F. Kennedy); Gray OH, 31–32.

9. Christian Herter, "The Problem of Cuba in the OAS," June 30, 1960, Box 4, WHO/OSS/IS, "Cuba (3) (May-July 1960)," DDEL.

10. On the Italian elections, see James E. Miller, *The United States and Italy, 1940–1950: The Politics and Diplomacy of Stabilization* (Chapel Hill, 1986); on Italy and the Philippines, see Allen W. Dulles, "Visit to the Honorable Harry S. Truman...," April 21, 1964, Box 122, Allen W. Dulles Papers (hereafter AWDP), "CIA 1964," Seeley Mudd Library, Princeton. Kermit Roosevelt, *Countercoup: The Struggle for the Control of Iran* (New York, 1979), is a CIA participant's account of the anti-Mossadegh plot. Thomas Powers, *The Man Who Kept the Secrets: Richard Helms & the CIA* (New York, 1979), sheds light on the Indonesian operation. Stephen E. Ambrose with Richard H. Immerman, *Ike's Spies: Eisenhower and the Espionage Establishment* (Garden City, NY, 1981), and Blanche Wiesen Cook, *The Declassified Eisenhower: A Divided Legacy* (Garden City, NY, 1981), offer comprehensive overviews of covert action under Eisenhower.

11. Lawrence R. Houston, interview with author, Washington, DC, February 20, 1984.

12. Richard M. Bissell, Jr., interview with author, Farmington, CT, January 14, 1981; E. Howard Hunt, *Undercover: Memoirs of an American Secret Agent* (New York, 1974), 86ff.

13. Quoted in Powers, *The Man*, 93–107; Peter Wyden, *Bay of Pigs: The Untold Story* (New York, 1979), 10–19.

14. Hayes Johnson, *The Bay of Pigs: The Leaders' Story of Brigade 2506* (New York, 1964), 33–38; Kesaris, *ZAPATA*, 4–5; Tad Szulc and Karl E. Meyer, *The Cuban Invasion: The Chronicle of a Disaster* (New York, 1962), 80–81.

15. Immerman, *The CIA in Guatemala,* 164ff; Schlesinger and Kinzer, *Bitter Fruit,* 167ff; Bissell, interview with author, Farmington, CT, May 18, 1984; "Brief History of Radio Swan" (n.d.; probably May 1961), DDRS 1985/001562.

16. Dwight D. Eisenhower, *The White House Years: Waging Peace, 1956–1961* (Garden City, NY, 1965), 525; Senate Committee on Foreign Relations, *Events,* 11–15; A. J. Goodpaster, "Memorandum of Conference with the President," May 16, 1960, Box 50, AWF/DDES, "Staff Notes Apr 60 (2)"; "Memorandum of Conference with the President," July 5, 1960, Box 4, WHO/OSS, Subject Series, State Department Subseries, DDEL.

17. "Memorandum for the Record," March 4, 1960, Box 47, AWF/DDES, "Staff Notes Feb 60 (1)"; Dwight D. Eisenhower note on Christian A. Herter, "Further Report on Status of Possible OAS Action on Cuba," April 23, 1960, Box 10, AWF, Dulles Herter Series (hereafter DHS), "Herter, C. Apr 60 (1)"; "The Declaration of San Jose, Costa Rica," Box 10, AWF/DHS, "Herter, C. Aug 60 (1)," DDEL.

18. "Legislative Meeting," August 16, 1960, Box 51, AWF/DDES, "Staff Notes Aug 60 (2)," DDEL.

19. Gray OH, 51–52.

20. Quoted in William Bragg Ewald, Jr., *Eisenhower the President: Crucial Days, 1951–1960* (Englewood Cliffs, NJ, 1981), 271. As early as 1956, a study mandated by the President's Board of Consultants on Foreign Intelligence Activities noted the CIA's "increased mingling in the internal affairs of other nations." No one, the report added, "other than those in the CIA immediately concerned . . . has any detailed knowledge of what is going on." Quoted in Arthur M. Schlesinger, Jr., *Robert Kennedy and His Times* (Boston, 1978), 455–456.

21. Richard M. Bissell, Jr., OH, John F. Kennedy Library, Boston, MA (hereafter JFKL), 30.

22. Ibid., 3.

23. Quoted in Wyden, *Bay of Pigs,* 69; Kesaris, *ZAPATA,* 7; message [CIA to Brigade trainers] (n.d.; probably November 1960), DDRS, 1985/001539.

24. Albert C. Persons, *Bay of Pigs* (Birmingham, AL, 1968), 34.

25. Kesaris, *ZAPATA,* 173; Wyden, *Bay of Pigs,* 46. After the election, defeated Republican candidate Richard M. Nixon asserted that the CIA had told Kennedy during the campaign that it was training exiles for an invasion. In a March 1962 memo to Kennedy, Special Assistant for National Security McGeorge Bundy wrote:

Allen Dulles reports that his notes for a July [1960] briefing do indicate that he was prepared to tell you that CIA was training Cuban exiles as guerrilla leaders and recruiting from refugees for more such training. He says he could not have briefed you on anything beyond that because nothing beyond this then existed. . . . it can be argued that what Nixon says is not wrong.

On the other hand, the impact of his charge remains entirely misleading, since it appears to refer to a briefing on the full scope of what was in the works in October. This you did not receive. . . . it appears that you had only sketchy and fragmentary information about covert relations to Cuban exiles and no briefing at all on any specific plan for an invasion.

McGeorge Bundy, "Nixon's Comments On Your Briefing On Cuba Before The Election," March 14, 1962, Box 35a/36, National Security Files (hereafter NSF), "Cuba, General," JFKL.

26. "Kennedy on Cuba" (n.d.; probably fall 1960), Box 991, John F. Kennedy Pre-Presidential Papers (hereafter JFKPPP), "Cuba," JFKL. On Cuba and the campaign, see Kent M. Beck, "Necessary Lies, Hidden Truths: Cuba in the 1960 Campaign," *Diplomatic History* 8 (Winter 1984): 46. Reports of the CIA training fueled concern in the Kennedy camp that, as one campaign memo put it, "the Administration might provoke some incident for Nixon's benefit before November 8." The candidate's brother, Robert F. Kennedy, resolved to "talk to Allen Dulles to make sure nothing being done [on] Cuba." A few days later, CIA Deputy Director Major General Charles P. Cabell met with the candidate. "Cuba, Latin American Prestige, Kennedy-Nixon TV Debate, Oct. 21, 1960," Box 991, JFKPPP, "Cuba"; "Telephone Calls-Tues. Oct 25," Box 34, Robert F. Kennedy Papers, Pre-Administration Political Files, JFKL; Huntington D. Sheldon, "Briefing of Presidential Candidates," November 1, 1960, Box 8, WHO/OSS, Subject Series, Alpha Subseries, "CIA, vol. III (5) Nov 60," DDEL.

27. Senate Committee on Foreign Relations, *Events*, 19.

28. Gordon Gray, memoranda of meetings with the President, November 10, November 28, December 5, 1960, and January 9, 1961, Box 5, WHO, Office of the Special Assistant for National Security Affairs (hereafter OSANSA), Special Assistant Series, Presidential Subseries (hereafter SAS/PS), "1960 Meetings with the President," A. J. Goodpaster, "Memorandum of Conversation with the President," January 6, 1961, Box 55, AWF/DDES, "Staff Notes Dec 60," DDEL; Whiting Willauer to John F. Kennedy, April 30, 1961, Box 4, Whiting Willauer Papers, Mudd Library; Schlesinger and Kinzer, *Bitter Fruit*, 156, 217.

29. Bissell interview, May 18, 1984; "Memorandum of Telephone Conversation with Secretary," November 14, 1960, Box 13, CAHP, "Christian Herter Tel Calls 9/11/60-1/20/61 (1)," DDEL.

30. Bissell quoted in Bundy, "Nixon's Comments On Your Briefing"; Wyden, *Bay of Pigs*, 68, 74; "Notes on Conversation of the President and General Persons November 3, 1960," Box 1, AWF, Presidential Transition Series, "Memos, Staff re Change of Adm"; "Memorandum of Call," January 3, 1961, Box 10, CAHP, "Presidential Telephone Calls 7/60-1/20/61," DDEL.

31. Wyden, *Bay of Pigs*, 46; Pat M. Holt, interview with author, Washington, DC, June 6, 1984; confidential interview.

32. Whiting Willauer, memorandum to Under Secretary Merchant, "The suggested Program for Cuba contained in the Memorandum to You Dated December 6, 1960," January 18, 1961, Box 5, White House Office, OSANSA, SAS/PS, "1960 Meetings with the President, vol. 2 (2)," DDEL.

33. Gordon Gray, "Memorandum of Meeting with the President," December 5, 1960, Box 5, WHO, OSANA, SAS/PS, "1960 Meetings with the President," DDEL; Clark M. Clifford, "Memorandum on Conference between President Eisenhower and President-elect Kennedy and Their Chief Advisers on January 19, 1961," January 24, 1961, Box 29a, President's Office Files (hereafter POF), "Eisenhower, D.D., 1/17/61-10/9/61," JFKL. After the invasion, Eisenhower distanced himself from the fiasco, emphasizing that during his administration "there were no plans yet based upon a particular area, particular numbers, or particular support." "Interview with President Dwight D. Eisen-

hower, Gettysburg, Pa.," November 8, 1966, Box 11, Eisenhower Post-Presidential Papers, "Augusta, Georgia," DDEL. The former president was correct that he had not bequeathed a project that had reached the point of no return. It is also true that by the time Kennedy took office, the project had become more than just another policy option he could readily dismiss. By giving the project strong support and allowing it to reach an advanced stage, Eisenhower created undeniable pressure for the new president to authorize the scheme.

Chapter 3

1. Paul L. Kesaris, ed., *Operation ZAPATA: The "Ultrasensitive" Report and Testimony of the Board of Inquiry on the Bay of Pigs* (Frederick, MD, 1981), 9, 12–13, 75–78; Thomas C. Mann, memorandum to the Secretary, "The March 1960 Plan," February 15, 1961, Box 35a–36, NSF, Cuba, General, JFKL; McGeorge Bundy, "Memorandum of Discussion on Cuba," January 28, 1961, DDRS, 1985/001542.

2. "Policy Decisions Required for Conduct of Strike Operations Against Government of Cuba," January 4, 1961, DDRS, 1985/001540.

3. Kesaris, *ZAPATA*, 75–78; Mann, "The March 1960 Plan."

4. Quoted in Robert Amory, Jr., OH, JFKL, 17; Dean Rusk, interview with author, Athens, GA, June 21, 1984; McGeorge Bundy, interview with author, New York, March 1, 1982; Arthur M. Schlesinger, Jr., interview with author, New York, March 8, 1982.

5. Amory OH, 9–20, and Walt W. Rostow OH, 39, JFKL; Peter Wyden, *Bay of Pigs: The Untold Story* (New York, 1979), 18; Schlesinger interview.

6. Quoted in Richard J. Walton, *Cold War and Counterrevolution: The Foreign Policy of John F. Kennedy* (New York, 1972), 6. On the administration's cold war mentality, see also Thomas G. Paterson, "Bearing the Burden: A Critical Look at JFK's Foreign Policy," *Virginia Quarterly Review* 54 (Spring 1978): 193–212.

7. Senate Committee on Foreign Relations, *Executive Sessions of the Senate Foreign Relations Committee (Historical Series) 1961* XIII, part I (Washington, DC, 1984), 339–341; McNamara quoted in Harry Rositzke, *The CIA's Secret Operations: Espionage, Counterespionage, and Covert Action* (New York, 1977), 199.

8. Mann, "The March 1960 Plan"; Arthur M. Schlesinger, Jr., *A Thousand Days: John F. Kennedy in the White House* (Boston, 1965), 240.

9. Kesaris, *ZAPATA*, 117; Schlesinger, *A Thousand Days*, 238–240; Arthur M. Schlesinger, memorandum for the President, February 11, 1961, Box 115, POF, Countries, Cuba, "Cuba Security 1961," JFKL; Richard M. Bissell, Jr., OH, JFKL, 5.

10. Adlai E. Stevenson, "Conf[erence] JFK and Blair, December 12 [1960]," Box 789, Adlai E. Stevenson Papers (hereafter AESP), Mudd Library.

11. Arthur M. Schlesinger, "Cuba," March 15, 1961, Box 35a–36, NSF, Cuba, General, JFKL; Wicker, cited in Arthur M. Schlesinger, Jr., *Robert Kennedy and His Times* (Boston, 1978), 453.

12. Kesaris, *ZAPATA*, 9; John F. Kennedy, "Memorandum for the Secretary of State re: Cuba," January 31, 1961, Box 115, POF, Countries, Cuba, "Cuba Security 1961," JFKL; Bundy, "Memorandum of Discussion on Cuba,"

January 28, 1961; McGeorge Bundy, "Memorandum of Meeting With President on Cuba," February 9, 1961, Box 35a–36, NSF, Cuba, General, JFKL. The JCS were generals Lyman L. Lemnitzer (Chairman), Thomas D. White (Air Force), George H. Decker (Army), and David M. Shoup (Marine Corps), and Admiral Arleigh A. Burke (Navy).

13. Admiral Arleigh A. Burke, interview with author, Bethesda, MD, October 1, 1983; Robert L. Dennison OH, U.S. Naval Institute, Annapolis, MD, 337.

14. David W. Gray, quoted in Wyden, *Bay of Pigs,* 88.

15. "Military Evaluation of the Cuban Plan," JCSM 57-61, February 3, 1961, "Annexes A and B," JCS Records (FOIA).

16. Ibid., and "Appendix E to Annex A."

17. Burke interview; General Lyman L. Lemnitzer, interview with author, Washington, DC, April 27, 1984; Earle Wheeler OH, 20, and Roswell Gilpatric OH, 47, JFKL. Gray thought that one reason that the CIA did not provide a written plan was that "the agency men had never assembled their ideas in one place." Wyden, *Bay of Pigs,* 88. Admiral Dennison believed the planners were "withholding" key information. Dennison OH, 334.

18. Burke interview.

19. General Lyman L. Lemnitzer, interview with author, Washington, DC, October 1, 1983; Wheeler OH, 23.

20. "U.S. Plan of Action in Cuba," JCSM 44-61, January 27, 1961, JCS Records (FOIA).

21. Wheeler OH, 20; Shoup testimony in Kesaris, *ZAPATA,* 247; "Military Evaluation of the Cuban Plan," JCSM 57-61. Reflecting on the JCS's evaluation that the operation "had a reasonable chance of initial success," Army Chief of Staff Decker later noted: "Well, this is true of any kind of an amphibious operation because the element of surprise is with the attacker, initially. This shifts to the defender, though, after the landing is made." George H. Decker OH, JFKL, 11.

22. "Military Evaluation of the Cuban Plan," JCSM 57-61.

23. Bundy, "Memorandum of Meeting," February 9, 1961; McGeorge Bundy, "Memorandum for the President," February 8, 1961, Box 35a–36, NSF, Cuba, General, JFKL.

24. "Evaluation of the CIA Volunteer Task Force," JCSM 146-61, March 10, 1961, JCS Records (FOIA).

25. Ibid.; Kesaris, *ZAPATA,* 154.

26. "Evaluation of the CIA Volunteer Task Force," JCSM 146-61.

27. Kesaris, *ZAPATA,* 14. Lemnitzer, accompanied often by General Gray and sometimes by Burke, usually represented the military at the White House meetings. Wheeler OH, 21; Kesaris, *ZAPATA,* 351. The chiefs, however, met as a body with the president at least twice before the invasion. Any of them could have voiced concern about the project directly to Kennedy. On the Taylor Board, see note 8, chapter 2.

28. Rusk interview; Kesaris, *ZAPATA,* 223; Arthur M. Schlesinger to Robert F. Kennedy, April 23, 1961, Box 3, Robert F. Kennedy Papers (hereafter RFKP), "RFK Attorney General Personal Correspondence, 1961, Salinger," JFKL.

29. Richard M. Bissell, Jr., interview with author, Farmington, CT, May 18, 1984; Bissell OH, JFKL, 8.

30. Richard M. Bissell, Jr., OH, DDEL, 5–7; McGeorge Bundy, "Memorandum for the President," February 25, 1961, Box 62, POF, Staff Memoranda, "McGeorge Bundy," JFKL.

31. Quoted in Tad Szulc and Karl E. Meyer, *The Cuban Invasion: The Chronicle of a Disaster* (New York, 1962), 103; Bundy in Kesaris, *ZAPATA*, 179; Bissell OH, JFKL, 5.

32. Sherman Kent, "Is Time on Our Side In Cuba?" January 27, 1961, and "Is Time on Our Side in Cuba?" March 10, 1961, CIA Records (FOIA).

33. Report 00-A 3177796, January 30, 1961, and report CS-3/461,320, March 16, 1961, CIA Records (FOIA). Shortly before the invasion, however, Dulles asked a few analysts from the Intelligence Directorate's Office of National Estimates to assess the Cuban population's likely reaction to a "hypothetical" exile landing. According to Bissell, they concluded that "spontaneous uprisings were unlikely . . . but that small groups of Castro opponents would take action. This estimate was very consistent with our expectations in organizational headquarters." Bissell interview, May 18, 1984.

34. Major General Edward G. Lansdale, interview with author, McLean, VA, June 1, 1984; Dulles, quoted in Cecil B. Currey, *Edward Lansdale: The Unquiet American* (Boston, 1988), 210–213.

35. Lyman B. Kirkpatrick, Jr., interview with author, Middleburg, VA, March 16, 1984.

36. Schlesinger, *A Thousand Days*, 237; Kesaris, *ZAPATA*, 305; Carlos R. Jones to Robert F. Kennedy, April 26, 1961, Box 2, RFKP, "RFK Attorney General Personal Correspondence, 1961, Jackson-Juliana."

37. Kennedy let Willauer go in February 1961. Willauer to Christian A. Herter, April 30, 1961, Box 4, Willauer Papers, Mudd Library.

38. Roger Hilsman OH, JFKL, 11; Colonel Richard Rogers, interview with author, Willington, CT, May 4, 1983.

39. Kesaris, *ZAPATA*, 16, 129–130.

40. Bundy in Kesaris, *ZAPATA*, 179–180. The planners were less than helpful when asked to justify their upbeat estimates. When White House adviser Richard N. Goodwin asked for evidence of the extent of dissaffection in Cuba, "Bissell said to General Cabell, Dulles's deputy, 'Don't we have an NIE [national intelligence estimate] on it?' Cabell: 'Yes.' The NIE, for obvious reasons, was not shown to the White House." Goodwin, quoted in Schlesinger, *Robert Kennedy*, 453. The JCS asked several times for a written study of the likelihood of uprisings but never received it. Lemnitzer interview, February 16, 1982.

41. Brigadier General David W. Gray, "Memorandum for the Record: Summary of White House Meetings," May 9, 1961, DDRS 1985/001550; "Proposed Operation Against Cuba," March 11, 1961, DDRS 1985/001543.

42. "Proposed Operation Against Cuba."

43. McGeorge Bundy, "Memorandum of Discussion on Cuba: National Security Action Memorandum 31," March 11, 1961, Box 328–330, NSF, Meetings and Memoranda, JFKL; Kesaris, *ZAPATA*, 12–13.

44. Kesaris, *ZAPATA*, 13.

45. "Evaluation of the Military Aspects of Alternate Concepts, CIA Para-Military Plan, Cuba," JCSM 166-61, March 15, 1961, JCS Records (FOIA); Kesaris, *ZAPATA*, 13–17; Richard M. Bissell, Jr., interview with author, Farmington, CT, January 14, 1981.

46. Rusk in Kesaris, *ZAPATA*, 220; Wheeler OH, 19; Arthur Schlesinger,

"Cuba: Political, Diplomatic, and Economic Problems," April 10, 1961, Box 65, POF, Staff Memoranda, "Arthur Schlesinger," JFKL.

47. Bissell OH, JFKL, 28. After the disaster, the CIA minimized the role uprisings were supposed to play. Bissell told the Senate Foreign Relations Committee that "with the disorganization that would have ensued if this beachhead had been maintained... you would have had quite widespread resistance activities. I prefer to call it that than a general uprising.... This, I think, would have been groups of initially hundreds of men in perhaps half a dozen different places in the island." Senate Committee on Foreign Relations, *Executive Sessions,* 436. Later, Bissell stated that popular reaction probably would have materialized "more in the form of guerrilla action than of an uprising." Richard M. Bissell, Jr., "Response to Lucien S. Vandenbroucke, 'The "Confessions" of Allen Dulles: New Evidence on the Bay of Pigs,' " *Diplomatic History* 8 (Fall 1984): 380.

Throughout the planning, however, the CIA counted on major uprisings and told the White House as much. The White House summarized its understanding in a draft cable of April 21, 1961: "Overthrow of Castro regime—depended on substantial internal uprisings against Castro to be stimulated by [the] admittedly limited military effort." Draft, "To All Latin American Diplomatic Posts" (April 21, 1961), Box 35a–36, NSF, Cuba, General, JFKL. During the invasion, Bissell apparently expected uprisings to occur soon. According to Robert Kennedy, on the first evening "we kept asking when the uprisings were going to take place. Dick Bissell said it was going to take place during the night." Robert F. Kennedy memo, June 1, 1961, quoted in Schlesinger, *Robert Kennedy,* 445. A CIA planner told the Taylor Board: "At Zapata we presupposed an uprising but the beachhead did not last long enough." Kesaris, *ZAPATA,* 78.

48. Kesaris, *ZAPATA,* 17–19, 29; David A. Phillips, *The Night Watch* (New York, 1977), 103; "Evaluation of the CIA Volunteer Task Force," JCSM 146-61; Wyden, *Bay of Pigs,* 258–259.

49. Bissell interview, May 18, 1984; Senate Select Committee to Study Operations with Respect to Intelligence Activities, *Alleged Assassination Plots Involving Foreign Leaders,* 72–82, 263–264.

50. "Evaluation of the Military Aspects," JCSM 166-61.

51. Kesaris, *ZAPATA,* 267.

52. Kesaris, *ZAPATA,* 14; "Proposed Operation Against Cuba"; Robert Kennedy memo in Schlesinger, *Robert Kennedy,* 443.

53. Kesaris, *ZAPATA,* 206, 228; Robert Kennedy memo in Schlesinger, *Robert Kennedy,* 443.

54. Kesaris, *ZAPATA,* 41–42.

55. "What briefing, if any, was given the Brigade or the Brigade's staff on going guerrilla," May 31, 1961, DDRS 1985/001554.

56. Kesaris, *ZAPATA,* 42; Richard M. Bissell, Jr., "Reflections on the Bay of Pigs: OPERATION ZAPATA" (book review), *Strategic Review* 12 (Winter 1984): 69.

57. Allen W. Dulles, handwritten notes, "Conclusion," Box 244, Allen W. Dulles Papers (hereafter AWDP), Mudd Library. Emphasis in original.

58. Dulles, handwritten notes, Box 244, AWDP, 2.

59. Eisenhower, quoted in "Damn Good and Sure," *Newsweek* March 4, 1963, 19; Dulles, handwritten notes, Box 244, AWDP.

60. Dulles, handwritten notes, Box 244, x, y, AWDP. Bissell denies that the planners "deliberately allowed Kennedy and his senior political advisers to ignore major weaknesses in the invasion plan." He acknowledges that they made "inaccurate" assumptions but says these "represented the best honest judgment of those in charge." Bissell, "Response to . . . Vandenbroucke," 377–380. Dulles explicitly states, however, that he kept his peace about key weaknesses of the plan. And the accumulation of "oversights"—the failure to note that the Bay of Pigs was not guerrilla terrain, to state that the Brigade was not interested in a guerrilla option, to dwell on morale problems among the trainees, or to point out that part of the Brigade would have next to no training—suggests that the same mechanism that led Dulles to try to silence Lansdale was again at work: the desire to sweep negative information under the rug.

61. There is other evidence that the CIA did not view the ban on Americans in combat as ironclad. It recruited American pilots for the operation, "feel[ing] that if there were great pressures, the prohibition on U.S. volunteers would be withdrawn." Bissell interview, January 14, 1981. As the invasion faltered, the CIA without authorization sent these pilots into action; several were killed. On the ground, the first man to land and open fire at the Bay of Pigs was—also unbeknownst to the White House—a U.S. CIA operative. "After Action Report on Operation Pluto," May 4, 1961, DDRS, 1985/001549; Wyden, *Bay of Pigs*, 218–219, 236–240.

62. Kesaris, *ZAPATA*, 11–15, 67, 80. McGeorge Bundy, "Meeting on Cuba, 4:00 p.m., March 15, 1961," March 15, 1961, Box 35a–36, NSF, Cuba, General, JFKL; Gray, "Memorandum"; Schlesinger, *A Thousand Days*, 243; Arthur Schlesinger, "Cuba," March 15, 1961, JFKL.

63. Diary entries, March 6 and 11, 1961, Adolf A. Berle Papers, "Berle Diary," Franklin D. Roosevelt Presidential Library, Hyde Park, NY.

64. Thomas C. Mann OH, JFKL, 18; Mann, "The Bay of Pigs Fiasco," unpublished manuscript provided by author; Mann, "The March 1960 Plan."

65. McNamara in Kesaris, *ZAPATA*, 200–201. On McNamara's involvement in and views on the plan, see also Wheeler OH, 3; Decker OH, 14; Kesaris, *ZAPATA*, 8, 14, 42, 200–205, 317.

66. Paul H. Nitze, *From Hiroshima to Glasnost: At the Center of Decision* (New York, 1989), 182–185.

67. Confidential source.

68. Bundy, "Meeting on Cuba . . . March 15, 1961," Bundy interview.

69. Rusk interview; Warren I. Cohen, *Dean Rusk* (Totawa, NJ, 1980), 96, 100–115; Dean Rusk, *As I Saw It: as told to Richard Rusk* (New York, 1990), 208–217.

70. Arthur Schlesinger, "Memorandum for the President," February 11, 1961, Box 115, POF, Countries, Cuba, "Cuba Security 1961," and Schlesinger, "Cuba," April 5, 1961, Box 115, POF, Countries, Cuba, "Cuba Security 1961," JFKL; Schlesinger, *A Thousand Days*, 255.

71. Pat M. Holt, interview with author, Washington, DC, June 6, 1984; Senator J. William Fulbright, interview with author, Washington, DC, March 21, 1984; J. William Fulbright and Pat M. Holt, "Cuba Policy," March 29, 1961, Box 114a, POF, Countries, Cuba, "General 1/61-3/61," JFKL.

72. Wyden, *Bay of Pigs*, 146–150; Gray, "Memorandum."

73. Wyden, *Bay of Pigs*, 195; Gray, "Memorandum."

74. Quoted in Schlesinger, *A Thousand Days*, 256.

75. Theodore Sorensen OH, JFKL, 25. Dulles denied giving such assurances. Hamilton F. Armstrong to Allen Dulles, September 7, 1965, Box 138, AWDP.

76. Quoted in Schlesinger, *A Thousand Days,* 258. Kennedy also was influenced by the enthusiastic report the Marine colonel with the CIA planning group cabled from Nicaragua on April 13. Hawkins called the Brigade a "formidable force," "more heavily armed and better equipped in some respects than U.S. infantry units." The officers, he wrote, were "motivated with a fanatical urge to begin battle. . . . they have utmost confidence in their ability to win. . . . I share their confidence." In "Memorandum for General Maxwell D. Taylor," April 26, 1961, DDRS 1985/001546. Robert Kennedy considered the cable "the most instrumental paper in convincing the President to go ahead." Quoted in Edwin O. Guthman and Jeffrey Shulman, eds., *Robert Kennedy In His Own Words: The Unpublished Recollections of the Kennedy Years* (Toronto, 1988), 241.

77. Schlesinger, *A Thousand Days,* 257; Lyman B. Kirkpatrick, Jr., "Paramilitary Case Study: The Bay of Pigs," *Naval War College Review* 2 (November–December 1972): 35.

78. Quoted in Wyden, *Bay of Pigs,* 155.

79. Schlesinger, *A Thousand Days,* 249.

80. Ibid., 259; Theodore C. Sorensen, *Kennedy* (New York, 1965), 307.

81. Fred M. Dean OH, Albert F. Simpson Historical Research Center, Maxwell AFB, AL, 224; William P. Bundy, interview with author, Washington, DC, February 9, 1984.

82. Confidential interview. Psychologist Irving Janis proposes a "groupthink" explanation of the Bay of Pigs. According to Janis, group dynamics can lead members of cohesive groups to slip into groupthink, or defective patterns of decision making, in which "the members' strivings for unanimity override their motivation to realistically appraise alternative courses of action." Irving L. Janis, *Groupthink: Psychological Studies of Policy Decisions and Fiascoes* (Boston, 1982), 9ff. Janis hypothesizes that to preserve their "esprit de corps" and comity, the Bay of Pigs decision makers lapsed into "illusions of invulnerability" and of "unanimity," suppressing doubts and suspending critical judgment when evaluating the plan.

Groupthink may be a recurrent decision-making pathology, but the record does not support the thesis that it was a major factor in the Bay of Pigs. Although Kennedy paid close attention to the views of his advisers, he made up his mind and gave the final go-ahead alone, not in the midst of any group. Nor were the Bay of Pigs decision makers especially cohesive. Some were friends and shared the buoyant mood that characterized the start of the Kennedy administration, but others, including Lemnitzer, Burke, Mann—all Eisenhower holdovers—and Rusk, Berle, and Schlesinger lacked close ties to Kennedy's inner circle or were uncertain of their standing. It seems doubtful that they felt, consciously or unconsciously, members of a cohesive group whose harmony had to be preserved, even at the expense of critical thinking. Janis also downplays the fact that despite the planners' upbeat assurances, Kennedy was up to the end highly ambivalent about the plan.

83. "Sequence of Events (D − 2 to D + 2), and Organization and Operation of Command Post," May 3, 1961, DDRS 1985/001548; "Policy Decisions Required for . . . Strike Operations"; Bissell OH, JFKL, 12–13. In a March 15, 1961, memo to the president, McGeorge Bundy wrote: "I think there is

unanimous agreement that at some stage the Castro Air Force must be removed." Bundy, "Meeting on Cuba...March 15, 1961."

84. Kesaris, *ZAPATA,* 15–16; "Sequence of Events"; Wyden, *Bay of Pigs,* 174–176; Bundy, "Meeting on Cuba...March 15, 1961."

85. Adlai E. Stevenson, "Conditions Given to JK by Phone 7 PM-Sat Dec 10," Box 789, AESP.

86. Wyden, *Bay of Pigs,* 156–157.

87. Adlai E. Stevenson, handwritten notes (n.d.; probably December, 1960), Box 836, AESP (emphasis in original); Wyden, *Bay of Pigs,* 156–157. Many of the trainers were lent by the U.S. Army Special Forces to the CIA for the operation. William P. Yarborough OH, vol. 9, William P. Yarborough Papers, U.S. Military History Institute, Carlisle Barracks, PA, 1–2.

88. Schlesinger, *A Thousand Days,* 271; Francis T. Plimpton OH, Box 90, AESP, 10; John Bartlow Martin, *Adlai Stevenson and the World: The Life of Adlai E. Stevenson* (Garden City, NY, 1977), 624.

89. Szulc and Meyer, *The Cuban Invasion,* 121; Wyden, *Bay of Pigs,* 176.

90. Martin, *Adlai Stevenson,* 626–628; Walter Johnson, ed., *The Papers of Adlai E. Stevenson,* vol. 8, *Ambassador to the United Nations, 1961–1965* (Boston, 1979), 53; Wyden, *Bay of Pigs,* 185–190. The day before the air attack, Castro's air force chief and a pilot genuinely defected and landed in Florida. Rusk says that, unaware of the staged defection scheme, he confused the landing of the B-26 in Miami with the authentic defections of the previous day. He thus told Stevenson the aircraft that landed on Saturday, April 15, was piloted by "genuine defectors." Rusk interview.

91. Wyden, *Bay of Pigs,* 185–190.

92. USUN New York 2892, April 16, 1961, Box 90, Stevenson Additional Papers, AESP; Newton Minow OH, Columbia OH Collection, Butler Library, Columbia University, New York, 91; Richard P. Graebel OH, Columbia OH Collection, 25; Mrs. Ernest Ives OH, Columbia OH Collection, 6.

93. Ralph G. Martin, *A Hero for Our Time: An Intimate Story of the Kennedy Years* (New York, 1983), 327; Barry M. Goldwater, *Goldwater* (New York, 1988), 136–137.

94. Kesaris, *ZAPATA,* 16–17, 129–130; "Sequence of Events"; Gray, "Memorandum."

95. Rusk interview; Hanson W. Baldwin, "Baldwin Memo of Telephone Conversation with Bobbie Kennedy," June 1961, Box 85, Hanson W. Baldwin Papers, Yale University Library, New Haven; Wyden, *Bay of Pigs,* 199. As part of the attempt to hide the U.S. hand, Dulles had left for a speaking engagement in Puerto Rico on the eve of the operation and was absent from Washington as these events unfolded.

96. Charles P. Cabell and Richard M. Bissell, Jr., "Cuban Operation," May 9, 1961, DDRS 1985/001551.

97. Ibid.

98. Kesaris, *ZAPATA,* 20; Cabell and Bissell, "Cuban Operation"; Wyden, *Bay of Pigs,* 199–200, 205–206.

99. Quoted in Wyden, *Bay of Pigs,* 205–206.

100. Kesaris, *ZAPATA,* 17–18; Johnson, *The Bay of Pigs,* 88, 95; "Sequence of Events."

101. Johnson, *The Bay of Pigs,* 103–108; Kesaris, *ZAPATA,* 21–23; Wy-

den, *Bay of Pigs,* 103–108, 217–222; Grayston Lynch, "After Action Report on Operation Pluto," DDRS 1985/001549. The exiles were supposed to land at three beaches, code-named Red, Blue, and Green, along a fifty-mile stretch of coast. The insertion at Green Beach never materialized. William Robertson, another paramilitary operative, accompanied the first exiles to Red Beach and also took part in the fighting. William Robertson, "Report of Activities on Barbara J," May 4, 1961, DDRS 1985/001549.

102. Johnson, *The Bay of Pigs,* 105–112; Kesaris, *ZAPATA* 21–23; Wyden, *Bay of Pigs,* 137, 217–222.

103. Lynch, "After Action"; Robertson, "Report"; Kesaris, *ZAPATA,* 21–23; Johnson, *The Bay of Pigs,* 112–113; Wyden, *Bay of Pigs,* 228–230. It is worth wondering how effective the D-Day raid would have been against the Castro aircraft that survived the D-2 strike. The D-2 attack by eight B-26s against three airfields destroyed five planes and damaged several others. Reconnaissance flights flown the next day showed that Castro had concentrated his remaining planes on one field. Kesaris, *ZAPATA,* 18, 135; Colonel L. Fletcher Prouty, letter to author, September 1, 1983. The CIA planned to use sixteen bombers against this target at D-Day, a large-scale attack that probably would have destroyed or grounded the remainder of the Cuban Air Force. Even if it failed to disable every remaining plane, any undamaged aircraft could not have taken off until it was checked, the runway cleared, and the confusion caused by the attack had abated. By then, the exile fleet probably would have finished unloading and departed the invasion area.

104. Kesaris, *ZAPATA,* 25; Johnson, *The Bay of Pigs,* 112–113; Wyden, *Bay of Pigs,* 228–235.

105. Johnson, *The Bay of Pigs,* 109–110; 121; Szulc and Meyer, *The Cuban Invasion,* 132–133.

106. Kesaris, *ZAPATA,* 41; Bissell, "Reflections," 69.

107. Lynch, "After Action"; Robertson, "Report"; Marion W. Boggs, "U.S. Policy Toward Cuba," May 4, 1961, Box 4, Vice Presidential Security File, "NSC-Cuba," Lyndon B. Johnson Papers, Lyndon B. Johnson Library, Austin, TX; confidential interview; Johnson, *The Bay of Pigs,* 115–133.

108. Wyden, *Bay of Pigs,* 229–231, 279–280.

109. Kesaris, *ZAPATA,* 35; 331; JCS message 994317 to CINCLANT, April 18, 1961, DDRS 1985/001524; Robert Kennedy memo in Schlesinger, *Robert Kennedy,* 445.

110. McGeorge Bundy, "Memorandum for the President," April 18, 1961, Box 35a–36, NSF, Cuba, General, JFKL.

111. Kesaris, *ZAPATA,* 25–26, 36–37. Edward E. Ferrer, *Operation Puma: The Air Battle of the Bay of Pigs* (Miami, 1982), 153, 203–204.

112. Johnson, *The Bay of Pigs,* 152–153; Wyden, *Bay of Pigs,* 270–271; Wheeler OH, 17; Robert Kennedy memo in Schlesinger, *Robert Kennedy,* 445. On April 10, 1961, Schlesinger warned the president that "if the rebellion appears to be failing, the rebels will call for U.S. armed help.... The first protection against step-by-step involvement is to convince the Cuban leaders that in no foreseeable circumstances will we send in U.S. troops." Arthur Schlesinger, "Cuba: Political, Diplomatic, and Economic Problems," Box 65, Staff Memoranda, A. Schlesinger File, "3/61-4/61," JFKL. In a press conference two days later, Kennedy stated, "there will not be, under any conditions, an intervention

in Cuba by the United States Armed Forces....The basic issue in Cuba is not one between the United States and Cuba. It is between the Cubans themselves." Quoted in Schlesinger, *A Thousand Days,* 262.

113. Wheeler OH, 17.

114. Brent Breitweiser OH, Simpson Center, 65.

115. Kesaris, *ZAPATA,* 330; Burke interview.

116. JCS message to CINCLANTFLT, 190837Z April 1961, DDRS 1985/001524; "A Brief Narrative of the Air Activity" (n.d.; probably May 1961), DDRS 1985/001547; Kesaris, *ZAPATA,* 29, 167; Schlesinger, *A Thousand Days,* 278; Ferrer, *Operation Puma,* 218. The most plausible explanation for the mix-up over the beachhead is confusion between Cuban and Nicaraguan time; Cuba was an hour ahead of Nicaragua.

117. L. L. Lemnitzer, "Bumpy Road," April 7, 1961, CM-179-61, and enclosure F, "Instructions for Destroyer Escort and Combat Air Patrol," DDRS 1985/001524; Dennison OH, 346, 365.

118. JCS message to CINCLANT, 172005Z April 1961, DDRS 1985/001524; Dennison OH, 351–352.

119. Johnson, *The Bay of Pigs,* 162; Wyden, *Bay of Pigs,* 276; Dennison OH, 358–361; Kesaris, *ZAPATA,* 164. Dennison also ignored an order to use unmarked boats and boat crews "in dungarees so that they will not be easily identified on beach." He believed that U.S. involvement was past concealment and that U.S. servicemen not in uniform were likely to be treated as "spies" if captured. He ordered his forces "to ignore further attempts at concealment...if we must fight to protect our forces in accomplishing a mission we will do so with our banner flying." JCS message to CINCLANTFLT, 210046Z April 1961, DDRS 1985/001524; Dennison OH, 364.

120. Dennison OH, 358.

121. Richard N. Goodwin, "Conversation with Commandante Ernesto Guevara of Cuba," August 22, 1961, Box 42–49, Theodore Sorensen Papers, Cuba, General, JFKL; Thomas G. Paterson, "Fixation with Cuba: The Bay of Pigs, Missile Crisis, and Covert War Against Fidel Castro," in Thomas G. Paterson, ed., *Kennedy's Quest for Victory: American Foreign Policy, 1961–1963* (New York, 1989), 137.

122. Baldwin, "Memo of Telephone Conversation." See also Robert H. Estabrook, "Background Dinner with Arthur Schlesinger, Jr., May 10, 1961," May 11, 1961, Box 1, Robert H. Estabrook Papers, JFKL; Arthur Krock, "Private Memorandum," May 5, 1961, Box 23, Arthur Krock Papers, Mudd Library; Walter Lippman, Diary Entries, April 27, 29, and May 3, Box 329, Walter Lippman Papers, Yale University Library; Henry R. Luce OH, JFKL, 28; Herbert M. Matthews, "Arthur Schlesinger, lunch," June 30, 1961, Box 27, Herbert M. Matthews Papers, "Important: My Notes Cuba for Columbia," Butler Library; Hugh Sidey, *John F. Kennedy, President* (New York, 1963), 141. For CIA views, see for instance, Kesaris, *ZAPATA,* 29n.

123. Kesaris, *ZAPATA,* 92, 123.

Chapter 4

1. Hambleton's episode appears in Earl H. Tilford, Jr., *Search and Rescue in Southeast Asia, 1961–1975* (Washington, DC, 1980), 117–119.

2. On U.S. POWs in Vietnam, see for example, Jeremiah A. Denton, Jr.,

When Hell Was in Session (Mobile, AL, 1982); Robinson Risner, *The Passing of the Night: My Seven Years as a Prisoner of the North Vietnamese* (New York, 1973).

3. Benjamin F. Schemmer, *The Raid* (New York, 1976), 28. Superbly researched and written, *The Raid* is the definitive study of the operation.

4. Ibid., 132–133.

5. William J. McQuillen, "Monograph Of Son Tay POW Rescue Attempt Operation," USAF Special Operations Force, Eglin AFB, FL, February 25, 1971, 1 (FOIA); Schemmer, *The Raid,* 26–37.

6. Schemmer, *The Raid,* 36–39, 51–56.

7. Schemmer, *The Raid,* 51–52. The Paris peace talks between the United States and North Vietnam began in May 1968. South Vietnam and the insurgent Vietcong joined in September 1968. Negotiations dragged on for five years before resulting in the Paris Agreement, a cease-fire accord the four parties signed on January 27, 1973. See Gareth Porter, *A Peace Denied: The United States, Vietnam, and the Paris Agreement* (Bloomington, IN, 1975).

8. Quoted in Schemmer, *The Raid,* 55.

9. "History Of The Aerospace Rescue & Recovery Service, 1 July 1970–30 June 1971, Annex: William R. Karsteter, The Son Tay Raid," USAF, Military Airlift Command, September 8, 1972, 1 (FOIA); McQuillen, "Monograph," 1; Commander, JCS Joint Contingency Task Group, "Report On The Son Tay Prisoner Of War Rescue Operation" (n.d.; probably 1971), part I, 2, and part I, A-2, JCS Records (FOIA); Schemmer, *The Raid,* 56, 64.

10. The other Joint Chiefs were Marine Corps Commandant General Leonard F. Chapman, Army Chief of Staff General William C. Westmoreland, Air Force Chief of Staff General John D. Ryan, and Chief of Naval Operations Admiral Elmo R. Zumwalt.

11. McQuillen, "Monograph," 2; JCS Joint Contingency Task Group, "Report On . . . Rescue Operation," part I, 2; Schemmer, *The Raid,* 65–71.

12. Admiral Thomas J. Moorer, interview with author, Washington, DC, March 13, 1984.

13. Ibid.; JCS Joint Contingency Task Group, "Report On . . . Rescue Operation," part I, 2.

14. Karsteter, "Son Tay Raid," 3; JCS Joint Contingency Task Group, "Report On . . . Rescue Operation," part I, 2, and part II, A-2, A-3; Schemmer, *The Raid,* 90–91.

15. Schemmer, *The Raid,* 82–83, 136–137; Brigadier General Donald D. Blackburn, interview with author, Mclean, VA, February 27, 1984.

16. Schemmer, *The Raid,* 82–83, 136–137; Brigadier General Leroy J. Manor, " 'Son Tay'—the POW Rescue Attempt," in *Aerospace Commentary,* Department of the Air Force, HQ Air University, Maxwell AFB, AL, 36 (n.d.), (FOIA); JCS Joint Contingency Task Group, "Report On . . . Rescue Operation," part I, 2–4.

17. Schemmer, *The Raid,* 40, 83; Lieutenant General John W. Vogt, interview with author, Washington, DC, April 13, 1984.

18. Schemmer, *The Raid,* 98–99.

19. Senate Committee on Foreign Relations, *Bombing Operations and the Prisoner-Of-War Rescue Mission in North Vietnam* (Washington, DC, 1971), 7; JCS Joint Contingency Task Group, "Report On . . . Rescue Operation," part II, C-4.

20. JCS Joint Contingency Task Group, "Report On...Rescue Operation," part I, III.

21. Manor, " 'Son Tay,' " 19; Simons, quoted in Heather David, *Operation Rescue* (New York, 1971), 30.

22. Lieutenant General Leroy J. Manor, interview with author, Alexandria, VA, February 29, 1984; Manor, " 'Son Tay,' " 21–22, 26; JCS Joint Contingency Task Group, "Report On...Rescue Operation," part I, IV.

23. Royal A. Brown OH, Simpson Center, 38; Richard A. Gabriel, *Military Incompetence: Why the American Military Doesn't Win* (New York, 1986), 46; "Operation Kingpin" (JCS briefing book) (n.d.; probably November 1970), 2, JCS Records (FOIA); JCS Joint Contingency Task Group, "Report On...Rescue Operation," part I, 19.

24. Blackburn interview; "Kingpin," 5–6.

25. "Kingpin," 6–7; Manor, " 'Son Tay,' " 34; Admiral Harry D. Train, II, interview with author, Norfolk, VA, June 6, 1984.

26. Karsteter, "Son Tay Raid," 12; Brown OH, 35.

27. "Kingpin," 3; Manor, " 'Son Tay,' " 31–32; McQuillen, "Monograph," 27.

28. Manor interview; "Kingpin," attachment: "Forces"; JCS Joint Contingency Task Group, "Report On...Rescue Operation," part I, 41.

29. Manor interview; "Kingpin," attachment: "Alternate Plans."

30. Karsteter, "Son Tay Raid," 7–9.

31. Confidential interview; Brigadier General Leroy J. Manor, "Commander's Comments," in McQuillen, "Monograph," viii.

32. JCS Joint Contingency Task Group, "Report On...Rescue Operation," part I, 15; Brigadier General Leroy J. Manor, "Oral Briefing to Charles Hildreth, Office of Air Force History, and William J. McQuillen, USAFSOF Historian," HQ USAFSOF, Eglin AFB, December 31, 1970, 6 (FOIA); Manor in McQuillen, "Monograph," V.

33. Karsteter, "Son Tay Raid," 4–5, 6–7; Brown OH, 35, 38; Manor, "Oral Briefing," 4–7; Manor in McQuillen, "Monograph," vi.

34. Moorer interview; Karsteter, "Son Tay Raid," 4–5; Brown OH, 35.

35. Train interview; Moorer interview; Vogt interview.

36. Manor interview.

37. Blackburn interview; David, *Operation,* 42; Senate Committee on Foreign Relations, *Bombing Operations,* 8.

38. Manor, " 'Son Tay,' " 24; McQuillen, "Monograph," 12–13; Brigadier General Leroy J. Manor, untitled briefing notes (n.d.; probably 1971), JCS Records (FOIA); Schemmer, *The Raid,* 133–134.

39. Moorer interview; Train interview; Manor, " 'Son Tay,' " 24; Schemmer, *The Raid,* 139–140; Brigadier General Donald D. Blackburn, letter to author, September 28, 1992.

40. Quoted in Schemmer, *The Raid,* 164.

41. Schemmer, *The Raid,* 134; Vogt interview. Created by Kissinger, the WSAG consisted of senior representatives from the Department of State, the CIA, and the U.S. Information Agency (USIA), as well as the Chairman of the JCS, another senior general, and Kissinger himself. The WSAG, which often met twice a day, played a key role coordinating the administration's military and diplomatic efforts in the Vietnam War. See Henry A. Kissinger, *White House Years* (Boston, 1979), 319; Allen E. Goodman, *The Lost Peace: America's Search for a Negotiated Settlement of the Vietnam War* (Stanford, 1978), 95.

42. Schemmer, *The Raid,* 135; McQuillen, "Monograph," 13; Manor, "'Son Tay,'" 24; Kissinger, *White House Years,* 699, 701. The Chinese reply signaled China's willingness to receive a U.S. envoy. Soon after, Kissinger made two secret trips to Beijing, paving the way for Nixon's 1971 visit to China.

43. Schemmer, *The Raid,* 59, 138, 160, 237–238.

44. Ibid., 161.

45. Kissinger, *White House Years,* 982; Schemmer, *The Raid,* 140.

46. Quoted in Schemmer, *The Raid,* 2–3; Moorer interview. Secure phones are configured to foil electronic eavesdropping.

47. David, *Operation,* 127; Schemmer, *The Raid,* 163.

48. Schemmer, *The Raid,* 163–164.

49. Senate Committee on Foreign Relations, *Bombing Operations,* 3, 23; Nixon quoted in Schemmer, *The Raid,* 163.

50. Moorer interview; Stuart H. Loory, "Story Behind the Raid on Sontay—The Problem of Intelligence," *Los Angeles Times,* February 5, 1971.

51. JCS Joint Contingency Task Group, "Report On . . . Rescue Operation," part II, C-4; Schemmer, *The Raid,* 137.

52. Schemmer, *The Raid,* 100–101, 170–172.

53. Ibid., 170–173.

54. Moorer interview; Blackburn interview; Robert K. Ruhl, "Raid at Sontay," *Airman* 19 (August 1975): 31; Schemmer, *The Raid,* 172–178; Vogt interview.

55. Quoted in Seymour M. Hersh, *The Price of Power: Kissinger in the Nixon White House* (New York, 1983), 305; Train interview. Writing about Sontay, columnist John Anderson alleged that Blackburn "told our associate Donald Goldberg years later: 'We knew they (the POWs) had been moved. We didn't want to give up the demonstration of power.' The real purpose of the raid, he said, was to show the North Vietnamese how vulnerable they were." John Anderson, "Military 'Fiasco' Was Really a Success," *Willimantic Chronicle,* July 9, 1985. In an 1984 interview, Blackburn was more circumspect. "The question," he noted, "was how empty was the camp? We knew the Vietnamese moved the POWs from time to time. . . . In the afternoon [of November 19] I learned of the possibility the camp might be empty. The intelligence teams went all over the information during the night and I met with them at five [A.M.]. I asked: 'Can you give me a 100 percent assurance the camp is clean?' I could not get a clear answer. I recommended that we go ahead with what we had. Suppose there had still been some [POWs]?" Blackburn interview.

56. Moorer interview; Train interview. In his memoirs, Kissinger writes:

> We knew the risk of casualties, but none of the briefings that led to the decision to proceed had ever mentioned the possibility that the camp might be empty. *After* the failure of the raid I was informed of a message sent in code by a prisoner of war that the camp was 'closed' on July 14. This was interpreted by military analysts to mean that the gates were locked; it had not been considered of sufficient importance to bring to the attention of the White House. (*White House Years,* 982)

Kissinger appears to be correct in saying that before the president authorized the raid on November 18, the military did not emphasize the possibility that the camp might be empty. His memoirs, however, suggest that the White House was never told the prisoners might have been moved. Key participants in the events recall otherwise. Chairman Moorer is certain Kissinger was informed of the intelligence findings of November 19 and 20, indicating that the POWs might no longer be at Sontay. As Moorer recalls, "[Kissinger] was there and he heard all of the evidence that was laid out to [CIA Director] Helms and [Defense Secretary] Laird and him. We had some doubts that the POWs were there.... Kissinger knew about it like the others." General Vogt likewise remembers that "Kissinger knew there were doubts.... In the final 48 hours we frankly exchanged with Laird and Kissinger all we had, including [DIA Director] Bennett's doubts." Moorer interview; Vogt interview.

57. Moorer was deeply anxious to do something for the POWs, and, given the choice, would not have stopped at the rescue mission. As he later explained: "I would have given the North Vietnamese six hours to give us the POWs then all hell would have broken loose. There were other means of pressure on North Vietnam: massive bombing and the mining of Haiphong harbor." Moorer interview.

58. Vogt interview; Train interview. At about the same time DIA received intelligence prompting the debate about Sontay, Washington learned about the death of still more POWs. Through surveillance of U.S. peace activists in close touch with the North Vietnamese, U.S. intelligence learned on November 19 that besides the deaths Hanoi had reported on November 12, eleven other POWs had died. Schemmer, *The Raid*, 174–175.

59. Vogt interview. However, with JCS approval, Blackburn briefed Admiral John S. McCain, Commander in Chief, Pacific (CinCPac), and General Creighton Abrams, Commander, U.S. Military Assistance Command, Vietnam (MACV), about the impending raid. Schemmer, *The Raid*, 145–146.

60. JCS Joint Contingency Task Group, "Report On ... Rescue Operation," part I, 75–76; Moorer interview; Schemmer, *The Raid*, 148.

61. Manor, " 'Son Tay,' " 23; McQuillen, "Monograph," 19–20; Manor, "Oral Briefing," 4–5; Schemmer, *The Raid*, 183.

62. Manor, "Oral Briefing," 4–5; JCS Joint Contingency Task Group, "Report On ... Rescue Operation," part I, 37–38; Karsteter, "Son Tay Raid," 24–26.

63. Karsteter, "Son Tay Raid," 25; JCS Joint Contingency Task Group, "Report On ... Rescue Operation," part I, 37–38; Manor interview.

64. McQuillen, "Monograph," 15; JCS Joint Contingency Task Group, "Report On ... Rescue Operation," part I, 67–68; Manor interview.

65. Lt. Col. Frederic M. Donohue, "Mission of Mercy," Air War College Report 4560, Maxwell AFB, 1972, 4–5; Karsteter, "Son Tay Raid," 29.

66. Manor, " 'Son Tay,' " 31; JCS Joint Contingency Task Group, "Report On ... Rescue Operation," part I, 8.

67. Tilford, *Search and Rescue*, 109–110; Schemmer, *The Raid*, 201, 204–208; Karsteter, "Son Tay Raid," 34–35; JCS Joint Contingency Task Group, "Report On ... Rescue Operation," part I, 49–53. The raiders reported that the occupants of the "school," while oriental, were taller and better equipped than the North Vietnamese guarding Sontay camp. The troops at the "school" may have been Chinese advisers. Schemmer, *The Raid*, 207, and "U.S. Raiders Killed 100–200 Chinese Troops in 1970 North Vietnam Foray," *Armed Forces Journal International* 117 (January 1980):32–34.

68. JCS Joint Contingency Task Group, "Report On ... Rescue Operation," part I, 53.

69. Ibid., 53–64.

70. Moorer interview; Schemmer, *The Raid*, 268–284.

Chapter 5

1. The JCS, Air Force, and Marine Corps records on the *Mayaguez* affair are now open for research; the bulk of the relevant White House archives, however, remain closed. Good studies on the affair include Christopher Jon Lamb, *Belief Systems and Decision Making in the* Mayaguez *Crisis* (Gainesville, FL, 1988); Richard G. Head, Frisco W. Short, and Robert C. McFarlane, *Crisis Resolution: Presidential Decision Making in the Mayaguez and Korean Confrontations* (Boulder, CO, 1978); Thomas D. Des Brisay, *Fourteen Hours at Koh Tang* (Washington, DC, 1975); and George R. Dunham and David A. Quinlan, *U.S. Marines in Vietnam: The Bitter End, 1973–1975* (Washington, DC, 1990). Roy Rowan's *The Four Days of Mayaguez* (New York, 1975) is a journalist's account written within weeks of the incident.

2. "Chronology of Events of the *Mayaguez* Incident," Box 33, White House Central Files (hereafter WHCF), "ND 18/CO/26," Gerald R. Ford Presidential Library, Ann Arbor, MI (hereafter GRFL).

3. Also present were Deputy Secretary of State Robert S. Ingersoll and Deputy Secretary of Defense William P. Clements, Jr. Subsequent NSC meetings also included presidential counselors John O. Marsh and Robert T. Hartmann, Presidential Counsel Philip W. Buchen, and other selected officials. "Daily Diary of President Gerald R. Ford," May 12, 13, and 14, 1975, Box 33, WHCF, "President's Daily Diary," and Box 14, WHCF, "Work Copy," GRFL.

4. Confidential interview; Ford, quoted in Lamb, *Belief Systems,* 66. On the mind-set of the decision makers, see Lamb, *Belief Systems,* 63–78.

5. Philip W. Buchen, interview with author, Washington, DC, March 20, 1984; confidential interviews; Gerald R. Ford, *A Time to Heal: The Autobiography of Gerald R. Ford* (New York, 1979), 275; Robert T. Hartmann, *Palace Politics: An Inside Account of the Ford Years* (New York, 1980), 324.

6. Kissinger, quoted in James A. Nathan, "The *Mayaguez,* Presidential War, and Congressional Senescence," *Intellect* 104 (February 1976): 361; Lee, quoted in William Shawcross, "Making the Most of Mayaguez," *Far Eastern Economic Review,* May 30, 1975, 11–12; Head, Short, and McFarlane, *Crisis Resolution,* 117; Lamb, *Belief Systems,* 184–187.

7. Buchen interview; Robert T. Hartmann, interview with author, Bethesda, MD, May 30, 1984.

8. Confidential interview. Ford had long been dogged by his image as a politician who, in President Lyndon B. Johnson's words, "could not walk and chew gum at the same time." Johnson, quoted in Richard E. Neustadt and Ernest E. May, *Thinking in Time: The Uses of History for Decision Makers* (New York, 1986), 59.

9. Confidential interview; Admiral James L. Holloway III, interview with author, Washington DC, June 25, 1984; quoted in Peter Goldman, "Ford's Rescue Operation," *Newsweek,* May 26, 1975, 17.

10. Quoted in Goldman, "Ford's Rescue Operation," 16. Kissinger has denied the quotation.

11. Quoted in Ford, *A Time to Heal,* 276. The day after the capture of the *Mayaguez,* "high ranking sources" confided to Philip Shabecoff of the *New York Times* "that the seizure of the vessel might provide the test of American determination in Southeast Asia . . . the United States has been seeking since the collapse of allied governments in South Vietnam and Cambodia." Quoted in Nathan, "The *Mayaguez,*" 362.

12. Hartmann, *Palace Politics,* 325–326; Head, Short, and McFarlane, *Crisis Resolution,* 110; Ron Nessen, *It Sure Looks Different from the Inside* (Chicago, 1978), 118; Congress, Reports of the Comptroller General of the United States, *Seizure of the Mayaguez, Part IV* (Washington, DC, 1976), 63–71; confidential interview.

13. Confidential interview.

14. Quoted in Ford, *A Time to Heal,* 279–280.

15. Ford found that Kennerly's observations "made a lot of sense." Ford was about to unleash U.S. airpower against the Cambodian mainland. Kennerly's comments prompted the president to opt for "surgical strikes" by carrier-based fighter-bombers, instead of B-52 strikes, which, Ford concluded, would be "overkill." Ibid.

16. Telegram, Norodom Sihanouk to Senator Mike Mansfield, April 7, 1975, Box 32, WHCF, "ND 18/CO/26 Wars—Cambodia 8/9/74–5/15/75," GRFL. Translation from French original. Former Cambodian ruler Sihanouk was allied with the insurgent Khmer Rouge Communists who, in the spring of 1975, toppled Cambodia's pro-Western Lon Nol regime.

17. Nathan, "The *Mayaguez,*" 361.

18. "Statement by the Press Secretary," Document A 12, Vertical File (Mayaguez), GRFL.

19. Confidential interview; Holloway interview; Goldman, "Ford's Rescue Operation," 19; Nessen, *Looks Different,* 118.

20. Comptroller General, *Seizure,* 66; Head, Short, and McFarlane, *Crisis Resolution,* 111.

21. J. A. Messegee, " 'Mayday' for the *Mayaguez:* The Patrol Squadron Skipper," *U.S. Naval Institute Proceedings* 102 (November 1976):95.

22. "After Action Report, US Military Operations SS Mayaguez/Kaoh Tang Island 12–15 May 1975: Narrative Summary" (n.d.; probably May 1975), 1, JCS Records (FOIA).

23. Comptroller General, *Seizure,* 66.

24. "Mayaguez Crisis" (notes of telephone calls), and memorandum, Bill Kendall, "Notification of action regarding S.S. Mayaguez," May 13, 1975, Box 17, Charles Leppert Files, GRFL.

25. Office of PACAF History, "History Of The Pacific Air Forces: 1 July 1974–31 December 1975, Volume 1," July 30, 1976, HQ PACAF, Hickam AFB, HI, 431–433 (FOIA).

26. Command History Branch, Office of the Joint Secretary, "Commander In Chief Pacific Command History 1975 Appendix VI—The SS MAYAGUEZ Incident," 1976, HQ CINCPAC, Camp H. M. Smith, HI, 16–17 (FOIA); USSAG/DOC, "A Compilation of Notes taken During the S.S. Mayaguez Seizure 13 May thru 15 May 1975: Tab C, UHF Link, Summary of S.S. Mayaguez Sitreps, 14 May 1975," in PACAF, "Mayaguez Operation, Miscellaneous Documents, 75/05/12–75/05/29," HQ PACAF, Hickam AFB, HI (FOIA).

27. "After Action Report: Narrative Summary," 1; Dunham and Quinlan, *Marines in Vietnam,* 239–240.

28. Buchen interview; Ford, *A Time to Heal,* 277.

29. Ford, *A Time to Heal,* 277; Head, Short, and McFarlane, *Crisis Resolution,* 113; Office of PACAF History, "History . . . Pacific Air Forces," 436–439.

30. Command History Branch, "Pacific Command History," 8; Urey W.

Patrick, "The Mayaguez Operation," Center for Naval Analyses, Arlington, VA, April 1977, 17.

31. Telephone call, "The President/General Scowcroft," 8:10 P.M., May 13, 1975, Box 1, Temporary Scowcroft Parallel File (hereafter TSPF), Scowcroft Office File, "Cambodia, Mayaguez Seizure," GRFL. Scowcroft's information at the time was not exact; the United States had not yet sunk any Cambodian craft. See "After Action Report: Results of Attacks Against Cambodian Naval Vessels."

32. "After Action Report: JCS Log of Significant Events," 3; Office of PACAF History, "History . . . Pacific Air Forces," 438–439.

33. Telephone calls, "General Wickham/General Scowcroft," 9:48 P.M., May 13, 1975; "The President/General Scowcroft," 9:50 P.M., May 13, 1975; Box 1, TSPF, Scowcroft Office File, GRFL.

34. Telephone call, "General Wickham/General Scowcroft," 9:54 P.M., May 13, 1975; Box 1, TSPF, Scowcroft Office File, GRFL. Ford writes that he ordered that the pilot "shoot across the bow but do not sink the boat." Ford, *A Time to Heal,* 278.

35. Confidential interviews; 388 Tactical Fighter Wing, "Narrative History 75/04/01 to 75/06/30," HQ Tactical Air Command, Langley AFB, VA, 28–30 (FOIA).

36. Office of PACAF History, "History . . . Pacific Air Forces," 436, 438–439; Ford, *A Time to Heal,* 277; "After Action Report: JCS Log of Significant Events," 3.

37. Comptroller General, *Seizure,* 66.

38. Quoted in Head, Short, and McFarlane, *Crisis Resolution,* 110–111. CIA Director Colby has confirmed that discussions during the crisis were open and extensive. William E. Colby, interview with author, Washington, DC, March 5, 1984.

39. Nessen, *Looks Different,* 123; Ford, *A Time to Heal,* 279; Head, Short, and Mc Farlane, *Crisis Resolution,* 123; Hartmann interview. As Ford later explained: "We had to assume a whole variety of possibilities because we weren't sure there were crew members on the fishing boat, and if there were, how many there were and whether there was part of the crew on the fishing boat and how many were back on the MAYAGUEZ." "Interview Of The President By Roy Rowan," June 23, 1975, Box 23, Ron Nessen Files, 9, GRFL.

40. Head, Short, and McFarlane, *Crisis Resolution,* 117; Message, CTF Seven Nine to CTG Seven Nine PT One, 130920Z May 1975, Mayaguez File, History and Museums Division, Headquarters, U.S. Marine Corps (hereafter USMCHMD), Washington, DC.

41. Jules Witcover, "The *Mayaguez* Decision: Three Days of Crisis for President Ford," *Washington Post,* May 17, 1975, quoted in Head, Short, and McFarlane, *Crisis Resolution,* 123; Rowan, *Four Days,* 141–142, 176.

42. Ford, *A Time to Heal,* 279; Rowan, *Four Days,* 178. In his memoirs, White House Press Secretary Ron Nessen recalls discussing with Pentagon spokesman Joseph Laitin the possible use of B-52s. According to Nessen, "Laitin said Schlesinger was arguing against them because he felt B-52s were so widely identified with the unpopular American bombings in Vietnam that their use in the *Mayaguez* episode would turn world opinion against the United States." Nessen, *Looks Different,* 122.

43. Head, Short, and McFarlane, *Crisis Resolution,* 122–123.

44. Ford, *A Time to Heal,* 280; Head, Short, and McFarlane, *Crisis Resolution,* 123–131; "After Action Report: Narrative Summary," 2–3.

45. "Interview Of President Ford By Hugh Sidey," May 16, 1975, Box 26, Nessen Files, 8, GRFL. A senior administration official subsequently recalled that despite the reports of atrocities that had been coming out of Cambodia after the Communist takeover, the Khmer Rouge did not have, at the time, the reputation for atrocities they later acquired. "[At the time of the *Mayaguez*] the bloodiness of the Khmer Rouge had not come out as it has now.... Our experience in the war had not been that overwhelming. During the hostilities in Cambodia they had not displayed the bestiality they exhibited after they took power." Confidential interview.

46. Admiral Harry D. Train, II, interview with author, Norfolk, Virginia, June 5, 1984.

47. Confidential interview.

48. Colby interview; Ford, *A Time to Heal,* 277; Hartmann, *Palace Politics,* 326; Holloway interview.

49. "Interview...By...Rowan," 3; "Interview...By...Sidey," 7–8; Scowcroft quoted in Chris Lamb, "Belief Systems and Decision Making in the *Mayaguez* Crisis," *Political Science Quarterly* 99 (Winter 1985): 693. In his memoirs Ford writes: "I remembered, the North Koreans had captured the intelligence ship U.S.S. *Pueblo* in international waters and forced her and her crew into the port of Wonsan. The U.S. had not been able to respond fast enough to prevent the transfer, and as a result, *Pueblo*'s crew had languished in a North Korean prison camp for nearly a year. I was determined not to allow a repetition of that incident" Ford, *A Time to Heal,* 277.

50. Ford, quoted in Head, Short, and McFarlane, *Crisis Resolution,* 117–118.

51. "Memorandum of Conversation: Bipartisan Congressional Leadership," May 14, 1975, Box 1, TSPF, Presidential Memcons, GRFL; Ford, *A Time to Heal,* 281; "Interview of the President By Representatives Of The New York Daily News," May 19, 1975, Box 26, Nessen Files, GRFL.

52. Ford was aware of these patrol boats and of the threat they posed. "Interview...By...Sidey," 5–6.

53. Defense Intelligence Report, "Weekly Intelligence Summary Distribution: Air Strike Damage During the Mayaguez Incident," C-6573/DI-GC, June 9, 1975, Defense Intelligence Agency, Washington, DC (FOIA); "After Action Report: Tacair Operations from Carrier Coral Sea and Bomb Damage Assessment, Mainland Strikes"; Comptroller General, *Seizure,* 97.

54. "After Action Report: Operational Concept," 2; Major General Charles F. Minter, "End of Tour Report," 8th Air Force/BAD 74/08/24–75/08/10, Simpson Center.

55. "Possible Scenarios for Recovery of Ship and Crew" (n.d.; probably May 13, 1975), Box 25, Philip W. Buchen Files, GRFL.

56. James R. Schlesinger, "Some Ruminations On The Office Of Secretary of Defense," unpublished paper (n.d.), 22; Scowcroft, quoted in Lamb, *Belief Systems,* 151.

57. Quoted in "Interview...By...Rowan," 5; Head, Short, and McFarlane, *Crisis Resolution,* 103; PACAF, "The SS Mayaguez Seizure: An Evaluation of Intelligence Factors," June 17, 1975, document 1026277, HQ PACAF, 2 (FOIA).

58. Holloway interview.

59. Comptroller General, *Seizure,* 69, Lamb, *Belief Systems,* 87. Lamb hypothesizes that Kissinger "chose not to pass along the information about the Chinese to the National Security Council in its last meeting." Lamb, *Belief Systems,* 123–124. The White House and senior NSC members could hardly have ignored this information, however, even if Kissinger did not raise it at a formal NSC meeting. Most substantive State Department cables, especially sensitive ones, are automatically disseminated upon receipt in Washington to a wide audience outside the State Department, including the White House. In a 1984 interview with the author, a senior White House official spontaneously mentioned the cable from Tehran, adding that the NSC had not given it much credence. Confidential interview.

60. Office of PACAF History, "History . . . Pacific Air Forces," 442; "After Action Report: Operational Concept," 1; Message, JCS to CINCPAC, Subject: "Draft Ultimatum," 142959Z May 75, in "After Action Report," Part Two.

61. Richard R. Brauer, Jr., "A Critical Examination of Planning Imperatives Applicable to Hostage Rescue Operations," April 16, 1984, student essay, U.S. Army War College, Carlisle Barracks, PA, 22–23; Shlomo Gazit, "Risk, Glory, and the Rescue Operation," *International Security* 6 (Summer 1981): 120–124.

62. Patrick, "Mayaguez Operation," 39.

63. "Interview . . . By . . . Sidey," 7.

64. Colby interview; Holloway interview; Colonel Zane Finkelstein, interview with author, Carlisle Barracks, PA, June 13, 1984.

65. Train interview.

66. On May 12 DIA estimated that there were "150–200 KC possibly on Kaoh Tang; 82 mm mortars, 75 mm recoilless rifles, 30 caliber, 7.62 mm and 12.7 mm machine guns, B40/41 Rocket Propelled Grenades." "After Action Report: DIA Intelligence Appraisal." Brigadier General Anderson W. Atkinson of the Joint Staff recalled receiving this estimate "within hours" of the outbreak of the crisis. Anderson W. Atkinson, interview with author, Niceville, FL, May 10, 1984. CinCPac's estimate was of a "reinforced company" of ninety to one hundred troops plus a weapons squad with a heavy mortar, recoilless rifle, machine guns, and rocket launchers. USSAG's estimates ranged from as few as twenty irregulars to a battalion of three hundred regular Khmer Rouge troops. Its last intelligence report of May 14 put the enemy strength on Koh Tang "as probably not exceeding 100," with small arms, automatic weapons, and possibly mortars. See BGen Johnson to Admiral Gayler, "SS Mayaguez Seizure," November 17, 1975, HQ PACAF, 1–2 (FOIA).

67. Command History Branch, "Pacific Command History," 451; Patrick, "Mayaguez Operation," 10, 16, 20.

68. Train interview; Schlesinger, "Ruminations," 21; Atkinson interview.

69. Confidential interview.

70. Lieutenant General John J. Burns, interview with author, Arlington, VA, May 8, 1984; Major General Earl J. Archer, interview with author, Washington, DC, May 29, 1984.

71. Johnson, "Mayaguez Seizure," enclosures: "Major General Earl J. Archer," and "Interview, Walter H. Baxter, III."

72. Train interview.

73. Confidential interviews. Jones got off to a bad start with the NSC after

the first meeting. As Head, Short, and McFarlane write, the NSC understood "that the JCS was asked to develop written military options and to present them to the White House later that afternoon (Monday). The JCS staff and General Jones operated under the assumption that the request for military alternatives was only a generalized one with no specific White House deadline." Head, Short, and McFarlane, *Crisis Resolution*, 111. Another example of White House frustration with the military's handling of events appears in the transcript of a 2.00 A.M. call May 13 to Ford by Scowcroft, informing the president that the *Mayaguez* was under way from Poulo Wai. Complaining that he had not been informed in a timely fashion, Scowcroft stated: "I am so mad, I'm just..." He did not finish the thought. Telephone call, "General Scowcroft/The President," 2:23 P.M., May 13, 1975, Box 1, TSPF, Scowcroft Office File, GRFL.

74. Colby interview.

75. Attachments "Present Situation" and "Options To Seize Island" to "Possible Scenarios for Recovery of Ship and Crew," Buchen Files, GRFL.

76. Office of PACAF History, "History...Pacific Air Forces," 453. Asked why the operation was not delayed another twenty-four hours, key Washington decision makers explained that they feared the Cambodians would use the extra night to transfer all of the captives to the mainland. They did not believe it feasible to seal off the area until the morning of May 16. Holloway interview, Train interview; confidential interview. The comptroller general report concluded that a blockade was a viable option. Comptroller General, *Seizure*, 103. Local U.S. commanders also thought they could cordon off Koh Tang successfully, even through another night. As General Burns recalled, "I think we could have developed a tight cordon around the island." Burns interview. General Archer was more emphatic: "We could have absolutely circled that island so that no living thing got out by the night of May 15th. We could have closed off the area entirely, and with C-130 flares, have lit it like daylight." Burns interview; Archer interview.

77. Head, Short, and McFarlane, *Crisis Resolution*, 117–118; 131; anonymous White House sources quoted in Aldo Beckman, "Longest Day—Decision, Dinner, Relief," *Chicago Tribune*, excerpted in "News & Comment: The President's Daily News Summary," May 19, 1975, Box 19, James Shuman file, GRFL. The Office of PACAF History's study observes that by 7:00 A.M. on May 14, "the final moves had been decided." "History...Pacific Air Forces," 440.

78. Train interview; George P. Steele OH, Naval Historical Center, Washington, DC. Admiral Weisner was himself in close contact with the Commander in Chief, Pacific, Admiral Noel A. M. Gayler. Gayler was in Washington when the crisis started, and from the outset was deeply involved in the military planning and preparations.

79. Command History Branch, "Pacific Command History," 21–23.

80. HQ USSAG, "Mayaguez Operation (Mayaguez Briefing—Draft, Working Papers)," 8 June [1975], in PACAF, "Mayaguez...Miscellaneous Documents."

81. Johnson, "Mayaguez Seizure," enclosure: "Walter H. Baxter, III."

82. Johnson, "Mayaguez Seizure," enclosure: "Col R. B. Janca"; Train interview.

83. Message, 56 SOW Nakhom Phanom Aprt Thai/DO to CINCPACAF Hickam AFB HI/XO, 191200Z May 75, CINCPAC Records (FOIA); Train in-

terview; confidential interview. Head, Short, and McFarlane state that by the end of the third NSC meeting there was strong sentiment within the White House to launch the operation without further delay. They write:

> Thus, the basic concept of an armed assault had been approved by the president at this midnight meeting [on May 13]. The question of timing then became the primary consideration. Secretary Kissinger pressed for the earliest possible commitment of forces.... The JCS was asked if the military could mount the operation one day earlier (which would have moved it from the morning of May 15 to the afternoon of May 14, Cambodian time). General Jones considered the proposal briefly, but replied to the White House that the JCS could not recommend such action. There were simply too many ships, aircraft, and ground forces to coordinate in such a short time, and most of them were still out of range of the target area. (*Crisis Resolution*, 118)

Chapter 6

1. Lieutenant General John J. Burns, interview with author, Arlington, VA, May 8, 1984; Major General Earl J. Archer, interview with author, Washington, DC, May 29, 1984.

2. BGen Johnson to Admiral Gayler, "SS Mayaguez Seizure," enclosure: "Walter H. Baxter, III," November 17, 1975, HQ PACAF; George R. Dunham and David A. Quinlan, *United States Marines in Vietnam; The Bitter End, 1973–1975* (Washington, DC, 1990), 240–241; Earl H. Tilford, Jr., *Search and Rescue in Southeast Asia, 1961–1975* (Washington, DC, 1980), 147. The CH-53 and HH-53 are slightly different versions of the H-53, the largest U.S. troop-carrying helicopter. The helicopters that deployed to Utapao had armor plating, offering some protection from ground fire, and high-speed Gatling guns, which deliver high volumes of machine gunfire.

3. CinCPac Ad Hoc Board, "Report on Intelligence and Operations in Contingencies," December 5, 1975, microfilm roll 32846, Simpson Center, 2–4 (FOIA).

4. Command History Branch, Office of the Joint Secretary, "Commander In Chief Pacific Command History 1975 Appendix VI—The SS MAYAGUEZ Incident," 1976, HQ CINCPAC, Camp H. M. Smith, HI, 5 (FOIA).

5. Archer interview; Burns interview. There was a good secure voice link between USSAG, CinCPac, and the NMCC.

6. Archer interview; CinCPac Ad Hoc Board, "Report: Sequence Of Events On Recovery Of S.S. Mayaguez."

7. Archer interview.

8. Colonel Robert R. Reed, "End of Tour Report," HQ Twelfth Air Force, Bergstrom AFB, TX (n.d.; probably summer 1975), 5 (FOIA). Talon Vise/Frequent Wind (TV/FW) was the evacuation of Americans from South Vietnam, which occurred days before the *Mayaguez* operation.

9. Archer interview.

10. Major General Carl W. Hoffman, interview with author, Rancho Bernardo, CA, June 11, 1984.

11. Colonel John M. Johnson, taped interview, May 19, 1975, USMCHMD.

12. Hoffman interview.

13. George P. Steele OH, Naval Historical Center, Washington, DC, 94–97.

14. Vice Admiral George P. Steele, interview with author, Philadelphia, PA, April 9, 1984; Steele OH, U.S. Naval Institute, Annapolis, MD, 492–493.

15. Lieutenant General John J. Burns, interview with author, Bethesda, MD, May 14, 1992.

16. CinCPac Ad Hoc Board, "Report: Command And Control Procedures." In the course of editing, "breakdown" became "confusion."

17. CinCPac Ad Hoc Board, "Report."

18. BLT 2/9, III MAF, "Koh Tang/*Mayaguez* Historical Report: Narrative Summary," September 12, 1975, USMCHMD; Johnson, "Mayaguez Seizure," enclosures: "Interview LT COL Randall Austin, USMC, BLT 2/9," and "Interview COL George A. Dugard, USAF, 901 ARS."

19. Command History Branch, "Pacific Command History," 13–16; Urey W. Patrick, "The Mayaguez Operation," Center for Naval Analyses, Arlington, VA, April 1977 39–40; Johnson, "Mayaguez Seizure," 4.

20. PACAF, "The S.S. Mayaguez Seizure: An Evaluation of Intelligence Factors," June 17, 1975, document 1026277, HQ PACAF, 9–10 (FOIA).

21. Johnson, "Mayaguez Seizure," 1–7, and enclosures: "Interview . . . Austin," "Interview COL John M. Johnson, USMC, HQ USMC," and "Interview, Col Alfred L. Merrell, USAF." Major Raymond E. Porter, commander of the unit that recaptured the *Mayaguez,* heard informally from an Air Force officer at Utapao of an estimate of ninety to one hundred Cambodians at Koh Tang. Porter recalls mentioning this to a colleague from the unit that was bound for Koh Tang the evening before the attack. The latter, however, has no recollection of hearing about the larger estimate. Johnson, "Mayaguez Seizure," enclosures: "Interview with Major Raymond E. Porter, USMC" and "Interview MAJ John B. Hendricks." All of the formal intelligence briefings the Marines received at Utapao gave estimates of no more than twenty to thirty Cambodians at Koh Tang.

22. Johnson, "Mayaguez Seizure," enclosures: "Interview . . . Austin" and "Interview . . . Porter."

23. Johnson, "Mayaguez Seizure," enclosures: "Interview with LCOL John I. Hopkins, USMC" and "Interview . . . Austin."

24. PACAF, "Evaluation of Intelligence Factors," 8, 10.

25. Johnson, "Mayaguez Seizure," enclosure: "Interview . . . Austin; BLT 2/9, "Koh Tang/*Mayaguez* Historical Report."

26. The lack of prelanding strikes against these gun emplacements caused a swirl of controversy after the operation. Senior officials said a high-level decision not to "prepare" the landing zones, so as to not endanger the *Mayaguez* crew, precluded such strikes. Indeed, there was a decision not to soften the landing zone with blanket artillery and/or aircraft fire; the JCS instructed to use "minimum force" during the landing. Message, Major General Earl J. Archer, "Lessons Learned—SS Mayaguez/Koh Tang Island Operation," AFSSO/USSAG/7AF/NKP TH/CS to AFSSO PACAF, 110915Z June 75 (FOIA); Command History Branch, "Pacific Command History," 26; DCS/Plans and Operations, "Assault on Koh Tang," HQ PACAF, June 23, 1975, 3 (FOIA); Congress, Reports of the Comptroller General of The United States, *Seizure of the Mayaguez, Part IV* (Washington, DC, 1976), 89. But there was no ban on limited preas-

sault strikes against identified targets. A CinCPac message stated that "TacAir will provide CAS [close air support] for Marine assault force (including pre-assault strikes as required)." Quoted in Patrick, "Mayaguez Operation," 92.

27. Johnson was led to believe none were available when he asked for the OV-10s. Johnson taped interview. But when the Marines ran into trouble, USSAG ordered OV-10s into action. Within hours they were on the scene. Message, USSAG/7AF to 56 SOW, 150315Z May 75, and message, USSAG/7AF to 56 SOW, 150740Z, May 1975, in Chronological Order Listing of Significant Message Traffic, 150001Z–151513Z, May 1975, in PACAF, "Mayaguez Operation, Miscellaneous Documents, 75/05/12–75/05/29," HQ PACAF, Hickam AFB, HI (FOIA).

28. "News & Comment: The President's Daily News Summary," Thursday, May 15, 1975, Box 19, James Shuman File, GRFL.

29. Message: "Story Background," 56 SOW Nakhon Phanom RTAFB TH/OI to CINCPACAF/HI/OI, 220115 May 1975 (FOIA).

30. Message: "Orders During SS Mayaguez Operation," CinCPac Honolulu HI to JCS WashDC, 201723Z May 1975, section 2, 2 (FOIA).

31. DCS/Plans and Operations, "Assault on Koh Tang," 3–11; Patrick, "Mayaguez Operation," 55–59; 92–93. General Burns explained after the operation that the fighters were refueling so they could cover the early stages of the landing. The AC-130 was returning to base because USSAG had a limited number of these planes, ideally suited for night action, and wanted to husband this resource, for it was unclear "how long the action would last." Burns interview, May 14, 1992.

32. DCS/Plans and Operations, "Assault on Koh Tang," 2–14; Patrick, "Mayaguez Operation," 55–59. In an interview shortly after the operation, Colonel Johnson exclaimed bitterly: "Wherever in the name of God was the fixed wing preparation of the landing zone that we requested the night before the landing? . . . What happened to the request, where were they, why was it not delivered?" Johnson taped interview.

33. Message, "56 Special Operations Wing Activities," 56 SOW Nakhon Phanom Airprt Thai/DO to CINCPACAF Hickam AFB HI/XO, 191200Z May 75, section 4, 3, and section 5, 2 (FOIA). The 3d ARRGp and the 21st SOS specialized in hazardous missions, but their pilots, though top-notch, were inexperienced in assault landings.

34. DCS/Plans and Operations, "Assault on Koh Tang," 2–26; Patrick, "Mayaguez Operation," 57–60; BLT 2/9, "Koh Tang/*Mayaguez* Historical Report;" Dunham and Quinlan, *Marines in Vietnam*.

35. Patrick, "Mayaguez Operation," 69–71.

36. Ibid., 47–51.

37. Ibid., 103. See also, "Informal Statements on the Operation, Cricket Problem Areas," in PACAF "Mayaguez . . . Miscellaneous Documents"; "Cricket 02 Mission Log" in 3 TFW, "AF History, Supporting Document," 75/04/01 to 75/06/30, vol. 6, Department of the Air Force, HQ 3D Combat Support Group (PACAF), APO SF 96274 (FOIA).

38. "Mayaguez/Koh Tang Operation, Pilot Interview," Iris1022548 pub. 75/06/01, PACAF, Hickam AFB (FOIA); Patrick, "Mayaguez Operation," 90. Each jet could spend no more than thirty to forty minutes over Koh Tang before refueling.

39. Transcript quotes from SS Mayaguez Recovery Operation, Tab C,

UHF Link, USSAG/INP, "Summary of the Mayaguez Sitreps," 14 May 1975, in PACAF, "Mayaguez... Miscellaneous Documents," and "Cricket 02 Mission Log"; helicopter pilot observations from "Personal Notes by Capt. Des Brisay, 5 June 1975," in PACAF, "Mayaguez... Miscellaneous Documents."

40. Patrick, "Mayaguez Operation," 72; message, "56 Special Operation Wing Activities," and message, "Superlative Performance of OV-10 A/C," 56 SOW NKP RTAFB TH/DO to CINCPACAF Hickam AFB HI/CC/XO, 180910Z June 1975 (FOIA). The following sums up the air-support situation until the OV-10s arrived: "At times, TacAir support would report that they (TacAir) were coming in. Friendly ground forces could not see the planes; bombs would hit. It was thought that Laser Guided Bombs (LGBs) were being used. In the afternoon, airstrikes continued without control from the ground." Patrick, "Mayaguez Operation," 72.

41. Further complicating close air support were the battlefield dimensions. The Marines landed on the northern tip of Koh Tang, a thin finger of land less than half a mile wide. The pockets of Marines on the east and west beaches were only a few hundred yards apart. In between were the Cambodians, some ten yards from the Marines. It often was difficult for the aircraft to attack enemy positions without endangering U.S. troops. DCS/Plans and Operations, "Assault on Koh Tang," 21; Patrick, "Mayaguez Operation," 73.

42. Lieutenant Colonel Randall W. Austin, taped interview, June 5, 1975, USMCHMD.

43. Austin taped interview; Major J. B. Hendricks, "Mayday for the Mayaguez: The Battalion Operations Officer," *U.S. Naval Institute Proceedings* 102 (November 1976): 105–108; Dunham and Quinlan, *Marines in Vietnam,* 250–255; BLT 2/9, "Koh Tang/*Mayaguez* Historical Report."

44. "After Action Report, US Military Operations, SS Mayaguez/Kaoh Tang Island 12–15 May 1975: JCS Log of Significant Events" (n.d.; probably May 1975), 6, JCS Records (FOIA).

45. Ibid., 5; Hu Nim, quoted in "Chronology of Thirteenth Air Force 1 July 1974–June 1975, Volume I-Narrative," Office of History, HQ, Thirteenth Air Force, Clark AFB, Philippines, 752–753 (FOIA).

46. Richard G. Head, Frisco W. Short, and Robert C. McFarlane, *Crisis Resolution: Presidential Decision Making in the Mayaguez and Korean Confrontations* (Boulder, CO, 1978), 133–138; Schlesinger, "Ruminations," 24–25; "After Action Report: JCS Log of Significant Events," 6.

47. Ford quoted in Head, Short, and McFarlane, *Crisis Resolution,* 133.

48. Command History Branch, "Pacific Command History," 27; Head, Short, and McFarlane, *Crisis Resolution,* 140–141; "After Action Report: JCS Log of Significant Events," 6. There is convincing evidence that the Koh Tang landing did not influence the decision to release the crew. According to the *Mayaguez's* captain, at 6:20 A.M. on May 15 the guards at Kompong Som received a radio message ordering the release of the crew. A Cambodian interpreter said the order came from the Cambodian high command in Phnom Penh. Given the poor communications in Cambodia at the time, it is unlikely that Phnom Penh knew about the landings on Koh Tang, which had begun moments before, when it issued its order. Even the troops guarding the crew seemed unaware that Koh Tang was under attack. "Seizure of the S.S. Mayaguez by Khmer Rouge Gunboat P 128: Statement of Facts as remembered by

Captain C. T. Miller," May 29, 1975, Box 27, White House Central Files, Case File, Ford to J. Paul Sticht, 4/22/76, GRFL.

49. Nessen, *Looks Different,* 128–129. Kissinger has denied the quotation. "After Action Report: Part II, Verbal Orders ... from SecDef."

50. "After Action Report: Part II, Verbal Orders ... from JCS," 4–5. Gayler, in Washington at the start of the crisis, flew back to Hawaii before the operation began.

51. Patrick, "Mayaguez Operation," 60–63; J. M. Johnson, Jr., R. W. Austin, and D. A. Quinlan, "Individual heroism overcame awkward command relationships, confusion and bad information off the Cambodian coast," *Marine Corps Gazette* 61 (October 1977): 31.

52. SS Mayaguez Recovery Operation, UHF Link/Tacair Log, in PACAF, "Mayaguez ... Miscellaneous Documents"; Burns interview, 1984.

53. Archer interview; message: "Orders During ... Operation," section 3, 2.

54. Johnson taped interview; message: "Orders During ... Operation," section 2, 1–6, and section 3, 1–3. In the morning, CinCPac told USSAG when to land individual helicopters on the island. CinCPac also tried to control the movements of the Marines. When they met stiff opposition, CinCPac ordered that "the GSF [Ground Security Force] Commander not hazard his force [and] not take offensive actions without waiting for reinforcements." Convinced, however, that his men would be less vulnerable in two pockets than in three, Austin decided on his own to link up with the Marines on the west beach. Soon after, CinCPac told USSAG to "pull back the GSF, so can provide suppressive Tacair support." Ibid.

55. Colonel Robert R. Reed, "End of Tour Report," HQ Twelfth Air Force, 5.

56. Message: "Orders During ... Operation," section 2, 2; Patrick, "Mayaguez Operation," 98.

57. DCS/Plans and Operations, "Assault on Koh Tang," 23; Patrick, "Mayaguez Operation," 60.

58. "After Action Report: Part II, Verbal Orders ... from JCS," 4; "ABCCC Mission Tapes ... ," transcribed 9 June 1975 by Capt. Des Brisay, in PACAF, "Mayaguez, Nail Forward Air Controller Message Traffic," Iris # 1022546, pub. 75/05/15, HQ PACAF (FOIA); Patrick, "Mayaguez Operation," 62–63; SS Mayaguez Recovery Operation, UHF Link/Tacair Log, in PACAF "Mayaguez ... Miscellaneous Documents"; Burns interview, May 14, 1992; message: "Orders During ... Operation," section 2, 4.

59. Burns interview, May 14, 1992; Johnson taped interview; Patrick, "Mayaguez Operation," 62–63.

60. DCS/Plans and Operations, "Assault on Koh Tang," 23–26; Patrick, "Mayaguez Operation," 60–62.

61. DCS/Plans and Operations, "Assault on Koh Tang," 26–28; Patrick, "Mayaguez Operation," 60–62. According to Burns, USSAG "felt that [Austin] had to consolidate himself, and we didn't need to worry him about the status of the crew." Burns interview, May 8, 1984.

62. "Mayaguez/Koh Tang Operation, Pilot Interview"; Patrick, "Mayaguez Operation," 65. The servicemen on the east beach were the passengers and crew of the helicopter that crashed on the east of the island early in the operation.

63. "After Action Report: Part II, "Verbal Orders...from CinCPac," 6; DCS/Plans and Operations, "Assault on Koh Tang," 28–29; "ABCCC Mission Tapes...""; "Personal Notes by Capt. Des Brisay." As one postmortem noted, "The arrival of the first OV-10s (Nail 68 and Nail 47) brought a marked improvement to the helicopter and TacAir control situation at Koh Tang." Patrick, "Mayaguez Operation," 90.

64. DCS, Plans and Operations, "Assault on Koh Tang," 28; message: "Orders During...Operation," section 2, 6, and section 3, 1.

65. DCS/Plans and Operations, "Assault on Koh Tang," 29–30; Thomas D. Des Brisay, *Fourteen Hours at Koh Tang* (Washington, DC, 1975) 142–144.

66. Message: "Orders During...Operation," section 3, 2.

67. Johnson taped interview; Des Brisay, *Fourteen Hours at Koh Tang*, 144–145; Hendricks, "Mayday for the Mayaguez," 104–107.

68. Patrick, "Mayaguez Operation," 65. After the operation, Lt. Col. Austin remarked: "I had the distinct feeling during that day that whatever was being decided about what was going to happen on the island was being decided essentially without my input...without any of my approval or consent." Austin taped interview.

69. BLT 2/9, "Koh Tang/*Mayaguez* Historical Report." Emphasis in text.

70. Austin taped interview; confidential interview; BLT 2/9, "Koh Tang/*Mayaguez* Historical Report; memorandum, "Missing in Action Status in the Case of Private First Class Gary C. Hall...Lance Corporal Joseph N. Hargrove ...and Private Danny Marshall...," July 31, 1975, USMCMHD.

71. Message, 56 SOW Nakhon Phanom Afld Thai/CC to CINCPACAF Hickam AFB HI/DP, 240716Z May 75, "Recommendation for Decoration for Heroism." Many of the helicopters that conducted the final evacuation had sustained considerable damage earlier that day. One was flying with a jerry-rigged fuel line of rubber and tape, which mechanics on the *Coral Sea* patched together after it lost its main fuel line in an rescue attempt at the east beach. Major General Leroy J. Manor, "Recommendation for Award of the Presidential Unit Citation," in 3 AFFG Air Force History, Narrative, 75/01/01-75/06/30, Simpson Center, 50 (FOIA).

72. BLT 2/9, "Koh Tang/*Mayaguez* Historical Report"; memorandum, "Jolly Green 43...Recommendation for Heroism," 4, in PACAF, "Miscellaneous Documents, 75/05/12 to 75/06/00," HQ PACAF (FOIA); Manor, "Recommendation for Award," 50.

73. DCS, Plans and Operations, "Assault on Koh Tang," 35; "ABCCC Mission Tapes...."

74. DCS/Plans and Operations, "Assault on Koh Tang," 33, 36; message, "56 SOW Operations Wing Activities," section 5, 3; pilot comments in "Personal Notes by Capt. Des Brisay: Conversation with 1 LT Donald R. Blacklund, Pilot JG 11, 6 June 75." Task Sergeant Wayne L. Fisk, a veteran of difficult missions, had been on the Sontay rescue mission. A Marine Corps history states a Marine officer and NCO also were with Fisk combing "the beach one last time for stragglers." Dunham and Quinlan, *Marines in Vietnam*, 262.

75. Confidential interview.

76. Hoffman interview; Steele interview; Burns interview, May 14, 1992. According to a subsequent Marine Corps investigation, the three missing men were last seen on May 15 at 8.00 P.M., ten minutes before the last helicopter left Koh Tang. What happened to them afterward is unknown. Memorandum,

"Missing in Action Status." A senior Marine Corps general later recalled that "there was a good deal of pressure" to have these "MIA" listed as "Killed in Action." Confidential interview.

77. Peter Goldman, "Ford's Rescue Operation," *Newsweek,* May 26, 1975, 16; "News & Comment," Friday, May 16, 1975, Box 19, Shuman File, GRFL; Michael Morrow, "Ford: Fastest Gun in the East," *Far Eastern Economic Review,* May 30, 1975, 10.

78. Had there been less haste to send in the Marines, however, the United States could have used forces trained in clandestine infiltration from the sea— such as Navy SEALs or Marine Corps reconnaissance forces—to scout the island beforehand for intelligence on the defenders and signs that the *Mayaguez* crew was there.

79. Quoted in "The Mayaguez—What Went Right, Wrong," *U.S. News and World Report,* June 2, 1975, 29; Steele OH, Naval Historical Center, 100.

Chapter 7

1. Gary G. Sick, *All Fall Down: America's Tragic Encounter with Iran* (New York, 1986), 50–166, 228–242; Pierre Salinger, *America Held Hostage: The Secret Negotiations* (New York, 1981), 28–29. Bazargan resigned two days after the embassy takeover, as it became apparent that the Iranian government would not force the militants to release the hostages.

2. On the struggle between "moderates" and "radicals" in the new regime, see for example James A. Bill, *The Eagle and the Lion: The Tragedy of American-Iranian Relations* (New Haven, 1988), 263–270, and Barry Rubin, *Paved with Good Intentions: The American Experience and Iran* (New York, 1980), 217–336.

3. Sick, *All Fall Down,* 243–253; Jimmy Carter, *Keeping Faith: Memoirs of a President* (New York, 1982), 457–463; Zbigniew Brzezinski, *Power and Principle: Memoirs of the National Security Adviser, 1977–1981* (New York, 1983), 477–478; Hamilton Jordan, *Crisis: The last year of the Carter Presidency* (New York, 1983), 25–26, 43; Cyrus Vance, *Hard Choices: Critical Years in America's Foreign Policy* (New York, 1983), 377; Stansfield Turner, *Terrorism and Democracy* (Boston, 1991), 25–26. Under Carter, the core NSC members were the president, vice president, the secretaries of state and defense, the national security adviser, the CIA director, and the JCS chairman. Others were sometimes invited for their specialized expertise.

4. Quoted in Jordan, *Crisis,* 43.

5. Carter, *Keeping Faith,* 459.

6. Quoted in Jordan, *Crisis,* 32.

7. Sick, *All Fall Down,* 228–293; Carter, *Keeping Faith,* 485; Turner, *Terrorism and Democracy,* 85–89. On the negotiations with Bourguet and Villalon, see Jordan, *Crisis,* pp. 93ff.

8. Carter, *Keeping Faith,* 496–497; Jordan, *Crisis,* 148–153; Sick, *All Fall Down,* 301–302, 311.

9. Khomeini quoted in Sick, *All Fall Down,* 316–317; Carter, *Keeping Faith,* 497–499; Jordan, *Crisis,* 162–178; Salinger, *America Held Hostage,* 168–186.

10. Carter, *Keeping Faith,* 499; text of letter in Sick, *All Fall Down,* 322.

11. Carter, *Keeping Faith,* 501–502; Jordan, *Crisis,* 223–226; Sick, *All Fall Down,* 322.

12. *Crisis,* 227; Sick, *All Fall Down,* 325–326.

13. Sick, *All Fall Down,* 327; Carter, *Keeping Faith,* 505.

14. Jordan, *Crisis,* 176. Switzerland represented U.S. interests in Iran after the takeover of the U.S. embassy, and Bourguet and Villalon relied extensively on the local Swiss embassy to communicate with Washington from Tehran.

15. Rosalynn Carter, *First Lady from Plains* (Boston, 1984), 319; Turner, *Terrorism and Democracy,* 99.

16. Carter quoted in Jordan, *Crisis,* 88, and Sick, *All Fall Down,* 326; Carter, *Keeping Faith,* 499.

17. Carter, *First Lady,* 323.

18. Brzezinski, *Power,* 490. CIA Director Turner likewise writes: "While the President and his political advisers must have been extremely conscious of the effect of the crisis on Jimmy Carter's prospects for re-election, I never saw any hint of his placing that consideration above what was in the best interests of the hostages." Turner, *Terrorism and Democracy,* 82.

19. Jordan, *Crisis,* 12.

20. Salinger, *America Held Hostage,* 88.

21. Quoted in Jordan, *Crisis,* 216. By late November 1979 Iran had released thirteen female and African-American hostages from among the sixty-six seized on November 4.

22. Sick, *All Fall Down,* 329; Vance, *Hard Choices,* 407.

23. Turner, *Terrorism and Democracy,* 82–84, 100, 106; Zbigniew Brzezinski, "The Failed Mission: The Inside Account of the Attempt to Free the Hostages in Iran," *New York Times Magazine,* April 18, 1982, 29; Carter quoted in Brzezinski, *Power,* 486. On growing popular impatience with the crisis, see also Carter, *First Lady,* 321; Carter, *Keeping Faith,* 489; Sick, *All Fall Down,* 329. Carter also had to contend with criticism from his Republican opposition. As early as November 1979, Republican presidential candidate Alexander M. Haig, Jr., had criticized Carter for "impulsively ruling out the use of force against Iran." That same month, Republican presidential candidate Ronald Reagan stated that Carter's "weakness and vacillation" had helped bring about the hostage crisis. Quoted in Turner, *Terrorism and Democracy,* 84.

24. Jordan, *Crisis,* 218–219. Much of the anti-Carter sentiment in these states, which have large Jewish populations, was in reaction to a U.S. vote in early 1980 at the UN for a resolution condemning Israel. In the winter of 1980, however, opinion polls showed that Carter's approval rating was low nationwide. The White House probably viewed the Connecticut and New York votes not just as an expression of dissatisfaction over the UN incident, but as a larger protest against the bulk of Carter's policies, including his handling of the economy, then in a serious recession, and of the hostage crisis.

25. Jordan, *Crisis,* 213.

26. Brzezinski, "The Failed Mission," 29; Sick, *All Fall Down,* 419–420. At the outset, CIA Director Turner was excluded from this planning cell. Turner quickly caught wind of its existence and was "livid" that he and the CIA were being left out. After he complained vehemently to Brzezinski, he was added to the group. Turner, *Terrorism and Democracy,* 38–40.

27. Paul B. Ryan, *The Iranian Rescue Mission: Why It Failed* (Annapolis, 1985), 17–28; James H. Kyle, *The Guts to Try* (New York, 1990), 15–29.

28. Special Operations Review Group, "Rescue Mission Report" (Washington, DC, 1980), 15–16. In May of 1980 the JCS appointed the Special Op-

erations Review Group, composed of six senior active duty and retired military officers, to investigate the failed mission. Although the original report remains classified, the Department of Defense released a declassified version, "Rescue Mission Report," in August 1980. See also Ryan, *Iranian Rescue,* 17–28; Kyle, *Guts,* 15–19, 29.

29. "Rescue Mission Report," 15–16.

30. Ibid., v. Emphasis in original.

31. Kyle, *Guts,* 47–48; Ryan, *Iranian Rescue,* 36–37.

32. Kyle, *Guts,* 94–97, 105–106; "Rescue Mission Report," 35–36; Ryan, *Iranian Rescue,* 41.

33. Lieutenant General James B. Vaught, interview with author, Arlington, VA, May 22, 1984; Seiffert and Fitch quoted in David C. Martin and John Walcott, *Best Laid Plans: The Inside Story of America's War Against Terrorism* (New York, 1988), 34–35. The planners have explained that from the time the JTF was first assembled, it had to be ready to go on very short notice because the captors could start harming the hostages at any time. The emphasis was on putting together an operational helicopter force quickly and keeping it primed. In such circumstances, Seiffert observed, "you do not have the option of taking all those people off to gain access to better qualified aviators." Vaught interview; Seiffert in Martin and Walcott, *Best Laid Plans,* 35.

34. "Rescue Mission Report," 42.

35. Ibid., 35. The Special Operations Review Group noted, however, that Air Force pilots aboard a carrier would have made it more difficult to keep mission preparations secret. Ibid., 36.

36. Charlie A. Beckwith and Donald Knox, *Delta Force* (New York, 1983), 253; Kyle, *Guts,* 102, 124–130, 140, 166–170, 178–180; Turner, *Terrorism and Democracy,* 69, 88–89, 105.

37. Beckwith and Knox, *Delta Force,* 253–256; Kyle, *Guts,* 181.

38. Beckwith and Knox, *Delta Force,* 253–256; Kyle, *Guts,* 181–183.

39. Beckwith and Knox, *Delta Force,* 256; Kyle, *Guts,* 183–184.

40. Beckwith and Knox *Delta Force,* 196; Admiral Stansfield Turner, interview with author, McLean, VA, May 21, 1984; Steven Emerson, *Secret Warriors: Inside the Covert Military Operations of the Reagan Era* (New York, 1988), 20–21. For a good account of intelligence gathering and other activities for the mission by CIA and military agents in Iran, see Martin and Walcott, *Best Laid Plans,* 6–12ff.

41. Turner interview; Turner, *Terrorism and Democracy,* 87.

42. Beckwith and Knox, *Delta Force,* 197.

43. "Rescue Mission Report," 19–20.

44. Vaught interview.

45. Quoted in Emerson, *Secret Warriors,* 20.

46. Ibid., 21.

47. Vaught interview. On the CIA's skepticism and reluctance to assist military agents, see also Martin and Walcott, *Best Laid Plans,* 7.

48. Vaught, quoted in Martin and Walcott, *Best Laid Plans,* 11; Beckwith and Knox, *Delta Force,* 264; Ryan, *Iranian Rescue,* 35. In *Secret Warriors,* Emerson writes:

In fact, Army officials have now revealed that the story [of the cook] was fabricated by the CIA. The information was actually provided by a deep-cover Iranian CIA source who had earlier gained access to the hostages. Only in 1985—five years after the mission—did a senior official of the Joint Task Force learn the real story: "The Agency had someone in Teheran the whole time and did not want to reveal their source's existence until they were sure the mission was taking place. But we never knew it at the time." Even when the mission was set to go, the CIA did not want to jeopardize his contacts or his life, so it falsely attributed its newly obtained information to the cook. Indeed, the Iranians had suddenly released a cook, but much of the information came from someone else. (Emerson, *Secret Warriors*, 21)

49. Vaught interview.
50. "Rescue Mission Report," 19.
51. Ibid., 39.
52. Ibid., 50.
53. Ibid., 26. The cohesion of the force might have been greater if, like the Sontay raiders, the various components of the rescue mission force had deployed to a single location where they would have devoted themselves exclusively to preparing for the mission. The JTF, however, had determined that only one U.S. training site could accommodate that large a force without risk of compromise. The JTF request to use the site was turned down with the explanation that "national security priorities precluded" its use. The planners also had qualms about isolating the force in one location, lest the members' prolonged absence from their normal bases arouse suspicion. Kyle, *Guts*, 72–73.
54. "Rescue Mission Report," 33.
55. Ibid., 33–34.
56. Admiral James L. Holloway III, interview with author, Washington, DC, June 25, 1984; Martin and Walcott, *Best Laid Plans*, 31. The eighth helicopter was added a few days before the mission. By then the JTF's calculations showed that the raiders needed seven helicopters to conduct the operation with an adequate safety margin. Brzezinski, *Power*, 495. General Pustay was concerned about this number. At an April meeting at the White House, Deputy NSC Director Aaron asked Pustay in an aside what was his greatest concern about the operation. Pustay replied: "The helicopters. I know [their fragility] well." Lieutenant General John S. Pustay, interview with author, Arlington, VA, March 3, 1984. This led to further discussion of the issue and a last-minute decision to add another helicopter. Brzezinski, *Power*, 495.
57. Beckwith and Knox, *Delta Force*, 241.
58. "Rescue Mission Report," 50.
59. The pilots would use these goggles, which intensify star- and moonlight, to enhance nighttime vision.
60. Kyle, *Guts*, 327; "Rescue Mission Report," 38–41. The JTF meteorologists had identified the dust storms as a potential flying hazard and included in the weather annex to the operational plan a chart listing the frequency, by month and location, of their occurrences. Although the helicopter pilots were not told about the storms, the JTF planners, who received the weather annex, knew they could occur.
61. "Rescue Mission Report," 38–40; Kyle, *Guts*, 327–328; Beckwith and Knox, *Delta Force*, 234.
62. "Rescue Mission Report," 38–42; Kyle, *Guts*, 328. Adding more nav-

igational aids, however, would have made even heavier helicopters already several thousand pounds overweight.

63. "Rescue Mission Report," 44–46.

64. Ibid., 44; Martin and Walcott, *Best Laid Plans,* 34.

65. "Rescue Mission Report," 44.

66. Ibid., 45. Seiffert, commander of the JTF helicopter detachment, was flying one of the training helicopters—a Marine Corps CH-53—when a BIM indication occurred. Martin and Walcott, *Best Laid Plans,* 34; Kyle, *Guts,* 115, 190.

67. "Rescue Mission Report," 22; Kyle, *Guts,* 33.

68. Beckwith and Knox, *Delta Force,* 237.

69. Colonel Charlie A. Beckwith, interview with author, Austin, TX, April 23, 1984.

70. Beckwith and Knox, *Delta Force,* 237.

71. Kyle, *Guts,* 173; David C. Martin, "Inside the Rescue Mission," *Newsweek,* July 12, 1982, 19.

72. Turner, *Terrorism and Democracy,* 110.

73. "Rescue Mission Report," 49.

74. Beckwith and Knox, *Delta Force,* 253–254; Kyle, *Guts,* 181–184.

75. Beckwith and Knox, *Delta Force,* 249–250.

76. Ibid., 233.

77. Confidential interview. Shortly after the operation, certain journalists gained access to a memorandum, allegedly written by the CIA before the raid, which predicted that 60 percent of the hostages were likely to die in a rescue attempt. Salinger, *America Held Hostage,* 237–238. CIA Director Turner, however, is emphatic that the CIA made no official estimate of the mission's chances of success or of the likelihood of casualties. Turner interview.

Chapter 8

1. Zbigniew Brzezinski, "The Failed Mission: The Inside Account of the Attempt to Free the Hostages in Iran," *New York Times Magazine,* April 18, 1982, 30.

2. Gary Sick, *All Fall Down: America's Tragic Encounter with Iran* (New York, 1986), 337; Stansfield Turner, *Terrorism and Democracy* (Boston, 1991), 67; James H. Kyle, *The Guts to Try* (New York, 1990), 140. According to the Special Operations Review Group, it was February when the military first had confidence "that a capability existed for the rescue." Special Operations Review Group, "Rescue Mission Report" (Department of Defense, Washington, DC, 1980), 7.

3. Jimmy Carter, *Keeping Faith: Memoirs of a President* (New York, 1982), 501. CIA Director Turner had on two previous occasions, in January and February, requested permission to send a reconnaissance flight to Desert One. Fearing that the negotiations then under way might be jeopardized if the flight were detected, Carter had turned down these earlier requests. Turner, *Terrorism and Democracy,* 89, 98.

4. Cyrus Vance, *Hard Choices: Critical Years in America's Foreign Policy* (New York, 1983), 408–409; Brzezinski, "Failed Mission," 30; Turner, *Terrorism and Democracy,* 101–102.

5. Hamilton Jordan, *Crisis: The last year of the Carter Presidency* (New York, 1983), 229.

6. Turner, *Terrorism and Democracy,* 105–106; Sick, *All Fall Down,* 338–341; Zbigniew Brzezinski, *Power and Principle: Memoirs of the National Security Adviser,* 1977–1981 (New York, 1983), 491–492; Carter, *Keeping Faith,* 504–505.

7. Turner, *Terrorism and Democracy,* 101; 106.

8. Memo quoted in Sick, *All Fall Down,* 341; Brzezinski, *Power,* 491–492.

9. Brzezinski, *Power,* 492–493; Carter, *Keeping Faith,* 506–507; Jordan, *Crisis,* 233–235; Vance, *Hard Choices,* 409; Turner, *Terrorism and Democracy,* 107.

10. Ibid.

11. Vance, *Hard Choices,* 409–410; Jordan, *Crisis,* 246.

12. Jordan, *Crisis,* 236; Vance, *Hard Choices,* 410; Brzezinski, *Power,* 494; Carter, quoted in Jordan, *Crisis,* 237; Carter, *Keeping Faith,* 507; Turner, *Terrorism and Democracy,* 108–109.

13. Lieutenant General James B. Vaught, interview with author, Arlington, VA, May 22, 1984; Charlie A. Beckwith and Donald Knox, *Delta Force* (New York, 1983), 7.

14. Christopher quoted in Beckwith and Knox, *Delta Force,* 7; Beckwith quoted in Jordan, *Crisis,* 246. Major Logan Fitch, who would lead Delta's assault on the embassy, was later quite explicit about what would have happened to the guards. "We were not there to arrest anybody," he said. "We were there to kill them. We were going to kill a lot of people." Quoted in David C. Martin and John Walcott, *Best Laid Plans: The Inside Story of America's War Against Terrorism* (New York, 1988), 4.

15. Carter, *Keeping Faith,* 507.

16. Carter, *Keeping Faith,* 507; Beckwith and Knox, *Delta Force,* 9–10; Brzezinski, *Power,* 495; Jordan, *Crisis,* 245–246; Turner, *Terrorism and Democracy,* 110–114.

17. Colonel Charlie A. Beckwith, interview with author, Austin, TX, April 23, 1984. According to one participant at the meeting, however, Beckwith stated: "We're going to get these people out, you can be sure of that." Frank Carlucci, Memorandum to Admiral Stansfield Turner, April 17, 1980, quoted in Turner, *Terrorism and Democracy,* 114.

18. Zbigniew Brzezinski, interview with author, Washington DC, June 8, 1984.

19. Confidential interview.

20. Among the civilian advisers, Brzezinski, Brown, and Turner, who met regularly to review the planning for the mission, had the best grasp of the plan. Even they, however, lacked the time to probe every detail.

21. "Rescue Mission Report," 21. To their credit, in an effort to spot the deficiencies in their product, the planners formed a "murder board" drawn from the JTF staff to review the planning for the mission. Kyle, *Guts,* 142. Evaluating one's own work is difficult, however. Not surprisingly, the JTF "murder board" overlooked significant shortcomings of its plan.

22. "Rescue Mission Report," 21. The chiefs were JCS Chairman General David C. Jones, Air Force General Lew Allen, Jr., Army General Edward C. Meyer, Marine Corps Commandant General Robert H. Barrow, and Navy Admiral Thomas B. Hayward.

23. Quoted in Martin and Walcott, *Best Laid Plans*, 32.

24. Carter, *Keeping Faith*, 512; Brzezinski, *Power*, 495–496; Beckwith and Knox, *Delta Force*, 262–266; Kyle, *Guts*, 205 ff; Jordan, *Crisis*, 249.

25. Carter, *Keeping Faith*, 513; Admiral Stansfield Turner, interview with author, Mclean, VA, May 21, 1984; Turner, *Terrorism and Democracy*, 118.

26. Turner, *Terrorism and Democracy*, 106. Turner points out, however, that up to the end the president, who had more at stake politically than the rest of the administration, was more reluctant than most of his advisers to use force. *Terrorism and Democracy*, 106.

27. W. Graham Claytor, Jr., interview with author, Washington, DC, April 17, 1984; Brzezinski interview.

28. Carter, *Keeping Faith*, 506; Sick, *All Fall Down*, 275–276; Betty Glad, "Personality, Political and Group Process Variables in Foreign Policy Decision-Making: Jimmy Carter's Handling of the Iranian Hostage Crisis," *International Political Science Review* 10 (January 1989): 44; Vance, *Hard Choices*, 410.

29. Jordan, *Crisis*, 232.

30. Ibid., 214, 234; emphasis in original.

31. Kyle, *Guts*, 238.

32. "Rescue Mission Report," 44–45; Paul B. Ryan, *The Iranian Rescue Mission: Why It Failed* (Annapolis, 1985), 69–70; Kyle, *Guts*, 249–250.

33. Pilot quoted in Ryan, *Iranian Rescue*, 70; Russell E. Rakip OH, Simpson Center, 2, 5; Martin and Walcott, *Best Laid Plans*, 13.

34. Kyle, *Guts*, 233–243; "Rescue Mission Report," 47.

35. Martin and Walcott, *Best Laid Plans*, 19–20.

36. "Rescue Mission Report," 45. Both the lead C-130 and Dash Five, the helicopter carrying Colonel Pitman, the overall helicopter force commander, carried satellite communications systems (SATCOM). The SATCOMs aboard the C-130 and Dash Five could not communicate with each other, but both could communicate with General Vaught and mission headquarters in Wadi Kena, Egypt. Wadi Kena thus could pass on to Dash Five information from the C-130. The C-130 communicators, however, were barely trained on the SAT-COM. When the lead C-130 encountered the suspended dust, its communicators tried to send out an encoded warning via SATCOM but could not use its special encryption system. Unwilling to send an uncoded message, they gave up. They did not realize that even unencoded SATCOM messages were secure. Kyle later termed the C-130 communicators' lack of familiarity with the SATCOM a "monumental disconnect." Kyle, *Guts*, 143, 223–224, 249–252, 273, 329–336; "Rescue Mission Report," 48.

37. Beckwith and Knox, *Delta Force*, 268–270; Martin and Walcott, *Best Laid Plans*, 14–17; Kyle, *Guts*, 255–262. The occupants of the fuel truck were not the only ones to stumble across the unusual activity at Desert One and get away. The driver of the truck that drove by as the lead C-130 activated the landing beacons at the strip undoubtedly noticed these unusual lights. Kyle, *Guts*, 258.

38. Brzezinski, *Power*, 497.

39. Carter, *Keeping Faith*, 515.

40. "Rescue Mission Report," 60. Dash Two suffered a hydraulic system failure en route to Desert One and, after its crew inspected the aircraft upon arrival, the helicopter flight leader determined it was unsafe to fly it any further. The raiders decided to abandon it at Desert One while they proceeded in the re-

maining helicopters to the hideaway near Tehran. The Iranian gendarmerie (paramilitary police) maintained a daytime presence in a town fifteen miles southwest of Desert One.

41. "Rescue Mission Report," 51; Beckwith and Knox, *Delta Force*, 270–275; Kyle, *Guts*, 277–282.

42. Quoted in Beckwith and Knox, *Delta Force*, 273–274. See also Kyle, *Guts*, 280, 285.

43. Rakip OH, 5; Kyle, *Guts*, 279; 284.

44. Ryan, *Iranian Rescue*, 81; "Rescue Mission Report," 50.

45. "Rescue Mission Report," 50–51; Beckwith and Knox, *Delta Force*, 275–276; Kyle, *Guts*, 283, 301.

46. "Rescue Mission Report," 45; Ryan, *Iranian Rescue*, 83–84.

47. Ryan, *Iranian Rescue*, 84; Kyle, *Guts*, 288, 336.

48. Beckwith and Knox, *Delta Force*, 275; Kyle, *Guts*, 285–288.

49. Beckwith and Knox, *Delta Force*, 276–278; Brzezinski, *Power*, 498; Carter, *Keeping Faith*, 515–516; Kyle, *Guts*, 287–291.

50. The helicopters used for the raid deployed to the carrier U.S.S. *Nimitz* in the Indian Ocean in early January 1980. One helicopter turned back after key navigational aids failed and another was abandoned en route because of rotor problems. Hydraulic problems on a third made it unsafe to fly past Desert One. This prompted widespread speculation that the helicopters had not been properly maintained. Like most Navy ships in the late 1970s and early 1980s, the *Nimitz* was short of skilled technicians. General Vaught maintains that poor and inadequately supervised maintenance aboard was a major cause of the mechanical problems. He points out that of the five flyable helicopters that reached Desert One, only three were in top, or "green," condition. The others, while still flyable, had had problems en route and were in only "amber" condition, after completing merely 65 percent of the flying planned for the mission. In his words, "This number of failures was unprecedented for so few helicopters." He stressed that in 2,200 hours of training with similar CH-53 helicopters in the United States, there had been only one mechanical problem forcing a helicopter to abort. He added that a senior JTF maintenance expert sent to the *Nimitz* in early 1980 found "many deficiencies," which the Navy had promised to correct. Vaught interview. Seiffert, commander of the JTF helicopter detachment and helicopter flight leader, likewise recalls that the JTF was "not happy" with the situation aboard the carrier in late 1979 and early 1980. Martin and Walcott, *Best Laid Plans*, 33.

Others dispute maintenance was a problem. According to former chief of naval operations Admiral James Holloway, who chaired the Special Operations Review Group, "Those planes were in the best material condition of any helicopter in the world. The best maintenance people in the U.S. [were aboard the carrier]. The *Nimitz*'s maintenance squadron had been quietly beefed up . . . and the maintenance personnel were handpicked. Then additional Marine Corps and Air Force maintenance went aboard. . . . Maintenance was not a factor." Admiral James L. Holloway III, interview with author, Washington, DC, June 25, 1984. Civilian technical representatives from the helicopter manufacturer were also sent aboard to deal with any special problem that might arise. According to one of the helicopter pilots who took part in the mission,

The maintenance people they had out there on the boat were taking good care of the aircraft already. Then we showed up on the carrier and went through the books on our aircraft, which had already been done before. Our dedicated maintenance officer flew out there and basically checked on the assumption of what we wanted done, could each aircraft perform.... We had twenty maintenance people who knew what they were looking for, i.e. one was a hydraulics specialist, another worked engines, etc....We scrutinized them and then flew them hard, as I have said. We did find a few items, but nothing major. I was impressed with the condition of my aircraft. We would not have flown them on that kind of mission had they not been so close to perfect as one can get. (Rakip OH, 4)

Another pilot recalled that after visiting the *Nimitz* in March, "I had no worries about maintenance when I left the ship." Quoted in Martin and Walcott, *Best Laid Plans,* 33. After some original problems, shipboard maintenance seems to have improved markedly in the first months of 1980.

51. Beckwith and Knox, *Delta Force,* 277–278; Kyle, *Guts,* 291–292.

52. Beckwith interview.

53. Martin and Walcott, *Best Laid Plans,* 24.

54. Rakip OH, 6–7; Beckwith and Knox, *Delta Force,* 278–279; Kyle, *Guts,* 295–299. Beckwith later commented: "God looked after us. I don't know why the helicopter closest to the blaze did not cook off." Beckwith interview.

55. Kyle, *Guts,* 298–301.

56. "Rescue Mission Report," 50.

57. Rakip OH, 7; Kyle, *Guts,* 304–305.

58. Turner, *Terrorism and Democracy,* 122.

59. Kyle, *Guts,* 302–304, 307–308; Turner, *Terrorism and Democracy,* 122–124.

60. Carter, *Keeping Faith,* 518; Aaron quoted in Sick, *All Fall Down,* 352.

61. "Rescue Mission Report," 22.

Chapter 9

1. "Prospects for the Castro Regime," Special National Intelligence Estimate (SNIE) 85-3-60, December 8, 1960, DDRS 1984/001524, 1–2. The SNIEs on political and military developments in Cuba were a joint product of the CIA, the National Security Agency (NSA), and the intelligence branches of the Departments of State, the Army, the Navy, the Air Force, the Joint Staff, and the Department of Defense.

2. Richard M. Bissell, Jr., "Reflections on the Bay of Pigs: OPERATION ZAPATA" (book review), *Strategic Review* 12 (Winter 1984): 69.

3. Benjamin F. Schemmer, *The Raid* (New York, 1976), 38, 40–41, 142–143.

4. Ibid., 100.

5. Charlie A. Beckwith and Donald Knox, *Delta Force* (New York, 1983), 196, 221.

6. Ibid., 264.

7. Bob Woodward, *Veil: The Secret Wars of the CIA, 1981–1987* (New York, 1987), 110, 114; James Coates and Michael Kilian, *Heavy Losses: The Dangerous Decline of American Defense* (New York, 1985), 350; Allen E. Goodman, "Dateline Langley: Fixing the Intelligence Mess," *Foreign Policy* 57 (Winter 1984–1985): 165–166.

8. Loch K. Johnson, *America's Secret Power: The CIA in a Democratic Society* (New York, 1989), 64–65, 84–86.

9. Quoted in Steven Emerson, *Secret Warriors: Inside the Covert Military Operations of the Reagan Era* (New York, 1988), 34–35.

10. David C. Martin and John Walcott, *Best Laid Plans: The Inside Story of America's War Against Terrorism* (New York, 1988), 47; James Adams, *Secret Armies: Inside the American, Soviet and European Special Forces* (New York, 1988), 210–211, 231; Arthur T. Hadley, *The Straw Giant. Triumph and Failure: America's Armed Forces. A Report from the Field* (New York, 1986), 14.

11. Gregory F. Treverton, *Covert Action: The Limits of Intervention in the Postwar World* (New York, 1987), 29; Jeffrey T. Richelson, *The U.S. Intelligence Community* (Cambridge, MA, 1989), 234–235; Johnson, *America's Secret Power,* 70–71; Roy Godson, *Intelligence Requirements for the 1990s: Collection, Analysis, Counterintelligence, and Covert Action* (Lexington, MA, 1989), 15–16.

12. Special Operations Review Group, "Rescue Mission Report" (Washington, DC, 1980), 19.

13. Graham T. Allison, *Essence of Decision: Explaining the Cuban Missile Crisis* (Boston, 1971), 81; Graham T. Allison and Peter Szanton, *Remaking Foreign Policy: The Organizational Connection* (New York, 1976), 180; I. M. Destler, *Presidents, Bureaucrats, and Foreign Policy: The Politics of Organizational Reform* (Princeton, 1974), 71–72; Morton H. Halperin and David Halperin, "The Key West Key," *Foreign Policy* 53 (Winter 1983–1984): 118–119; Samuel P. Huntington, "Defense organization and military strategy," *Public Interest* 75 (Spring 1984): 21, 45.

14. Beckwith and Knox, *Delta Force,* 295; Edward N. Luttwak, Steven L. Canby, and David L. Thomas, *A Systematic Review of "Commando" (Special) Operations, 1939–1980* (Potomac, MD, C & L Associates, n.d.), I:26–27; Edward N. Luttwak, *The Pentagon and the Art of War: The Question of Military Reform* (New York, 1985), 44–45.

15. The *Mayaguez* operation was an exception: much of the JCS Joint Staff in Washington was involved in the planning. Admiral Harry D. Train, II, interview with author, Norfolk, VA, June 5, 1984.

16. General Lyman L. Lemnitzer, interview with author, Washington, DC, April 27, 1984; Beckwith and Knox, *Delta Force,* 252ff.

17. Quoted in Hamilton Jordan, *Crisis: The last year of the Carter Presidency* (New York, 1983), 246.

18. Martin and Walcott, *Best Laid Plans,* 32; BGen Johnson to Admiral Gayler, "SS Mayaguez Seizure," enclosure: "Interview, Walter H. Baxter, III," Headquarters, Pacific Air Forces, Hickam AFB, HI.

19. George E. Reedy, *The Twilight of the Presidency* (New York, 1970), 12–13.

20. Quoted in Thomas G. Paterson, "Fixation with Cuba: The Bay of Pigs, Missile Crisis, and Covert War Against Fidel Castro," in Thomas G. Paterson, ed., *Kennedy's Quest for Victory: American Foreign Policy, 1961–1963* (New York, 1989), 134–135.

21. On wishful thinking, see Irving L. Janis and Leon Mann, *Decision Making: A Psychological Analysis of Conflict, Choice, and Commitment* (New York, 1977), 52–54ff.; Robert Jervis, *Perception and Misperception in International Politics* (Princeton, 1976), 356–381; Otto Klineberg, *The Human Dimension in International Relations* (New York, 1966), 91; Richard Ned Lebow, *Between Peace and War: The Nature of International Crisis* (Baltimore, 1981), 169–222.

22. Theodore C. Sorensen, *Kennedy* (New York, 1965), 307. Unlike Bissell and other senior CIA officials, Kennedy did not engage in wishful thinking out of enthusiasm for the venture, about which he had his doubts. Convinced, however, that he had no choice but to proceed, he closed his eyes to key flaws in the scheme.

23. Jordan, *Crisis,* 214.

24. H. J. Jackson, ed., *Samuel Taylor Coleridge* (New York, 1985), 314.

25. Henry A. Kissinger, *White House Years* (Boston, 1979), 994.

26. The question arises as to what exactly causes wishful thinking to occur. A considerable body of theoretical decision-making literature, much of it drawing from psychological theory, offers various hypotheses regarding why this and other decision-making pathologies arise. For examples, see footnote 21 above as well as Alexander L. George, *Presidential Decisionmaking in Foreign Policy: The Effective Use of Information and Advice* (Boulder, CO, 1980); Charles Hermann, ed., *International Crises: Insights from Behavioral Research* (New York, 1972); Ole R. Holsti and Alexander L. George, "The Effects of Stress on the Performance of Foreign Policy Makers," *Political Science Annual* 6 (1975).

27. Arthur M. Schlesinger, Jr., *Robert Kennedy and His Times* (Boston, 1978), 445.

28. Carl von Clausewitz, *On War* (Princeton, 1984), 87.

29. General Lyman L. Lemnitzer, interview with author, April 27, 1984, Washington, DC; Peter Wyden, *Bay of Pigs: The Untold Story* (New York, 1979), 205.

30. Colonel Robert R. Reed, "End of Tour Report," HQ Twelfth Air Force, Bergstrom AFB, TX (n.d.; probably summer 1975), 5.

31. General Bruce Palmer, Jr., *The 25-Year War: America's Military Role in Vietnam* (Lexington, KY, 1984), 206. The only instance in which tight, "blow-by-blow" centralized control over the execution of a tactical operation is warranted is a confrontation with another nuclear power, where the operation could escalate into nuclear war.

32. Robert A. Manning, "Casey's CIA: New Clout, New Danger," *U.S. News and World Report,* June 16, 1986, 26–27; John Prados, *Presidents' Secret Wars: CIA and Pentagon Covert Operations Since World War II* (New York, 1986), 369; Martin and Walcott, *Best Laid Plans,* 47–48; Woodward, *Veil,* 304–312, 386–387; Edward C. Meyer, "Low-Level Conflict: An Overview," in Brian M. Jenkins (conference director), *Terrorism and Beyond: An International Conference on Terrorism and Low-Level Conflict,* Rand Report R-2714-DOE/DOJ/DOS/RC (Santa Monica, CA, 1982), 41.

33. ISA first came to the attention of the press in 1982, when various sources alleged it was supporting private groups running clandestine missions into Laos in search of U.S. MIAs (service personnel missing in action). In 1983 ISA came under further public scrutiny when some of its members were charged with misusing government funds. Adams, *Secret Armies,* 214–217; Richelson, *The U.S. Intelligence Community,* 61–64. For a detailed account of the covert activities of the U.S. armed forces since 1980, see Emerson, *Secret Warriors.*

34. Adams, *Secret Armies,* 231; Richard A. Gabriel, *Military Incompetence: Why the American Military Doesn't Win* (New York, 1985), 168. On intelligence problems in Grenada, see Gerald Hopple and Cynthia Gilley, "Policy without Intelligence," in Peter M. Dunn and Bruce W. Watson, eds., *American Intervention in Grenada: The Implications of Operation "Urgent Fury"* (Boulder, CO, 1985), 55–71.

35. House Committee on Armed Services, *National Defense Authorization Act for Fiscal Year 1991* (Washington, DC, 1991), 246. Noriega remained at large for several days after the invasion, then took refuge at the residence of the papal nuncio in Panama City before eventually turning himself in to U.S. forces. On intelligence shortcomings in Panama, see also Malcolm McConnell, *Just Cause: The Real Story of America's High-Tech Invasion of Panama* (New York, 1991), 55–73ff.; and Lorenzo Crowell, "The Anatomy of *Just Cause:* The Forces Involved, the Adequacy of Intelligence, and Its Success as a Joint Operation," in Bruce W. Watson and Peter G. Tsouras, eds., *Operation Just Cause The U.S. Intervention in Panama* (Boulder, CO, 1991), 67–104.

36. Senate Committee on Armed Services, *Department of Defense Authorization for Appropriations for Fiscal Years 1992 and 1993* (Washington, DC, 1991), 156; Bruce Van Voorst, "We See a World of More, Not Fewer, Mysteries," *Time,* April 20, 1992, 62 (interview with Director of Central Intelligence Robert M. Gates); David H. Hackworth, "The Lessons of the Gulf War," *Newsweek,* June 24, 1991, 23; Norman Friedman, *Desert Victory: The War for Kuwait* (Annapolis, 1991), 237.

37. Beginning in the mid-eighties, Congress moved to tighten control over ISA and other military intelligence activities. Emerson, *Secret Warriors,* 235–236; Senate Committee on Armed Services, *Nominations Before the Senate Armed Services Committee* (Washington, DC, 1991), 262–263.

38. On the special operations mind-set, see Luttwak, Canby, and Thomas, *A Systematic Review of "Commando" (Special) Operations,* I-18–I-28; Ross S. Kelly, "Special Operations Reform in the Reagan Administration," in Neil C. Livingstone and Terrell E. Arnold, eds., *Beyond the Iran-Contra Crisis: The Shape of U.S. Anti-Terrorism Policy in the Post-Reagan Era* (Lexington, MA, 1988), 86–87.

39. Special Operations Review Group, "Rescue Mission Report," 61.

40. Quoted in Adams, *Secret Armies,* 209; Gabriel, *Military Incompetence,* 153; Melinda Beck, "America's Secret Military Forces," *Newsweek,* April 22, 1985, 23; Robert A. Manning and Steven Emerson, "Special Forces: Can They Do the Job?" *U.S. News and World Report,* November 3, 1986, 41.

41. Adams, *Secret Armies,* 238–239, 243–244, 253–254; Gabriel, *Military Incompetence,* 153, 156–161.

42. Quoted in Adams, *Secret Armies,* 263; William S. Cohen, "A Defense Special Operations Agency: Fix for an SOF Capability That Is Most Assuredly Broken," *Armed Forces Journal International* 123 (January 1986): 38; Clinton H. Schemmer, "House Panel Formed To Oversee Special Ops Forces," *Armed Forces Journal International* 122 (October 1984): 15.

43. R. Lynn Rylander, "ASD-SOLIC: The Congressional Approach to SOF Reorganization," *Special Warfare* 2 (Spring 1989): 12; Stephen D. Goose, "Low Intensity Warfare: The Warriors and Their Weapons," in Michael T. Klare and Peter Kornbluh, eds., *Low-Intensity Warfare: Counterinsurgency, Proinsurgency, and Antiterrorism in the Eighties* (New York, 1987), 82.

44. Quoted in Cohen, "Fix," 39.

45. On Congress's role in special operations reform, see House Committee on Armed Services, *Special Operations Forces* (Washington, DC, 1988), 41ff; Rylander, "ASD-SOLIC," 10–17; Henry L. T. Koren, Jr., "Congress Wades into Special Operations," *Parameters* 18 (December 1988): 62–74.

46. Senate Committee on Armed Services, *Department of Defense Authori-*

zation... 1992 and 1993, 135; James J. Lindsay, "USSOCOM: Strengthening the SOF Capability," *Special Warfare* 2 (Spring 1989): 4–5.

47. Senate Committee on Armed Services, *Department of Defense Authorization... 1992 and 1993,* 135; Rylander, "ASD-SOLIC," 14–15.

48. House, *Special Operations Forces,* 63; Rylander, "ASD-SOLIC," 16–17.

49. *United States Special Operations Forces Posture Statement,* presented by Honorable James R. Locher, III, Assistant Secretary of Defense for Special Operations and Low-Intensity Conflict, and General Carl W. Stiner, U.S. Army Commander in Chief United States Special Operations Command (Washington, DC, 1992), 22, B-1; Senate Committee on Armed Services, *Department of Defense Authorization... 1992 and 1993,* 135–136; Carl W. Stiner, "The Strategic Employment of Special Operations Forces," *Military Review* 71 (June 1991): 2–13. Not all the forces under USSOCOM, however, specialize in raids and other *coups de main.* A large proportion of these forces specialize in counterinsurgency and psychological warfare. For a breakdown of USSOCOM's forces and capabilities, see Ross S. Kelly, *Special Operations and National Purpose* (Lexington, MA, 1989), 5–16; United States Special Operations Forces, C-1 ff.

50. On Operation "Just Cause" and special operations therein, see House Committee on Armed Services, *National Defense Authorization Act... 1991;* 244–245; McConnell, *Just Cause,* 53ff.; Crowell, "Anatomy," 67–104; Stiner, "Strategic Employment," 8–9.

51. On special operations in the Persian Gulf war, see "Special Operations in Desert Storm: Separating Fact from Fiction," *Special Warfare* 5 (March 1992): 2–6; E. M. Flanagan, Jr., "Hostile Territory Was Their AO in Desert Storm," *Army* 41 (September 1991): 12–30; Douglas Waller, "Secret Warriors," *Newsweek,* June 17, 1991, 20–28.

52. Special Operations Review Group, "Rescue Mission Report," 61.

53. Neither the 1973 War Powers Resolution nor the 1980 Intelligence Oversight Act significantly affect the quality of review of strategic special operations. The War Powers Resolution requires the president to consult with Congress in every possible instance before introducing U.S. forces into hostilities or into situations where involvement in hostilities is imminent. In practice, presidents have waited until the last minute to advise Congress of strategic special operations. In the *Mayaguez* operation, the White House did not inform congressional leadership of its decision to recover the crew by force until the Marines were ordered into action. In the Iran rescue mission, the White House did not advise Congress before sending the rescue force to Desert One. The administration later stated that it intended to inform Congress once the force had made it past Desert One and before it stormed the embassy.

The Intelligence Oversight Act requires the White House to inform the House and Senate intelligence committees of important covert actions. Although some committee members expect prior notification, the executive does not believe that all covert actions require prior notice. In several cases it has notified the committees after the fact; in the Iran-Contra episode, it did not notify them at all. In the best of cases, then, Congress is likely to be notified only shortly before a strategic special operation occurs. Moreover, it can only comment on the political advisability of such missions and is not in a position to probe into the planning. Philip W. Buchen, "Memorandum for Ron Nessen," May 16, 1975, Box 32, White House Central Files, ND 18/CO/26 5/16/75-5/18/75, GRFL; Johnson, *Secret Power,* 107–129; Robert F. Turner, *The War*

Powers Resolution: Its Implementation in Theory and Practice (Philadelphia, 1983), 59–64, 69–72.

54. Christopher A. Abel, "Controlling C³," *U.S. Naval Institute Proceedings* 116 (July 1990): 38–42; Friedman, *Desert Victory,* 144–146.

55. Evan Thomas, "A Warrior Elite For the Dirty Jobs," *Time,* January 13, 1986, 17. On the suspicion of special forces, see also Adams, *Secret Armies,* 262–288; Emerson, *Secret Warriors,* 30–32; Neil C. Livingstone, "A New U.S. Antiterrorism Strategy for the 1990s," in Loren B. Thompson, ed., *Low-Intensity Conflict: The Pattern of Warfare in the Modern World* (Lexington, MA, 1989), 97.

56. Quoted in Emerson, *Secret Warriors,* 30.

57. John D. Waghelstein, "Post-Vietnam Counterinsurgency Doctrine," *Military Review* 65 (May 1985): 45–49; Thomas, "Warrior Elite," 18.

58. Bruce Palmer, Jr., OH, January 5, 1976, U.S. Army Military History Institute, 145.

59. Quoted in Noel Koch, "Objecting to Reality: The Struggle to Restore U.S. Special Operations Forces," in Loren B. Thompson, ed., *Low-Intensity Conflict,* 53–54.

60. Senate Committee on Armed Services, *Department of Defense Authorization for Appropriations for Fiscal Years 1988 and 1989* (Washington, DC, 1988), 3675–3676.

61. Thomas, "Warrior Elite," 17; Benjamin F. Schemmer, "December Was Not a Good Month for USAF Special Operations," *Armed Forces Journal International* 123 (January 1986): 46–47.

62. Adams, *Secret Armies,* 268; Deborah J. Meyer and Benjamin F. Schemmer, "An exclusive AFJ interview with: Noel C. Koch Principal Deputy Assistant Secretary of Defense International Security Affairs," *Armed Forces Journal International* 122 (March 1985): 42, 46; Thomas, "Warrior Elite," 17; Michael Ganley and Deborah Gallagher, "DOD Special Operations Airlift Plan Draws Mixed Reviews on Capitol Hill," *Armed Forces Journal International* 123 (May 1986): 19.

63. House Committee on Armed Services, *National Defense Authorization Act . . . 1991,* 255; Stiner, "Strategic Employment," 10–11.

64. Rylander, "ASD-SOLIC," 16; House Committee on Armed Services, *Special Operations Forces,* 39.

65. On the influence of culture on foreign policy behavior, see for example Akira Iriye, "Culture and International History," in Michael J. Hogan and Thomas G. Paterson, eds., *Explaining the History of American Foreign Relations* (Cambridge, U.K., 1991), 214–225, and Michael H. Hunt, *Ideology and U.S. Foreign Policy* (New Haven, 1987).

66. See for example John Spanier, *American Foreign Policy Since World War II* (New York, 1985), 9–10.

67. On this point, see for instance Glen Fisher, *Mindsets: The Role of Culture and Perception in International Relations* (Yarmouth, ME, 1988), 52–53.

68. Clausewitz, *On War,* 101.

69. Richard F. Brauer, Jr., "A Critical Examination of Planning Imperatives Applicable to Hostage Rescue Operations" (U.S. Army War College, Carlisle Barracks, PA, April 16, 1984), 17.

Selected Bibliography

General

Personal Interviews

Beckwith, Colonel Charlie A., April 23, 1984.
Blackburn, Brigadier General Donald D., February 27, 1984.
Drain, Richard, March 2, 1984.
Holloway, Admiral James L., III, June 25, 1984.
Komer, Robert, W., June 22, 1984.
Lansdale, Major General Edward G., June 1, 1984.
Locher, James R., III, September 9, 1992.
Manor, Lieutenant General Leroy J., February 29, 1984.
Moorer, Admiral Thomas J., March 13, 1984.
Mountel, Colonel Robert, February 13, 1984.
Phillips, David A., March 20, 1984.
Vaught, Lieutenant General James B., May 22, 1984.
Train, Admiral Harry D., II, June 6, 1984.
Vogt, Lieutenant General John W., April 13, 1984.
Yarborough, Lieutenant General William P., February 14, 1984.
Confidential interviews.

Unpublished Papers and Documents

Collins, John M. "The Essence of Special Operations." Congressional Research
   Service, Library of Congress, Washington, DC, June 2, 1986 (draft).
Luttwak, Edward N., Steven L. Canby, and David L. Thomas. *A Systematic Re-*

view of "Commando" (Special) Operations, 1939–1980. C & L Associates, Potomac, MD, n.d.

Harned, Glenn M. "Army Special Operations Forces and AIRLAND Battle." MMAS thesis, U.S. Army Command and General Staff College, Fort Leavenworth, KS, 1985.

Published Records and Official Sources

Brauer, Richard F., Jr. "A Critical Examination Of Planning Imperatives Applicable To Hostage Rescue Operations." U.S. Army War College, Carlisle Barracks, PA, April 16, 1984.

Collins, John M. "United States and Soviet Special Operations." A study prepared by the Congressional Research Service, Library of Congress, at the request of the Special Operations Panel of the Readiness Subcommittee of the House Committee on Armed Services. 100th Cong., 1st sess., 1987.

———. "U.S. Low-Intensity Conflicts 1899–1990." A study by the Congressional Research Service, Library of Congress, prepared at the request of the Readiness Subcommittee of the House Committee on Armed Services. 101st Cong., 2d sess., 1990.

Department of the Army. Headquarters, United States Army Training and Doctrine Command. "US Army Operational Concept for Special Operations Forces (SOF)." Tradoc Pamphlet 525–34. Fort Monroe, VA, July 26, 1984.

Department of Defense. *Conduct of the Persian Gulf Conflict: Final Report to Congress.* Washington, DC, 1992.

———. *United States Special Operations Forces Posture Statement.* Presented by Honorable James R. Locher, III, Assistant Secretary of Defense for Special Operations and Low-Intensity Conflict, and General Carl W. Stiner, U.S. Army Commander in Chief United States Special Operations Command. Washington, DC, 1992.

Hoffman, Bruce. "Commando Raids: 1946–1983." Rand Note N-2316-USDP. Santa Monica, CA, 1985.

Meyer, Edward C. "Low-Level Conflict: An Overview." In *Terrorism and Beyond: An International Conference on Terrorism and Low-Level Conflict* (Brian M. Jenkins Conference Director). Rand Corporation Report R-2714-DOE/DOJ/DOS/RC. Santa Monica, CA, 1982.

Orr, George E. *Combat Operations C³I: Fundamentals and Interactions.* Research Report. Air University Press, Maxwell Air Force Base, AL, 1983.

Stiner, Carl W. "United States Special Operations Forces: A Strategic Perspective." U.S. Special Operations Command, MacDill Air Force Base, FL, January 1992.

U.S. Congress. House. Committee on Armed Services. Readiness Subcommittee. *National Defense Authorization Act for Fiscal Year 1991—H.R. 4739 and Oversight of Previously Authorized Programs.* Title III—Operation And Maintenance. 101st Cong., 2nd sess., 1991.

———. *National Defense Authorization Act for Fiscal Years 1992 and 1993—H.R. 2100.* Title III—Operation and Maintenance. 102d Cong., 1st sess., 1991.

———. Special Operations Panel and Readiness Subcommittee, *Special Operations Forces.* 100th Cong., 2d sess., 1988.

―――. Subcommittee on Department of Defense. *Department of Defense Appropriations for 1992.* Part 2. 102d Cong., 1st sess., 1991.

―――. Senate. Committee on Armed Services. *Department of Defense Authorization for Appropriations for Fiscal Years 1988 and 1989.* Part 7. 100th Cong., 1st sess., 1988.

―――. *Department of Defense Authorization for Appropriations for Fiscal Years 1992 and 1993.* Part 1. 102d Cong., 1st sess., 1991.

―――. *Nominations Before the Senate Armed Services Committee, Second Session, 101st Congress.* 101st Cong., 2d sess., 1991.

―――. Subcommittee on Sea Power and Force Projection. *To Combat Terrorism and Other Forms of Unconventional Warfare.* 99th Cong., 2d sess., 1986.

Published Oral History

Palmer, General Bruce, Jr. Oral History. Bruce Palmer Papers, U.S. Army Military History Institute, Carlisle Barracks, PA.

Books

Adams, James. *Secret Armies: Inside the American, Soviet and European Special Forces.* New York, 1988.

Allison, Graham T. *Essence of Decision: Explaining the Cuban Missile Crisis.* Boston, 1971.

Allison, Graham T., and Peter Szanton. *Remaking Foreign Policy: The Organizational Connection.* New York, 1976.

Bamford, James. *The Puzzle Palace: A Report on America's Most Secret Agency.* Boston, 1982.

Barnett, Frank R., B. Hugh Tovar, and Richard H. Shultz, eds. *Special Operations in US Strategy.* Washington, DC, 1984.

Beaumont, Roger A. *Special Operations and Elite Units, 1939–1988: A Research Guide.* New York, 1988.

Betts, Richard K. *Soldiers, Statesmen, and Cold War Crises.* Cambridge, MA, 1977.

―――. "Analysis, War, and Decision: Why Intelligence Failures Are Inevitable." In *Power, Strategy, and Security: A World Politics Reader,* edited by Klaus Knorr. Princeton, 1983.

Blechman, Barry M., and Stephen S. Kaplan. *Force without War: U.S. Armed Forces as a Political Instrument.* Washington, DC, 1978.

Bok, Sissela. *Secrets: On the Ethics of Concealment and Revelation.* New York, 1982.

Bolger, Daniel P. *Americans at War: 1975–1986, an Era of Violent Peace.* Novato, CA, 1988.

Cable, James. *Gunboat Diplomacy: Political Applications of Limited Naval Force.* London, 1971.

Clifford, J. Garry. "Bureaucratic Politics." In *Explaining the History of American Foreign Relations,* edited by Michael J. Hogan and Thomas G. Paterson. Cambridge, U.K., 1991.

Coates, James, and Michael Kilian. *Heavy Losses: The Dangerous Decline of American Defense.* New York, 1985.

Cohen, Eliot A. *Commandos and Politicians: Elite Military Units in Modern De-
mocracies.* Boston, 1978.

Destler, I. M. *Presidents, Bureaucrats, and Foreign Policy: The Politics of Organizational Reform.* Princeton, 1974.

Emerson, Steven. *Secret Warriors: Inside the Covert Military Operations of the Reagan Era.* New York, 1988.

Evans, Ernest. *Wars Without Splendor: The U.S. Military and Low-level Conflict.*
New York, 1987.

Fisher, Glen. *Mindsets: The Role of Culture and Perception in International Relations.* Yarmouth, ME, 1988.

Friedman, Norman. *Desert Victory: The War for Kuwait.* Annapolis, 1991.

Gabriel, Richard A. *Military Incompetence: Why the American Military Doesn't
Win.* New York, 1985.

George, Alexander L. *Presidential Decisionmaking in Foreign Policy: The Effective
Use of Information and Advice.* Boulder, CO, 1980.

Godson, Roy, ed. *Intelligence Requirements for the 1990s: Collection, Analysis,
Counterintelligence, and Covert Action.* Lexington, MA, 1989.

———. *Intelligence Requirements for the 1980's: Covert Action.* Washington DC,
1981.

Gooch, John, and Amos Perlmutter, eds. *Military Deception and Strategic Surprise.* London, 1982.

Hadley, Arthur T. *The Straw Giant. Triumph and Failure: America's Armed
Forces. A Report from the Field.* New York, 1986.

Halperin, Morton H. *Bureaucratic Politics and Foreign Policy.* Washington, DC,
1974.

Hayden, H.T., ed. *Shadow War: Special Operations and Low Intensity Conflict.*
Vista, CA, 1992.

Hermann, Charles, ed. *International Crises: Insights from Behavioral Research.*
New York, 1972.

Holsti, Ole R., and Alexander L. George. "The Effects of Stress on the Performance of Foreign Policy-makers." In *Political Science Annual,* vol. 6, *1975,*
edited by Cornelius P. Cotter (Indianapolis, 1975).

Hopple, Gerard, and Cynthia Gilley. "Policy without Intelligence." In *American
Intervention in Grenada: The Implications of Operation "Urgent Fury,"* edited
by Peter M. Dunn and Bruce W. Watson. Boulder, CO, 1985.

Hunt, Michael H. *Ideology and U.S. Foreign Policy.* New Haven, 1987.

Iriye, Akira. "Culture and International History." In *Explaining the History of
American Foreign Relations,* edited by Michael J. Hogan and Thomas G. Paterson. Cambridge, U.K., 1991.

Janis, Irving L. *Groupthink: Psychological Studies of Policy Decisions and Fiascoes.*
Boston, 1982.

Janis, Irving L., and Leon Mann. *Decision Making: A Psychological Analysis of
Conflict, Choice, and Commitment.* New York, 1977.

Jervis, Robert. *Perception and Misperception in International Politics.* Princeton,
1976.

Jordan, Amos, and William J. Taylor, Jr. *American National Security: Policy and
Process.* Baltimore, 1981.

Johnson, Loch K. *America's Secret Power: The CIA in a Democratic Society.* New
York, 1989.

Kelly, Ross S. *Special Operations and National Purpose.* Lexington, MA, 1989.

———. "Special Operations Reform in the Reagan Administration." In *Beyond* the *Iran-Contra Crisis: The Shape of U.S. Anti-Terrorism Policy in the Post-Reagan Era*, edited by Neil C. Livingstone and Terrell E. Arnold. Lexington, MA, 1988.

Klare, Michael T., and Peter Kornbluh, eds. *Low-Intensity Warfare: Counterinsurgency, Proinsurgency, and Antiterrorism in the Eighties*. New York, 1987.

Klineberg, Otto. *The Human Dimension in International Relations*. New York, 1966.

Lebow, Richard Ned. *Between Peace and War: The Nature of International Crisis*. Baltimore, 1981.

Luttwak, Edward N. *The Pentagon and the Art of War: The Question of Military Reform*. New York, 1985.

Marchetti, Victor, and John D. Marks. *The CIA and the Cult of Intelligence*. New York, 1974.

Martin, David C., and John Walcott. *Best Laid Plans: The Inside Story of America's War Against Terrorism*. New York, 1988.

McConnell, Malcolm. *Just Cause: The Real Story of America's High-Tech Invasion of Panama*. New York, 1991.

Neustadt, Richard E., and Ernest R. May. *Thinking in Time: The Uses of History for Decision Makers*. New York, 1986.

Paddock, Alfred H., Jr. *U.S. Army Special Warfare. Its Origins: Psychological and Unconventional Warfare 1941–52*. Washington, DC, 1982.

Palmer, General Bruce, Jr. *The 25-Year War: America's Military Role in Vietnam*. Lexington, KY, 1984.

Paschall, Rod. *LIC 2000: Special Operations & Unconventional Warfare in the Next Century*. Washington, DC, 1990.

Prados, John. *Presidents' Secret Wars: CIA and Pentagon Covert Operations Since World War II*. New York, 1986.

Ranelagh, John. *The Agency: The Rise and Decline of the CIA*. New York, 1986.

Record, Jeffrey. *Beyond Military Reform: American Defense Dilemmas*. Washington, DC, 1988.

Reedy, George E. *The Twilight of the Presidency*. New York, 1970.

Reisman, W. Michael, and James E. Baker. *Regulating Covert Action: Practices, Contexts, and Policies of Covert Coercion Abroad in International and American Law*. New Haven, 1992.

Richelson, Jeffrey T. *The U.S. Intelligence Community*. Cambridge, MA, 1989.

Roosevelt, Kermit. *Countercoup: The Struggle for the Control of Iran*. New York, 1979.

Ryan, Michael C. "Combat Rescue Operations." In *The Future of Conflict in the 1980s*, edited by William J. Taylor, Jr. and Steven A. Maaranen. Lexington, MA, 1982.

Sarkesian, Sam C., and William L. Scully, eds. *U.S. Policy and Low-Intensity Conflict: Potentials for Military Struggles in the 1980s*. New Brunswick, NJ, 1981.

Sarkesian, Sam C., and John Allen Williams, eds. *The U.S. Army in a New Security Era*. Boulder, CO, 1990.

Shackley, Theodore. *The Third Option: An American View of Counterinsurgency Operations*. New York, 1981.

Shulsky, Abram N. *Silent Warfare: Understanding the World of Intelligence*. Washington, DC, 1991.

Smist, Frank J., Jr. *Congress Oversees the United States Intelligence Community, 1947–1989*. Knoxville, TN, 1990.

Spanier, John. *American Foreign Policy Since World War II*. New York, 1985.

Thompson, Loren B., ed. *Low-Intensity Conflict: The Pattern of Warfare in the Modern World.* Lexington, MA, 1989.

Treverton, Gregory F. *Covert Action: The Limits of Intervention in the Postwar World.* New York, 1987.

Turner, Robert F. *The War Powers Resolution: Its Implementation in Theory and Practice.* Philadelphia, PA, 1983.

von Clausewitz, Carl. *On War.* Edited by Michael Howard and Peter Paret. Princeton, 1984.

Wagoner, Fred E. *Dragon Rouge: The Rescue of Hostages in the Congo.* Washington, DC, 1980.

Watson, Bruce W., and Peter G. Tsouras, eds. *Operation* Just Cause: *The U.S. Intervention in Panama.* Boulder, CO, 1991.

Weigley, Russell F. *The American Way of War: A History of United States Military Strategy and Policy.* New York, 1973.

Weiner, Tim. *Blank Check: The Pentagon's Black Budget.* New York, 1990.

Winkates, James E. "Hostage Rescue in a Hostile Environment: Lessons Learned from the Son Tay, Mayaguez, And Entebbe Missions." In *Political Terrorism and Business: The Threat and Response,* edited by Yonah Alexander and Robert A. Kilmarx. New York, 1979.

Wise, David, and Thomas B. Ross. *The Invisible Government.* New York, 1964.

Woodward, Bob. *Veil: The Secret Wars of the CIA, 1981–1987.* New York, 1987.

Articles and Newspapers

Abel, Christopher A. "Controlling C³." *U.S. Naval Institute Proceedings* 116 (July 1990).

Adams, James. "Our No-Fault Military Keeps Making the Same Mistakes." *Washington Post,* September 6, 1987.

"America's Secret Soldiers: The Buildup of U.S. Special Operations Forces." *Defense Monitor* 14 (1985).

Beck, Melinda. "America's Secret Military Forces." *Newsweek,* April 22, 1985.

Bolger, Daniel P. "Special Operations and the Grenada Campaign." *Parameters* 18 (December 1988).

Burgess, William H., III. "Special Operations Forces and the Challenge of Transnational Terrorism." *Military Intelligence* 12 (April–June 1986).

Cohen, William S. "A Defense Special Operations Agency: Fix for an SOF Capability That Is Most Assuredly Broken." *Armed Forces Journal International* 123 (January 1986).

Crane, Barry, Joel Leson, Robert Plebanek, Paul Shemella, Ronald Smith, and Richard Williams. "Between Peace and War: Comprehending Low-Intensity Conflict." *Special Warfare* 2 (Summer 1989).

Daniel, Dan. "The Case for a Sixth Service." *Armed Forces Journal International* 123 (August 1985).

Dudney, Robert S. "Can't Anybody Here Run a War?" *U.S. News and World Report,* February 27, 1984.

Flanagan, E. M., Jr. "Hostile Territory Was Their AO in Desert Storm." *Army* 41 (September 1991).

Foster, Stephen Oliver (pseud.) "Pentagon Slow-Rollers Stymie SOF Improvements." *Armed Forces Journal International* 126 (October 1988).

Ganley, Michael, and Deborah Gallagher. "DOD Special Operations Airlift Plan Draws Mixed Reviews on Capitol Hill." *Armed Forces Journal International* 123 (May 1986).

Gazit, Shlomo. "Risk, Glory, and the Rescue Operation." *International Security* 6 (Summer 1981).

Gellman, Barton. "Amid Winds of War, Daring U.S. Rescue Got Little Notice." *Washington Post,* January 5, 1992.

George, Alexander L. "The Case for Multiple Advocacy in Making Foreign Policy." *American Political Science Review* 66 (September 1972).

Godson, Roy. "Intelligence Requirements for the 1990s." *Washington Quarterly* 12 (Winter 1989).

Goodman, Allen E. "Dateline Langley: Fixing the Intelligence Mess." *Foreign Policy* 57 (Winter 1984–1985).

Hackworth, David H. "The Lessons of the Gulf War." *Newsweek,* June 24, 1991.

Halperin, Morton H., and David Halperin. "The Key West Key." *Foreign Policy* 53 (Winter 1983–1984).

Huntington, Samuel P. "Defense organization and military strategy." *Public Interest* 75 (Spring 1984).

Hyde, James C. "SOCOM Procurement Drops 31% in FY 93." *Armed Forces Journal International* 129 (March 1992).

Isby, David C. "Special Operations Forces Response." *Military Intelligence* 11 (January–March 1985).

Kelly, Peter A. "Raids and National Command: Mutually Exclusive!" *Military Review* 60 (April 1980).

Kelly, Ross S. "US Special Operations." *Defense & Foreign Affairs* 12 (September 1984).

———. "US Special Operations II: Issues, Challenges, Trends." *Defense & Foreign Affairs* 12 (October 1984).

Koren, Henry L. T., Jr. "Congress Wades into Special Operations." *Parameters* 18 (December 1988).

Lindsay, James J. "USSOCOM: Strengthening the SOF Capability." *Special Warfare* 2 (Spring 1989).

Livingstone, Neil C. "Fighting Terrorism and 'Dirty Little Wars.' " *Air University Review* 35 (March–April 1984).

Manning, Robert A. "Casey's CIA: New Clout, New Danger." *U.S. News and World Report,* June 16, 1986.

Manning, Robert A., and Steven Emerson. "Special Forces: Can They Do the Job?" *U.S. News and World Report,* November 3, 1986.

Meyer, Deborah J., and Benjamin F. Schemmer. "An exclusive AFJ interview with: Noel C. Koch Principal Deputy Assistant Secretary of Defense International Security Affairs." *Armed Forces Journal International* 122 (March 1985).

Motley, James B. "Washington's Big Tug-of-War Over Special Operations Forces." *Army* 36 (November 1986).

Olsen, William J. "Organizational Requirements for LIC." *Military Review* 68 (January 1988).

Rylander, R. Lynn. "Special Operations Forces After the Rise." *Military Review* 69 (February 1989).

———. "ASD-SOLIC: The Congressional Approach to SOF Reorganization." *Special Warfare* 2 (Spring 1989).

Sarkesian, Sam C. "The Myth of US Capability in Unconventional Conflicts." *Military Review* 68 (September 1988).

Schemmer, Benjamin F. "December Was Not a Good Month for USAF Special Operations." *Armed Forces Journal International* 123 (January 1986).

———. "Special Ops Teams Found 29 Scuds Ready to Barrage Israel 24 Hours Before Cease-Fire." *Armed Forces Journal International* 128 (July 1991).

Schemmer, Clinton H. "House Panel Formed To Oversee Special Ops Forces." *Armed Forces Journal International* 122 (October 1984).

Schoch, Bruce P. "Four Rules for a Successful Rescue." *Army* 31 (February 1981).

Shani, Joshua. "AIRBORNE RAIDS: a potent weapon in countering transnational terrorism." *Air University Review* 35 (March–April 1984).

Siegel, Adam B. "Lessons Learned From Operation EASTERN EXIT." *Marine Corps Gazette* 76 (June 1992).

"The Special Ops Transfer: An Idea Whose Time Has Come?" *Armed Forces Journal International* 122 (October 1984).

Starry, General Donn A. "A Perspective on American Military Thought." *Military Review* 69 (July 1989).

Stiner, Carl W. "The Strategic Employment of Special Operations Forces." *Military Review* 71 (June 1991).

Thomas, Evan. "A Warrior Elite For the Dirty Jobs." *Time,* January 13, 1986.

U.S. Army Special Operations Command, Public Affairs Office. "Special Operations in Desert Storm: Separating Fact from Fiction." *Special Warfare* 5 (March 1992).

Van Voorst, Bruce. "We See a World of More, not Fewer, Mysteries" (interview with Director of Central Intelligence Robert M. Gates.) *Time,* April 20, 1992.

Waghelstein, John D. "Post-Vietnam Counterinsurgency Doctrine." *Military Review* 65 (May 1985).

Waller, Douglas. "Secret Warriors." *Newsweek,* June 17, 1991.

Bay of Pigs

Unpublished Papers and Documents

Acheson, Dean, Harry S. Truman Presidential Library, Independence, MO.

Baldwin, Hanson W., Yale University Library.

Bar-Joseph, Uri. "Out of Control: Intelligence Intervention in Politics in the USA, Britain and Israel." Ph.D. dissertation, Stanford University, Palo Alto, CA, 1990.

Berle, Adolf A., Franklin D. Roosevelt Library, Hyde Park, NY.

Bowles, Chester, Yale University Library.

Central Intelligence Agency, Report 00-A 3177796, January 30, 1961, and Report CS-3/461,320, March 16, 1961. Obtained through Freedom of Information Act (FOIA).

———. Kent, Sherman. "Is Time on Our Side in Cuba?" January 27, 1961. FOIA.

———. "Is Time on Our Side in Cuba?" March 10, 1961. FOIA.

Decker, General George H., U.S. Army Military History Institute, Carlisle Barracks, Carlisle, PA.

Dulles, Allen W., Princeton University Library.

Eisenhower, Dwight D., Ann Whitman File, Dwight D. Eisenhower Presidential Library (DDEL), Abilene, KS.

Eisenhower, Dwight D., Post-Presidential Papers, DDEL.

Estabrook, Roger H., John F. Kennedy Presidential Library (JFKL), Boston.

Gray, Gordon, DDEL.

Herter, Christian H., DDEL.

Johnson, Lyndon B., Vice Presidential Security File, Lyndon Baines Johnson Presidential Library, Austin, TX.

Joint Chiefs of Staff, "U.S. Plan of Action in Cuba." JCSM 44–61, January 27, 1961, FOIA.

———, "Military Evaluation of the Cuban Plan." JCSM 57–61, February 3, 1961, FOIA.

———, "Evaluation of the CIA Volunteer Task Force," JCSM 146–61, March 10, 1961. FOIA.

———, "Evaluation of Military Aspects of Alternate Concepts, CIA Para-Military Plan, Cuba," JCSM 166–61, March 15, 1961. FOIA.

Kennedy, John F., Pre-Presidential Papers, JFKL.

Kennedy, Robert F., JFKL.

Krock, Arthur, Princeton University Library.

Lippmann, Walter, Yale University Library.

Mann, Thomas C. "The Bay of Pigs Fiasco," unpublished manuscript provided by author.

———, letter to author, June 30, 1983.

Matthews, Herbert M., Columbia University Library.

National Security Files, 1961–1962, JFKL.

President's Appointment Book, Jan–Jun 1961, Office Files, JFKL.

President's Office Files, 1961, JFKL.

Rusk, Dean, "Reflections on the Bay of Pigs," unpublished paper provided by author.

Smith, Walter Bedell, DDEL.

Sorensen, Theodore C., JFKL.

Stevenson, Adlai E., Princeton University Library.

U.S. Marine Corps, Cuba File, Reference Section, History and Museums Division, Headquarters, U.S. Marine Corps, Washington DC.

White House, Office of the Special Assistant for National Security Affairs, Records, 1959–1961, DDEL.

White House, Office of the Staff Secretary, Records, 1959–1961, DDEL.

Willauer, Whiting, Princeton University Library.

Yarborough, Lieutenant General William P., U.S. Army Military History Institute.

Personal Interviews and Correspondence

Amory, Robert, Jr., interview, February 16, 1982.

Bissell, Richard M., Jr., interviews, May 18, 1984, and January 14, 1981.

Bundy, McGeorge, interview, March 1, 1982.

Bundy, William P., interview, February 9, 1984.

Burke, Admiral Arleigh A., interview, October 1, 1983.

Dillon, Douglas C., letter to author, January 30, 1984.

Drain, Richard, interview, March 4, 1984.
Fulbright, J. William, interview, March 21, 1984.
Garthoff, Raymond L., interview, April 26, 1984.
Goodpaster, General Andrew J., interview, January 27, 1984.
Halpern, Samuel, interview, May 22, 1984.
Holt, Pat M., interview, June 6, 1984.
Houston, Lawrence R., interview, February 20, 1984.
Kirkpatrick, Lyman D., Jr., interview, March 16, 1984.
Krisel, Captain Lionel, interview, June 9, 1984.
Lansdale, Major General Edward G., interview, June 1, 1984.
Lemnitzer, General Lyman L., interviews, April 27, 1984, and February 16, 1982.
Mann, Thomas C., letter to author, June 30, 1983.
Murphy, Charles J. V., telephone conference, May 4, 1984.
Parrott, Thomas A., interview, May 30, 1984.
Pforzheimer, Walter L., interview, February 20, 1984.
Phillips, David A., interview, March 20, 1984.
Plank, John, interview, May 2, 1983.
Prouty, Colonel L. Fletcher, letter to author, September 1, 1983.
Rogers, Colonel David, interview, May 3, 1983.
Rusk, Dean, interview, June 21, 1984; letter to author, March 8, 1982.
Schlesinger, Arthur M., interview, March 8, 1982.
Taylor, General Maxwell D., letter to author, February 15, 1982.
Yarborough, General William P., interview, February 14, 1984.

Published Records and Official Sources

Declassified Documents Reference System. Carrollton, MD, 1984–1986.
U.S. Congress. Senate. Committee on Foreign Relations. *Events in United States–Cuban Relations: A Chronology*. 88th Cong., 1st sess., 1963.
———. *Executive Sessions of the Senate Foreign Relations Committee (Historical Series) 1961*, XIII, part I, 87th Cong., 1st sess., 1984.
———. Select Committee to Study Government Operations with Respect to Intelligence Activities. *Alleged Assassination Plots Involving Foreign Leaders*. New York, 1976.

Published Oral Histories and Interviews

Acheson, Dean. OH. JFKL.
Amory, Robert, Jr. OH, JFKL.
Brentweiser, General Brent. OH. Albert F. Simpson Historical Research Center, Maxwell AFB, AL.
Bissell, Richard M., Jr. OH. JFKL.
———. OH. DDEL.
Bohlen, Charles. OH. JFKL.
Dean, Lieutenant General Fred M. OH. Simpson Center, Maxwell AFB.
Decker, General George H. OH. JFKL.
———. OH. U.S. Army Military History Institute.
Dennison, Admiral Robert L. OH. U.S. Naval Institute, Annapolis, MD.
Gilpatric, Roswell L. OH. JFKL.

Graebel, Richard P. OH. Columbia University Library.

Gray, Gordon. OH with Maclyn Burg. DDEL.

———. OH with Paul Hopper. DDEL.

Hill, Robert C. OH. DDEL.

Hilsman, Roger. OH. JFKL.

Holt, Pat M. OH. Senate Historical Office, Washington, DC.

Ives, Mrs. Ernest. OH. Columbia University Library.

Luce, Henry R. OH. JFKL.

Mann, Thomas C. OH. JFKL.

Newton, Minow. OH. Columbia University Library.

Pawley, William D. OH. Herbert H. Hoover Presidential Library, West Branch, IA.

Pell, Claiborne. OH. JFKL.

Plimpton, Francis T. OH. Columbia University Library.

Sorensen, Theodore C. OH. JFKL.

Yarborough, Lieutenant General William P. OH. U.S. Army Military History Institute.

Wheeler, General Earle G. OH. JFKL.

Wirtz, Willard. OH. Columbia University Library.

Books and Articles

Ambrose, Stephen E., with Richard H. Immerman. *Ike's Spies: Eisenhower and the Espionage Establishment*. Garden City, NY, 1981.

Beck, Kent M. "Necessary Lies, Hidden Truths: Cuba in the 1960 Campaign." *Diplomatic History* 8 (Winter 1984).

Bell, Jack. *The Johnson Treatment: How Lyndon B. Johnson Took Over the Presidency and Made It His Own*. New York, 1965.

Bernstein, Barton J. "Kennedy and the Bay of Pigs Revisited—Twenty Four Years Later." *Foreign Service Journal* 62 (March 1985).

Bissell, Richard M., Jr. "Response to Lucien S. Vandenbroucke, 'The "Confessions" of Allen Dulles: New Evidence on the Bay of Pigs.' " *Diplomatic History* 8 (Fall 1984).

———. "*Reflections on the Bay of Pigs:* OPERATION ZAPATA, Paul L. Kesaris, Editor" (book review). *Strategic Review* 12 (Winter 1984).

"Damn Good and Sure." *Newsweek,* March 4, 1963.

Cohen, Warren I. *Dean Rusk*. Totawa, NJ, 1980.

Cook, Blanche Wiesen. *The Declassified Eisenhower: A Divided Legacy*. Garden City, NY, 1981.

Currey, Cecil B. *Edward Lansdale: The Unquiet American*. Boston, 1988.

Eisenhower, Dwight D. *The White House Years: Waging Peace, 1956–1961*. Garden City, NY, 1965.

Etheredge, Lloyd S. *Can Governments Learn? American Foreign Policy and Central American Revolutions*. New York, 1985.

Ewald, William Bragg, Jr. *Eisenhower the President: Crucial Days, 1951–1960*. Englewood Cliffs, NJ, 1981.

Ferrer, Edward E. *Operation Puma: The Air Battle of the Bay of Pigs*. Miami, 1982.

Goldwater, Barry M. *Goldwater*. New York, 1988.

Goodwin, Richard N. *Remembering America: A Voice from the Sixties*. Boston, 1988.

Gott, Richard. *Rural Guerrillas in Latin America*. Middlesex, U.K., 1973.

Guthman, Edwin O., and Jeffrey Shulman, eds. *Robert Kennedy In His Own Words: The Unpublished Recollections of the Kennedy Years*. Toronto, 1988.

Higgins, Marguerite. "Kennedy Was Critical of Bay of Pigs Advisers." *Washington Star,* July 21, 1965.

Higgins, Trumbull. *The Perfect Failure: Kennedy, Eisenhower, and the CIA at the Bay of Pigs*. New York, 1987.

Hinckle, Warren, and William W. Turner. *The Fish Is Red: The Story of the Secret War Against Castro*. New York, 1981.

Hunt, E. Howard. *Undercover: Memoirs of an American Secret Agent*. New York, 1974.

————. *Give Us This Day*. New Rochelle, NY, 1973.

Immerman, Richard H. *The CIA in Guatemala: The Foreign Policy of Intervention*. Austin, TX, 1982.

Johnson, Hayes. *The Bay of Pigs: The Leaders' Story of Brigade 2506*. New York, 1964.

Johnson, Walter, ed. *The Papers of Adlai E. Stevenson*. Vol. 8, *Ambassador to the United Nations, 1961–1965*. Boston, 1979.

Kesaris, Paul L., ed. *Operation ZAPATA: The "Ultrasensitive" Report and Testimony of the Board of Inquiry on the Bay of Pigs*. Frederick, MD, 1981.

Kirkpatrick, Lyman B., Jr. "Paramilitary Case Study: The Bay of Pigs." *Naval War College Review* 2 (November–December 1972).

Lazo, Mario. *Dagger in the Heart: American Policy Failures in Cuba*. New York, 1968.

Mahoney, Robert B. *U.S. Navy Responses to International Incidents and Crises, 1955–1975*. Arlington, VA, 1977.

Martin, John Bartlow. *Adlai Stevenson and the World: The Life of Adlai E. Stevenson*. Garden City, NY, 1977.

Martin, Ralph G. *A Hero for Our Time: An Intimate Story of the Kennedy Years*. New York, 1983.

Miller, James E. *The United States and Italy, 1940–1950: The Politics and Diplomacy of Stabilization*. Chapel Hill, 1986.

Nitze, Paul H. *From Hiroshima to Glasnost: At the Center of Decision*. New York, 1989.

Paterson, Thomas G. "Bearing the Burden: A Critical Look at JFK's Foreign Policy." *Virginia Quarterly Review* 54 (Spring 1978).

————. "Fixation with Cuba: The Bay of Pigs, Missile Crisis, and Covert War Against Fidel Castro." In *Kennedy's Quest for Victory: American Foreign Policy, 1961–1963,* edited by Thomas G. Paterson. New York, 1989.

Persons, Albert C. *Bay of Pigs*. Birmingham, AL, 1968.

Phillips, David A. *The Night Watch*. New York, 1977.

Powers, Thomas. *The Man Who Kept the Secrets: Richard Helms & the CIA*. New York, 1979.

Prouty, L. Fletcher. *The Secret Team: The CIA and Its Allies in Control of the United States and the World*. Englewood Cliffs, NJ, 1973.

Ranelagh, John. *The Agency: The Rise and Decline of the CIA*. New York, 1986.

Rosenberg, David A. "Arleigh A. Burke." In *The Chiefs of Naval Operations*, edited by Robert E. Love, Jr. Annapolis, 1980.

Rositzke, Harry. *The CIA's Secret Operations: Espionage, Counterespionage, and Covert Action.* New York, 1977.

Rusk, Dean. *As I Saw It: as told to Richard Rusk.* New York, 1990.

Schlesinger, Arthur M., Jr. *A Thousand Days: John F. Kennedy in the White House.* Boston, 1965.

———. *Robert Kennedy and His Times.* Boston, 1978.

Schlesinger, Stephen, and Stephen Kinzer. *Bitter Fruit: The Untold Story of the American Coup in Guatemala.* Garden City, NY, 1982.

Sidey, Hugh. *John F. Kennedy, President.* New York, 1963.

Sorensen, Theodore C. *Kennedy.* New York, 1965.

Szulc, Tad, and Karl E. Meyer. *The Cuban Invasion: The Chronicle of a Disaster.* New York, 1962.

Vandenbroucke, Lucien S. "Anatomy of a Failure: The Decision to Land at the Bay of Pigs." *Political Science Quarterly* 99 (Fall 1984).

———. "The 'Confessions' of Allen Dulles: New Evidence on the Bay of Pigs." *Diplomatic History* 8 (Fall 1984).

Walton, Richard J. *Cold War and Counterrevolution: The Foreign Policy of John F. Kennedy.* New York, 1972.

Wyden, Peter. *Bay of Pigs: The Untold Story.* New York, 1979.

Sontay

Unpublished Papers and Documents

Commander, JCS Joint Contingency Task Group. "Report On The Son Tay Prisoner Of War Rescue Operation." (N.d., probably 1971.) Office of the Joint Chiefs of Staff. FOIA.

Karsteter, William R. "The Son Tay Raid." Annex to "History of the Aerospace Rescue & Recovery Service 1 July 1970—30 June 1971." U.S. Air Force Military Airlift Command, September 8, 1972. FOIA.

Luttwak, Edward N., Steven L. Canby, and David L. Thomas. "A Systematic Review of 'Commando' (Special) Operations 1939–1980." C & L Associates, Potomac, MD.

Manor, Brigadier General Leroy J. " 'Son Tay'—the POW Rescue Attempt." *Aerospace Commentary* (classified USAF periodical), Department of the Air Force, HQ Air University, Maxwell AFB, AL. FOIA.

———. Untitled briefing notes. (N.d.; probably 1971.) Office of the Joint Chiefs of Staff, 1971. FOIA.

McQuillen, William J. "Monograph of Son Tay POW Rescue Attempt Operation." USAF Special Operations Force, Eglin AFB, FL, February 25, 1971. FOIA.

"Operation Kingpin." (JCS briefing book; n.d., probably November 1970.) Office of the Joint Chiefs of Staff. FOIA.

Personal Interviews

Blackburn, Brigadier General Donald D., February 27, 1984.

Manor, Lieutenant General Leroy J., February 29, 1984.

Moorer, Admiral Thomas J., March 13, 1984.

Rogers, William P., telephone interview, April 16, 1984.

Train, Admiral Harry D., II, June 6, 1984.
Vogt, Lieutenant General John W., April 13, 1984.
Confidential interviews.

Published Records and Official Sources

Donohue, Lt. Col. Frederic M. "Mission of Mercy." Air War College Report 4560, 1972, Maxwell AFB, AL.
U.S. Congress. Senate. Committee on Foreign Relations. *Bombing Operations and the Prisoner-of-War Rescue Mission in North Vietnam.* 91st Cong., 2d sess., 1970.

Published Oral Histories and Interviews

Brown, Colonel Royal A. OH. Simpson Center, Maxwell AFB. FOIA.
Manor, Brigadier General Leroy J. "Oral Briefing to Charles Hildreth, Office of Air Force History, and William J. McQuillen, USAFSOF Historian," HQ USAFSOF, Eglin AFB, FL, December 31, 1970. FOIA.

Books and Articles

Anderson, John. "Military 'Fiasco' Was Really a Success." *Willimantic Chronicle,* July 9, 1985.
David, Heather. *Operation Rescue.* New York, 1971.
Denton, Jeremiah A., Jr. *When Hell Was in Session.* Mobile, AL, 1982.
Gabriel, Richard A. *Military Incompetence: Why the American Military Doesn't Win.* New York, 1986.
Garrett, Richard. *The Raiders: The Elite Strike Forces That Altered the Course of War and History.* New York, 1980.
Goodman, Allen E. *The Lost Peace: America's Search for a Negotiated Settlement of the Vietnam War.* Stanford, 1978.
Hersh, Seymour M. *The Price of Power: Kissinger in the Nixon White House.* New York, 1983.
Kissinger, Henry A. *White House Years.* Boston, 1979.
Loory, Stuart H. "Story Behind the Raid on Sontay—The Problem of Intelligence." *Los Angeles Times,* February 5, 1971.
Palmer, General Bruce, Jr. *The 25-Year War: America's Military Role in Vietnam.* Lexington, KY, 1984.
Porter, Gareth. *A Peace Denied: The United States, Vietnam, and the Paris Agreement.* Bloomington, IN, 1975.
Powers, Thomas. *The Man Who Kept the Secrets: Richard Helms & the CIA.* New York, 1979.
Risner, Robinson. *The Passing of the Night: My Seven Years as a Prisoner of the North Vietnamese.* New York, 1973.
Ruhl, Robert K. "Raid at Sontay." *Airman* 19 (August 1975).
Schemmer, Benjamin F. *The Raid.* New York, 1976.
———. "U.S. Raiders Killed 100–200 Chinese Troops in 1970 North Vietnam Foray." *Armed Forces Journal International* 117 (January 1980).
Tilford, Earl H., Jr. *Search and Rescue in Southeast Asia, 1961–1975.* Washington, DC, 1980.

Westmoreland, General William C. *A Soldier Reports*. Garden City, NY, 1976.
Wise, David. *The Politics of Lying: Government Deception, Secrecy, and Power*. New York, 1973.

Mayaguez

Unpublished Papers and Documents

BLT (Battalion Landing Team) 2/9, III MAF, "Koh Tang *Mayaguez* Historical Report: Narrative Summary." September 12, 1975, U.S. Marine Corps, Reference Section, History and Museums Division.

Buchen, Philip W., Files, Gerald R. Ford Presidential Library, Ann Arbor.

CinCPac [Commander In Chief Pacific] Ad Hoc Board, "Report on Intelligence and Operations in Contingencies," December 5, 1975, microfilm roll no. 32846, Simpson Center, Maxwell AFB. FOIA.

CinCPac Honolulu HI, message: "Orders During SS Mayaguez Operation," to JCS WashDC, 201723Z May 1975. FOIA.

Command History Branch, Office of the Joint Secretary, "Commander in Chief Pacific Command History 1975 Appendix VI—The SS Mayaguez Incident," 1976, HQ CinCPac, Camp H. M. Smith, HI. FOIA.

CTF Seven Nine, message to CTG Seven Nine PT One, 130920Z May 1975, Mayaguez File, U.S. Marine Corps, Reference Section, History and Museums Division.

Defense Intelligence Agency, "Weekly Intelligence Summary Distribution: Air Strike Damage During the Mayaguez Incident," C-6573/DI-GC, June 9, 1975, Washington, DC. FOIA.

Joint Chiefs of Staff, "After Action Report, US Military Operations SS Mayaguez/Kaoh Tang Island, 12–15 May 1975" (n.d.; probably May 1975). Office of The Joint Chiefs of Staff. FOIA.

Leppert, Charles, Files, GRFL.

Minter, Major General Charles F., "End of Tour Report." 8th Air Force/BAD 74/08/24-75/08/10, Simpson Center, Maxwell AFB. FOIA.

Nessen, Ron, Files, GRFL.

PACAF [Pacific Air Forces], "Chronological Order Listing of Significant Message Traffic," 150001Z–151513Z, May 1975, HQ, PACAF. FOIA.

———, "Mayaguez, Nail Forward Air Controller Message Traffic," Iris # 1022546, 75/05/15, HQ, PACAF. FOIA.

———, "Mayaguez Operation, Miscellaneous Documents," 75/05/12 to 75/05/29, Iris # 1022536, HQ, PACAF, FOIA.

———, "Miscellaneous Documents," 75/05/12 to 75/06/00, Iris # 1022544, HQ, PACAF. FOIA.

———, "The SS Mayaguez Seizure: An Evaluation of Intelligence Factors," June 17, 1975, HQ, PACAF. FOIA.

———, BGEN Johnson to Admiral Gayler, "SS Mayaguez Seizure," November 17, 1975, HQ, PACAF. FOIA.

———, DCS/Plans and Operations, "Assault on Koh Tang," June 23, 1975, HQ, PACAF, Hickam AFB, HI. FOIA.

———, Office of PACAF History, "History Of The Pacific Air Forces: 1 July 1974–31 December 1975, Volume 1," July 30, 1976, HQ, PACAF, FOIA.

Patrick, Urey W., "The Mayaguez Operation," Center for Naval Analyses, Marine Corps Operations Analysis Group, Arlington, VA, April 1977.

Reed, Colonel Robert R., "End of Tour Report," HQ Twelfth Air Force, Bergstrom AFB, TX (n.d.; probably summer 1975). FOIA.

Schlesinger, James R., "Some Ruminations on the Office of Secretary of Defense," unpublished manuscript (n.d.).

Scowcroft, Brent, Temporary Parallel File, GRFL.

Shuman, James, Files, GRFL.

U.S. Marine Corps, memorandum, "Missing in Action Status in the Case of Private First Class Gary C. Hall...Lance Corporal Joseph N. Hargrove... and Private Danny Marshall," July 31, 1975, U.S. Marine Corps, Reference Section, History and Museums Division.

USSAG, Major General Earl A. Archer, message: "Lessons Learned-SS Mayaguez/Koh Tang Island Operation," AFSSO/USSAG/7AF/NKP TH/CS to AFSSO PACAF, 110915Z June 75. FOIA.

Vertical File, GRFL.

White House Central Files, GRFL.

3 AFFG Air Force History, Narrative, 75/01/01-75/06/30, Iris # 1006850, Maxwell AFB. FOIA.

3 TFW, "Cricket 02 Mission Log," in "AF History, Supporting Document," 75/04/01 to 75/06/30," vol. 6, Department of the Air Force, HQ 3D Combat Support Group (PACAF), APO SF 96274.

9th Marines, Third Marine Division, "Koh Tang Assault/Operation Mayaguez Report," Part 1, Narrative Summary Koh Tang Assault/Operation Mayaguez, September 12, 1975, U.S. Marine Corps, Reference Section, History and Museum Division.

13th Air Force, "Chronology of Thirteenth Air Force 1 July 1974–June 1975, Volume I-Narrative," Office of History, HQ, 13th AF, Clark AFB, Philippines. FOIA.

56 SOW Nakhom Phanom Aprt Thai/DO, message to CINCPACAF Hickam AFB HI/XO, 191200Z May 75, FOIA.

56 SOW Nakhon Phanom RTAFB TH/OI, message, "Story Background," to CINCPACAF/HI/OI, 220115 May 1975. FOIA.

56 SOW Nakhon Phanom Airprt Thai/DO, message, "56 Special Operations Wing Activities," to CINCPACAF Hickam AFB HI/XO, 191200Z May 75. FOIA.

56 SOW Nakhon Phanom Aprt Thai/DO, message, "Superlative Performance of OV-10 A/C," to CINCPACAF Hickam AFB HI/XO, 191200Z May 1975. FOIA.

56 SOW NKP RTAFB TH/DO, message to CINCPACAF Hickam AFB HI/CC/XO, 180910Z June 1975, FOIA.

56 SOW Nakhon Phanom Afld Thai/CC, message, "Recommendation for Decoration for Heroism," to CINCPACAF Hickam AFB HI/DP, 240716Z May 75. FOIA.

56 SOW Nakhon Phanom Aprt Thai/DO, message to CINCPACAF Hickam AFB HI/XO, 191200Z May 75. FOIA.

388 Tactical Fighter Wing (TFW), "Narrative History 75/04/01 to 75/06/30," HQ Tactical Air Command, Langley AFB, VA. (FOIA).

———, Korat AB TH/IN, message to AIG 913, 151030Z May 75. FOIA.

Personal Interviews

Archer, Major General Earl J., May 29, 1984.
Atkinson, Brigadier General Anderson W., May 10, 1984.
Burns, Lieutenant General John J., May 8, 1984, and May 14, 1992.
Colby, William, E., March 5, 1984.
Buchen, Philip W., March 20, 1984.
Finkelstein, Colonel Zane, June 13, 1984.
Hartmann, Robert T., May 30, 1984.
Hoffman, Major General Carl W., June 11, 1984.
Holloway, Admiral James L., III, June 25, 1984.
Houghton, Major General Kenneth J., June 11, 1984.
Quinlan, Colonel David A., June 20, 1984.
Schlesinger, James R., June 1, 1984.
Scowcroft, Brent, June 15, 1984.
Steele, Vice Admiral George P., April 9, 1984.
Train, Admiral Harry D., II, June 5, 1984.

Published Records and Official Sources

U.S. Congress. House. Committee on Foreign Affairs. Subcommittee on International Security and Scientific Affairs. *War Powers: A Test of Compliance.* 94th Cong., 1st sess., 1976.
————. Reports of the Comptroller General of the United States Submitted to the Subcommittee on International Political and Military Affairs, Committee on International Relations. *Seizure of the Mayaguez, Part IV.* 94th Cong., 2d sess., 1976.

Published Oral Histories and Interviews

Austin, Lt. Col. Randall W. Taped interview by Major J. B. McIppeny, Camp Courtney, Okinawa, June 5, 1975. U.S. Marine Corps, History and Museums Division.
Johnson, Colonel John M., Jr. Taped interview by Major J. B. McIlleny, Camp Courtney, Okinawa, 19 May 1975. U.S. Marine Corps, History and Museums Division.
PACAF. "Mayaguez/Koh Tang Operation, Pilot Interview" (taped interview). Iris # 1022548, Hickam AFB. FOIA.
Steele, Vice Admiral George P. OH. Naval Historical Center, Washington, DC.

Books and Articles

Baral, Jaya Krishna. "The *Mayaguez* Incident: A Study of Crisis Management." *International Studies* 19 (January 1980).
Bartlett, Tom. "Mayaguez." *Leatherneck: Magazine of the Marines* 68 (September 1975).
Carlile, Donald E. "The Mayaguez Incident—Crisis Management." *Military Review* 56 (October 1976).

Colby, William E., and William Forthbath. *Honorable Men: My Life in the CIA.* New York, 1978.

Des Brisay, Thomas D. *Fourteen Hours at Koh Tang.* Washington, DC, 1975.

Dunham, George R., and David A. Quinlan. *U.S. Marines in Vietnam: The Bitter End, 1973–1975.* Washington, DC, 1990.

Ford, Gerald R. *A Time to Heal: The Autobiography of Gerald R. Ford.* New York, 1979.

Gazit, Shlomo. "Risk, Glory, and the Rescue Operation." *International Security* 6 (Summer 1981).

Goldman, Peter. "Ford's Rescue Operation." *Newsweek,* May 26, 1975.

Hartmann, Robert T. *Palace Politics: An Inside Account of the Ford Years.* New York, 1980.

Hamm, Michael J. "The Pueblo and Mayaguez Incidents: A Study of Flexible Response and Decision-Making." *Asian Survey* 17 (June 1977).

Head, Richard G., Frisco W. Short, and Robert C. McFarlane. *Crisis Resolution: Presidential Decision Making in the Mayaguez and Korean Confrontations.* Boulder, CO, 1978.

Johnson, J. M., Jr., R. W. Austin, and D. A. Quinlan. "Individual heroism overcame awkward command relationships, confusion and bad information off the Cambodian coast." *Marine Corps Gazette* 61 (October 1977).

Kelly, Peter A. "Raids and National Command: Mutually Exclusive!" *Military Review* 60 (April 1980).

Lamb, Christopher J. *Belief Systems and Decision Making in the* Mayaguez *Crisis.* Gainesville, FL, 1988.

———. "Belief Systems and Decision Making in the *Mayaguez* Crisis." *Political Science Quarterly* 99 (Winter 1985).

"The Mayaguez—What Went Right, Wrong." *U.S. News and World Report,* June 2, 1975.

"The Mayaguez Test." *Washington Post,* October 11, 1976.

Messegee, J. A., Robert A. Peterson, Walter J. Wood, J. B. Hendricks, and J. Michael Rodgers. " 'Mayday' for the *Mayaguez.*" *United States Naval Institute Proceedings* 102 (November 1976).

Morrow, Michael. "Ford: Fastest Gun in the East." *Far Eastern Economic Review,* May 30, 1975.

Nathan, James A. "The *Mayaguez,* Presidential War and Congressional Senescence." *Intellect* 104 (February 1976).

Nessen, Ron. *It Sure Looks Different from the Inside.* Chicago, 1978.

Puryear, Edgar F., Jr. *George S. Brown, General, U.S. Air Force: Destined for Stars.* Novato, CA, 1983.

Rowan, Roy. *The Four Days of Mayaguez.* New York, 1975.

Simmons, Robert R. "Case Studies: The *Pueblo,* EC-121, and *Mayaguez* Incidents." In *The Use of the Armed Forces as a Political Instrument,* edited by Barry Blechman and Stephan Kaplan. Washington, DC, 1976.

———. *The Pueblo, EC-121, and Mayaguez Incidents: Some Continuities and Changes.* College Park, MD, 1978.

Shawcross, William. "Making the Most of Mayaguez." *Far Eastern Economic Review,* May 30, 1975.

Taylor, John B. "Air Mission Mayaguez." *Airman* (February 1976).

Tilford, Earl H., Jr. *Search and Rescue in Southeast Asia.* Washington, DC, 1980.

Witcover, Jules. "The Mayaguez Decision: Three Days of Crisis for President Ford." *Washington Post,* May 17, 1975.

Iran

Personal Interviews

Beckwith, Colonel Charlie A., April 23, 1984.
Brzezinski, Zbigniew, June 8, 1984.
W. Graham Claytor, Jr., April 17, 1984.
Holloway, Admiral James L., III, June 25, 1984.
Komer, Robert, W. June 22, 1984.
Powell, Jody, May 30, 1984.
Pustay, Lieutenant General John S., March 3, 1984.
Sick, Gary G. June 7, 1983.
Turner, Admiral Stansfield, May 21, 1984.
Vaught, Lieutenant General James B., May 22, 1984.

Published Records and Official Sources

Public Papers of the Presidents of the United States: Jimmy Carter, 1980–81. Washington, DC, 1981.
Special Operations Review Group. "Rescue Mission Report." Washington, DC, August 1980.

Published Oral History

Rakip, Captain Russell E. OH. Simpson Center, Maxwell AFB.

Books and Articles

Armstrong, Scott, George C. Wilson, and Bob Woodward. "Debate Rekindles on Failed Iran Raid." *Washington Post,* April 25, 1982.
Beckwith, Charlie A., and Donald Knox. *Delta Force.* New York, 1983.
Bill, James A. *The Eagle and the Lion: The Tragedy of American-Iranian Relations.* New Haven, 1988.
Brzezinski, Zbigniew. *Power and Principle: Memoirs of the National Security Adviser, 1977–1981.* New York, 1983.
———. "The Failed Mission: The Inside Account of the Attempt to Free the Hostages in Iran." *New York Times Magazine,* April 18, 1982.
Carter, Jimmy. *Keeping Faith: Memoirs of a President.* New York, 1982.
Carter, Rosalynn. *First Lady from Plains.* Boston, 1984.
Cogan, Charles G. "Not to Offend: Observations on Iran, the Hostages, and the Hostage Rescue Mission—Ten Years Later." *Comparative Strategy* 9 (1990).
Christopher, Warren, Harold H. Saunders, Gary Sick, Robert Carswell, Richard J. Davis, John E. Hoffman, Jr., and Roberts B. Owen. *American Hostages in Iran: The Conduct of a Crisis.* New Haven, 1985.

Earl, Robert L. "A Matter of Principle." *U.S. Naval Institute Proceedings* 109 (February 1983).

Emerson, Steven. *Secret Warriors: Inside the Covert Military Operations of the Reagan Era.* New York, 1988.

Glad, Betty. "Personality, Political and Group Process Variables in Foreign Policy Decision-Making: Jimmy Carter's Handling of the Iranian Hostage Crisis." *International Political Science Review* 10 (January 1989).

Hadley, Arthur T. *The Straw Giant. Triumph and Failure: America's Armed Forces. A Report from the Field.* New York, 1986.

Janis, Irving. "In Rescue Planning, How Did Carter Handle Stress?" *New York Times,* May 18, 1980.

Jordan, Hamilton. *Crisis: The last year of the Carter Presidency.* New York, 1983.

Keisling, Phillip. "Desert One: The Wrong Man and the Wrong Plan." *Washington Monthly* (December 1983).

Kyle, James H. *The Guts to Try.* New York, 1990.

Martin, David C. "Inside the Rescue Mission." *Newsweek,* July 12, 1982.

———. "New Light on the Rescue Mission." *Newsweek,* June 30, 1981.

Martin, David C., and John Walcott. *Best Laid Plans: The Inside Story of America's War Against Terrorism.* New York, 1988.

McFadden, Robert D., Joseph B. Treaster, and Maurice Carroll. *No Hiding Place: The New York Times Inside Report on the Hostage Crisis.* New York, 1981.

McClellan, David S. *Cyrus Vance.* Totowa, NJ, 1985.

Powell, Jody. *The Other Side of the Story.* New York, 1984.

Pustay, John S. "The Problem Is Systemic." *Armed Forces Journal International* 121 (February 1984).

Rubin, Barry. *Paved with Good Intentions: The American Experience and Iran.* New York, 1980.

Ryan, Paul B. *The Iranian Rescue Mission: Why It Failed.* Annapolis, 1985.

Salinger, Pierre. *America Held Hostage: The Secret Negotiations.* Garden City, NY, 1981.

Schlesinger, James R. "Some Lessons of Iran." *New York Times,* May 6, 1980.

Schemmer, Benjamin F. "Presidential Courage—And the April 1980 Rescue Mission." *Armed Forces Journal International* 118 (May 1981).

———. "Beckwith Blasts *Newsweek* Account of Iranian Rescue Mission." *Armed Forces Journal International* 119 (August 1982).

Scott, Alexander. "The Lessons of the Tehran Raid for American Military Policy." *Armed Forces Journal International* 117 (June 1980).

Sick, Gary G. *All Fall Down: America's Tragic Encounter with Iran.* New York, 1986.

Smith, Steve. "Policy preferences and bureaucratic position: the case of the American hostage rescue mission." *International Affairs* 61 (Winter 1984–85).

———. "The Hostage Rescue Mission." In *Foreign Policy Implementation,* edited by Steve Smith and Michael Clark. London, 1985.

Summers, Harry J. "Delta Force: America's Counter-Terrorist Unit and the Mission to Rescue the Hostages in Iran" (review essay). *Military Review* 63 (November 1983).

Taylor, Maxwell D. "Analogies (II): Was Desert One Another Bay of Pigs?" *Washington Post,* May 12, 1980.

Turner, Stansfield. *Secrecy and Democracy: The CIA in Transition.* Boston, 1985.
––––––. *Terrorism and Democracy.* Boston, 1991.
Valliere, John E. "Disaster at Desert One: Catalyst For Change." *Parameters* 22 (Autumn 1992).
Vance, Cyrus. *Hard Choices: Critical Years in America's Foreign Policy.* New York, 1983.

Index